Praise for *Beyond Secular Order*:

'Exploratory, daring, irritating and illuminating by turns, John Milbank cannot be compared with anything else in the intellectual life of our times. Whatever our conclusions on the positions he has defended, he has succeeded in posing the questions that have really mattered, so that those who have simply wished not to know, have risked being all too obviously granted their wish. Now in a work of synthesis he revisits his early modernity-criticism, enriching it with the reflections on ontology, politics and theology that have occupied him since. It will become the cardinal text for interpreting him and arguing with him.'

Oliver O'Donovan, University of Edinburgh

'This rich and many-sided work documents the remoter origins of modern Western philosophy in the theological controversies of the later Middle Ages, arising out of the nominalist rebellion against Aquinas' synthesis. But tracing this connection has much more than an antiquarian interest. Milbank goes on to show how we can understand the strains and tensions within modern philosophy, and the contemporary attempts at critique, in new and fruitful ways in the light of this history. And he extends these insights to our contemporary understanding of politics. New and exciting avenues of exploration open again and again in this richly suggestive work.'

Charles Taylor, McGill University

Illuminations: Theory and Religion

Series editors: Catherine Pickstock, John Milbank, and Graham Ward

Religion has a growing visibility in the world at large. Throughout the humanities there is a mounting realization that religion and culture lie so closely together that religion is an unavoidable and fundamental human reality. Consequently, the examination of religion and theology now stands at the centre of any questioning of our western identity, including the question of whether there is such a thing as 'truth'.

Illuminations aims both to reflect the diverse elements of these developments and, from them, to produce creative new syntheses. It is unique in exploring the new interaction between theology, philosophy, religious studies, political theory, and cultural studies. Despite the theoretical convergence of certain trends they often in practice do not come together. The aim of *Illuminations* is to make this happen, and advance contemporary theoretical discussion.

Published

Sacrifice and Community: Jewish Offering and Christian Eucharist
Matthew Levering

The Other Calling: Theology, Intellectual Vocation, and Truth
Andrew Shanks

The State of the University: Academic Knowledges and the Knowledge of God
Stanley Hauerwas

The End of Work: Theological Critiques of Capitalism
John Hughes

God and the Between
William Desmond

After Enlightenment: The Post-Secular Vision of J.G. Hamann
John R. Betz

The Theology of Food: Eating and the Eucharist
Angel F. Mendez Montoya

No God, No Science: Theology, Cosmology, Biology
Michael Hanby

Beyond Secular Order

The Representation of Being and the Representation
of the People

John Milbank

WILEY Blackwell

This edition first published 2013
© 2013 John Wiley & Sons, Ltd

Registered Office
John Wiley & Sons, Ltd, The Atrium, Southern Gate, Chichester, West Sussex,
PO19 8SQ, UK

Editorial Offices
350 Main Street, Malden, MA 02148–5020, USA
9600 Garsington Road, Oxford, OX4 2DQ, UK
The Atrium, Southern Gate, Chichester, West Sussex, PO19 8SQ, UK

For details of our global editorial offices, for customer services, and for information about
how to apply for permission to reuse the copyright material in this book please see our
website at www.wiley.com/wiley-blackwell.

The right of John Milbank to be identified as the author of this work has been asserted in
accordance with the UK Copyright, Designs and Patents Act 1988.

Library of Congress Cataloging-in-Publication Data applied for.

Hardback ISBN: 978-1-118-82523-5
Paperback ISBN: 978-1-118-82529-7

A catalogue record for this book is available from the British Library.

Cover image: Inside the Ca' d'Oro, Venice. Photo © John Milbank.
Cover design by www.cyandesign.co.uk

Set in 10/12.5pt Galliard by SPi Publisher Services, Pondicherry, India
Printed in Malaysia by Ho Printing (M) Sdn Bhd

1   2013

In the groves of their *academy, at the end of every visto, you see nothing but the gallows.*

Edmund Burke, from *Reflections on the Revolution in France*

Contents

viii   *Contents*

Acknowledgements

I am indebted to Conor Cunningham and Aaron Riches for the initial suggestion for this book – though in the end it has turned out very differently – and to my head of department, Simon Oliver, for his support while finishing it. Also to Sam Kimbriel for his comments on the project during this period. My other intellectual debts are now too numerous and deep to be readily recorded, but my thinking here has been profoundly informed by continual conversation with my wife Alison and my children Arabella and Sebastian. Also by frequent interchanges with my former student Catherine Pickstock of Emmanuel College, Cambridge, and with her former student Adrian Pabst, now of the University of Kent. Finally, my great thanks go to Rebecca Harkin and Karen Raith at Wiley Blackwell for enabling this book quickly to appear in print, to Janet Moth, project manager, and to Eric Lee for compiling the index.

J.M.

Preface:
The Hidden Dimension
of Humanity

This book is a successor volume to *Theology and Social Theory*, and seeks to deepen its analyses.[1]

Like that book, it is in part an exercise in tracing the roots of 'the secular'. The first 'sequence' of the current book does so in terms of philosophy. A proposed sequel, *On Divine Government*, will further do so in terms of theology and the history of religion. The reason for this triple division we shall shortly see.

There is an intrinsic difficulty in any such genealogical endeavour. Human existence is split between actions and verbal or other symbolic performances on the one hand, and reflexive verbal theorisations (in whatever degree of abstraction) on the other. Apparently, we usually act without reflection and without reference to our theoretical assumptions. Equally, we often present our theoretical musings as if these arose from a void and were not intended as pragmatic interventions. Yet in reality all our actions assume a mythical, metaphoric, or rational framework, while all our theoretical utterances and writings are practical interventions in human history, whether deliberately so or not.

This means that both acting and thinking typically occur in the shadows, always with half-concealment. As a result, human history but rarely comes to the light of day and we remain unable clearly to see ourselves. The task of the genealogist is therefore to penetrate these shadows, and to reach a level where we can regard actions in the light of their presuppositions and theories in the light of their practical tendencies.

[1] John Milbank, *Theology and Social Theory*, 2nd edn. (Oxford: Blackwell, 2006).

Beyond Secular Order: The Representation of Being and the Representation of the People, First Edition. John Milbank.
© 2013 John Wiley & Sons, Ltd. Published 2013 by John Wiley & Sons, Ltd.

Yet precisely because this dimension of full daylight is hidden, to try to reach it can appear to be a further venture into the murk, a departure from the apparently clear evidence of events on the one hand, and the exegetical perusal of texts on the other. For the problem is that presuppositions have generally gone unsaid in actions, while practical contexts and implications have been obfuscated on the page. It follows that both mere empiricism and mere philology are self-defeating: in seeking to reach the objective, they fail to reach the real.

By contrast, the assumption of my genealogy is that there can be perspectives from which one can see the homology between human theory and human action. Yet this truly illuminating light is hidden under a divided bushel, and can be glimpsed but fleetingly, because what history most disguises through division into thought and event is the deepest substance of its own occurring. Hence, in the name of truth, one must run the risk that any claim to illuminate human history at depth will present conclusions that can seem excessively abstruse or even implausible. Yet it may be this very abstruseness that is the mark of their authenticity.

Such a circumstance is not a licence for guesswork, even if it reveals the unavoidable need for interpretative 'abduction' that necessarily goes (one hopes with caution and good judgement) 'beyond the evidence'. Of course as much evidence as can be gleaned should be gleaned, yet the most relevant evidence here is the witness of elusive echo back and forth between the two registers of *verba* and *pragmata*.

Given my argued position therefore, it is not simply a matter of seeing whether or not these echoes can be traced. Rather, it is taken to be the case, for reasons of historical ontology, that a deep homology *must* exist, since specifically human action is theoretically informed and all human words have a performative dimension. Also, given the fact that human beings can communicate with each other in greater or lesser degrees, one must apply this principle at a more collective level: there will always be a shared hidden horizon of coincidence between act and meaning, whether at the level of a locality, a culture, or the entire human race – which undoubtedly shares, at some level, a single culture.

In consequence, the presupposition of this book is that there has to exist a concealed symmetry between the most rarefied expressions of modern thought in 'philosophy', on the one hand, and modernity's collective 'political' deeds on the other. A further presupposition is that it is possible to take a short cut to locating this isomorphism by looking at specifically 'political philosophy' or 'political theory' in the broadest sense (as much of it is the work of jurists and not of philosophers). For it is likely that within this discourse metaphysical abstraction and lived events will theoretically come together in a markedly acute fashion

It should be noted that this is a different proposal from that of reading the history of political thought 'contextually', though that is involved and by no means disparaged. Instead, it is rather that political thought is taken to be a level of writing that begins to disclose a concealed, more ultimate 'context' that is itself theoretical as much as practical.

The focus of the present book is therefore on a certain homology between metaphysical philosophy, on the one hand, and political philosophy on the other. Within the scope of theory at least, it is intended to show how ideas about being coincide with ideas about human action. What is 'seen' corresponds to what is done or made, in accordance with the Aristotelian understanding that, while an *ergon* proceeds from an essence, an essence is something that always performs an *ergon*, such that a blinded eye is for Aristotle no longer an eye at all.[2]

These are the formal dimensions of my enquiry. Substantively, as in *Theology and Social Theory*, I shall try to show that what is apparently 'secular' in modern general ontology, and then in political ontology, in reality derives from specific currents of theology, questionable from the point of view of the most authentic Christian tradition. It is, ironically, certain particular modes of theology which first invent and encourage 'secularisation' and then, because of their unbelievability, invite an agnostic and atheist scepticism which eventually engenders nihilism as a kind of truncated theological *via moderna*.

More specifically, in the first sequence, 'On Modern Ontology', I identify four assumptions of modern philosophy, which all derive from late medieval, largely Franciscan-inspired currents, besides early modern scholasticism and Baroque Augustinianism which themselves lie within their slipstream. These are: (1) the univocity rather than analogy of being; (2) knowledge by representation rather than identity; (3) the priority of the possible over the actual; and (4) causality as 'concurrence' rather than 'influence'. These assumptions are all profoundly linked to the equally important invention of a novel space of 'pure nature', independent of the human natural orientation to the supernatural as taught by the Church Fathers and the high Middle Ages, but then largely abandoned by late medieval and early modern theology.

In each instance we have a rationalist reduction of real mystery, which itself tends to render the real rationally problematic. In the first case, everything is now seen as unambiguously 'the same' or else, with equal unambiguity 'different'; in the second case, to know something is seen as an unproblematic and, it is hoped, exact 'copying'; in the third case, mystery is drained from actual depths since anything existent is seen as a mere instantiation of a logical

---

[2] Aristotle, *Meteorologia* 390.10. See also *Nicomachean Ethics*, 1097a15–b2.

or mathematically definable instance; in the fourth case, co-operating causes are seen as lying extrinsically side by side and not as obscurely interfering with each other. As to the notion of 'pure nature', it opens out the space of secular autonomy itself, within which all transcendent reference will eventually be denied.

These four aspects of modern ontology, as linked to the theology of *natura pura*, are traced in the first sequence of the book, along with their ramifications and several main developments. The alternative, more traditional, positions are also sketched out and defended, along with some initial suggestions for how these might be updated (for the criticisms of these positions are not always simply 'wrong' and cannot just be dismissed and ignored).

Already, however, of these four aspects it is 'representation' which is given the longest consideration, because modern ontology is so constituted that (not without contradiction) it gives primacy to the theory of knowledge rather than to the theory of being.

The second sequence, 'On Political Ontology', then traces the assumptions about, and recommendations for human action in the political field, in the case of both modern and pre-modern western thought. In the case of modern thought it is constantly indicated how there are correlations between the four general ontological assumptions and more specific political ones. The field of 'pure nature' is here adumbrated in terms of procedures at once univocally constructive according to a *mathesis* of human rational artifice and representationally mimetic both of a supposed human nature and of human society reduced to measurable *quanta*. Political power is defined as a reserve of potential that is enacted through will, rather than by an actualising 'eruption' of human society (as the Thomistically influenced John Fortescue put it in the late Middle Ages) that is already contingently actual, like an embryo with a heart that later gives rise to its own head.[3] Finally, the formal and material aspects of human social existence are seen as concurrently coinciding, rather than as organically blended.

These correlations are, however, complex and overlapping, while 'representation', unsurprisingly, is, in political terms, a particularly crucial contested category. The importance of 'representative' democracy in the modern era is shown to correlate with the reign of epistemology in philosophy, while older, medieval notions of political representation are shown to correlate with an earlier 'knowledge by identity' in which the representation of being played a very different role. For medieval political thought,

---

[3]   John Fortescue, *In Praise of the Laws of England*, ch. XIII in *On the Laws and Governance of England*, ed. Shelley Lockwood (Cambridge: Cambridge University Press, 2002), 20.

'representation by identity' is the most crucial ontological category, but there is no equivalent domination of 'identity' over analogy, actuality and influence in the ontological field at large, precisely because in the pre-modern era ontology held unequivocal priority over the theory of understanding.

It is also the case that my perspective necessarily means that politics intrudes already in the first sequence, while the second often continues to expound the nature of general ontology, both pre-modern and modern. In the case of both sequences, I have tried to aid the reader by concentrating on essentials – referring frequently to some of my published articles for those in search of more details.

Since it is the case that in political theory the human *ergon* as at once envisaged and enacted comes particularly to view, the most crucial category of political thought can be considered to be the anthropological. So in this sequence a second theme of my theoretical symphony more clearly emerges, alongside the fourfold contrast of ontological perspectives. This second theme is the relation of humanity to animality.

Here the rationalisation and eventual secularisation of political ontology further surfaces in terms of (1) the sundering of human life from human reason; (2) the sundering of human nature from human society; (3) the sundering of human nature from human culture; and (4) the sundering of human nature from supernatural grace. There is a broad correspondence between these four categories of modern anthropology and the four categories of modern ontology plus the invention of *natura pura*, but not a one-to-one correlation.

By contrast, pre-modern Christian thought defined Man as a rational animal, as a social animal, as a fabricating animal (*homo faber*), and as destined to the beatific vision. In every case, I argue that one is dealing with an 'addition' that is seen as paradoxically essential: this is what I dub 'trans-organicity'. It is such a realistic paradoxicality that modern rationalism, whether theological or secularist, is most of all unable to stomach.

All this can sound as if what I am proposing is a straightforward defence of the ancients against the moderns. But that is not exactly the case. Rather, what I wish to do is thoroughly to upset the usual duality of periodisation which sets a very recent modernity against all that has gone before in western human history, and perhaps human history *in toto*.

This revisionary perspective is articulated in the following ways:

1   The Christian-versus-pagan axis continues to be seen as fundamental for western history, right up to the present. In the first place, this is because Christianity 'democratises' the antique commitment to trans-organicity and virtue.

2 In the second place, antiquity by and large knew of no 'pure nature', but already referred the natural to the supernatural, albeit this was too confined to intra-cosmic terms. Thus, as Eric Voegelin intimated, any notion (even those sometimes entertained by the high Middle Ages themselves) that Christian revelation simply 'added' the supernatural to a 'nature' known to the pagans is historically too simple.[4]

3 In consequence, the 'nature' to which modern secularists appeal is a post-Christian phenomenon of dubious stature outside a Christian framework. For even if neo-scholastic theology falsely proclaimed the autonomy of a natural end, the self-contained coherence and the validity of this end still only made sense as something ordained by God. In purely secular terms there really can be no such regulated or self-regulating nature – only the randomness and contingency of matter and force. In this sense there is no 'modern' that one might care to defend, since it has always already been the 'postmodern' and always been prepared to accept, with Nietzsche, that without nature one might after all envisage matter as guided by a darkly supernatural, neo-pagan vitality.

4 The normal 'Whig' periodisation which sees a smooth transition from Renaissance to Enlightenment (still retained by Michael Allen Gillespie, even though he recognises the nominalist origins of modernity[5]) to the various modes of positivism, is false. I argue instead that some lines of the Christian Renaissance consummated medieval thinking (even though there were also nominalist humanist currents, to be fair to Gillespie), while the main line of modernity is derived from late medieval nominalist-voluntatist theology and from the quasi-Augustinian 'Counter-Renaissance' of the seventeenth century.

5 The Enlightenment (which is not treated in detail in this book) needs to be more diversely analysed in 'long Renaissance', 'long Reformation', and 'long Counter-Renaissance' perspectives. In this light it can be divided into (a) a Christian and sometimes post-Christian Ciceronian-Stoic reaction against the voluntarism of 'modern Christian' thought; (b) a perpetuation of Reformation and Counter-Renaissance currents in a more Unitarian, Arian-Newtonian idiom (most so-called 'deists' having actually been heterodox Christians) which was often also Masonic; (c) a 'Radical Enlightenment' which was Brunonian-Hermetic and Spinozistic and frequently likewise Masonic; (d) a fully atheist Enlightenment

---

[4] Eric Voegelin, *Science, Politics and Gnosticism: Two Essays* (Washington, DC: Regnery, 1997), 11–13.

[5] Michael Allen Gillespie, *The Theological Origins of Modernity* (Chicago: Chicago University Press, 2008), 19–100.

which broke with immanentist vitalism in favour of cosmic mechanism. Only the final and most minority branch is non-religious.[6]

6 By contrast, pre-Romanticism and early Romanticism (in Germany especially, but also in France and Britain) cannot at all be understood as a straightforward further extension of any of these modes of enlightenment. It rejected both the 'disenchanted transcendence' of (b) and the 'enchanted immanence' of (c) in favour of a newly enchanted transcendence which effectively reinstated medieval gothic and Renaissance currents in new poetic guise. Despite or even because of its syncretism which might reincorporate pagan elements, its impulse was fundamentally in the direction of orthodox Christianity, showing many intimations of what had been lost since the high Middle Ages.[7] The later 'dark' Romanticism of Schopenhauer and Nietzsche was, by contrast, largely due to the renewed influence of the Enlightenment thinkers Kant and Goethe. It follows that, as Charles Taylor has suggested, our current modernity is the product of several competing Enlightenment visions, the tension between them and Romanticism, and finally the division within Romanticism itself.[8] It is largely because my sympathies lie with the spirit of early Romanticism and its attempt considerably to re-envision Christian orthodoxy, that my position cannot be considered simply 'reactionary' or 'nostalgic'.

7 Since modern philosophy is informed mainly by nominalism and the Counter-Renaissance, it does not, as is usually thought, favour the activity and the constructivism of the human intellect, save in a bastardised sense which I explain in this book.[9] To the contrary, it is antique and medieval

---

[6] On the radical Enlightenment and Freemasonry, see Jan Assmann, *Moses the Egyptian: The Memory of Moses in Western Monotheism* (Cambridge, Mass.: Harvard University Press, 1997), 91–143; Margaret C. Jacob, *The Radical Enlightenment: Pantheists, Freemasons and Republicans* (Los Angeles: University of California Press, 2006); Martin Bernal, *Black Athena: The Afroasiatic Roots of Classical Civilisation*, vol. 1: *The Fabrication of Ancient Greece, 1785–1985* (London: Vintage, 1987), 161–223. For the exaggeration of the reality of 'Deism' and the downplaying of the importance of Unitarianism in Britain and continued Jansenism in France and Italy, see S.J. Barnett, *The Enlightenment and Religion: The Myths of Modernity* (Manchester: Manchester University Press, 2003).

[7] See, for example, Novalis, *Philosophical Writings*, trans. Margaret Mahony Stoljar (New York: SUNY, 1997); Friedrich Schlegel, *Philosophical Fragments*, trans. Peter Firchow (Minneapolis: Minnesota University Press, 1991). For the important distinction between German idealism and the dynamic realism of the German Romantics, see Manfred Frank, *The Philosophical Foundations of Early German Romanticism*, trans. Elizabeth Millain-Zaibert (New York: SUNY, 2008).

[8] Charles Taylor, *A Secular Age* (Cambridge, Mass.: Harvard University Press, 2007), 299–419.

[9] See the first sequence, section 9, and the second sequence, section 15, below.

thought which truly envisages the activity of reason. So if such a perspective gets much extended by Renaissance and Romantic notions, this is in continuity with tradition and *not* in the name of anything modern – if modernity is paradigmatically understood in terms of the dominance of *mathesis* and *techne* over *poesis*. Perhaps this conclusion is what most of all upsets the usual contrast of the moderns with the ancients.

8   For related reasons, *historicism* cannot straightforwardly be considered as something specifically modern. To begin with, the sense of estranged distance from the past is initially the fruit of the Christian contrast between old and new covenants and with the pagan world. Even the Renaissance sense of a loss of pagan glories is not unanticipated by Patristic accounts of the general decline of the human race and the way that pagans often put contemporary Christians to shame. Partly for this reason, the first attempt to 're-gather' pagan wisdom was made as early as the Anglo-Saxon period in England, and this impulse was then sustained through the influence of the Englishman Alcuin at Charlemagne's court in the tenth century and in various monastic and cathedral schools in the twelfth. The sense faintly present later on in 'the' Renaissance and then more emphatically in the Enlightenment of a distance of the modern world from a superstitious and benighted past cannot be considered to be fully fledged historicism (as I am defining it) because it is more a celebration of a final *exit* from historicity. By contrast, true historicism from Herder onwards concerns the truth that we can never escape specific historical roots or presuppositions. As later elaborated by Søren Kierkegaard and Charles Péguy, it also implies (beyond any reductive sense that people are 'confined by their epoch') that the lived history of memory and non-identical repetition is truer to the *reality* of the past than the work of the academic historian.[10] For if, as I have argued, enacted events have imaginative and theoretical horizons, then even the 'facts' of what has occurred only get clarified in the light of later re-enactments and later recallings. To say that these can 'falsify' is true, but superficial; more fundamentally they alone establish the truth of the occurrence of what has occurred. There can be no storming of the Bastille as a *historical event* (as opposed to a clashing of material atoms) without its annual commemoration, as Péguy famously concluded.[11] It is indeed collective memory and re-enactment which get initially closer to 'the hidden dimension of humanity' where vision

---

[10]   See Catherine Pickstock, *Repetition and Identity* (Oxford: Oxford University Press, 2013), 85–107.

[11]   Charles Péguy, *Clio* (Paris: Gallimard, 1932), 114, 135–136, 195–196.

and act form a single essence-*ergon*. However, such memory always requires a re-purging, both at a popular and a critical academic level. The latter is part of what I am trying to undertake in the current book.

9   If such critical historicism is rooted in the organic and popular historicism of memory and non-identical repetition, then it becomes possible to see how the Middle Ages, both as a traditional culture and as a Christian culture rooted in a commemorated event of rupture with an older past, were latently historicist through their activist account of memory and thought. For this reason the early Romantic historicist predilection for the gothic was in a way a tautologous predilection for an incipiently historicist culture.

10   Even with respect to the truth that historicism involves an awareness that 'humans make history' and so that the human being is a fabricating, creative animal, I shall show, following Ernst Kantorowicz, that the root of this awareness lies in the pre-Renaissance gothic period.[12] It arises not only under Christian auspices, but initially with specifically *legal and political* reference. Once more the idea of a 'passive' past and an 'active and creative' modernity is disturbed. For this contrast is used to conceal the way in which the modern dominance of *techne* is linked *not* with a Promethean pride in production, but with a falsely pious inflation of passive theory that exalts both the autonomy of a humanly available subjective *a priori* and an empiricist reduction of reality to manipulable 'objectified' items. In either case it is exactly *ars*, or creative activity envisaged as participating in the divine creation – and so as teleologically guided by the inspired vision of the emerging artefact itself – that is suppressed.

11   Conservatism, I contend, is just as *modern* a category as progressivism. Pre-modernity knew of neither. Thus to appeal, to some degree, to the pre-modern is no more a 'conservative' than it is a 'progressive' gesture. This can be explicated in terms of the fact that pre-modernity typically favoured in politics a 'mixed constitution' of 'the One', 'the Few', and ' the Many', with the blend varying according to circumstance. But, as André de Muralt has pointed out, nominalism-voluntarism, founded on the univocity of being, cannot mediate the one with the many, any more than it can analogically mediate the same with the different.[13] Accordingly, the role of the few – both the 'aristocratic' wise and what I call the 'extended few' which are the mediating institutions of the Christian era – is suppressed in modern times. Instead, one gets a battle

[12]   See the second sequence, sections 10–12, below.
[13]   See the second sequence below.

between a 'conservative' and 'right-wing' advocacy of 'the One' and a 'liberal' and 'left-wing' advocacy of 'the Many' – even if Right and Left can sometimes change places in this respect. By contrast, as Jean-Claude Michéa and others have shown, 'socialism' was not originally situated on this spectrum at all.[14] It rejected the 'conservatism' of advocates of a return to the entirely modern, unity-obsessed, technocratic and spectacular *ancien régime*, but also criticised the new tyranny of liberal industrial modernity. For this reason it tended indeed to appeal by contrast to the pre-modern, and to resurrect the role of 'the Few', even if it wished for a more radical and in a different, non-liberal, sense, a more 'left-wing' version of mixed constitution.

So what is it that this book then favours politically for the future? In keeping with a Christian socialist vision (where I want to insist on the co-belonging of both terms), a recovery but transformation of an antique medieval politically ontological vision. 'Trans-organic' humanity is also a humanity which needs freely to blend the life and implicit wisdom of the social many with the guidance of the virtuously rational few and the unifying artifice of the personal one, under the orientation of all to the transcendent Good and final vision of the Godhead. I consistently argue that the viability of democracy itself depends upon a continued constitutional commitment to 'mixed government'. However, the Christian democratisation of virtue as charity implies a transfigured version of mixed government that newly promotes the creative flourishing of all and the combined shaping of an earthly city that might remotely image the eternal.

In the proposed sequel, *On Divine Government*, the perspective will shift and seek to penetrate further into the 'hidden dimension'. This has to do with the final theme of the symphony which is 'divine government', already intimated towards the end of this volume. In the sequel, the second theme of 'human animality' will be continuously sustained, while the initial theme of the 'four contrasting philosophical categories', and especially the contrast of 'representation as mirroring' versus 'representation as symbolic identity' will echo throughout in the lower registers.

Political discourse displays, in a pale theoretical fashion, the homology of ontology with action. However, this isomorphism is displayed more directly, though with a double display, by religion – both religious discourse and religious ritual, which are of course intimately linked. It is in religious expression and liturgical performance that any given human society most of

---

[14]   See the second sequence, section 27, below.

all admits and confesses 'the hidden dimension'. But this may often be in a still obscure fashion, whose darkness may appear all too 'advised' from the point of view of detached critical suspicion, or alternatively, as authentically respectful of genuine mystery, for an inner-cultural understanding. This darkness is marked by the still twofold idiom: on the one hand religious discourse (mythical or theological) remains relatively theoretical, if less so than that of ontology, since it is more likely to acknowledge action and events at the level of primary reality. On the other hand, religious ritual, like political theory, has a relatively practical bent. Yet just as religious discourse speaks of divine performances, besides 'the way things are', so religious ritual steps beyond theoretical reflection upon social practice towards ideal, normative, or paradigmatic instantiations of such practice.

These observations, then, begin to suggest that religion is always the most fundamental domain of human history and specifically human experience. Here the hidden but assumed emerges partially into the light.

However, from a strictly critical and objective perspective, it turns out that not all religions are on the same level in this respect. Many human religions relate themselves, both theoretically and practically, to a cosmic level which they take to be less than ultimate – often marked by a mythically narrated violent 'break' which leaves a reserved space of mystery that is sometimes occupied by a posited but unknown 'high god'. Effectively they deal with metonymic or synecdochic substitutes for this ultimacy.[15] And just such 'reservation' can allow, as in the case of Greece and India, 'philosophy' to emerge as a discourse that does, often controversially, claim to deal with this ultimate level.

While philosophy usually remained linked to modes of ritual and *ascesis*, it nevertheless tended (especially to begin with) to reserve 'being' as a contemplated reality beyond and above 'practice'. Insofar as it did so, however, this 'being' tended to be construed in immanentist terms, since the removal of ancient reserve initially coincided with a new boldness of myth itself that tended to identify the 'high' with the 'all' through concepts of the Macranthropos (or cosmic man – evidenced in ancient India, the ancient Near East and in ancient Greece) which allowed the transition from myth to philosophy – or from the rule of synecdoche and metonymy to that of a univocalist monism – to occur.[16] The revision of myth nonetheless also generally involved a revision of mythical violence, since the finite cosmos as we know it was envisioned

---

[15]   See John Milbank, *The Religious Dimension in the Thought of Giambattista Vico*, vol. 2: *Language, Law and History* (Lewiston: Edwin Mellen, 1992), 38–117.
[16]   See Thomas McEvilley, *The Shape of Ancient Thought* (New York: Allworth, 2002), 23–28.

as the divine or titanic tearing apart of the cosmic man. Such violence was later rationalised in philosophical doctrines like that of the Stoic periodic conflagration and reconstitution of physical reality.

A complicating factor here is that the more 'being' was distinguished from 'nature' and so philosophy as 'metaphysics' (though the word was not yet used) from 'physics', then the more a level of transcendence that only an element of reconstrued original myth could invoke in terms of an independent 'activity' was appealed to – as by Socrates, Plato and Aristotle and to a degree also by the *Upanishads* and the traditions of the *Vedanta*. In this sense original philosophy was a monistic revolt against myth (whose impulse is sustained by Stoicism, with the same disconnect between normal ethical action and the indifference of being, to which one must just be resigned) whereas later more humanistic and political philosophies were 'conservative' hybrids of philosophy and mythology.[17]

By almost unique contrast with other cultures, the ancient Hebrews refused what they saw as the 'idolatry' of metonymic or synecdochic substitution. Instead, they risked an open-ended metaphoric tension with the ultimate, whereby figurative substitutions of finite for infinite had also to be suspiciously negated, since they were not simply of part for whole or effect for cause, but rather of obscure symbol for the obscurely symbolised. In consequence, new and more adequate substitutions had to be constantly sought and then negated in their turn. Thus neither the exclusive worship of the high god, nor the refusal of 'idolatrous' substitutions is what truly marks the novelty of Israel, but rather its invention of not just a *mythos*, but also a restrained *cultus* of the ultimate. The ark of the covenant may have been unspectacular and frail, but *that* was Israel's crucial invention.

Precisely because its ritual referred to the one creator God, there developed in Israel no 'philosophy', since reflexivity was not here alienated to the level of abstraction. Instead, because it was retained at the level of linguistic tropes, reflexivity was also doubled, since the import of metaphorical rule is that the ultimate as 'being' lies both (as for philosophy) beyond action and contingency, and yet also (unlike philosophy) not beyond, since only in action and event is reality ever manifest.[18] As Hebrew rituals peculiarly

[17]   This contrast is today played out (perhaps in incoherently secular terms) in the contrast between Heidegger's 'Presocraticism' or Deleuze's 'Stoicism', on the one hand, and Badiou's 'Platonism' on the other, which seeks to find an irreducible place for subjectivity within the ontological order.

[18]   One might remark here that philosophy is perfectly capable of apophaticism, but not of 'mystical theology' in Dionysius the Areopagite's sense: that is, not of the negation of the negation, of the surpassing of negation *as well as* affirmation. For affirmation of what lies beyond the unknown requires an appeal to *mythos* and *symbolon*.

claimed to reach the absolute, the blend of representation of being with enacted norm proper to ritual was naturally never negated even in the projection of transcendence.

When, with Philo and others, the Jewish tradition met with Greek philosophy, it arrived at an explicit third moment of reflection beyond its own implicit double reflexivity from narrated action to being and back again to action. As it had so far tacitly taken God to be being (as in Exodus) and his law to be an ontology of the Creation (as in Numbers, Leviticus and the Wisdom literature), so now it openly proclaimed that Greek being was in fact God, and the Greek order of the cosmos a matter of divinely willed legality. Christian and later Islamic thought duly followed suit.

But as we have already intimated, this synthesis of *nomos* with *ousia* was only possible because Plato and Aristotle had already to some degree, by reinvoking a *mythos* of a transcendent realm 'activated' the ultimate *ousia* and in Plato's case identified the ultimate more as the active source of radiating normativity than of 'abiding' being. This new note of peaceful donation of the cosmos contrasts both with the violent generative break with transcendence enshrined in earlier myth, and with the alternative myths of sacrificial partition of the cosmic man that continued to inflect the perspectives of the first immanentist philosophy. However, the new philosophical mythographers of transcendence had not quite arrived at the monotheistic sense of God as an outgoing will and self-deliberating intelligence.

For this reason, as Giorgio Agamben has argued in the wake of the remarkable twentieth-century Catholic theologian Eric Peterson, theology, as the dominant discourse of the west in the Christian era, is a kind of celestial fusion of metaphysical with political understanding.[19] What political theory is, in a veiled way, to human history, theology is to the entire understanding of reality, but with a more perfect blending of universally theoretical with practical considerations.

For this reason one can say that the first sequence of the current book is about metaphysics, the second is about political theory, while *On Divine Government* will be about religion and theology – precisely insofar as one can define theology as the coincidence of political theory with metaphysics. Because of this coincidence it is changes traceable within theology, still more than those within philosophy or political theory, that tend to reveal the hidden genesis of modern theoretical perspectives.

---

[19] Giorgio Agamben, *The Kingdom and the Glory: For a Theological Genealogy of Economy and Government*, trans. Lorenza Chiesa and Matteo Mandarani (Stanford, Calif.: Stanford University Press, 2011), 53–67.

But the turn to theology has also a practical equivalent. The immanent pride of place accorded to political action is dislodged by that of liturgical or ecclesial performance which extends far beyond church walls in an ambition (initially most shown by monasticism) to embrace the whole of human life on earth. One can say, following Eric Voegelin, that all human politics deliberately or reflectively 'represents' cosmic order, but Christian liturgy much more explicitly and continuously enunciates this, through a sustained effort (as, again, Agamben has argued) to fuse the practical performance of truth with the theoretically based transformation or 'reforming' (as Gerhart Ladner put it) of human society.[20] Here the cult of the ultimate is taken to a new pitch which seeks to blend being and action in terms of the mediation of a truth that is no longer even 'law' because it is not 'over against' either action or being – not commanding the former, as a possibility seeking to master actuality, nor representing the latter at a mimetic remove from it.

Even though 'law' has been thereby downgraded or perhaps transfigured, the primacy of action remains or is even enhanced, since it is all the more personalised as intimate to the merely self-constrained subject – primarily divine, secondarily human. Such radicalism arguably prevents the reversal of priority between act and potential, besides the slippage of knowledge by identity towards knowledge by representation. By contrast, the intensified legalism of Islam (as compared even with Judaism) proved one seedbed for the first beginnings of such philosophical developments, which later infected the west, even if its own home-grown legalisations, from the twelfth century onwards, provided another important root. (Correspondingly it can be said that Sufism and the mystical currents of Shi'ism have at many times crucially tempered the more legal dispositions of Islamic faith and practice.[21])

---

[20]   Eric Voegelin, *The New Science of Politics: An Introduction* (Chicago: Chicago University Press, 1987); Gerhart Ladner, *The Idea of Reform: Its Impact on Christian Thought and Action in the Age of the Fathers* (New York: Harper & Row, 1967).

[21]   As David Burrell and others have so rightly emphasised, it is both sad and ironic that some later, more Persian and Neoplatonic-Gnostic rather than Aristotelian-influenced directions of Islamic thought, for example in Al Ghazali, Sourawardi, Ibn Arabi, and Mulla Sadra, are far more in potential harmony with the metaphysics of the Church Fathers, Aquinas, and the 'Dominican' legacy than the Islamic philosophies which earlier exerted an actual influence on the west. One can note here especially Mulla Sadra's rejection of Ibn Sina's essentialism and embrace of something rather akin to Aquinas's 'existentialism'. Moreover, the Islamic reflection on the importance of the imagination in understanding the superiority of revelation to philosophy is more developed than nonetheless highly equivalent reflections in Christian tradition (for example in Augustine, who like Al Ghazali relates them to the resurrection body in his *De Genesi ad Litteram*), besides resonating with this tradition's embrace of 'theurgic' currents after Dionysius the Areopagite. See Henri Corbin, *Histoire de la philosophie islamique* (Paris: Gallimard, 1986), 285–305, 393–496.

For the above reasons one can argue that all Christian theology is not so much 'political theology' as it is 'politicised metaphysics' or 'metaphysical politics'. Whether or not this new degree of coincidence is revelatory or sinister, it opens up the claim that Christianity is not only 'the most religious of religions', but also the most human of specifically human processes. Therefore, to reject Christianity inevitably opens to view (as Agamben contends) 'post-human' perspectives. (Between Christianity and post-humanism, his own position is perhaps uncertainly located.) For even though it is true that Christianity secularised law, politics, language, science and artistic representation, it did not initially do so in the name of an autonomous secular space – this eventual upshot was only the result of the inauthentic doctrine of *natura pura*. Instead, this secularisation much more implied a negative qualification of *any* stable claims to capture the sacred, and at the same time a relativisation of the Durkheimian sacred/profane boundary (frequent in many cultures), with a consequent sacralisation of all nature as Creation and all culture as divinisable because human. In this way Christianity exalts and extends the religious (in keeping with its borrowing and redefinition of the Roman word 'religio' as now a seamless binding to the true God) precisely by making it more coincide with the human – which is also thereby elevated.

The third sequence will explore these issues consequent upon the idea of Christianity as a theory of 'divine government' which was central for several of the Church Fathers and later for Thomas Aquinas. It is equally a practice of divine government which seeks liturgically to enact and mediate it. This rule of God ranges over soul, city and cosmos. It extends also to human history, because the coincidence of being with action in God requires that metaphysics now become also a philosophy of history, an account of God's actual providential supervision of human events, to the degree that this can be discerned. (Without any such attempt there would be no doctrine of Christ or of the Church.) Thus if political theory surreptitiously reflected and reinforced this empirical level of actual event, now, when articulating a theology, it must be directly engaged and even elevated to co-primacy with being on account of the doctrine of the Incarnation. For this doctrine resolves the *aporia* of an impossible yet necessary difference between the omnipresent God's action *ad intra* and his action *ad extra*, thereby capping 'the more religious because more coincident' character of Christianity.

The two sequences of the present book continually raise the question of the secular as an internal corruption of the theological. In the sequel this question will also appear from the new angle of divine government. For one must now search, not just for a shift in the shared underlying assumptions of both theory and practice, but for a more superficial – and yet equally crucial – level where these assumptions are as much ritually enacted as they are expounded in theory: though in either case, not with entire obviousness. For an 'assumption' more fundamental than either theory or practice must perforce be also a meta-practice, an archetypally 'commanding' action, just as much as it is a paradigmatic theoretical command.[22]

Thus, for example, in *On Divine Government* the question will become less one of the peculiarities of the scholastic thought of the Franciscans as of the possible idiosyncrasies of their entire way of life: their 'habit' of being as well as of thinking. More generally, the question becomes one of whether the idea of a divine government through love eventually becomes perverted in the course of the wholly necessary attempt to incarnate it. In other words, as Ivan Illich asked, does an institutionalisation of the personal come to displace the personalisation of institutions?[23]

Such shifts might undergird the theoretical embrace of the *mathesis* of univocity, possibility, representation and concurrence. And one might either see this decadence as inevitably implied in the initial claimed coincidence of willed loving action and eternal state of being – as Agamben tends to do, though with complex qualifications – or instead as arising later and contingently, in various datable stages, as claimed by Illich and echoed by myself.

Yet if one espouses the latter position, the question remains as to how such drastic deviation, leading in the end to secular apostasy and dereliction of the sacred, within the very culture that uniquely claimed that God had become flesh, could have been possible. Here a 'Romantic' self-critique of Christianity can identify almost from its inception (for all that it newly pointed in the reverse direction) a still excessive bias towards abstraction, towards an ascetical world-refusal and towards action as *stasis*. These biases arguably left its defences too weak against rationalism and an eventual (late medieval and Baroque) idolatry of God as but 'another' ontic reality, however immense. Equally they left Christianity too little safeguarded against a tendency to secularise piously abandoned nature, accompanied by a failure to discern divine inspiration at work in the dynamism of life and the power of human creativity. Both tended in consequence to be handed over to immanentising construals.

---

[22]   See Michel Foucault, *The Archaeology of Knowledge*, trans. A.M. Sheridan Smith (London: Tavistock, 1986).
[23]   Ivan Illich and David Cayley, *The Rivers North of the Future: The Testament of Ivan Illich* (Toronto: Anansi, 2005).

It is notable that, by contrast, the modern restorers of the tradition (from the best of the Christian Renaissance – Cusanus, Mirandola – through the more poetic Christian Baroque – Thomas Browne, Thomas Traherne – to Christian Romanticism – Novalis, Friedrich Schlegel – and post-Romanticism – Félix Ravaisson, Charles Péguy)[24] have tended to emphasise the priority of feeling over reason; a horizontal dilation towards the cosmos and the sexual other as not abandoned by a vertical dilation towards God; the continuity of humanity with a vitalised nature and the reworking of *methexis* in terms of the participation of natural and human creative powers in the Trinitarian emanation of Word and Spirit. It has been more acutely seen that thought and consciousness are lodged at once in our given embodiment and yet also in our 'invention' of language, while the mystery of the ability of imagination and symbol to conjure up truth in resonance with the real has gradually pointed towards a need to engage with the 'suppressed orthodoxies' of the Christian tradition – the more material and magical mysticisms of angel, daemon, star, element, tincture, flower, jewel, humour, letter and number, which echoes in the 'mainline' thinkers more than is often allowed.

All this amounts to a predilection not only for a 're-enchantment' of reality, but for a deepened enchantment, and a yet more generous consideration of pagan religion and other faiths than was entertained in the Patristic era (though in extension of its better impulses). In many ways the crucial theological issue today is whether or not the historically attested Christian tendency to 'disenchant' cosmologies is entirely loyal to its own nature. Might it not be, despite Christianity's indeed authentic and salutary breaking of fetishistic boundaries and questioning of pagan metonymic-synecdochic closure, that this religion does not rather, at its liturgical and sacramental heart, propose a heightened enchantment able to charm down even the absolute (though by and through his ordaining of such cultic means), and therefore able also to include, resume and perfect all local enchantments which it must perforce respect out of its own very incarnating logic? So whereas historical Christianity has excessively tended to wreck all local 'magic', in such a way as to give rise to an abstractly formal secularity or 'enlightenment' as the only shared human discourse and practice, it might be argued that a genuine Christianity uniquely offers a shared theurgic carapace.

Within such a theoretical horizon, analogy newly becomes metaphor and paradox, identity becomes artistic enactment, activity also active potential, and influence a greater synergic engagement of the creative primacy

---

[24]   Many other authors might of course be named.

of the first cause itself. In these ways what is valid in the rationalistic critique undertaken by nominalism is allowed, but met with a questioning of the rationalistic premises themselves. Equally, what is salutary in voluntarism and its heir, political liberalism, is admitted, since if freedom is once again integrated with teleology, ends themselves are now more construed in terms of the freely creative.

These shifts in the construal of the four traditional ontological perspectives must be as much enacted ecclesially and politically as thought through theologically and philosophically, if Christianity and the legacy of the west are to be renewed, and humanity itself sustained in its bizarrely amphibious dignity.

Sequence on Modern Ontology

1 From Theology to Philosophy

If theology is concerned with being in its entirety in relation to God, then we must say that it is also concerned with philosophy in its entirety as the science of being as such, of the way in which being appears, can be known about, acts and can be acted upon, besides those fundamental modes of being which 'divide nature' (to echo Eriugena) into the metaphysical, the biological and the physical. This concern with philosophy in its entirety does not mean, however, that philosophy straightforwardly provides a foundation upon which theology builds, or that philosophy gives an adequate, non-revisable account of being to which theology merely adds the further insights of revelation concerning the nature of the creative cause and the manner in which the creation has fallen and later come to be redeemed. One could even say that the latter model at once accords too much autonomy to philosophy and too much superiority to theology.

For this notion of philosophy as foundational and autonomous is notably ahistorical. In practice it usually means that Christian theology becomes subservient to the dominant philosophy of the day, as still too often prevails. The problem here is that these contemporary philosophies frequently turn out to be not at all theologically neutral, for example in their conception of the relation of God to being, or of the nature of language and of human understanding.

The fundamental reason for this is that an entity called 'philosophy' has never, as a matter of fact, really existed in pure independence from religion or theology. One can even go further, to claim that the idea, or rather the

Beyond Secular Order: The Representation of Being and the Representation of the People, First Edition. John Milbank.
© 2013 John Wiley & Sons, Ltd. Published 2013 by John Wiley & Sons, Ltd.

illusion, of a sheerly autonomous philosophy is twice over the historical invention of certain modes of theology itself.

In the first place, as Pierre Hadot and others have shown, Greek philosophy was always a mode of spiritual practice and never an 'interest-free' enquiry involving a 'view from nowhere'.[1] To quote Eric Voegelin:

> Platonic-Aristotelian analysis did not in the least begin with speculations about its own possibility, but with the actual insight into being which motivated the analytical process. The decisive event in the establishment of *politike episteme* was the specifically philosophical realisation that the levels of being discernible within the world are surmounted by a transcendent source of being and its order. And this insight was itself rooted in the real movements of the human spiritual soul toward divine being experienced as transcendent. In the experiences of love for the world-transcendent origin of being, in *philia* toward the *sophon* (the wise), in *eros* toward the *agathon* (the good) and the *kalon* (the beautiful), man became philosopher.[2]

Of course Voegelin is only speaking here about one philosophical trajectory, albeit the most historically important one, namely the realist-spiritualist tradition of the Academy. However, the materialist Stoics distinguished between philosophy proper, 'as the lived practice of the virtues of logic, physics and ethics' and '"discourse according to philosophy" which was theoretical instruction in philosophy',[3] and they sought to attune both their practical and their theoretical attitudes to the divine character of the cosmos. Even the more nakedly materialist Epicureans did not, according to Hadot, 'conceive physics as a scientific theory, intended to reply to objective, disinterested questions', but rather pursued the study of terrestrial and celestial phenomena in order to secure peace of mind in the face of death, by arguing that the gods never intervene in a self-sustaining physical universe. A free moral adjustment of attitude to this fact is possible because a genuine freedom of the will is grounded in the original, spontaneous, ungrounded and un-determined 'swerve' (*clinamen*) away from an original equilibrium and isonomy of the atoms themselves, which engenders all the differentiations of the universe.[4]

[1] Pierre Hadot, *What is Ancient Philosophy?*, trans. Michael Chase (Cambridge, Mass.: Harvard University Press, 2002).
[2] Eric Voegelin, *Science, Politics and Gnosticism: Two Essays* (Washington, DC: Regnery, 1997), 12.
[3] Hadot, *What is Ancient Philosophy?*, 172.
[4] Hadot, *What is Ancient Philosophy?*, 117–120. See also Michel Serres on Lucretius's moral purposes in *The Birth of Physics*, trans. Jack Hawkes (Manchester: Clinamen Press, 2000), 165–192, especially 176 on the *clinamen*.

Thus even the antique materialists were not trying to adjust their spiritual outlooks to awkward natural facts, but rather were searching for an account of nature that would allow for an experience of beatitude for the individual in this life – omitting the more political, relational and hyper-cosmic perspectives of the Academic tradition which Christianity later greatly augmented. As Robert Spaemann puts it: 'Striving after pleasure and striving after self-preservation were not for Epicurus or the stoic simply naturalistic data, as they were for the French materialists of the eighteenth and for the evolutionary biologists of the nineteenth century; rather, they were aspects of reflection through which life is grasped as a whole which can turn out well or badly.'[5] So, as Spaemann argues, because Epicurus did not assume that real pleasure was merely sensory, but rather sought for an untrammelled and undisturbed personal sensation of happiness (*eudaimonia*), he sought it in a pure present moment uncontaminated by painful memory or fearful anticipation. However, such an ideal moment must paradoxically turn out to be unconscious, mystically transcending the mere experience of pleasure, just as our hedonistic enjoyment of friends will only sustain itself if we show some sort of disinterested regard for them which will guarantee that they can remain friends. Hence Epicurus deduces from a pleasure-seeking basis the duty to die for friends and the greater blessedness of giving as compared with receiving. Likewise, the Stoic pursuit of self-preservation, *conatus*, is not based in the first place upon an ontological anthropology, but upon an attempt to secure stability by maximising our power and range of connections. Yet, since such an effort will never guarantee security, it turns paradoxically into an attitude of resignation towards fate and indifference as to what happens to oneself.[6]

So in a way that seems very counter-intuitive to us moderns, it was antique *materialism* which encouraged pure sacrificial altruism and noble ascetic indifference towards all suffering, whereas the more spiritual, Academic tradition tended to allow more for the ultimate value of relationality and friendship, of 'being-with' the cosmos and the other, rather than self-obliteration in the face of these realities. One can only grasp why this was the case if one sees that these different philosophical stances were just as much different practices and different modes of religious belief as they were divergent argumentative conclusions. In the Academic case one has a philosophy which makes life in the *polis* and (sometimes) friendship with the cosmically transcendent divine ultimate;

---

[5] Robert Spaemann, *Happiness and Benevolence*, trans. Jeremiah Alberg SJ (Notre Dame: Notre Dame University Press, 2000), 50.
[6] Spaemann, *Happiness and Benevolence*, 28–50.

in the materialist case one has philosophies grounded on a life of ascetic retreat or else solitude, and which preclude any ultimate association with the gods (whose existence is still not denied). Perhaps, as was indicated in the Preface, Deleuze and Guattari were right to identify the first and purest philosophy with an anti-mythical and monistic thinking of immanence, incorporating both matter and mind, both energy and image; however, insofar as their models for this are necessarily *antique* materialism (and Spinoza in certain ways in the wake of antiquity), then one could say that such pure philosophy is also a kind of theology, a mode of religiosity and even of *hyper* religiosity, insofar as it is materialism which tends to demand a discontinuity between the ethics of practical involvement and the theoretical stance of unification with reality.[7]

Paradoxically, it might seem, it was only when Jews, Muslims and then Christians rediscovered aspects of Greek philosophy, especially Aristotle and certain fragments of Neoplatonism, that they projected back onto antiquity a purely 'rational' enquiry that was somewhat of their own invention. This was because antique philosophy could be viewed as at least problematically legitimate if it was taken as the work of human reason, but not if it was taken as linked to specifically pagan religious reflection. In this way a category of 'pure reason' started to come into being only as the shadow of the notion of 'faith'. To cite Hadot once more: 'modern philosophy has come to consider itself a theoretical science because the existential dimension of philosophy no longer had any meaning from the perspective of Christianity, which was simultaneously both doctrine and life'.[8]

In many ways this rediscovery of antique thought disturbed an older Christian model for the integration of philosophy within Christian doctrine. In the case of the Greek Fathers from the apologists onwards, and of Augustine, little distinction was made between *philosophia Christiana*, 'doctrine' and 'theology'. Truth was seen as one, and revelation as the restoration of a fullness of truth, insofar as this is accessible for finitude, to fallen human beings. This sometimes entailed nevertheless a distinction between pagan (i.e. mainly Greek) and 'revealed' philosophy. However, the former – in the case of those Platonic authors held, by the Christian apologists like Justin Martyr to have already intuited monotheism – was less regarded as a replete natural philosophy than as a kind of mental typological anticipation of a full, revealed theoretical illumination. For with the incarnation of the *Logos* itself, and the more general descent of *Sophia*

[7] Gilles Deleuze and Félix Guattari, *What is Philosophy?*, trans. Hugh Tomlinson and Graham Burchell (New York: Columbia University Press, 1994), 35–61.

[8] Hadot, *What is Ancient Philosophy?*, 259.

in the joint arrival in time of the *Logos-Ecclesia* (a theme more rarely but nonetheless sometimes entertained), it was considered that a more complete human reasoning, or 'philosophy' became possible. But this more complete reasoning was itself situated within an entire 'life according to the *Logos*', such that the monastic life was often equated with *philosophia*.[9]

There is indeed much evidence to suggest that, before the year 1300 or so, there was no clear duality between theological and philosophical reason. This is witnessed, as Jean-Luc Marion has pointed out, by the quite cautious and limited use of the term 'theology' itself, given that this term would have been seen, in its pagan philosophical use, as tending dangerously to subordinate theology to philosophy.[10] This is particularly true for the Aristotelian legacy which divided theoretical science up into the mathematical, the physical and the theological and which also, on at least one reading, regarded the study of God as a regional division of the study of being in general.[11] Thus the Latin tradition prior to 1300 tended to favour terms like *sacra pagina* and *sacra eruditio* and later *doctrina sacra* to the term *theologia*.

In Aquinas nonetheless, in the wake of Maimonides, Ibn Sina and Ibn Rushd, there is apparently a much greater distinction made between philosophy, including its rational mode of doing theology, and *sacra doctrina*, which reflects upon revelation. But to regard this seemingly sharp distinction as simply a gain, with time, of a greater clear-sightedness, is surely naïve.[12] For the new divide rather reflects the challenge posed by Aristotelianism as a philosophy seemingly true according to reason, and yet less easily assimilable in certain ways with the conclusions of faith than an earlier Platonic mode of thinking. Often this circumstance later gave rise to various modes of a 'double truth' doctrine, as in so-called 'Latin Averroism'. It also eventually helped to encourage a new mode of theologico-philosophical reflection which not only dared to criticise Aristotle himself, but also the entire actualist and realist bias of the Greek philosophical legacy, in the name of an increasingly positivistic and voluntarist account of God, creation and revelation by vastly extending the scope and ontological primacy of logical possibility: I am thinking of Scotus and then of the nominalists. However, in the case of

---

9   Hadot, *What is Ancient Philosophy?*, 237–270.
10   Jean-Luc Marion, 'What are the Roots of the Distinction between Theology and Philosophy?', lecture given at Georgetown University, 20 Apr. 2011, available on YouTube. Last viewed 12 June 2012.
11   Aristotle, *Metaphysics* V.1026a19, X.1064b3; Boethius, *De Trinitate* II.1–20.
12   See John Milbank and Catherine Pickstock, *Truth in Aquinas* (London: Routledge, 2001), 19–59.

Aquinas, the new circumstance rather encouraged him to show how basically Aristotelian reasons, when properly considered, themselves supported the conclusions of faith.

Yet Aquinas was only here successful because he was able to show that the implications of Christian doctrine were more 'materialist' than had hitherto been supposed – or at least consistently supposed. The material creation was not only good, its material character was also for us vital in assisting the processes of mental deliberation, reasoning to God and the bringing about of our salvation. Even if most certainly Aristotle uniquely enabled him to state these conclusions in a bold new fashion, they were nonetheless supported both by a more accurate reading of Augustine than that provided by more spiritualist and dualistic interpretations, and by deployment of the Proclean strand of Neoplatonism (mediated in part by Dionysius the Areopagite) which already permitted an integration of a more 'materialist' view within a framework that remained fundamentally emanationist and participatory in a Platonic mode, but now assumed more emphatically theurgic and cosmological dimensions. The picture Aquinas is always arguing for concerns fundamentally the logic of creation *ex nihilo*, along with the gracious raising of spiritual creatures to a supernatural end that is, nonetheless, paradoxically an integral implication of their spiritual existence as such.[13]

Thus while Aquinas appears to deploy 'purely rational' arguments, the conclusions which he is supporting are always those consistent with faith – like, for example, the diversity and autonomy in different created spirits of the operation of the active intellect, which, against the Arab scholastics, he took to be required in order to sustain both the freedom of spiritual beings and the ultimate significance of the material distinctness and individuality of human spiritual creatures.[14] Furthermore, Aquinas was not a modern rationalist: he understood good reason to be an attentive reception, via the mediation of the senses and discursive operations, of the divine light of the *Logos*, in fundamental keeping (despite many scholarly denials) with the view of St Augustine.[15] Finally, for Aquinas, good reason can only be such if implicitly it desires, and therefore mysteriously intimates in advance, that which can only be received as a gift: namely the supernatural light of faith.[16]

[13]   See for this point and the entire account of Aquinas here given, Milbank and Pickstock, *Truth in Aquinas*.

[14]   Aquinas, *De Unitate Intellectus Contra Auerroistas*.

[15]   See Jacob Schmutz, 'La Doctrine médiévale des causes et la théologie de la nature pure (XIIIe–XVIIe siècles)', *Revue Thomiste*, special issue on the *Surnaturel* (Jan.–Feb. 2001), 217–264.

[16]   See John Milbank, *The Suspended Middle: Henri de Lubac and the Debate Concerning the Supernatural* (Grand Rapids, Mich., and London: Eerdmans/SCM, 2005, 2006), 88–108.

In these ways Aquinas effectively restored the Patristic integration of philosophy with theology, albeit he now more distinguished to unite. Unlike some of his contemporaries and many later medieval theologians, he did not locate the rational study of God within the field of metaphysics. Instead, he saw metaphysics as concerned with 'being' as its object and as concerned with God only insofar as it must posit a causal principle for being itself, in the sense of being as *ens commune*, or that abstract 'generic' existence which is displayed in various different essential modes amongst finite creatures, and in real distinction from them. Metaphysics understands that this ultimate cause of being, which is 'God' – as the coincidence of *ens* and *essentia* in *esse* or the 'to be' itself – must be the subject of a higher science which is in fact God's own self-knowledge, since a science of the absolute uncaused ground of all things can only be self-reflexive and for us esoteric. So for any substantive knowledge of 'theology proper' at all, we depend upon divine revelation. Yet this, it turns out, for Aquinas concerns simply a heightened degree of the participation of both disclosive historical events and human mental illumination in the divine reality.[17] Grace-given revelation, which is nothing other than the creation's awareness of itself in humanity as destined to return to God ('deification') is inseparable for Aquinas from the outgoing of creation, which can only proceed forth in the exact measure that it is bound to return, since at its depth its only reality is the gift of divine existence, which is 'all in all'.[18] However, angelic, cosmic and human fallenness conceals this reality from view, and it must be shown again through the re-making of humanity and the cosmos (only achievable through Man the Microcosm) in the Incarnation of the *Logos*. It is uniquely the sight of Christ on earth and the tasting of Christ in the Eucharist which now restores to the intellect through the senses that 'certainty' of anticipating the beatific vision which is obscurely implied even by the rational appeal to God as first cause.[19]

Rational theology and revealed theology are not, then, for Aquinas, even from a human perspective, simplistically discrete 'stages', but rather always imply each other in different degrees and with different intensities along a continuum of coming-to-know within historical time. But from a divine point of view it is Aquinas's central doctrine of divine simplicity (which means that all and every distinction we make as to the inner divine life applies only to our limited cognitive or 'grammatical' perspective) which ensures that the two theologies are only aspects of a single divine knowing.

[17]   *ST* II-II. q. 171 a. 1 ad. 4 a. 2 resp.; a. 3 resp.; a. 6 resp.
[18]   See Milbank, *The Suspended Middle*, 88–103.
[19]   See Frédéric Nef, *Qu'est-ce que la métaphysique?* (Paris: Gallimard, 2004), 281–378; Milbank and Pickstock, *Truth in Aquinas*, 19–65.

For God the creator and revealer is one: his emanation of created being and his call to creation and humanity to return to him are a single same eternal unchanging action. Within God they are indeed further identical with the inner (relationally distinguished) Paternal generation of the Word, and the 'returning' procession of the Spirit through the Son from the Father. For in his *Sentence Commentary* Aquinas remarkably stated, anticipating Eckhart, that the Trinitarian and created outgoings are 'essentially' the same, and only distinguished by 'the addition of a sort of relation to the temporal effect'.[20]

And even from the human, created point of view, as has just been stated, creation and deification (of humanity and of the cosmos in various proper degrees through humanity) are perceived as but finitely distinguished facets of the single divine act, although the teleological relation involved in the natural/supernatural distinction also embodies (one might add, to Aquinas) a trace of the distinction by substantive relation between the metaphorically 'natural' or 'biological' generation of the Son and the metaphorically 'willed' procession of the Spirit.[21]

This unifying perspective is reflected in Aquinas's pedagogic practice, which rarely shows a strong division between the two modes of discourse, but rather tends constantly to shuttle between both. Reason, for him, always has an obscure onlook towards faith, while faith, which is relatively more intuitive, can never, in this life, fully leave behind the discursiveness proper to philosophy.

It follows that, for Aquinas, philosophy is not straightforwardly foundational and neither is theology straightforwardly superior.

Instead theology, whenever it intimates the heights, must humbly return to the depths and forever in time start all over again with the relatively prosaic problems posed by philosophy. Its transcendence of the philosophical

---

[20] Thomas Aquinas, *In Sent.* I, dist. 16 q. 1 a. 1 resp.

[21] On divine simplicity and our *modus significandi* in Aquinas, see David B. Burrell CSC, *God and Action* (London: RKP, 1979) For the argument that Aquinas ultimately, like Eckhart, 'identifies' from the divine perspective Trinitarian inner and creative outer emanation, at least in his earlier writings and possibly also in his later ones, see Philipp Rosemann, *Omne ens est aliquid: Introduction à la lecture du 'système philosophique' de Saint Thomas d'Aquin* (Louvain and Paris: Peeters, 1996), 202–203. I have taken the Trinitarian distinction of nature and will from the Franciscan tradition in Bonaventure and Scotus, but tried to reconcile it with the tradition of substantive relation, whereas the Franciscans intended to use this distinction to distinguish the persons *instead of* distinction by substantive relation. This involved a divide between non-voluntary natural generation and sheerly voluntary procession which I am not endorsing. I merely want to suggest a remote analogy between natural and supernatural orientation – or indeed natural and cultural orientation – on the one hand, and the relation between Son and Spirit on the other.

perspective is always, for now, merely provisional. Inversely, philosophy offers no secure self-contained foundation, because it always necessarily gestures beyond itself, in accordance with the Augustinian version of the 'Meno problematic' which Aquinas several times invokes: we can only seek God who is beyond all reach if in some strange sense we have already arrived at this destination, because he has always already reached down to us.[22] The scope of this problematic for him embraces both reason and revelation and transcends their division, as likewise does the entire framework of the participation of beings in Being and of spiritual beings in the divine light, which is in itself one and simple.

It can be argued, then, that Aquinas warded off the threat of duality posed by those Islamic philosophers with which he was familiar – even if one should point out that various mystically Sh'ite and Sufi figures later offered more integrating perspectives. Aquinas indeed, at times, when assessing the rational opinions of Plato and Aristotle, suggests that one must take account of the pagan character of their thought, though no doubt, with historicist hindsight, he did not do this to anything like a sufficient degree.

For these reasons it is not entirely clear that Aquinas fully accepted the retrospective invention of the rational autonomy of philosophy.

However, this autonomy was much more decisively confirmed in a second historical moment. In a gradual process stretching from Scotus through Suárez to Báñez, theology started to conclude that human beings not only have two distinct final ends (as Aquinas formally allows), a natural and a supernatural one, but that the former remains substantially independent of the latter. If previously the notion of a purely rational philosophy had been shadowed by a sense of something pagan and unredeemed, now, especially after Francisco Suárez, this was seen as an entirely legitimate exercise, within the bounds of 'pure nature', so long as it was undertaken in ultimate expectation of 'serving' the higher truth of faith.[23] A fully autonomous theoretical philosophy, in principle independent of any existential orientation or quest for beatitude, had at last arrived.[24] In a certain way, then, we must qualify Deleuze and Guattari: philosophy as concerned with purely immanent, univocal being (whether this is taken as including a transcendent 'god' or not) and so with a theoretical primacy of indifferent facts that we must come to terms with – an immanentism that is eventually much more nakedly

---

22   See Milbank and Pickstock, *Truth in Aquinas*, 36–37.
23   Hadot, *What is Ancient Philosophy?*, 255.
24   See Milbank, *The Suspended Middle*.

spelled out in all its implications by David Hume than by Baruch Spinoza – is the bastard offspring of a theology which has embraced a dualism of natural and supernatural ends. It is not, after all, a pure but abandoned child of Greek antiquity.

So the paradox is that the theoretically secularising gesture, which permitted the arrival of a pure, autonomous philosophy, was entirely a theological gesture, and even one which sought to conserve the transcendence of God and the priority of the supernatural, by mistakenly insisting on the sheer 'naturalness' and self-sufficiency of human beings without grace, as a backdrop for augmenting grace's sheer gratuity.

2   The Four Pillars of Modern Philosophy

This circumstance then poses a crucial question for theology today. Far from it being the case that theology is necessarily at the mercy of philosophical fashions, it is now, thanks to new historical research, in a position to ask whether the fundamental assumed shape of modern philosophy as such is not the result of buried and forgotten past theological decisions. Decisions which, in theological terms, were highly questionable, if, indeed, not outrightly erroneous.

Here one needs to see that the invention of a double human end (natural and supernatural) was itself embedded in earlier and equally doubtful theological options, which all tended to suggest the comprehensibility of finite being, essences, knowledge and causality entirely in their own terms, without reference to their created and supernatural origin. These were, primarily, the substitution of: (1) univocity for analogy in ontology; (2) mirroring representation for knowledge by identity in gnoseology; (3) the primacy of possibility for the primacy of actuality in modal theory; and finally (4) in the case of the theory of causality, the 'concurrence' of created with divine causality on the same ontological plane for an earlier notion of finite and infinite causation operating synergically on different ontological levels, with the latter conceived as transcendentally all-determining of finite causes in their very independence, through a process of 'in-flowing' or *influentia*. This model extended also to intra-ontic strata: thus matter and form were now seen as 'concurrently' working causes operating in the same dimension, whereas by Aristotle and Aquinas they were seen as 'reciprocally' operating causes, meaning causes acting in incommensurably different fashions and yet each indispensable to the other. We shall later see the acutely practical and social implications of this seemingly esoteric point.[25]

In all four cases one has a new set of philosophical theses which dictate the entire consequent course of modern philosophy – as several of the major historians of philosophy now agree. But, in all four cases also, it is arguable that the fundamental reasons for the adoption of these theses were theological.

(a) Univocity

First of all, as regards univocity, Ibn Sina (Avicenna in Latin usage) and later Scotus were concerned not just with questions of logic but with the security of proofs for God's existence which, in order to be fully apodeictic, can be held to require a stable middle term. Scotus was in addition concerned to defend the coherence of predicating terms like 'goodness' of God by insisting upon their core stability of meaning and projecting this supposed semantic identity upon the ontological level. This meant that our understanding of evaluative or 'perfection' terms had already become divorced from human experience and the spiritual life. In Aquinas it was still the case that an exploration of the meaning of the word 'good' involved entering on an existential journey towards an inaccessible plenitude of perfect goodness in God. So to delve into the richness of the meaning of good was also to ascend towards a higher contemplation and practice of goodness, and that ascent in its turn simply *was* the ascent towards God. Semantic and logical exploration was, in consequence, also here an ontological one and, in addition, an entering into a pedagogic *paideia*, beyond any merely detached, passionless enquiry. With the shift towards univocity, however, the meaning of the word 'good' can be known about sufficiently once and for all, in independence from any spiritual stance. This means that 'to become better', in practical terms, is no longer also to achieve a greater theoretical insight into the meaning of goodness,

---

[25] See, for all these four points and much of the following explication of them, Olivier Boulnois, *Être et représentation: Une généalogie de la métaphysique moderne à l'époque de Duns Scot* (Paris: PUF, 1999); Nef, *Qu'est-ce que la métaphysique?*, 314–415; Schmutz, 'La Doctrine médiévale des causes'; Catherine Pickstock, 'Duns Scotus: His Historical and Contemporary Significance', *Modern Theology*, 21/4 (Oct. 2005), 543–575; John Milbank, 'The Thomistic Telescope: Truth and Identity', *American Catholic Philosophical Quarterly*, 80/2 (2006), 193–227; David Burrell, 'Aquinas and Scotus: Contrary Patterns for Philosophical Theology', in *Faith and Freedom: An Interfaith Perspective* (Oxford: Blackwell, 2004), 91–113; André de Muralt, *L'Unité de la philosophie politique: De Scot, Occam et Suarez au libéralisme contemporain* (Paris: J. Vrin, 2002).

in line with that union of the theoretical with the practical which, we have already seen, defined 'philosophy' as such – as both 'love of knowledge' and 'knowledge of love' – ever since classical antiquity.[26] Instead, it implies a merely quantitative increase in the exemplification of a goodness already fully known about.

It is easy to see here how the ground for the Kantian finitisation and formalisation of practical reason has already been prepared. Similarly, Scotus anticipated in some measure the Cartesian thesis of an 'equal measure of freedom' pertaining between God and humanity, infinite and finite, since already for him the will is formally defined as 'indifferent' to the choice it makes – whether for or against what still for him (and still even for Descartes) should be its proper final end. Since later for Kant the 'morally right' consists, both for God and humanity, in an ungrounded decision of the will for a primary goodness (now reduced tautologously to mere respect for freedom itself as 'moral right'), conceivable and definable independently of this decision, of any habitual formation, or teleological orientation of the affections, one can say that Scotist univocity opened the way here also for a further rationalist abolition of the qualitative distance between God and creatures.

Finally, Duns Scotus considered that his idea of being in the abstract, rather than materialised being as the natural first object of human understanding both guaranteed our spiritual nature and indicated the difference between a pre-fallen and a fallen, sensually debased, exercise of intelligence.[27]

It was especially in terms of this new, less ontological concept of the transcendentality of being (which already edges towards the Kantian sense of 'transcendental') that metaphysics as ontology came to be considered independent of theology and transcendentally prior to it, in the course of a long process that culminated with Suárez in the early seventeenth century.[28] And this was no mere procedural matter, for it meant that concepts of 'height' were no longer identical with concepts of 'the most universal' and that the former was now logically situated within the transcendental space of the latter. Excellence has been reduced to one more fact within a field fundamentally defined by facts – whereas previously all facts pointed ultimately towards the highest excellence and were only 'there' at all in

---

[26]   This transposition is suggested by Luce Irigaray, in *The Way of Love*, trans. H. Bostic and S. Pluháček (London: Continuum, 2002). Even if the term was never quite used in that way, something of such a reversal was implied in it. See also Jean-Luc Marion, *Le Phénomène érotique* (Paris: Grasset, 2003), 9–23. I am indebted here for discussions with Tony Baker of the Episcopal Divinity School, Austin, Texas.

[27]   See Boulnois, *Être et représentation*, 223–291.

[28]   See J.-F. Courtine, *Suarez et le système de la métaphysique* (Paris: PUF, 1990).

their various ways of being because they were literally *facta*, made things or gifts suspended from this height, and symbolically signed with a trace of their sublime origin.

(b) Representation

Secondly, as regards knowledge by representation, the new model was much encouraged by Scotus's view that one can formally distinguish the divine intellect, as representing truth, from the divine being, which enjoys a certain metaphysical primacy. It was especially in relation to the paradigmatic model of divine knowledge that Scotus distinguished the *esse objectivum* of known being as something 'caused to be known' by God and as intending a represented object, from the *esse formalis* of the actual representation itself. Through his 'objective' knowledge of things, God now *precisely* and univocally represents them, whereas, for Aquinas, God's eminent 'representation' of things as *identical* with his very being (not formally distinct from it, as for Scotus), knows things through a heightened *dissimilarity* to them – knows them truly by achieving them in himself as more than themselves and only knowable in their alien finitude as the participability of their infinitely perfect exemplary instance. It was just this traditional Platonic 'exemplarism' which Scotus abandoned: no longer is the stone as known by God 'nobler' than the stone as it finitely exists.[29]

In the older exemplarist view it can most of all be seen that Platonic-Aristotelian 'knowledge by identity' implies also a 'knowledge through transformation'. But with Scotus this becomes a knowledge through literal 'copying', even in the case of God, who 'mirrors' those things which he has willed to bring into being, yet in such a way that the mirror has ontological precedence over that which it mirrors.[30] This means that God can 'efficiently' produce the ideal objects of his knowledge independently of their formal reference or their formally eminent real pre-containment of created things. In addition, since his knowledge of actual things is merely consequent upon his willed production of them, rather than being – as for Aquinas – identical with his essence and with his *Verbum* (the second person of the Trinity), it has acquired a discursive as well as an intuitive aspect (and so in this respect also comes more univocally to resemble human knowledge).

[29]   Duns Scotus, *Opus Oxoniense* IV, dist. 1 q. 1 para. [20]. See also, for a fine account of this point, Rosemann, *Omne ens est aliquid*, 48–72.

[30]   Duns Scotus, *Ordinatio* I, dist. 32 §23.

Such an account of divine understanding encourages the possibility that human knowledge also is essentially the subjective efficient and discursive production of an image, and only secondarily an intuited image 'of' something.[31] Gradually, this came to displace the Aristotelian and Thomist view that human understanding does not primarily depend on an accuracy of copying, but rather is guaranteed to be true (unless something 'unnaturally' interferes with this reality) by the unmediated identity of the abstracted form in the mind with the form as it exists when combined with matter in the material substances of which we have knowledge.

This switch from knowledge by identity to knowledge by representation was equally encouraged, from Scotus through to Ockham, by the increasing consideration that God, through exercise of his *potentia absoluta*, can sever the normal link between our mind's understanding of things and the way they are in themselves. This helps to ensure that, in Scotus, the primary thing that is known through cognitive intention is not the real, external form-matter compound as for Aquinas, but rather, for the first time in history, an 'object', the *esse objectivum* which is a fundamentally inward reality, a 'copy' in principle detachable from external reference, because it no longer involves a real transmission of form from the external reality.[32] Following Ibn Sina, and what Étienne Gilson rightly called *augustinisme avicennisant*, most Franciscan theologians had already (unlike Aquinas) rejected Aristotle's view that a form could pass as *species* all the way from matter to the immaterial intellectual capacity of the soul (or 'mind'). This was because they considered it inappropriate to assign to the intellect such a degree of passivity in the face of a non-reflexive and so non-intellectual source: for their various alternative explanations, sensation is seen as somehow occasioning or triggering an auto-activation on the part of the mind. All these theories tended to involve, in consequence, some sort of notion of a direct co-ordination by God of material with spiritual causality at the immanent level itself. (In this way a theory of 'causality by concurrence' was invoked: see (d) below).[33]

This fear of ascribing any sort of passivity to the human mind in the face of non-cognitive and material sources can be seen as essentially linked to Plotinian tradition, which rejected the full descent of the human soul into a material body, in contrast to the 'theurgic' construal of Plato (Iamblichus, Proclus and Damascius), which allowed this, and therefore much more embraced a receptivity of the human mind in the face of the material

---

[31]   For all this paragraph see Boulnois, *Être et représentation*, 405–457.
[32]   Duns Scotus, *Quodlibetal Questions*, 13 par. [12] 39 (461).
[33]   See Boulnois, *Être et représentation*, 72.

cosmos, often indeed seen as in some sense 'greater' and more intellectual (as animated by the world soul, following Plato's *Timaeus*) than the human mind itself.[34] The latter perspective (known to him via Dionysius, John Damascene and the Proclean *Liber de Causis*), almost as much as his Aristotelianism, encouraged Aquinas's 'materialist' emphasis, and allowed him much more to stress a humility of the human mind before the material creation, despite the truth that it is the noblest thing within that creation. Since the latter is the work of God, proceeding from an infinite mind with which the human mind is not commensurate, it could not therefore be formed by us (even if we had the materials to hand, in contrast to the later Renaissance claims of Ficino and Galileo).[35] Aquinas's position here seems to do more justice to credal theology. Hence the Franciscan rejection of knowledge by identity for knowledge by representation is linked to a theology that is Platonising *in a bad sense*, one which underrates the nobility of the material creation.

The new Franciscan idea that we know primarily an object which intentionally 'represents' reality through copying it, producing a kind of phenomenal *simulacrum*, ultimately ensures the modern turn from ontology to epistemology, although this turn usually followed Ockham rather than Scotus in abandoning the 'intentional' moment in favour of a passively present atomic sensation, or else a phantasmic 'idea' in the case of René Descartes and John Locke – here following remotely Peter Auriole (just before Ockham) and Nicholas of Autrecourt (Ockham's follower) rather than Ockham himself.[36] For Ockham, the human mind engages in an act of understanding by fictively substituting a 'name' for the thing known through sensation, in a way that further opens up a sceptical prospect (again by invoking God's *potentia absoluta*) of doubting any intrinsic connection between names and things whatsoever. However, Scotus's intentionalist variant returns much later with the thought of Husserl, and forms the basis both for his phenomenological *epoché* and curious combination of a quasi-realist receptivity with a transcendentally idealist closure against transcendent reference to the real. This Scotist scheme is only mutated, not abandoned, by Heidegger, since he

---

[34]   See Gregory Shaw, *Theurgy and the Soul: The Neoplatonism of Iamblichus* (University Park, Pa.: Penn State University Press, 1995).
[35]   On Ficino and Galileo in this respect, see J.-L. Chrétien, 'From God the Artist to Man the Creator', in *Hand to Hand: Listening to the Work of Art*, trans. Stephen E. Lewis (New York: Fordham University Press, 2002), 94–130.
[36]   See André de Muralt, 'Kant, le dernier occamien: Une nouvelle définition de la philosophie moderne' (1975), in *La Métaphysique de la phénomène* (Paris: J. Vrin, 1985), 138–159, specifically 146.

identifies the human phenomenological openness towards – and anxiety in the face of – being, with the 'there' of being as such: *Da-Sein*.[37]

In the Scotist instance, an older sense that knowledge is an event which, through formal participation, 'really relates' us to the ontological form in its mode of 'being known', and so to its intentional 'rebound' back to the form/matter compound, is lost: now what is 'intended' by the act of understanding and its correlative object is merely a 'represented' being in the world, since the formality of the known object may 'copy' the real external thing, but has no real formal identity or continuity with it. And the newly invented 'object' sustains an ontological novelty through all its later transmutations: as primarily (following the divine paradigm) a 'possibility' it is prior to either actual essence or to existence, and yet as *aliquid* ('something') rather than *res*, it still shares with real things a parity of univocal being. Thus Scotus alternates in different places as to whether the first object of the intellect is real being or, rather, both real and objective being, and he opens the way for Suárez's placing of *res* itself under the aegis of the *aliquid*, defined since Scotus as the 'not nothing', while leaving it unclear as to whether there is now a 'transcendental object' embracing both 'things' and 'concepts'. In this way being starts to be reduced to the representable and ontology to give way to epistemology: a transition that will be consummated by Descartes and Kant.[38]

(c)   Possibilism

In the third case of the modal priority of the possible over the actual it is, once again, a matter of stressing the *potentia absoluta* as God's primary attribute, along with an elevation of the divine will over the divine intellect, as well as, still more significantly, the formal distinction of the two. The latter notion ensures that reasoning, sundered from the erotic (in the sense of the desiring) will be more and more thought of in terms of the consideration of

[37]   See de Muralt, *L'Unité de la philosophie politique*, 7–26 (esp 24), 154–157; 'La Critique de la notion scotiste d'*esse objectivum*, le "psychologisme" et le "nominalisme" occamiens', in *Métaphysiques médiévales: Cahiers de la Revue de Théologie et de Philosophie* (Geneva, Lausanne and Neuchâtel, 1999), 20. De Muralt's work is only marred by his refusal to accept that there is a significantly Neoplatonic dimension in Aquinas and that this is needed to enhance his Aristotelianism, with which it is not, however, essentially at variance. Curiously, such a recognition would render more powerful the general drift of de Muralt's genealogy – especially in relation to the issue of causality, where the rise of concurrence was directly linked to the decline of Neoplatonic *influentia*. See Schmutz, 'La Doctrine médiévale des causes'. See also for the above paragraph, Boulnois, *Être et représentation*, 88–105, 405–457.

[38]   Boulnois, *Être et représentation*, 405–457.

an *a priori* repertoire of logical possibilities, while, equally, willing, sundered from an intrinsic determination by the rationally best, starts to become reduced to an arbitrary choice that precedes any necessities endemic to an order of actuality.[39]

For Aristotle, the actual was primary in terms of definition, time and substance.[40] We can define things because we encounter them. Possibilities arise only because certain things are already actual and these are the most basic realities, the primary instantiations of being. Accordingly, potentiality cannot actualise itself but must be actualised by what is already in being. This means that the possible is defined in terms of its tendency to the realisation of an actual *telos*.

Such an outlook was taken over and even augmented by Aquinas. For he understood the contingency of the created world in terms of the dependency of its *partial* actualisations (and so its partial *perfections*), upon the divine simple and infinite actuality. In this manner he considered the actualised 'necessities' of the created order which conformed to the regularities of eternal reason to be just as contingent – since they are dependent on the divine creative act – as its apparently more accidental or aleatory features.

For many of the Franciscan theologians, and pre-eminently Duns Scotus, this outlook paid too much tribute to pagan fatality. Yet one can argue that they only thought this because, in the wake of a conceptual paradigm shift from a more allegorical to a more literalist apprehension of biblical content, they were *reinterpreting* the biblical legacy rather than attending to it more precisely.

'More literalist' here means in part that the *sensus literalis* itself (which does not quite coincide with our contemporary meaning of 'literal') was less and less taken to include also the symbolic participation of natural realities 'literally' referred to (in our modern sense) in the divine. It means in addition that the allegorical, tropological and anagogical – that is, Christological, ethical and eschatological – senses (that are covertly implied by the *sensus literalis*) were increasingly reduced to a positive meaning of 'literal prophecy'.[41]

This degeneration, as Henri de Lubac argued, destroyed in quasi-Nestorian fashion the Christological possibility of theology as such, which is grounded in a pointing of all created reality to the *comunicatio idiomatum*

---

[39] For all of this section, see Nef, *Qu'est-ce que la métaphysique?*, 314–411.

[40] Aristotle, *Metaphysics* 1049b4–5.

[41] See Henri de Lubac, *Exégèse médiévale: Les Quatre Sens de l'écriture* (Paris: Aubier, 1964), II-II, 263–302. See also Peter Candler, *Theology, Rhetoric, Manuduction* (Grand Rapids, Mich.: Eerdmans, 2006).

between Christ's divine and human natures, within which divine realities are translated into the terms of created symbolic echo and counter-echo – and are not left as 'separately' divine, conveyable only to human beings in positive, arbitrary, authoritarian terms.[42] If one takes account of the fact (which the best modern scholarship confirms) that the Bible is *internally* constituted through a typological apprehension of the cosmos, history and language, then this gradual slide towards 'Nestorian' literalism by no means implies an increase in 'biblical' influence at the expense of Neoplatonising metaphysics.

Indeed one should argue just the contrary: the very theologians (from Scotus through to Ockham and then to Suárez) who abandoned a meta-physically participatory framework were the same theologians who tended to abandon also a grounding of *quaestio* in *lectio*, or of scholastic dispute in scriptural commentary (whereas Aquinas commented with great exegetical and theological acumen on at least nine books of the Bible, while also compiling a *Catena Aurea* of Patristic commentaries on the Scriptures). This was because they increasingly tended to reduce revelation to the divine disclosure of isolated facts and logically linked propositions which could be distilled from the narrative and typological flow of Scripture, whose significance was in consequence downplayed and left to the musings of more 'mystical' writers. So it is precisely the more classical Christian sensibility, which tends to think of the disclosive role of the symbol as irreducible, and of revelation as given in signs whose horizontal *semiosis* (linked always to inter-bodily communication) cannot be elided from their vertical import, which will tend also to be sympathetic to the metaphysical mysteries of participation. For in the latter case it is taken that we 'see in part', and cannot ever travel to the back of the 'dark glass' in order to compare image with original, or the precise way in which our minds are able obscurely 'to envisage' the divine.

So the later Franciscan theologians tended to be suspicious of *both* partici-pation *and* allegory as impairing our acknowledgement of the absolute free-dom of God by supposing that various created realities, by their very nature, disclose something of the eternal divine essence. Instead of the notion of a partial reflection of created glory, they preferred to stress the sheer arbitrary electedness of every aspect of the created order. Hence the very notion of 'contingency' started to be redefined, with archiepiscopal backing at Paris and Canterbury, as a pure possibility that might not have been instantiated

---

[42]   De Lubac, *Exégèse médiévale*, II-II, 198–207, 317–328, 349–352.

at all, or else instantiated otherwise.[43] For Aquinas, as for Aristotle, an actuality realises a possibility, but does not *continue* to be synchronically shadowed by a real possibility that is a hypostasised logical possibility, since for Aquinas an actuality fulfils in some measure a divinely intended good and therefore 'cancels out', through its very fulfilment, the genuinely possible. By contrast, for Duns Scotus, the contingency of a finite actual moment is only guaranteed by the *persistence* in some sense of the real possibility of an alternative actuality which is therefore *synchronous* with that actuality.[44]

One could say that the latter view ignores the non-punctuality of events: the way in which, for a single actuality to have been different, everything would have had to be different, all the way back to the outset of time. But this is just why, with Leibniz, Scotist modalism eventually shifts into the idiom of possible-worlds theory – the set of compossibles of this world is perennially shadowed by the sets of compossibles of infinite other worlds. An entirely aleatory construal of this situation is, however, prevented in Leibniz by his mathematicised Avicennian view that possibility in itself constitutes essences which urge towards existence; equally by his view that being is still, as for Aquinas, a perfection, and finally by the affirmation that God chooses the best of all possible worlds.[45]

But already before Leibniz, with Descartes, a voluntarism more radical even than that of Ockham had pointed the way to an overcoming of any essentialist possibilism, which supposes that God is presented with an *a priori* range of essential possibilities that he has not merely 'made up'. Once Descartes had suggested that even the principle that 2 and 3 make 5 is the result of a divine decree for our world only, the prospect emerged of a more anarchic possibilism which thinks in terms of an absolutely open possibility of myriad conceivable axiomatisations for myriad varying systems corresponding to myriad various worlds.[46] It is within this lineage that, in our own day, a 'plural worlds' theorist like David Lewis can now

---

[43] See *La Condamnation parisienne de 1277*, trans. and ed. David Piché (Paris: J. Vrin, 1999), condemned articles 58–60, p. 98; 96, p. 108; 99, 103, p. 110; 107, 111, p. 112; 130, p. 118; 135–136, p. 120; 140–141, p. 122; 159, p. 126; 186, p. 136. These condemnations frequently targeted positions held by nearly everyone to be heterodox, generally Averroistic perspectives affirming the eternity of the world and the absolute eternal necessity of celestial motions, but in such a manner as to bring within their range incorporations of Hellenic philosophical perspectives concerning finite reflections of the eternal rational order such as those entertained by Aquinas.

[44] Duns Scotus, *Lectura* I, 39. And see Nef, *Qu'est-ce que la métaphysique?*, 347–371, and David B. Burrell CSC, *Freedom and Creation in Three Traditions* (Notre Dame, Ind.: Notre Dame University Press, 1993), 25–37, 43–46.

[45] Nef, *Qu'est-ce que la métaphysique?*, 379–411.

[46] Descartes, *Meditations on First Philosophy*, trans. John Cottingham (Cambridge: Cambridge University Press, 1986), 21, p. 14.

ontologically subordinate all experienced actuality to the status of mere examples of the possibility that we know about in the instantiated possible world that we inhabit, implying that there very likely really 'are' infinitely many other instantiated worlds.[47] Atheism has no reason to invoke any transcendent prior actuality, and therefore it must revert in a more anarchic mode to Ibn Sina: there can be no reason why any possible system is actualised and therefore we must, on the whole (a certain agnosticism intrudes at this point), assume that what is possible is also (somewhere, somehow) actual, or from 'its own point of view' grants another mode of actuality. Therefore, this 'modal realism' implies that *no* world truly exists at all, and its multi-nihilistic atheism perfectly combines an ultimately theologically derived voluntarism – converted into a random instantiation of all possible sets of compossibles – with an equally theologically derived possibilism (from the same theological stock), which reduces the actual to a mathematically or logically comprehensible mode of organisation.

In this way, as in so many others, it is the legacy of *a certain type of medieval theology* which has ensured the modern triumph of atheism: (1) in reaction against its arbitrary, authoritarian God,[48] (2) in recognition of his redundancy within a voluntarist-possibilist outlook, and finally (3) in essential continuity with such a theology after all, given the fact that any assertion of an ultimate void of virtual potential can readily be given a 'western Buddhist' sort of gloss.

But what it is further crucial to note is the link between attitudes to the modal on the one hand, and attitudes to the existential on the other, already discussed in section (a) above. If metaphysics on the post-Scotist view is about being, and being concerns just the bare given instance of 'not nothing' (as in Suárez), then actuality can no longer be construed as a rising order of perfections, and the complete 'nature' of a thing is fully determined, not by the arriving 'gift' of actuality, but by a preceding inert, 'given' possibility. It follows that metaphysics defined as the science of univocal being quickly becomes in effect (again, as already in Suárez), or even in name, the science not so much of every *ens*, but rather of every *res*, whether actual or possible, with priority given to the possible – and so also to formal logic, to a sheerly indeterminate notion of will as choice (instead of the idea of will only being possible through a fundamental lure towards a *telos*) and eventually, as with Kant, to the priority of knowledge over being, since knowledge has prior access to possibilities and to the 'formally

---

[47]   David Lewis, *On the Plurality of Worlds* (Oxford: Blackwell, 1986).
[48]   See Michael Buckley, *At the Origins of Modern Atheism* (New Haven, Conn.: Yale University Press, 1990).

distinguished' transcendental categories within which alone it is supposedly 'possible' for us to know, but to know, theoretically, only phenomena.

By these modes the rise of possibilism aligns exactly with the shift in meaning of the term 'transcendental'. If actual existence is merely the instantiation of existential possibility, then *ens* denotes a predetermined range of meaning for being as a cognitive category (either infinite or finite with all its sub-divisions) rather than an infinite mysterious depth of actuality which finite things all participate in, to some limited degree. The same applies to all the other transcendental terms: *unum, verum, bonum, pulchrum, res, quid* and *aliquid*. (The latter term denotes the fact that every *res*, in order to be a 'thing', must have some sort of identity – in the infinite case inclusive of 'all' identity, in finite cases identified in relation to other, different finite identities.)[49] After Scotus, all these transcendental terms were generally no longer held to be fully 'convertible' with each other, such that (as for Aquinas), we only distinguish their infinite uncreated, or even their finite, created, instances from each other from our limited cognitive point of view. Instead, it was now held that these terms must be 'formally distinguished' from each other, on pain of losing their separate meanings, since it was now supposed that we have a *full and complete insight* into those meanings, precisely because 'transcendental' had already come to denote, long before Kant, an *a priori* grasp of the possible range of meaning of these terms. This implies, questionably, that we can comprehend categorically the mode of that 'truth' or 'goodness' or 'beauty' which it is possible for us to comprehend, and that we can know in advance what formal shape it will take: this is exactly what Kant seeks to define for the three 'transcendental' realms, now formally distinct from each other (and no longer intra-convertible), in each of his three critiques.[50]

This entire 'critical' enterprise is questionable, because one can point out, 'metacritically', that it has simply assumed a particular axiomatic system according to which the empirical contents that fulfil the criteria for possible truth, goodness and beauty are always hierarchically conditioned by these criteria, and cannot reciprocally qualify these very criteria themselves. And such an axiomatic system is counter-intuitive, because we know (or at least post-classical cultures know) that, for example, a single particular actual work of art may redefine for us our sense of the possible 'range' of the beautiful, while equally a single passage in a human life may do the same thing for our sense of the ethical, and even the possible modes of theoretical

---

[49] See Rosemann, *Omne ens est aliquid.*
[50] See Ludger Honnefelder, *La Métaphysique comme science transcendentale*, trans. from the original German by Isabelle Mandrella (Paris: PUF, 2002).

truth have been redefined by the invention of non-Euclidean geometries, transfinites and space-time relativity – which all render problematic Kant's Euclidean- and Newtonian-based *a priori* categories of possible understanding.

Yet despite the way in which developments in modern mathematics, physics, aesthetics and politics (in the latter case revealing, since Hegel, the links between Kant's supposedly universal ethical principles and the dubious assumptions of a liberal political system) all tend to call the Kantian approach into doubt, most modern philosophy has continued to be characterised by an alliance between the redefined transcendental and the priority of the possible. This is as true for phenomenology as it is for the analytic tradition. So cognitively speaking, as was already suggested above, we remain caught within a 'certain Middle Ages'. It follows that to oppose to this a genuinely Thomistic or other mode of traditional theological-philosophical realism (all indebted to the Neoplatonic fusing of Plato with Aristotle) is not to be anachronistically nostalgic, but rather to appeal to a different strand of medieval tradition which, to a degree, resurfaced during 'the Renaissance'. (For example, it is arguable that Pico della Mirandola was more Thomistic than many early modern 'Thomists'.)[51]

In this way, the idea that natural necessities, essences, inherent formal meanings (*eide*) and so forth arrive only with actualisation as 'gift' from God is lost sight of. Instead, one has a doubly arid mere *givenness* without tint of generosity or gratitude. Possibilities are sheerly 'there' without real receiving, while actualities are non-predicamental existential instantiations of essences, equally just 'there' as if a description of 'how' they are was sufficient in itself, and did not require any raising of the issue as to 'why' they are in being at all, on the valid assumption that ascription of derivation colours our sense of the way things are 'in themselves'.

An adequate (if not provable) answer to the question 'Why?' must be in terms of personal donation. For to say, with Heidegger, who lies still fully within the univocalist-possibilist paradigm, that an impersonal being, identical with the virtual void and with temporal passage, 'gives' limited existences is futilely to try to describe how Being itself is merely 'given' in its destiny to both reveal and conceal itself in the ontic.[52] It is not explained why this should be the case, nor why this reality should only become apparent and so truly 'be' at all (for Heidegger's still phenomenological outlook) for human *Dasein*. Still less is it explained why this *Dasein* should

---

[51]   Henri de Lubac, *Pic de la Mirandole* (Paris: Aubier-Montaigne, 1964).

[52]   See Antonio López, FSCB, *Gift and the Unity of Being* (Washington, DC: CUA Press, 2013); Martin Heidegger, *On Time and Being*, trans. Joan Stambaugh (New York: Harper, 1972).

happen to coincide with a living being, in contrast to Aristotle's account of the coincidence of reason, self-moving soul and heightened sensitivity of animal 'touch' in his 'rational animal'.[53] And nothing is explained at all (in contrast to Neoplatonism) as to why exactly the ontic should take physical and non-rational as well as rational biological forms, while the possibility of non-temporal rational existences ('angels') is illogically left out of consideration.

Finally, Heidegger supplies us with no reason as to why Being as exhausted by temporal instantiation should not be considered as but one more dimension of the ontic, since it concerns only the interplay between the actual and the possible. 'Being as such' suggests rather the self-standing, the replete and plenitudinous, which already contains in eminent mode all of the reality of mere beings. If, by contrast, as for Heidegger, it is only 'there' in the ontic, then it is still merely a Scotist univocal abstraction which occurs always in the 'same' fashion, *qua* being, in a myriad series of ontic differences whose differences are metaphysically indifferent, and therefore require, for a perfected atheism, the 'flatter', more explicitly nihilistic treatment of a Deleuze or a Badiou, without any privileging of humanity, nor of oracular sites of spatial disclosure (as in Heidegger's later writings).[54]

In this way we can come to see how *both* phenomenology (when it has not already covertly trespassed upon theology) *and* analytic philosophy, as we saw with David Lewis, logically conclude that a pure transcendental ontology without God must point in an entirely aleatory and nihilistic direction. Where the post-Scotist transcendental is logically allowed, beyond Kant and Husserl (and ultimately in the lineage of Descartes and Spinoza), once more (as with Scotus himself) to determine the range of possible being and not simply the range of possible knowing, then, in atheistic terms, this must imply an anarchic virtuality, bounded only by the inner-axiomatic constraints of logical necessity. Hume was absolutely correct to argue that, outside any theologically supported framework, including the Aristotelian-Neoplatonic doctrine of the hylomorphic shape of material reality, there can be no room for any notion of 'natural necessity'.[55]

---

[53] See Didier Franck, *Heidegger et le problème de l'espace* (Paris: Éditions de Minuit, 1986); *Heidegger et le Christianisme* (Paris: PUF, 2004) I am indebted to discussions with David Bentley Hart concerning Heidegger. More will be said about Heidegger and animality in *On Divine Government*.

[54] See Gillian Rose, *Dialectic of Nihilism* (Oxford: Blackwell, 1984), 104–108.

[55] See Quentin Meillassoux, *Après la finitude: Essai sur la nécessité de la contingence* (Paris: Éditions du Seuil, 2006).

(d) Concurrence

In the fourth case, that of concurrence, the more divine freedom is construed in univocal and so ontotheological terms as guaranteed by its power to out-compete and trump created freedom the more – as an indirect, paradoxical consequence – created freedom, is then also granted an autonomous space outside divine causation.

The older medieval model of causation, as Jacob Schmutz has explained, was essentially Neoplatonic.[56] Its central notion was that of *influentia*, which remained true to the metaphoric basis of the word. According to this notion, a higher cause in a chain of causes (for example the heat and light of the sun as opposed to the nutritive power of the earth) is not merely a (de-metaphorised) external 'influence' upon a cause lower down in a causal series, which would therefore act as but one 'factor', albeit a predominant one, in bringing about a certain effect – like a man pushing along a supermarket trolley, but being slightly assisted by his toddler son. Instead, the higher cause is a 'flowing into' the entire lower causal scenario, such that it conditions, at a qualitatively higher level, *both* the lower effect *and* the lower cause, just as the sun's heat has already determined in large part the shapes taken by the surface of the earth which allows plants to grow within it. For the Neoplatonic outlook, a hierarchy of forms meant that lower forms were determined by higher ones, such that the causality of the higher ones only operated *through* the lower ones, even though, as Aquinas following Proclus taught, higher cases are always, in a covert fashion, more powerfully at work, even at lower levels.[57]

Thus higher causes operate unilaterally, even though they of themselves give rise, at a lower level, to a certain 'response' to their influence. In the case of material reality however, matter itself is not given by form, but is either a surd residue or else (and always, of course, for the three biblically based monotheistic traditions) something whose existence is directly derived from the highest cause of all, the Creator himself. This means that between 'formal' and 'material' cause a certain irreducible *reciprocity* pertains: for Aquinas, for example, matter is only actualised through form, while in the terrestrial sphere form can only be realised and 'individuated' through material limitation. However, this

---

[56]   Schmutz, 'La Doctrinè médiévale des causes'. On the emergence of causality as concurrence see also Burrell, *Freedom and Creation in Three Traditions*, 94.

[57]   Aquinas, *ST* I q. 65 a. 3 resp.: 'the thing that underlies primarily all things [Being] belongs properly to the causality of the supreme cause'.

reciprocal causality is still not causality by concurrence, precisely because form and matter do not both contribute actual parts or aspects of the causal sufficiency required in order to produce a certain effect. To the contrary, the formal cause is only working when it is already conjoined with matter and vice versa. This is because, as with the hierarchy of forms, formal and material causality operate at qualitatively different levels. All the *actual* 'influence' is supplied by form; matter provides only a mysterious field of passive potentiality that limits and so particularises the active potential of form in its abstract essential reach. In the case of Aquinas, it is more strongly insisted (in accord with his creationism) that material potential itself only exists 'through' the transmission of form, since *forma dat esse*,[58] while the 'designated' or spatial dimension of matter crucial for individuation only arrives *with* the composite.[59] In the most ultimate perspective, for Aquinas, the individuation of a particular material thing is fully achieved through the entire participation of form and matter in being, which allows it to

---

[58] *ST* I q. 65 a. 4 resp.: 'composites have being through forms'. ('Composites' comprise material potential and formal actuality.) See also *De Potentia Dei* q. 5 a. 4 ad. 1: *quantum unicuique inest de forma, tantum inest ei de virtute essendi*; *ST* I q. 17 a. 3: 'a thing has being by its proper form'. Finally see *ST* I q. 66 a. 1 resp., where it is denied that formless matter has ever existed, even at the 'beginning' of creation, since if matter exists it is in act and 'act itself is a form'. Hence, beyond Aristotle, matter is only actualised, is only in existence at all, through form.

[59] Aquinas *De Ente et Essentia* II (4); in *Boeth. de Trin.* q. 4 a. 1 Aquinas considers that the definition of 'man in general' as a species involves 'matter in general' or 'undesignated matter'. So if the latter alone individuated, that would mean contradictorily that man as species was already an individual. On the other hand, if pure matter individuated man from 'outside' his specificity, that would suggest that the individual – in nominalist fashion – did not share in universal specificity and therefore that universal essences 'could not be defined', because they would then be just empirical generalisations that might be falsified. Designated space, therefore, it seems is a kind of 'bridge' which for Aquinas constitutes a necessary relation of matter as activated and individualising to form. The spatial or the quantitative supplies a mysterious transitional terrain between material potential and formal actuality – which is *not* as later for Descartes, building on Scotus (see below in the main text) itself 'mere' matter as pure extension, a matter *falsely* etherealised into geometric form. In other words a Cartesian reduction of all non-thinking reality, including all life, to 'matter', in reality *loses* matter in a quasi-idealistic way. This is just the kind of thing which the Cambridge Platonists Henry More and Ralph Cudworth pointed out against Descartes. See Adrian Pabst, *Metaphysics: The Creation of Hierarchy* (Grand Rapids, Mich.: Eerdmans, 2012), 125–150; John Milbank, 'The Thomistic Telescope: Truth and Identity', in Peter Candler and Conor Cunningham, eds., *Transcendence and Phenomenology* (London: SCM, 2007), 288–333.

'exist' as this or that. Here the individuality provided by material limit is converted into a positive value exceeding the generic and the specific at the existential level.[60]

However, the model of causality by *influentia*, as exemplified in both the unilateral series of emanating forms and the reciprocal interplay of form with matter, is only undergirded by a specific sort of classical theology. This ensures, as I have already mentioned, that the most general derives from the highest. Not only does a higher rank pre-form the causal sphere of a lower rank; its influence also pre-forms in a more eminent, more powerful sense, the entire series of lower ranks as compared with the influence of the immediate higher rank at any level whatsoever. It is for this reason, to invert the principle just mentioned, that the highest cause is also the most universal: its influence is more at work than anything else even at the very base of the hierarchy. Indeed for Proclus, and still more for Aquinas, who affirms creation, the highest cause, which is also the highest form coincident with the *actus essendi*, *continues* to operate at the lowest level when the virtuality of all other, lesser causes is exhausted: 'Being is innermost [*magis intimum*] in each thing and most fundamentally inherent in all things [*quod profundus omnibus inest*] since it is formal in respect of everything found in a thing.'[61] This is exactly why there is matter: one can legitimately gloss Aquinas to say that it is a kind of vast shadow of all created being which reminds creatures, negatively, of the inexhausted and simple, unified divine active potential beyond the scope of created act and form.

This is, perhaps, the ultimate ground for the need of corporeal sacraments: beneath all our corruption an untouchable 'innocence' of matter always returns us to God, because undesignated matter as potential, like a kind of photographic negative of finite being, is alone the pure work of the first

---

[60]   *ST* I q. 47 a. 1. Here Aquinas *denies* that the 'distinction' of things comes from matter and attributes it directly to the creative act of God, who can alone directly know singulars through an act of intuition which is identical to his act of causing them participatively to be: see *ST* I q. 14 a. 11; *SCG* I 54. 4. This is why Aquinas has no need for the Scotist *haeccitas*, which is an unexplained positive principle sheerly extrinsic to the Scotist 'common nature' of an essence. The latter somehow exists extra-mentally and can be instantiated either in mental universals or in material particulars no longer individuated by matter alone, since matter in itself for Scotus now causally contributes merely a quasi-actual aspect of an item. (See immediately below in the main text.) (The 'common nature', as involving free-floating hypostasised forms outside the mind – in contrast to Aquinas, who only has universal forms in the mind and materialised forms in things – seems 'too Platonic' in the usual crude sense of 'Platonic' as involving isolated hypostasised abstractions existing outside a knowing subject.) See Alain de Libera, *La Querelle des universaux de Platon à la fin du Moyen Age* (Paris: Éditions du Seuil, 1996), 330–351. I am indebted here to discussions with Adrian Pabst and Phillip Blond.
[61]   *ST* I q. 8 a. 1 resp.

cause operating without any secondary assistance, even in the sense of assistance at a qualitatively lower level (rather than in the sense of 'concurrence'). It is just for this reason that, at the base of the ontological pyramid, the unilateral descent of qualitatively different formal causes gives way to the reciprocal interaction between descending form and a matter which lies, as it were, even beneath the reach of this descent, since its depths are plummeted by God alone. Even though form gives to matter its existence as potency, it cannot actually give this potency in its categorial essence through the exercise of any 'influence' whatsoever. And this is why our *sheerly* 'negative' knowledge of matter as that which is privated of form echoes in the depths the apophatic approach to the heights – which, however, in the case of the upward reference, is also in constant dialectical oscillation with a positive attribution.

It is therefore the eminence of God as *esse* which undergirds causal influence both as unilateral descent and as reciprocal interaction.

But within the scope of the Scotist univocal ontology, as already partially instigated by his Franciscan forebear Bonaventure,[62] this undergirding is lost, and in consequence the new causal model of 'concurrence' emerges,[63] which continues to dominate all of western philosophy up till and beyond Immanuel Kant. Since, for univocity, finite being fully 'is' in its finitude, outside of participation, it becomes possible to think of infinite and finite causes as each contributing distinct if unequal shares to any particular causal upshot, within a paradigm of flattened quantitative uniformity

---

[62]   Bonaventure's incipient univocalism is shown in the way in which he thinks that all finite beings possess the same basic ontological structure as regards substance and accident, genus, species and individuation etc. Thus he equates the surplus of existence over essence in creatures with the potentiality of matter (to which he attributes a quasi-form), ascribing to angels and human souls a 'spiritual matter'. Again, he does not think, as Aquinas does, that for angels species coincides with individuality, nor that humans' souls are only aspects of the entire human substance, because he does not think that matter, as the potentiality of being, can be an intrinsic limitation of being, but instead regards it as an extrinsic addition. Aquinas by contrast thinks of being as pure act which is limited by the potentiality of form (as genus and species) and of matter (as individual). In this way Bonaventure essentialises and univocalises finite existence by identifying it with fixed 'quantitative' degrees of material potential rather than the limited but dynamic participation of form in act, as according to Aquinas. The latter's sense of hierarchic metaphysical difference is far more truly Neoplatonic, as is his view that the addition of intellect to animal being and the modifications of intellect are 'accidental' only in some sort of radically 'proper' sense. The Franciscan General accordingly starts to view the activities of angels in a more voluntarist, contingent sort of fashion which is only tendentiously 'more biblical'. See Bonaventure, *In II Sent.* dist. 3, p. 1, a. 1 q. 1, concl.; dist. 3, p. 1, a. 2, q. 3.

[63]   In Bonaventure it does so with respect to the doctrines of intellectual illumination and divine grace: Bonaventure, *De Scientia Christ.* q. 4 resp.; *In II Sent.* dist. 24, p. 1 a.1 q. 2. And see Schmutz, 'La Doctrine médiévale des causes'; Milbank, *The Suspended Middle*, 89–97.

rather than of levels of qualitative differentiation.[64] Thus the metaphor of two horses pulling one barge, explicitly refused by Aquinas, was now embraced to describe the co-operation of God and creatures in bringing about finite created results, including that of human redemption.[65] Within the older view, to the contrary, it had been accepted that at every level of being, and supremely in the case of the Creator-created relationship, a cause at one lower level could be doing 'all the work', while at another, higher level, 'all the work' was equally being done by a higher cause – like the ultimate principles of motion (vital and physical) which allow the horses to pull the barge and the barge to be pulled at all. Here it should be noticed that the eminent cause not only fully determines the lower formal cause, but also the receptive capacity of the lower thing that is causally effected – in the case of material things this will mean the potential of designated matter, or the 'material cause' (the receptive capacity of matter as such being determined by the highest cause – God – alone). In this way reciprocal exchange is unilaterally given from a higher level.[66] But now, within the univocal outlook, the mystery of non-competing yet co-functioning replete causalities at different levels was abandoned for a theory which worked in terms of a 'zero-sum game' – the more of divine, the less of created causality at work, and vice versa.

The theory of causality by concurrence does not apply only to the Creator-created level. As with the case of causality by influence, the divine model provides the paradigm and guarantee for all lesser causality, while inversely the way one conceives the latter provides indispensable metaphors for thinking about the former. Here, again, theology provides the ultimate vision and yet its appeal to philosophical examples, both discursive and empirical, is indispensable. In the present instance, with respect to causes immanent to the created order, the notion of qualitatively different causes operating simultaneously and synergically at different hierarchical levels is abandoned. No longer do the planetary bodies entirely bring about terrestrial movements

---

[64]   See Nef, *Qu'est-ce que la métaphysique?*, 314–411.

[65]   Aquinas, *Contra errores Graecorum*, 23; Scotus, *Quodlibetal Questions*, q. 5; Peter John Olivi, *Sentence Commentary*, q. 72. The metaphor became yet more standard in the seventeenth century.

[66]   From this it can be seen that there is a subtle linkage between two different and apparently unrelated monisms. That is to say, between *uni*vocalist metaphysics and a merely *uni*lateralist and impossibly purist account of the gift, whereas an analogical metaphysics both entertains reciprocity as not contaminating the reality of gift and points to perspectives of asymmetrical and hierarchically instigated reciprocity which deny the absolute contrast of the reciprocal with the unilateral. See Milbank, *The Suspended Middle*, 53, 90–98, and 'The Gift and the Mirror: On the Philosophy of Love', in *Counter-Experiences: Reading Jean-Luc Marion* (Chicago: Chicago University Press, 2007), 253–317.

in a higher idiom; instead, they simply provide a 'general' causal context, which no longer has such clearly hierarchic connotations. They can then 'concur' with more specific mechanical or vital or psychic causes on one and the same univocal plane of being.

In this way, the subtlety of the older account of a descending series was lost. For that account, causality was 'one-way', a unilateral path of downward descent, since the higher causes were complete in themselves and for this reason did *not* really 'casually effect' things in our modern sense (the sense which Hume criticised) at all; rather they 'gave', through qualified emanation of their own reality, the subordinate 'effect' itself.[67] Nothing at a lower level assisted the higher cause, and in this sense there was no reciprocation. On the other hand, the lower-level causality which is proper to the effect itself (like the nutritive power of plants as granted by the sun), is a kind of 'response' to the higher cause, which is nonetheless itself 'granted' by that higher cause, just as, at the very highest level of all, and with the most completeness, it is God who gives the response of creatures to himself which establishes and defines their very being, besides that further response through grace which ensures our justification and deification. So it becomes proper to speak here of a paradox of 'unilateral exchange'.[68]

The new *concursus* model, however, renders the interaction of higher and lower formal causes 'reciprocal' in a far cruder sense. For now the two causes are both contributing different aspects of one reality in a way that is simply complementary in a banal, everyday sense: the co-operation between a more 'general' and a more 'special' (specific) mode of determining. However, if the concurrence model compromises unilaterality with respect to the embedded series of formal causes – both within this series itself[69] and between this entire series and the first cause – it also compromises reciprocity in the case where, for the older (Platonico-Aristotelian) view it more genuinely applies: namely in the case of form-matter interaction.

In the first case, there is concurrence because, after Duns Scotus, higher and lower co-operating forms are no longer melded by participation into one single, architectonically shaping form in the instance of a distinct substantive entity – as for example the form of a man integrates an entire series of physical forms which participate in this form, while the form of the man itself includes a share in the psychic, in intellection and in the

[67] See Jean-Luc Marion, 'Saint Thomas d'Aquin et l'Onto-théo-logic', *Revue Thomiste* (Jan.–Mar. 1995), 31–66.

[68] See Milbank, *The Suspended Middle*, 89–97.

[69] Scotus applies this model to the co-operation of humans and the sun in the case of human generation: *Ordinatio* I, dist. 3, pa. 3, q. 2, no. 503.

divine *esse*. Instead, for Scotus, if a series of constituting forms are mentally separable, then there is some ground for this in the real. They cannot any longer be absolutely unified in reality, because the ineffable bond of *influentia* which renders two formal causes absolutely necessary at two different levels, according to different analogical degrees, has been sundered, in favour of the idea that the higher cause exerts a merely more 'general' rather than specific influence, thereby fatally identifying the superior with the vaguer rather than (as for Proclus and Aquinas) the more intimate.[70] There can be no such bond because there is no analogy in being: rather, a higher existential reality can univocally meet a lesser one within the same 'plane of immanence', to use Deleuze's appropriate phrase.[71] It follows that a series of formal causes which are all just 'doing a bit' can in theory operate without each other, and that God could, according to his *potentia absoluta*, bring about just this state of affairs. Moreover, *esse* is not uniquely and exclusively a divine effect, as for Aquinas, for whom co-operating finite causes only contribute in an analogical and participatory way that is entirely subsumed within the self-sufficient action of God. Instead for Scotus, since finite creatures equally exist, though with less 'intensity' alongside the infinite, their causal contribution to the existence of things must genuinely 'add' something to the divine initiative.[72]

When it comes to the second case, of formal-material interaction, then here also Duns Scotus abandoned the *influentia* model which was inseparable from the analogical conception of being. Form could no longer 'entirely' give being to matter. If matter is not only mentally distinguishable from form, but distinguishable as generically different, then in the concrete it must be not just really distinct, but also potentially separable from form, since if form and matter interact, this has to occur on the same univocal plane of being and both must contribute 'something' to the existence of a material substance.[73] For the 'something' that is matter to be real it cannot be a kind of mysterious negative shadow of form which makes sense only as the rebound to the One at the base of a descending formal series. (Here Aquinas, by contrast, clearly follows the Neoplatonists in trying to make more metaphysical sense, through deployment of such a scheme, of Aristotelian matter as 'pure potency'.)

---

[70]   Duns Scotus, *Ordinatio* II, dist. 3, pa. 2. q. 1, and I, dist. 36, q. unica no. 65. On these grounds Scotus denies, against Aquinas, that *esse* is entirely and exclusively a divine effect,.

[71]   Gilles Deleuze and Félix Guattari, *A Thousand Plateaus: Capitalism and Schizophrenia*, trans. Brian Massumi (London: Athlone, 1987), 266.

[72]   Scotus, *Opus Oxoniense* IV, dist. I, q. 1 §7.

[73]   Scotus, *Opus Oxoniense* II, q. 1, n. 11 (121); *Quaestiones in Metaphysicae* 7, q. 5; *Lectura* II, dist. 12, q. unica. And see Eric Alliez, *Capital Times: Tales from the Conquest of Time*, trans. Georges Van den Abbeele (Minneapolis: Minnesota University Press, 1996), 206–207.

Instead, it must 'fully exist' in its own right, and the potential of matter must after all have a kind of actuality and a kind of general formality. It is for this reason, in part, that Scotus affirms that God *could* have created pure matter without form and likewise specific form that can be individualised (by 'haecceity') without matter.[74] Nevertheless, one can also reverse the priority here. Because Scotus wishes to say that everything is possible for God, and the current order of the world is merely the result of his decision for a certain set of compossibles, he is encouraged to embrace the *concursus* model of causality and the real separability of form from matter.

So for Scotus and his successors, matter and form reciprocally interact in a somewhat similar way to the series of embedded formal causes. However if, in the latter case, unilaterality was lost in favour of 'partial co-operation', in the former case, the same notion actually displaces a *more radical* reciprocity, for which totally asymmetrical and non-continuous realities interact without hierarchical interval to produce a single material substance. Again, following the *influentia* model, both realities are indispensable, and therefore the existence of separated matter is impossible even for God. Later we shall see the political implications of this shift.

For now it can be clearly seen that a theologically encouraged account of causality has long survived a loss of interest in divine causality and the memory of this genealogical origin.

3 Modern Philosophy: A Theological Critique

It has been shown how the modern philosophical preference for univocity, for representation, for possibility (including the division of the transcendentals and the sundering of will from intellect) and causal concurrence, possesses not always fully acknowledged theological roots – even if these roots were reciprocally encouraged to grow within the soil of a certain philosophical outlook.

From a Christian point of view, the buried theological stratum of modern thought does not obviously represent a progressive advance in Christian reasoning, but is rather thoroughly questionable. Equally, its more philosophical aspect does not seem rationally obvious as compared with older realist metaphysical outlooks.

---

[74] Scotus *Opus Oxoniense* II, dist. 17. The possible existence of form as we know it in this temporal and sublunar world without matter is affirmed (against Aquinas, amongst others) in Archbishop Étienne Tempier's Parisian condemnations of 1277 which helped to shift the European mind in favour of the *via moderna*. See *La Condamnation parisienne de 1277*, condemnations nos. 96 and 103, pp. 108–111.

So one is left with a picture of two competing existential visions, which were originally elected for reasons of conjoined theological-philosophical preference, in which the theological factor in the end carried most weight, since this had to do with the most ultimate individual and social orientations. The choice between these visions has never been a matter of pure rational argument.

The theological and philosophical objections to the fourfold vision of the *via moderna* extended into 'modern philosophy' will now be summarised in the subsequent sections of the first sequence, beginning with the defence of analogy versus univocity. The treatment of 'identity versus representation' will be the most extensive, extending into several further sections, since 'representation' shapes the space of epistemology, which is the most determinative space of modern philosophy.

4   Analogy versus Univocity

Theologically speaking, univocity breaks with the entire legacy of negative theology and eminent attribution, which also undergirded doctrines of deification. God can only be mysterious for this new outlook as infinitely 'more', while if the quality of this 'more' is to us unknown, then it proposes a voluntarist rupture to our understanding, not an eminent continuity. Thus for Scotus the phrase 'God is good' can only be meaningful if God is good with an infinite degree of precisely that perfection we know as 'good' with exactly the same meaning. No 'ascent' to God will here deepen that meaning, encouraged by the lure of an ever greater negative mystery.

Univocity also obliterates the sense that creation is through and through a divine gift with its claim that being as such, as opposed to finite being, is not created, since the term 'being' has now become a logically transcendental place-holder that precedes any existentially actual reality. Hence both infinite and finite being are now held to presume the formal possibility 'to be'.[75] For Aquinas, by contrast, the divine infinite being is an absolutely unprecedented (logically as well as existentially) and mysterious simple actuality that is identical with infinite intelligence, while abstract being in general, *ens commune*, is first of all a created actuality and only thereby a subject of possible becoming or even of fictional speculation.

Philosophically speaking, univocity is only one possible *reading* of the ontological difference between Being and beings. It represents an existential orientation more than it does any conclusive mode of argument. For it is in

[75]   See Honnefelder, *La Métaphysique comme science transcendentale*.

part the result of an ungrounded decision that there can be no 'middle' in *meaning* between identity and difference – and therefore also the result of a decision against any specific, irreducible meaning for poetic metaphor and any grounding of meaning in a depth which for us must remain not fully fathomable. Since the beautiful in its excess to rational analysis and empirical verification is precisely a strange 'shining through' of infinite, inaccessible meaning to finite, locatable meaning, this decision is also a decision against the objective reality of beauty and a decision for the subordination of the appearance of beauty (now confined to epistemological epiphenomenon) to the reality of the sublime as our experience of the margin of an infinite which is simply inscrutable. For the reality of beauty in which the terrible is strangely the consoling, one substitutes simply the aesthetic of the terrible and the continuously interruptive and yet absolutely withheld.[76]

Univocity is equally a decision against a middle in *being* between identity and difference. Since the meaning of beauty is reduced to the subjective (something, after Kant, to do with the experience of the co-ordination of our diverse faculties), an aesthetically neutral objective reality is seen as always parcelled out (in line with the 'concurrence' model) between a general conditioning sameness on the one hand, which is ultimately the sameness of being as such, and a particular conditioned and yet reciprocally conditioning difference on the other. The connecting link or 'correlation' between conditioning and conditioned now becomes sheerly esoteric – hence the mystery of 'schematism' in Kant – within the very mode of philosophising that refuses to allow or to theorise any sort of occult connection.[77]

Alternatively, by a simple act of sceptical reversal (the 'postmodern'), difference can become the primary conditioning factor and sameness the factor which is transcendentally determined by difference and yet, through its reciprocal causal power, always succeeds in betraying its 'virtual' pressure towards pure otherness. This terminally negative dialectic (which it remains, despite denials and aspirations) offers to its devotees an unexplained mediation of ontological violence posing as evident *gnosis* to the initiated.

Yet the decision to refuse 'the between' (*metaxu*) of mediation, remains the same in either case, while the modern Hegelian 'dialectical' option is but a counterfeit mediation which involves a constant agonistic shuttle between sameness and difference that ultimately issues both in a swallow-

---

[76] See John Milbank, 'Sublimity: The Modern Transcendent', in Regina Schwartz, ed., *Transcendence: Philosophy, Literature and Theology Approach the Beyond* (London: Routledge, 2004), 211–234.

[77] On 'correlation' see Meillassoux, *Après la finitude*.

ing of the different by the same and in an abjection of pure difference as totally contingent and irrelevant for the comprehension of truth.[78] In the case of *both* Hegel *and* the postmodern exacerbations of his reasoning, this irrelevant untruth is eventually proclaimed to be the nihilistic truth itself.[79]

If one follows these reflections, then one can see how one might deconstruct the typical 'analytic' claim that being is not a predicate and therefore is always said in the same fashion. Since, in terms of this claim, being is in no sense a quality, then the predication of being is simply the upshot of a double negation – dialectic being always latent to analysis as the only thing which prevents it from being sheerly tautological. What is, is only what is not 'not', not nothing at all. But this conceals an arbitrary decision to make but one aspect of existential grammar fundamental: the direct contrast between all the parts of the verb 'to be' and pure nullity. For as Plato taught, 'there is a swallow' (for example), stands in an indeterminate (semantic and phenomenological) contrast not only with 'no swallow at all', but also with 'not a wagtail', 'not a magpie', 'not a blackbird', 'not a seagull'.[80] In this way the vertical of the predication of being over against nullity always gets horizontally diverted into the labyrinth of essential and particular differences. And ultimately, the decision to make 'is not not' normative is a decision for the *priority* of the not, since such a decision is linked to the new priority of the possible over the actual. This means that the mark of a thing's being is that it instantiates a 'can be this' in such a way that the fate of 'there will not be a this' always hovers over it as the shadow of death, and fundamentally defines it. Such a definition in turn implies an equality between nullity and being (as also affirmed by the modern mathematical embrace of zero as a fully fledged number in the 'natural' number series) and therefore a kind of incipient nihilism.[81] Actuality is here not permitted to do any work in revealing essence or unique characteristics: as with the case of

---

[78]   See William Desmond, *Being and the Between* (New York: SUNY, 1995) for an elaboration of a 'metaxological' point of view against univocal (i.e. 'analytic') and equivocal (i.e. postmodern) and dialectical (i.e. Hegelian) philosophies. Since his metaxological' is at once the mediating, the analogical and the participatory, rearticulated in such a way as to take more account of temporal dynamics as compared with medieval metaphysics, his subtle but luminous project is profoundly similar to that of 'Radical Orthodoxy'. On the abjection side to Hegel, see Slavoj Žižek's now classic statement, 'Not only as *Substance*, but also as *Subject*', in *The Sublime Object of Ideology* (London: Verso, 1989), 201–231.

[79]   See John Milbank, 'The Double Glory, or Paradox Versus Dialectics', in Slavoj Žižek and John Milbank, eds., *The Monstrosity of Christ: Paradox or Dialectic?* (Cambridge, Mass.: MIT, 2009), 110–233.

[80]   Plato, *Sophist* 1003e–1007b.

[81]   See Conor Cunningham, *Genealogy of Nihilism* (London: Routledge, 2002); Jacob Klein, *Greek Mathematical Thought and the Origins of Algebra* (New York: Dover, 1993).

Kant's bourgeois conclusion, an actual reality is no more than its abstract numismatic equivalent. It is surely incredible that the famous 'thousand thalers' example is so readily accepted, because were one, say, to substitute 'daughters' (not perhaps in such great quantities), one would see the monstrosity of what he is saying. Is a number of actual daughters qualitatively and essentially the same as a number of possible daughters? This would only follow were it really conceivable that one could reduce their actual phenomenality to either the abstract mathematical ratios which they embody or else the causes (willed or otherwise) which went into their formation, or a combination of both. But if one wishes to 'save their appearances', then the specificity of the way they show themselves in the world is inseparable from their actuality, from their specific embodiment, movements and history of motions, physical and psychic.

It follows that the univocalist (ultimately Scotist and derivatively Kantian) version of the view that 'being is not a predicate' reduces to the idea that an actuality can be exhaustively defined in its essence and qualities as an instantiation of a preceding possibility, which must be either a *mathesis* or a virtuality or else both.[82] But in that case what an entity really is for us in its

---

[82]   By contrast, the Thomist version of this view simply states that inevitable existential instantiation never follows, in either logic or reality, from the definition of a finite entity. But it does not unwarrantedly deduce from this, in Avicennian fashion, that the essential character of a thing is *ontologically* prior to its actuality – a deduction which smuggles back a covert 'existence' and even 'inevitable existence' of the essence, even though the real distinction of *esse* from *essentia* should preclude according any existence to essence as such, far less any existence that is bound to be – which belongs to God alone, wherein *esse* and *essentia* alone coincide. But God's existence follows from his essence only because an infinitely defined essence equally follows from his existence – whereas the essence of any contingently existing thing must always be somewhat fluid. See Aquinas, *De Ente et Essentia*, 4. Although he says here that one can understand 'man' or 'phoenix' without knowing whether they exist in reality, he does not say (and his whole outlook would deny) that one first knows these things as logical possibilities, rather than as either real or imagined actualities – given Thomas's Neoplatonic-Aristotelian and Augustinian view (so strange to most today) of both the imagination and of thought as realms containing ontologically real entities. The reality of intellectual beings lies indeed at the heart of the argument of this early treatise. So whether essences are instantiated as merely imaginary or as humanly (as opposed to angelically) intellectual, or as fully real (as materially embodied or else existing as angelic separate spiritual substances) is a matter of degree of existential actualisation. This is not, for Aquinas, as it is for Scotus and Kant, an affair of simple either/or. Thus at the maximum degree of divine full existence, which is self-instantiating, being is not emptily existential, but coincides with an infinite qualitative determination of essence, an unimaginably saturated determination. In this pure *esse*, creatures participate in various extents. And only this hierarchically differentiated sharing in an infinitely actualised qualitativeness constitutes for Aquinas 'existence'. His 'real distinction' of *esse* from *essentia* does not mean that in reality the one can occur without the other, only that the two do not entirely coincide, except in God.

phenomenality is after all *not* what it really is.[83] How it 'looks' is not what truly defines it, moves it and renders it real – and it is clear that modern physical science mostly works within this univocalist model (which renders its conclusions valid only up to a point). Hence if being is not (in this sense) a predicate and qualities do not proceed from actuality, the full actuality of a thing is abolished in favour of that spectral ghost of the actual which is the possible. And like a ghost, this also means that the essence and qualities of a thing hover exactly between life and death, redemption and damnation, or more precisely something and nothing. So what a thing uniquely is, equally may not be, and therefore, from an ontological point of view, equally is not. Actuality is therefore now twice abolished – first thinned out by possibility, it has now been hollowed out by a nullity that gnaws always at its heart. As Scotus put it, in terms which were later still more empha-sised by William of Ockham, 'everything which is unqualifiedly nothing includes in itself the essence of many'.[84]

So if affirmation of univocity is only a decision, then it is also a decision against common sense, because we persistently believe that what we see is a reality, and that the most real, the most vivid, lies on the surface or constantly rises to it. Here one can envisage a certain seemingly strange alternative conjunction of phenomenology, postmodernism and Thomism. For one may validly assume that what appears is real, and what is 'superficial' is fundamental and cannot be reduced to a more basic – but inevitably more thinned-out, more misty – depth. But to hold on to these positions one must perforce insist (against Deleuze, as thinkers as diverse as Michel Henry, Alain Badiou and François Laruelle now see) upon the priority of the actual against that of either the possible or the virtual (the latter being a kind of potential that has been supplied with both a subtle body and an outboard motor).[85] If we hang

---

[83]   Phenomenology, as with Heidegger, tends to espouse the priority of possibility over act, precisely because the claim to reduce being to describable appearance must reduce it to the structures of its possibility, even if these be understood in wholly negative and 'saturated' terms. For this reason pure phenomenology is latently of itself 'structuralist' and this is why it can only think the excess of what does not appear as a sublime void in contrast to the figuration of the beautiful. Ironically, it is Merleau-Ponty, who openly engaged with structuralism, who also escaped this collapse. This was just because he did not make possibility prior to act, nor reduce being to phenomenality. Instead for him the excess of what does not appear can be spoken about in ontological, structural or semiotic terms, but this very formal acknowledgement of distance allows that there is something in the experience of that distance which cannot be reduced to subjective capture or structural formulation. The point where an ineffable experience of the absent coincides with attempts to figure the absent is the point where the sublime is integrated with the beautiful as glory.

[84]   Duns Scotus, *Ordinatio* I, dist. 43 q. unica n. 18. See also Cunningham, *Genealogy of Nihilism*, 3–43.

[85]   See John Mullarkey, *Post-Continental Philosophy: An Outline* (London: Continuum, 2006).

on to the reality of that which superficially appears in all it richness, then it cannot be reduced to anything which precedes it either in time or place. It is radically 'uncaused' and is in consequence either 'self-caused' in its single seamless occurrence, which exceeds any causal contrast of conditioning and conditioned (as Laruelle's 'non-philosophy' demands),[86] or arrives to us as an emanated gift. The first, immanentist, option will always reinstate a dualism between the causing and caused self which will generally resort to some sort of idea of a single cosmic general self, reducing the world of the conscious individual who knows things and interacts with things other than itself – and sometimes affects things while being sometimes affected by them – to epiphenomenal appearance (as seems to occur with both Laruelle and Henry). And in that case, the fundamental self-caused actuality which is 'just there' seems, in its basic spontaneity, which determines that there will be such a world of illusions (and cannot escape from determining this), after all to reduce to an underlying virtuality which exposes the delusory and half-true character of what appears as visible, moving, inter-acting and so forth.

One only escapes this dualism and this virtualism by allowing that each actual thing with all its superficial vividness is the direct gift of an ultimate infinite actuality which is God. This is exactly why Chesterton was right to think that only creationist theism coincides with everyday common sense, in saving the appearance of appearances as such.[87]

It is this rendering which alone lines up with a decision to sustain the complex grammar of the existential by giving the 'is' in 'there is a swallow' equal weight as a marker of difference to the semantic freight it carries as a marker of sheer presence. For if being only occurs as *aliquid*, as Aquinas taught, as something that is distinguishable in relation to something else, then we have no objective reason to decide that we can abstract 'sheer being' from all the differently inflected beings, as though that gave us 'the essence' of being, even in semantic terms.[88] Indeed the pure 'is' over against 'not' of univocity is a fundamental grammar only likely to be adopted by a certain kind of non-mystical theologian, or else an agnostic or an atheist. It remains *possible*, at the very least, to decide that, if being always arrives to us in differentiated qualitative terms, it is in itself a kind of mysterious hyper-quality (an eminence of all differences), which as an infinite actuality conveys an absolute plenitude of qualities, just as we know that only

[86] François Laruelle, *Principles of Non-Philosophy*, trans. Nicola Rubczak and Anthony Paul Smith (London: Bloomsbury, 2013).
[87] See G.K. Chesterton, 'The Ethics of Elfland', in *Orthodoxy* (London: The Bodley Head, 1957), 66–103.
[88] See Rosemann, *Omne ens est aliquid*, 13–48.

actual beings first realise those qualities which poetry can capture, and any possibilism must deny or refuse.

There is one final but crucial point. Beings in the world do not all appear with equal intensity. Some are more vividly in act than others and therefore some things exist more than others – that is, if we decide not to reduce the reality of appearances. At the phenomenological level (if we elect to remain there) this is not just subjective waffle, since things only appear to us at all in a coherent pattern through which we can move and converse intelligibly (as Badiou has shown), because certain things in certain situations (and certain things consistently so) are dominant over other things, while some things dominate in one way and yet are dominated by others in other respects.[89] Hence one can say that some things exist more intensely in some fashions, less so in others. So a hierarchy of being may be complex and entangled, but the actuality of phenomena, when we remain with it, presents itself always as such a degree-differentiated series. Light dominates the day, but the garden frames my labour; the colours of women's dresses illumine the street along which they are propelled, yet they could not do so were not the street wide enough to allow their passage, and yet constrained enough not to engulf their flaring in the wastes of an already vivid desert.

So while the differences of being may often be egalitarian, they can only strike us at all within certain complex hierarchical patterns of overarching and overarched, predominantly influencing and subtly inflecting. Therefore, if common sense intimates to us that the actual is ultimate, and common experience suggests to us that being which is always qualified may be in itself hyper-qualitative, then the hierarchical structures which 'transcendentally' permit this common experience suggest that finite being as such is hierarchical, because it 'participates' in various analogical degrees (and in different aspects in different degrees) in that infinite actuality which, for Dionysius the Areopagite, was 'thearchy' beyond hierarchy, and which alone gives and saves the finitely self-grounded actualities which appear before our eyes.

For these reasons it follows that it is – at the minimum – equally rational to decide that being is always the same in its fundamental virtuality, or to decide, instead, that it is copiously yet harmoniously differentiated in its fundamental actuality, and that to this difference is always added in its finite actual instantiations a more and a less, but always also varyingly as to a here and a there, and in ever more teasing oscillations.

---

[89] Alain Badiou, *Logiques des mondes: L'Être et l'événement*, 2 (Paris: Éditions du Seuil, 2006), 119–153.

5   Identity versus Representation

The theory of knowledge by representation is just as theologically questionable as the theory of the univocity of being.

First of all because, in God, since he is simple, intellect cannot 'follow', even metaphysically, upon being.

Secondly, as regards human knowledge, because the harmonious continuity between the way things exist in matter and the way they exist in our mind embodies a certain pan-sacramental order that is part of the divine government of the world, reflecting the divine reason as such, and therefore not liable to be interrupted by even a divine whim.

Thirdly, because the theory of knowledge by identity respects the partially spiritual, because integrally formed, character of all created things as proceeding from God. Knowledge, from a theological point of view, as Aquinas taught, has the spiritual purpose of raising and enhancing reality; it is not primarily, in its *raison d'être*, a neutral Sherlock Holmes-like capacity for observation and accurate inference.[90]

Furthermore, it turns out that knowledge by representation is by no means a 'neutral' philosophical theory which theology may or may not find to be a congenial inheritance. To the contrary, as we have already seen, the theory became dominant for overwhelmingly theological reasons. In the case of God this has to do both with the formal distinction and with univocity – metaphysical positions which, as has already been explained, are intimately linked with stances in both rational and revealed theology. In the case of human understanding, the rise of the theory of the object is inseparable from the invocation of the absolute power of God and an accompanying diminution of any sense of 'natural necessity', or of structures within the creation which inherently reflect and participate in the divine example. This means that the will is no longer, of its very natural 'weight' or *pondus*, drawn to a natural and ultimately supernatural *telos* which practical reason dimly intimates in advance. Likewise, the intellect is no longer seen as 'intending' its object of understanding, in such a way that, via the ministrations of the intellectual 'word' or concept, and the imaginary 'phantasm', the mind achieves an immediate 'identity' with the object known which is a kind of ecstatic relation to that object, expressing an aesthetic affinity or 'convenience' between things as existing and things as formally comprehended.

In these terms Aquinas modified the Aristotelian view that the concept in the mind is, in a purely formal mode, the same as the thing which is

---

[90]   See Milbank and Pickstock, *Truth in Aquinas*, 1–18.

known by the concept, with the Augustinian teaching (linked to his view that our understanding echoes the Trinitarian relations) that the mind through intention really 'returns' to the thing known and establishes a kind of bond with it.[91] Accordingly, a subtle balance was achieved between the idea that a form as known exists in a higher mode, and the equally important idea that this form-as-known is lacking in that full existentiality which only the matter-form compound possesses within the sub-angelic realm. In God alone do these two aspects fully coincide.[92]

If one ignores this Augustinian dimension then one will tend, like André de Muralt (whose work is nonetheless crucial and on the whole exemplary), to regard the Scotist and Ockhamite revolutions as simply abandoning Aquinas's Aristotelian metaphysics, as if 'intentionality' were an Aristotelian doctrine, which it is not.[93] But on a purely Aristotelian view, the teleology

---

[91]   Augustine, *De Trinitate* XI.1.2. Here Augustine gives the case of looking at an object as a remote image of the Trinity and suggests (following the Stoics) that in the case of looking at an object there are three aspects: the object seen, the act of seeing – including the image in the eye – and finally 'what holds the sense of the eyes on the thing being seen as long as it is being seen, namely the conscious intention'. So here intentionality is linked with imaging the Holy Spirit as directive will. (The object seen being the 'Father'; the act and image of seeing being the 'Son'.) The intentional aspect of understanding is for him closely linked with the 'carrying' of knowledge by desire, just as the *Verbum* is uttered by God through the breath of the *Pneuma*.

[92]   See Milbank and Pickstock, *Truth in Aquinas*, 1–18; Milbank, 'The Thomistic Telescope', in *American Catholic Philosophical Quarterly*.

[93]   See the excellent article 'Intentionality in Ancient Philosophy', in the *Stanford Encyclopaedia of Philosophy*, at <http://Plato.Stanford.edu/entries/intentionality-ancient/>, which corrects several earlier misapprehensions. Aristotelian knowledge by identity of form is not the same as intentionality, which, rather, has Stoic roots. It is closely linked with the Stoic doctrine of signs and the idea that the sign indicates a *lekton* or 'signified' in modern parlance, which is not itself immediately the real referent but an 'incorporeal' position within a system of signification. Augustine sustained this connection, speaking of the sign-word as *dictio*, which indicates or intends a *dicibile*: *De Dialectica*, V. At the same time, intentionality could also for Augustine explicate the meaning of a sign-word directly in terms of reference: thus he speaks of *intentio digitis*, a pointing by the finger, as establishing the meaning of a word in his early *De Magistro* at X.34. So 'intentionality' for Augustine, as later often for the scholastics, hovers between indication of the signified and indication of the referent. The Stoics also spoke of *enteinein*, a cognate of the Latin *intentio* within the context of their theory of vision. This was also followed by Augustine in his *De Genesi ad Litteram* (I.31 and VII.20), where he speaks of a medium of *pneuma* which carries a beam from the eye to the thing known. Such a notion is probably echoed in Book XI of the *De Trinitate*. The fact that, in its origins, intentionality has to do both with semiotics and with the theory of vision is fascinating with respect to some debates in twentieth-century phenomenology. It would seem that there were also Arabic sources for the notion – perhaps these also were ultimately of Stoic derivation. See Sarah Catherine Byers, *Perception, Sensibility and Moral Motivation in Augustine: A Stoic-Platonic Synthesis* (Cambridge: Cambridge University Press, 2012).

of knowledge tends to run in one direction only, which is the inverse of the teleology of the will: the thing known is the fulfilment of the thing as merely existing. Aquinas, to be sure, echoes this view,[94] but it is as if, for him, such fulfilment is always provisional, and is for now qualified by a kind of counter-teleology which is intentionality – and indeed this notion in its first Latin variant in Augustine lies close to the idea of knowledge as always accompanied by a directing desire.[95]

This counter-teleology involves, however, three distinct moments. First of all the concept, as Augustinian *verbum*, has become more of an inner emanation than it was for Aristotle. Despite the continued identity of the act of knowledge with the thing known, this identity (echoing the Father-Son relation in the Trinity) now also involves a real relational interval between the knower and the concept which he expresses. Secondly, the expressed concept is not only 'word' as uttered, but also 'word' (again following Augustine) as inner sign which points beyond itself to the real thing known by way of an invocation of that thing's (partial) knowability: this is the conjunction of the thing as known with the thing as intended (or 'signified' in semiotic terms). The 'intentionalisation' of the Aristotelian concept therefore involves also its 'linguistification'.[96]

But in a third moment one might say that the inner sign expands into an inner 'icon', because the intentional reference of the concept back to the thing known involves also the *conversio ad phantasmata* which links the universality of the concept with the sensory intuition of a particular reality by recalling this in an act of imagination (roughly that which Samuel Taylor Coleridge much later described as 'the primary imagination', by which we concretely envisage the coherent unity of a sensed thing or state of affairs).[97]

If intentionality in Aquinas involves an element of 'reverse teleology' as regards knowledge, which places it more in parallel to the path of the will which is teleologically directed from the willing person to a real external end,

---

[94]   *ST* I q. 8 a. 3 resp.

[95]   *ST* I q. 8 a. 3 resp.

[96]   *ST* I q. 34 a. 2, resp.; q. 85, a. 2 ad. 2. And see Mark Jordan, *Ordering Wisdom: The Hierarchy of Philosophical Wisdom in Aquinas* (Notre Dame, Ind.: Notre Dame University Press, 1986), 31–39. Jordan here exposes Bernard Lonergan's a prioristic and therefore anachronistic obfuscations of the Thomistic *verbum*.

[97]   Aquinas, *ST* I q. 86 a. 1 resp.: 'even after abstracting the intelligible species [from the phantasms] the intellect, in order to understand [the singular], needs to turn to the phantasms in which it understands the species'. Aquinas here cites in support Aristotle, *De Anima* 7, but while the Philosopher does indeed there insists that the soul never thinks without imagined images, it is not perhaps clear that he affirms a 'return' to these images in the way that Aquinas does. Also *ST* q. 84 a. 7 resp. See in addition Milbank and Pickstock, *Truth in Aquinas*, 1–18; John Milbank, 'On Thomistic "Kabbalah"', *Modern Theology*, 27/1 (Jan. 2011), 147–185.

then this is precisely because knowledge is borne by desire for relation with the thing known, both intrinsically (since even God desires to know) and provisionally (since in knowing we are always returned to the thing known as not yet adequately known). It is because knowledge must seek to know further, and more specifically, that which it first obscurely knows through desire (following Augustine's reworking of the Meno problematic)[98] that our intentional understanding echoes also the role of the Holy Spirit in the Trinity as that loving 'breath' of the Father upon whose air-current the second person of the Trinity is both 'borne' as 'Word' and 'born' as Son.

Inversely, while the will 'immediately' and blindly through its *pondus* intends its practical goal, here an opposite and equivalent 'reverse teleology' is at work for Aquinas, since the very notion of a practical teleology requires an intellectual moment: the will must be in some fashion informed in advance through its conjunction with the intellect of the nature of the goal to be pursued, if it is to recognise it as desirable. Thus for Aquinas, again following Augustine, the will, on a Trinitarian analogy, emerges in procession 'through' knowledge as well as from the 'Paternal' source of knowledge in the memory, which Augustine had said occurs insofar as it puts these things to good 'use' through right desire.[99]

Hence the will is but *relatively* more ecstatic than the intellect, while the intellect is but *relatively* a more self-sufficient terminus than is the will.

Once one has taken this Augustinian dimension in Aquinas's theory of intentionality into account, then one can see how, in one respect, the modification of, and eventual movement away from, intentionality in Scotus and Ockham involves augmenting one potentiality of Aristotle's teaching itself, with a relative *neglect* of the Augustinian supplement. For if form fulfils itself in our understanding, in an approximation to the 'thought thinking itself' of the first mover, then it is possible to take this in a more empiricist-cum-idealist direction. Without the Thomist (and ontologically Trinitarian) intentional 'return' of the reimagined concept to the real, the way lies open for the real to be bracketed altogether in favour of what we 'seem' to know, or know internally within certain *a priori* constraints. But since the Aristotelian relative neglect of 'return' (although this may be somewhat less true of the *De Anima*) is bound up with his view that

---

[98]   Aquinas, *ST* I q. 2 a. 1 ad. 1.

[99]   Augustine, *De Trinitate* X.4.17; Aquinas, *ST* I q. 93 a. 6 resp. Also *ST* I q. 8 a. 5 ad. 1: 'these powers include one another in their acts, because the intellect understands that the will wills, and the will wills the intellect to understand. In the same way good is contained in truth, inasmuch as it is an understood truth, and truth in good, inasmuch as it is a desired good'. See in addition Pierre Rousselot SJ, *The Intellectualism of St. Thomas*, trans. James E. O'Mahoney (London: Sheed & Ward, 1935).

material reality does not emanate from a divine source – is not 'created', does not bear a negative trace of transcendence and therefore should be increasingly 'left behind'– this late medieval shift seems dubious from a theological point of view.

Moreover, just why should it have been made by thinkers, from Scotus onwards, who are often seen as having a strongly 'Augustinian' aspect to their thought? An adequate answer here would have to be complex, but it is at least partially to do with Duns Scotus's mode of understanding of the *vestigium trinitatis*. Scotus, in the wake of Richard of St Victor, other Franciscan theologians including Bonaventure, and also and supremely the lay cleric Henry of Ghent (who consummated this trend), differenti-ated the persons not by means of substantive relations, but instead in terms of qualitatively different emanations prior to either relationality or personhood. This qualitative distinction was made in terms of a suppos-edly exegetically based contrast between the generation of the Son *per naturam* on the one hand, and the procession of the Spirit *per voluntatem* on the other hand.[100] The character of the Son as *Logos* is in effect seen as more secondary by Scotus than by Augustine and Aquinas, because he believes that the Father as Father is 'habitually' in possession of the divine understanding, which the emanation of the *Verbum* merely actual-ises. The formally precedent divine intellect is, in turn, 'formally distinct' from the divine infinite essence which for Scotus actually *grounds* a Paternal *Monarchia* (which he insists on, following John Damascene) as superior to any relational engagement. The Son as 'naturally' generated is thoroughly secondary: he is held to be not formally infinite, since he is consequent upon the essence and even the formally distinguished divinely essential understanding and will which 'quasi-emanate' from this essence ('before' the Trinitarian emanations), and finally to be consequent upon the Father's absolute personal priority. Hence the Son as Word simply 'expresses' and conveys like an instrument the essential divine intellect, just as the Spirit does the essential divine will.[101]

This means that while, in a sense, for Scotus, the most obvious analogue for the Trinity would be natural human birth combined with human 'cultural' willing, the psychological 'illustration' of the Trinity is in fact much more heavily psychologised by him than it was by Augustine and

---

[100]   See Boulnois, *Être et représentation*, 107–114.
[101]   Duns Scotus, *Quodlibetal Questions*, q. 1 aa. 2–3; q. 3 a. 2; q. 4 a. 3; q. 5 aa. 1–3. In effect, Scotus like many other of his contemporaries, downplays the Trinitarian qualification of monotheism. It is difficult not to see the impact of Islamic philosophy as a factor here – though it is by no means the only one and not necessarily the main one.

becomes much more literal in import – especially because the intellect is seen as emanating more spontaneously and so more 'naturally' than the will. (For Augustine the analogue remained a metaphor, even if a *necessary* metaphor, which a good exegesis of the Scriptures demands, rather than a mere 'illustration' of a positive dogma.)[102] In the case of Augustine, the memory, understanding and love of oneself which remotely mirror the divine aseity are nonetheless concerned with faculties that are through and through ecstatic: truly to recall, understand and love oneself is to recall the true self who recollects, intends and aims towards God and the neighbour.[103] But if these three faculties are not relationally understood within the divine *exemplum* as referring to each other and constituting each other, then the resulting non-relationality and self-sufficiency will tend also to elide the ecstatic aspect. Memory that does not intrinsically understand or recall is just a passive trace that might bear no clue as to 'the past'; understanding that does not always remember something and desire something is complete in its own solipsism, like the Cartesian *cogito*. Love that does not understand anything, but affectively (and unilaterally) exceeds reason (in the tradition of Bernard of Clairvaux, under the long-term and somewhat baneful influence of John Cassian)[104] will be a love grounded upon a pure choice, not swayed by any mode of rational persuasion.

---

[102]   See Lewis Ayres, *Augustine and the Trinity* (Cambridge: Cambridge University Press, 2010).

[103]   Augustine, *De Trinitate* VIII–X. See also Michael Hanby, *Augustine and Modernity* (London: Routledge, 2003), 27–72, for a fine summation and development of the work of Rowan Williams, Lewis Ayres, myself and others on the question of how to understand the Augustinian self in the image of the Trinity.

[104]   See Hanby, *Augustine and Modernity*, 106–133, and Rowan Williams, *The Wound of Knowledge* (London: DLT, 1990), 9–118. And more specifically see Bernard of Clairvaux, *The Twelve Steps of Humility* (London: Hodder & Stoughton, 1985), 7–8, pp. 37–41. Here, the reason as instructed by the divine Son arrives at true self-knowledge in self-indictment of guilt which prepares the soul for the work of the Holy Spirit, who instructs the will in humility and loving submission to God the Father. This *schema* already departs from Augustinian complexity: it over-distinguishes the work and existence of both the Trinitarian persons and the human faculties which mirror them and encourages too much the onto-theological notion that we meet God when we leave the self behind, as if God and self were in ontic rivalry. Where the intellect is seen as somewhat less important for access to God than the loving will (whereas they are both equally essential for Augustine), then the crucial realities of participation and mediation are subtly diluted. By contrast, the true Augustinian and Dionysian traditions as perpetuated by the Cistercian tradition at its best (William of St Thierry's 'enlightened love': see *The Mirror of Faith*, trans. Thomas X. Davis (Kalamazoo: Cistercian Publications, 1979), 13 and 17) and the later Rhenish, Spanish and French 'humanist' currents (following Bérulle) do not make this mistake. Even John of the Cross's 'dark night' afflicts the soul in its entirety and does not betoken a simple passage from derelict self to the advance into an unknown God, because the night is already obscurely the night

Therefore such an understanding will not necessarily be intentional and such a willing will not necessarily be teleological.

It follows that, shorn of the relational dimension of reciprocal echo between the three faculties, the psychological analogue to the Trinity loses also its ecstatic, extra-psychological aspect. It becomes more the case that the three faculties in isolation echo the three persons of the Trinity, and that they do so within a solipsistic completeness, so ensuring that now, indeed (as not at all with Augustine), God is modelled by 'the solitary mind' in accordance with the priority Scotus gives (again unlike Augustine)

of erotic wounding which begins to transfigure human knowledge and will into their true ecstatic identity. (See, for example, *The Dark Night of the Soul*, trans. Benedict Zimmermann (Cambridge: James Clarke, 1973), Book II, XIII, 10). So while, indeed, John of the Cross like Luther reflects that 'crisis of the self' caused by the breakdown of organic society as identified by Michel de Certeau, he does so in a manner that, in the wake of Eckhart, insists more radically on the inherent 'nothingness' of created things as already taught by Augustine: this does not in the end downgrade the role of our own proper activities and emotions, whereas in the case of Luther the nothingness of our activity as such is perverted into the passivity of our created being over against a grace received within the same univocal plane. Hence it was the more voluntarist mystical current that helped in the end to encourage the Lutheran onto-theological delusion that we receive an unmediated, uncreated grace (hovering impossibly and idolatrously 'between' God in his essence and the creation, like the Palamite uncreated energies, formally distinguished from the divine essence) that precedes our meritorious response. By contrast, the latter, for Catholic doctrine, is the entirely grace-given and created work of the supernatural habit of charity, which involves the establishment of reciprocal bonds of friendship with others, and not simply the notion of the ethical deed as an echo of the supposedly purely unilateral divine bestowal of grace. Where the intellect retains an equilibrium with the will, there love retains its link with circumstance, preference, recognition and discernment – of all creatures in myriad ways by God, of God remotely by us, of humans by each other. But without circumstance and preference (the Augustinian *ordo amoris* which demands that finite creatures must love some more than others) love reduces to a blind act of the will which can in the end be no more than mere choice or election. This is exactly why, as Michel Hénaff shows, the Magisterial Reformers twice abolished gift, and therefore compromised love as the heart of Christianity – replacing it with a loveless trust in an inscrutable deity (*Le Prix de la Vérité* (Paris: Éditions du Seuil, 2002), 351–380). First of all they compromised grace by substituting whimsical 'election' for unilateral charity (albeit for a true view this 'gives' the reality of our thankful and meritorious return), and secondly they compromised reciprocal charity as the organising principle of society, opening the path to the general sway of capitalist contract. This seems to me to be a problem even with William Tyndale's positions, albeit that he qualifies Luther with the more Augustinian and metaphysically realist Wycliffite legacy according to which all authority, clerical and 'secular' (relating to our time on earth), is by divine gift, and must be exercised responsibly according to the laws of charitable distribution. For he has still lost the sense of charity as 'state of being' or as reciprocal bond, rather than one-way gesture, and it is just this which causes him to condemn, with all the Reformation, practices like the meritorious endowment of chapels and almshouses as 'selfish' and 'idolatrous' because mainly concerned with prayers for one's to the essence over the persons, and the way in which he idolatrously categorises God as an individual, comparing him to 'Socrates'.[105]

In this complex way, a very deficient understanding of the Trinity crucially helped to incite the model of representation, because it entirely altered Aquinas's understanding of intentionality. In the case of Duns Scotus, the expressive word which always in Augustine and Aquinas involves a disclosive relation between known and knower (even in the case of God), is no longer seen as essential for every act of understanding. Instead there is, for humans, an immediate – though not entirely reliable – intuitive knowledge of particulars, without active intellectual translation and universalisation (as there is for Aquinas) by analogy with sensory awareness (here Scotus anticipates Hobbes and Locke), and in a fashion which mimics the immediate external orientation of human willing.[106] When it comes to reflective abstraction which achieves knowledge of real universals and intends 'common natures' (indifferent to universality of particularity, and somewhat like immanentised impersonal Platonic ideas), then the concept as object of knowledge is more complete in itself than it is for Aquinas, and only 'intends' through the act of representation which somehow cognitively 'mirrors' the material object.[107] (In Aquinas, there is indeed some aspect of 'picturing', but this only serves to convey the real ineffable proportion that exists between the knowing-imagining 'icon' and the real thing in the world.)

---

own soul. His real failure here (which is all of a piece with the strained and anti-scriptural denial of practices like anointing which could only be condemned through the equally un-biblical claim that miracles ceased in the apostolic age) is to grasp the 'festive' dimension of charity and the way an exchange need not be a mere calculus (even though it had so often degenerated into that in the late Middle Ages) because it is concerned with establishing bonds between the living and the dead, between the living and the living, and between material and spiritual benefit. See William Tyndale, *The Obedience of a Christian Man* (London: Penguin, 2000), and Rowan Williams's fine and sympathetic exposition of Tyndale in his *Anglican Identities* (London: DLT, 2004). Later chapters in this book are implicitly clear that Richard Hooker later took Anglicanism in a much more Catholic direction. See also, on the Protestant distortion of charity, John Bossy's seminal remarks in *Christianity in the West 1400–1700* (Oxford: Oxford University Press, 1975), 140–152.

[105] Duns Scotus, *Opus Oxoniense* I, dist. 3 q. 1 a. 2.

[106] Duns Scotus, *Ordinatio* IV, dist. 45 q. 3. n. 17; *Quodlibetal Questions*, 6 a. 1 [8] 19. And see de Muralt, *La Métaphysique du phénomène*, 60. In the second of Duns Scotus's passages referred to, Scotus sees this sort of intuition as a model for the beatific vision which again suggests that he too much thinks of God as 'another thing' and plays down the Pauline 'we will see as we are seen', which implies (as Aquinas read it) the most extreme possible intensification of knowledge by identity, whereby the reality known entirely displaces the normal function of the intellectual *species*.

[107] See de Muralt, *La Métaphysique du phénomène*, 57–76, and de Libera, *La Querelle des universaux*, 321–351.

This means that Scotus has already ceased to think, in genuinely Aristotelian terms, of understanding as belonging to an existential 'world' of its own – in keeping with which vision, Augustine (and Aquinas after him) had declared that 'knowledge is a kind of life in the reason of the knower'.[108] Instead, it has become a sort of *substitute reality*, the 'best that we can do' in the face of the fullness of the real – now thought of as if it was pre-intellectual and could exist altogether without the governance of created mind (which it cannot, for Aquinas),[109] just as, for Scotus, the divine infinite being 'formally precedes' the divine intelligence.

One might say that, on Aquinas's view, the material world is like a kind of 'day' which is nonetheless of itself 'dark' with the density of black soil, since no light will phenomenally shine there unless there are minds to regard it. By contrast, the human understanding is like a kind of night, within which nonetheless, as for the opening of St John's Gospel, a light always shines, the light of the *Logos* which 'lighteth every man'. Or equally one could say that the material world is the state of being awake which is yet asleep without the wakened who walk through it, while the intellectual world (*esse intellectuale*) is like a state of sleep which nonetheless continuously enjoys a dream: the dream of consciousness itself. In Aquinas the very order of governance of this world involves the constant oscillation, as it were, of day and night: wakefulness amongst the sleeping stones and the semi-somnolence within the dream which inhabits a panpsychic reality. The day lacks its own light and awareness, which the night of the intellect supplies. And yet the night-powers can only see 'in' the daylight, can only dream 'of' the daytime.

But for Scotus, already, 'night' and 'sleep' have been defined at once by deficiency and instrumentality – perhaps echoing the fact that this is also for him literally the case, since he also flattened time (long before Newton) into an abstract passing, such that it could exist in independence of the movement of bodies and of rhythmic, liturgical oscillations that constitute as well as measure temporal *diastasis*.[110] Just as literal night has come in the modern west to mean merely an annoying lack of light, and literal sleep has come to mean merely a regular tiresome need to replenish the powers of mind and body, so that we have lost the ritual pattern of 'segmented sleep' punctuated by prayerful, studious or erotic 'watches',[111] so also for

---

[108]   Augustine, *De Trinitate* IX.1.4.

[109]   See Milbank, *The Suspended Middle*, 88–103.

[110]   See Pickstock, 'Duns Scotus'.

[111]   See A. Roger Ekirch, *At Day's Close: A History of Nighttime* (London: Weidenfeld & Nicolson, 2005), and Craig Koslofsky, *Evening's Empire: A History of the Night in Early Modern Europe* (Cambridge: Cambridge University Press, 2011).

Scotus the intellectual realm as 'the dream of night' primarily lacks that reality which it tries to grasp, and seeks to make up for the deficiencies of sensory intuitive apprehension. It is reduced in consequence to the status of 'a virtual day'.

Thus the concept which only intends by representation is no longer the intellectual *verbum* which has 'elevated' (after Aristotle) form itself and in addition expresses an ineffable intentional relation (after Augustine) to the greater existential fullness of materialised form. Instead, it is a kind of ersatz substitute for the real thing, a mere model, a coding or 'representation'. In the long term this gives rise to that sort of playschool pseudo-realism (so beloved of modern theologians) which speaks of the linguistic and the symbolic in terms of 'inadequate but necessary models of the real' and so forth.

6   Intentionality and Embodiment

But it also, as André de Muralt argues, gives rise to the Husserlian account of intentionality, which is ultimately traceable to Scotus, insofar as it effectively abandons the mediating role of the concept as inner (or indeed outer) sign. Husserl's notion of understood *eidos* comes very near, as de Muralt points out, to the Aristotelian-Thomist notion that an understood form is identical with an existing form. In this respect Husserl began to break with the theory of knowledge as representation. Thus against idealism he insisted on the 'separateness' of the known object from the knower, and concomitantly that in knowing an idea we are 'intending' some aspect of reality. This is especially the case because we can only make sense, in his famous example, of the sides of a cube which are visible to us, *as* sides of a cube if we mentally and so 'intentionally' supply the missing sides and also intend the glimpsed sides as sides of the entire invisible figure. Since we can never fully experience, nor fully supply, the absent aspects of any phenomenon (even a cube, whose entire range of properties we cannot exhaust), phenomenological research and analysis becomes 'an infinite task'.[112]

However, what is intended here is still fundamentally what can be 'represented', and not the real in its ontologically resistant reality. When Husserl wrote that 'the presentation I have of Greenland's icy wastes certainly differs from the presentation Nansen had of it', he did not mean to draw attention to Nansen's direct confrontation with the cold, isolation

---

[112]   De Muralt, *La Métaphysique du phénomène*, 10–76.

and sublime vastness of the Arctic Circle.[113] Instead, by declaring that the 'object is the same' in either case, he makes it chillingly clear that reference to an intentional essence is indifferent to such direct encounter. Hence the contrast between 'intentional essence' and 'semantic essence' is not one between how a thing is in itself and the various different ways in which it can appear to observers, but is rather a sheerly phenomenological distinction that consciousness makes between the stable identity of a thing, on the one hand, and the differing and changing modes in which it may present itself to us on the other. The former is never exhaustively presented to us and yet it can be precisely grasped in its essence – like the cube which we never see all at once. Hence the intended geographical location 'Greenland' remains the same, even though we may be pointing to it on a map by a warm fireside, or else we may be referring to it as that which palpably surrounds us in all its desolation. Although we understand a geographical location to be a real place, external to our thought processes, it preserves, according to Husserl, its intentional consistency merely in the way that the ideal object presented by the description 'straight line' is identical with the ideal object presented by the description 'shortest line'.[114] Only later would Maurice Merleau-Ponty save the reality of Greenland (for example) by arguing that it exists as the real but shifting intersection of multiply real and really related perspectives which are at once physical and ideational.[115]

From this comparison we can see that Husserl did not think, like Augustine and Aquinas, of all mental concepts as inner signs or 'mental words' which 'intentionally' point away from the mental itself, but instead (in an ultimately Scotist lineage) as blends of cognitive and imaginary intuition which do not signify a presumed extra-mental reality towards which sign and thought are inextricably open, but rather display to a degree the intended essence itself which is a Scotistic *esse objectivum*, defined by being the object of the mind's regard.[116]

---

[113]   Edmund Husserl, *Logical Investigations*, vol. 2, trans. J.N. Findlay (London: Routledge, 2001), Investigation V, ch. 2, §21, p. 123. Alasdair MacIntyre misreads this passage in a realist sense as indicating that 'the object as presented always may be and often is an object quite apart from its being presented to some consciousness' – see Alasdair MacIntyre, *Edith Stein: A Philosophical Prologue* (London: Continuum, 2006), 46.

[114]   Husserl, *Logical Investigations*, vol. 2, Investigation V, ch. 2, §21, p. 123.

[115]   I hope to say more about these matters in *On Divine Government*.

[116]   Jacques Maritain once remarked that 'The dependence certain characteristics of phenomenology seem to have on Duns Scotus might also be noted, particularly his [Husserl's] theory of ideas and *esse objectivum*'. See *The Degrees of Knowledge*, trans. Gerald B. Phelan (Notre Dame, Ind.: Notre Dame University Press, 1998), 109 n. 77. In the same place (109–110)

Yet this less than realist version of intentionality is insufficient, because it is the very excess of intended being over the realm of the mental which alone makes sense of the very idea of knowability. As Adorno argued against Husserl, it is because real things remain densely other and cannot be *fully* known that the mind registers them as the proper objects of cognitive awareness; it is finally the very unknowability of things as things which gives them to us as things-to-be-known.[117] (Only in the divine Trinity do knowing and alterity entirely coincide.) Even though Husserl in part recognised this, because he allowed that the offering of aspects is never completed, he nevertheless did not allow that this indicates an ulti-mate *apophasis* about the actual essences of things, which cannot be made the object of an eidetic reduction, since their given 'reserve' is simply the excess of existence itself over what we can think about existence. Greenland is after all the same place for Nansen out there in the Arctic wastes and for me ensconced in snug domesticity, because we are both lured not just by a denomination but by a name secured in semantic constancy only because it is affixed to a real, if never univocally seizable, global orientation.

And since Greenland is a real mystery and not a cognitively defined reality (just as 'globe' and 'place' are abstract mysteries more than they are grasp-able 'essences'), *all* that we can know of it are its various geological, geographical, meteorological, historical and mythical aspects which are indeed like 'signs' through which we 'intend' a drastically absent reality which we nonetheless fully trust to 'be really there'. So if one justifiably ref-uses any Husserlian notion of an 'intentional essence', one requires instead a sense, lacking in Husserl, of the manifest and yet undemonstrable way in which the visible aspects of things mediate to us their invisible reserve of self-sustaining unity and consistency which helps to integrate the endless revisability of perspectival shifts through which they are apprehended. This sense was later articulated by Merleau-Ponty, precisely because he balanced the primacy of phenomenology with an equal primacy for ontology.[118]

he well defined the difference between Husserlian and Augustinian/Thomist intentionality: 'Intentionality is not only that property of my consciousness of being-directed transparency, of aiming at objects in the depth of itself. Above all, intentionality is a property of thought, a prerogative of its immateriality, whereby being in itself, posted "outside it", i.e. being which is fully independent of the act of thought, becomes a thing existing within it, set up for it and integrated into its own act through which, from that moment, they both exist in thought with a single, self-same suprasubjective existence.'

[117] Theodor W. Adorno, *Against Epistemology*, trans. Willis Domingo (Oxford: Blackwell, 1982).
[118] Maurice Merleau-Ponty, 'The Intertwining – The Chiasm', in *The Visible and the Invisible* trans. Claude Lefort (Evanston, Ill.: Northwestern University Press, 1968), 130–155. I am indebted to discussions with Jennifer Spencer, formerly of Emmanuel College, Cambridge, on all this.

But within the Husserlian scheme, by contrast, it is at once the case that the intending concept is really but a representational substitute for the real and so is 'existentialised' – such that it lacks the formal dignity that it possesses in Aquinas – and that the intending displaces the real altogether. Thus Husserl defines even a 'real object' as 'the possible object of a straightforward percept'.[119] Here a nominalist empiricism and a transcendentalist idealism are in exemplary collusion: ideas at the horizon would efface themselves before perfectly present facts, and merely instrumental universal notions before particulars, but correlatively such facts would be noetically entirely constitutable by our minds, since all that our minds can understand is the unfolding of what was always *a priori* latent in terms of the inherent manifestness of the essences of all knowable objects that can appear to us. Intentionality would therefore 'eschatologically' vanish and representation finally triumph as ideal construction. This means that not only does the concept (in a Scotist lineage) here 'substitute' for reality, like a dream for waking consciousness, but also all we are left with is the substitution, all we can do all day is day-dream. For within Husserl's later 'transcendental turn' it is recognised that representation carries no guarantee of verisimilitude, and that this is rather delivered by the quasi-Fichtean assumption that the *a priori* structure of our intellection, which has an inexhaustible power precisely to intuit phenomena, is the road to the constitution of the real (which ultimately requires a divine guarantee, supplied by Husserl in his unpublished writings).

At this point Husserl threatens to betray one of the very imperatives of phenomenology, which rescues the integrity of immediate, surface phenomena against scientific reduction (which occurs only under a certain intentional bias). However, his later recognition of the way in which the body already cognises things through being itself an object in the world (and yet a peculiarly reflexive object), and consequently the way in which the opening up of a new aspectual and intentional field is contingently situated in space, time and human bodily interaction (his simultaneously corporeal and historicist turn), starts to work against this 'substitutionalism' – although this new turn was only fully followed up by Merleau-Ponty. For in the threshold reality of embodied life, which is at once 'subjective' and 'objective', material and conceptual *eidos* are mingled, and therefore every comprehension tends to be immediately a relational return to ecstatic engagement with other realities, while comprehension itself ceases

---

[119]   *Logical Investigations*, vol. 2, Investigation VI, ch. 6, §47, p. 285; *Ideas Pertaining to a Pure Phenomenology and to a Phenomenological Philosophy*, trans. R. Rojcewicz, A. Schuwer and F. Fersten (Dordrecht: Kluwer, 1983–1989), Book I, §85, pp. 246–250.

to be instrumentalised and regarded as a 'substitute', since it is an integral part of the flow of intra-corporeal reality and the interaction between bodies and unconscious objects which together constitute an ultimate transcendental horizon. The intercorporeal also ensures that human understanding is fundamentally inter-subjective, since the knowledge inscribed in bodies is always a relation to other conscious bodies via shared attention.[120] All these dimensions – the orientation of bodies to things, bodies to bodies and subjects to subjects – make up 'the life-world' from which precise, logical scientific knowledge is only abstracted, upon which it obscurely depends, and to which it must always return as the source of new stimuli for research and exploration.

Both the dependency upon, and the return to, the 'life-world' now suggest a very different and 'non-reductivist' sense for the 'phenomenological reduction', since this is now more a matter of becoming aware of the full reality implied in the 'natural attitude' than of leaving the latter behind once and for all in favour of a superior vantage-point.[121] In this way the path to a richer, non-empiricist intentionalist realism is once again opened up by Husserl in a newly more 'materialist' and socio-historical fashion – although one which is somewhat anticipated by Aristotle's *De Anima* and Aquinas's deployment of this work.[122]

This late shift in Husserl's outlook involves, therefore, an intensification of his initial recovery of the intentional. It is almost as if he travelled in reverse steps the road taken by modern philosophy after Scotus. He starts by rejecting the non-intentionalism of both empiricism and idealism, which was historically the result of the logic of the 'substitutionist' outlook: if representations are what we must 'make do with', then they are also all that we know – such was already the conclusion of William of Ockham against Scotus, in declaring that signs directly stand for things without the mediation of intentional concepts,[123] and it was later echoed by Descartes and the rationalists, besides Locke and the empiricists, and finally Kant and his idealist heirs. All these currents were haunted by scepticism: it seems to be apparent to our senses that there is a world beyond our awareness, but how can we know that our thoughts and our sensations have anything to do with this world as it really is, as opposed to our pragmatic negotiations with it? And if all is merely

120   Husserl, *Ideas*, Book II, §18 a–b and c–h, pp. 60–70, 82–95.
121   Husserl, *The Crisis of European Sciences and Transcendental Phenomenology: An Introduction to Phenomenological Philosophy*, trans. David Carr (Evanston, Ill.: Northwestern University Press, 1970), Part IIIA, 28–55, pp. 103–189.
122   See Milbank and Pickstock, *Truth in Aquinas*, 60–87.
123   See de Libera, *La Querelle des universaux*, 286–287.

pragmatic, why, then, is there a conscious mental realm at all, given that everything functional might be performed unconsciously? That appears to be an unsolvable problem for the materialist psychologism against which Husserl reacted, and thus he reasserted the view that thought is inherently 'thought of something': an irreducibly constitutive relation to something of an intimate extremity unknown in corporeal nature.

But as we have seen, he first of all recovered intentionality in a Scotist mode, which naturally suggested the reversal from an empirical to an idealist outlook. Only much later did questions of embodiment, society and historicity (significantly enough) edge him back towards something like a more Thomistic and genuinely realist perspective upon intentionality. Husserl nonetheless failed formally to abjure a transcendentalist horizon of historically unfolding 'necessary' traditions of ideation, like that of Euclidean geometry or Galilean physics, thereby suppressing the problem of the contingency of axiomatic decisions which, however much they may prove their worth within a certain problematic field, are nonetheless tied from the outset to a certain material or 'written' construction of *problemata* – parallel lines which only never meet, for example, on a two-dimensional finite plane – as Derrida rightly pointed out against him.[124]

All the same, if we recall that we live in the body which both wakes and sleeps, then it is likely that we will realise how conscious mental 'night' does not simply reflect, or substitute for, the fully real but unconscious 'day', but is rather intertwined with it. The world is intercorporeal and intersubjective as well as being divided between the mental and the physical. Moreover, all our 'private' mental interactions with unconscious bodies tend to be interfused with, and also remotely modelled upon, the for us transcendentally primary sphere of the inter-corporeal. In the body (to which the phantasmatic always returns) to think is always obscurely to receive and in turn to give again, to act through that sacrificial self-restriction towards the other that is yet the only path to self-fulfilment.[125]

Such a perspective indicates a contemporary road back to a theological vision of a meaningful universe that is inherently related according to an aesthetic order and comprises teleological goals, including the goal of intentional knowledge. The latter, genuinely understood, holds in a tensional balance both the dignity of thought and the dignity of material existence. Moreover, the greater understanding of the body as a 'threshold' reality,

---

[124]   Husserl, *Crisis*, Part II, 8–10, pp. 21–61. Jacques Derrida, *Edmund Husserl's Origin of Geometry: An Introduction*, trans. P. Leavey (Brighton: Harvester, 1978), includes Husserl's text.
[125]   See Chesterton, *Orthodoxy*, 45. Obviously one can see many of Wittgenstein's reflections as promoting these sorts of perspectives.

opened up by a mode of phenomenology which is entirely compatible with a realist metaphysic, permits one better to understand how the divine *Logos* could have descended not just into intelligent mind at the angelic level, but into the corporeal soul and body of a living human being and have perpetuated this embodiment in the intercorporeity of the Church.

For embodiment best reveals divine reason in the created order, since it is in the body that one comes *nearest* to that divine synthesis of reason with existential reality that does not simply 'swallow' such reality in thought, thereby paradoxically leaving thought with nothing to think about. The body performs thought through its gestures, like an actor upon a stage, in such a way that embodiment iconically enlarges the thought and yet does not abolish thought as sign. Instead, the body in its very density ecstatically points away from itself to other bodies which are also living, enacted processes of signification for which being is itself a thinking and so an intentional referring. Even the angelic is in one respect here surpassed, because body is always darkly traced by that shadow of intellectual light which is matter – and it is just for this reason that the human being, not the angel, is the microcosm, and therefore can be appropriately hypostasised in Christ by the exemplary person of the Son. Yet it remains the case that the coincidence of being and thought is not perfect, as it is for the angels and for God: bodies oscillate between their daytime siesta of impenetrable material density and their nighttime operatic gestures of lucid meaning, under the spotlight of reason.

7   Intentionality and Selfhood

Advocacy of Merleau-Ponty's perspective can seem to run foul of later developments in phenomenology associated with the names of Michel Henry, Emmanuel Levinas and Jean-Luc Marion. These all have in common the view that intentionality cannot be regarded as phenomenologically fundamental. The reasoning here is entirely rigorous, since it is pointed out that, while the object of an intention, if it is regarded (in 'Scotist' terms) as merely the mental object, can become fully manifest, the process of intending itself can never be brought to full awareness. This is because any attempt to round upon our intending opens up the prospect of an infinite regress, since the intentionality of intending can only be preserved if something in the experience of intending escapes experiential awareness. Therefore the intentional core of our thought processes would always elude any phenomenological grasp.[126]

---

[126]   Michel Henry, *Phénoménologie matérielle* (Paris: PUF, 1990), 13–59.

Undoubtedly, Husserl failed to resolve this conundrum and therefore Henry et al. are so far correct: intending itself would not appear to be reducible to a passive donation as the very heart of phenomenological ambition demands. However, at this juncture two alternatives clearly open to view: either, in order to have a pure phenomenology which will be coterminous with the whole of philosophy, intentionality must be grounded in something prior to intention, or else, in order to save the primacy of intentionality (which alongside 'givenness' is Husserl's other primary philosophical stress), pure phenomenology must be abandoned, and it must be seen to be 'crossed' by both ontology and semiotics. This is the route taken by Merleau-Ponty, for whom intending (in an Augustinian and Thomistic lineage) is once more of real objects, and now by a fully embodied self. These objects can never be fully manifest, but must to some degree be 'conjectured' through the reading of intentions as signs which also involves a 'perceptual faith', since the sign function is not prised apart from the phenomenological register of 'the shown'. Something mysteriously 'comes through' when we know, which is simultaneously 'seen' and yet 'judged'.

However, this option with regard to known realities is also an option with respect to self-awareness. If nothing is known save through an intention, and the *ecstasis* of intention exceeds manifestation, then we cannot be fully manifest to ourselves, any more than we can have a transparent insight into the essence of other things and people. Thus for Merleau-Ponty we cannot know ourselves 'inwardly' apart from the awareness of our body.[127] The latter is a threshold between subjectivity and objectivity, which cannot be known internally (not even in the instances of dream, pathology or mystical ecstasy, which do not evade the imagination) without a simultaneous knowing of it externally. I understand for example my hand at once as something I can move and as something I can see. Without being able to move my hand I would not realise what it is that I am seeing before my eyes, but without being able to see my hand I would not understand what it is to move it. It follows that, if I only know myself as an embodied self and there is no uncontaminated 'inner self', then I can only ever know my 'I' as always already a 'me' and only grasp myself as a reflection of an already commenced distance. This distance includes all the relations in which my embodied self stands to other finite realities and all their influences upon my embodied situation. I constantly have to 'claim myself back' from this distance, and yet also reaffirm the distance, unless I am to

---

[127] Maurice Merleau-Ponty, *Phenomenology of Perception*, trans. Colin Smith (London: Routledge, 1992), vii–xxi, 148–153, 369–409.

admit that my only possible self is always alienated from a 'real' self which, however, is not really there.

The latter was Jean-Paul Sartre's position, for which it is the 'bad faith' of 'the spirit of seriousness' to identify with one's distanced self as authentic rather than temporarily if necessarily entertained.[128] The only possibility here of escape from alienation and a trumping of irony is to embrace the alien as the decided, or to opt for an altogether new decision and diversion. Here one can say that the option of intentionality and its ontologisation is embraced, but in nihilistically existentialist guise. Following Heidegger's implicit abandonment of Husserl's anti-psychologism by now situating the cognitive subject fully in 'the world' as an environment to which she is ineluctably related, every intentional investment of self in this world none-theless eventually confronts the 'nauseous' reality of the intended world's absolute indifference to our subjective human interests.

Michel Henry's avoidance of this bleak existentialism comes at the cost of a total retreat from the intentional, in order to perfect the purity of the phenomenological project. Husserl had spoken of the indeterminate *hyle* of sensory and cognitive impressions that precede an intentional under-standing.[129] Henry suggested that the awareness of this *hyle* continues to accompany every intention and to allow its instance.[130] In fact, the intending of objects is always a diminution of genuine cognition, since there we know only their exteriors and we know these in a mode of domineering distantiation which tends to obliterate real experience. Genuine cognition in awareness of the *hyle* is 'auto-affection'. Despite the nomenclature, this is in no way anything reflective, but is rather an immediate and primordial awareness of self, through which we can also directly apprehend everything else insofar as it (through alien external channels) affects the self and entirely penetrates it.[131] Thus auto-affection is not a reflexive 'inner-sensing' or 'self-sensing' as expounded by Aristotelian tradition up until the time of Descartes and later revived

---

[128]   Jean-Paul Sartre, *Transcendence of the Ego: A Sketch for a Phenomenological Description*, trans. Sarah Richmond (London: Routledge, 2011).

[129]   Husserl, *Ideas*, Book II, §85, pp. 246–250.

[130]   Henry, *Phénoménologie matérielle*.

[131]   Henry effectively revives (through the overwhelming influence of Schopenhauer on his thought) Goethe's view that a true natural philosophy knows natural realities by sympathy from within ourselves. Merleau-Ponty's perspective is rather compatible with the more balanced attempts by German Romantics like Novalis and Friedrich Schlegel to com-bine's Goethe's importantly corrective view with the more externalising considerations of empirical natural science. See Pierre Hadot, *Le Voile d'Isis: Essai sur l'histoire de l'idée de nature* (Paris: Gallimard, 2004), 321–364.

against Descartes by Xavier Bichat and Maine de Biran (in whose lineage Merleau-Ponty profoundly lay). It is instead a 'materialised' and 'affectivised' version of the Cartesian 'self-consciousness' – the *cogito* itself, supposedly reborn.

However, whether auto-affection is pre-conscious or conscious, pre-cognitive or cognitive, is not entirely clear in Henry. As Peter Ashworth has pointed out, with the retreat from intentionality goes also a retreat from disclosive 'mood' – such as anxiety, melancholia, or boredom – as we find in Kierkegaard, Heidegger and Sartre.[132] For a mood is a general intentional comporting of the self towards the world. But auto-affection is entirely indeterminate, indeed like Aristotelian matter, and its pure *pathos* is indifferent to either suffering or joy, evil or goodness. As Ashworth says, this means that the price Henry must pay for securing an absolutely unbreachable and inalienable citadel of subjectivity is the total loss of character and individuation of this subject. Once the 'I' is liberated from the 'me', the internal from the external body, and my abiding interiority from shifting worldly relationships, I am ironically left with only a person-hood 'in general', and therefore all that we normally understand by subjectivity has been entirely surrendered. The heart of the self may be for the later Henry a mystical identity with God, but it is no longer truly an individuated self who is identical with God, as it most certainly was for Eckhart (whom Henry likes to invoke).[133]

The upshot is a negative agreement with Sartre after all: where the latter rejects the reverse 'bad faith' of refusing to invest the empty self in arbitrary worldly decisions, Henry's espoused religious faith sanctifies this emptiness. Such a gesture would undergird that dubious and prevalent contemporary spirituality which obsessively and one-sidedly stresses our need to rid ourselves of self-illusion. This runs the risk of characterising as such deception every single one of our worldly investments and 'trying on of parts', either in external reality or in the imagination. Played out to the end – as it was with great brilliance by the English novelist John Cowper Powys – such a spiritual stance suggests a plurality of illusory if necessary and enticing mythological options on the one hand, and a Gnostic retreat to an absolute otherness that is both inward and infinitely remote, on the other.[134] By contrast, the real and genuinely strenuous spiritual task (as intimated by T.S. Eliot in *The Confidential Clerk*) is constantly to sort out

---

[132] Peter Ashworth is a psychologist who has studied philosophy with me. This entire section is deeply indebted to his acute insights.
[133] See Milbank, 'The Double Glory'.
[134] See especially John Cowper Powys, *Wolf Solent* (London: Penguin, 2000).

which of the entertained 'fictions' one is naturally fit to inhabit by virtue of natural personal endowment, cultural situation and their genuine teleological desirability. Some illusions have to turn out to be real and operable, else nothing would be achieved at all and we would never acquire any characterisable or consistent identities.

It follows that externalisation of self is essential for the recouping of a characterisable self and any inward sense of who we are. The latter is somehow (and problematically) realised in the obscure interval and conjuncture between the inter-corporeal and the linguistic. And there is no relation to self more fundamental than such reflexivity, because, as Merleau-Ponty asserted, there is no originally perceived *hyle* that is not already suffused with meaning or with intentional reference, which already (as Augustine thought) informs all human sensation. Moreover, our most fundamental perceptions and sensations already involve an active attempt by the body to orientate itself and to operate within its environment. The latter impinges not in terms of passively received 'givens', but in terms of 'affordances' or opportunities for self-preservation and self-development.[135] Not just our hands but also our other sensory organs 'seize hold' of things in a way that cannot be reduced to an equivalent sensory input received in a sheerly receptive 'internal space'. Thus what the eye attains to is not just information received through a sensory organ, but a specific orientation or 'look' upon a thing that is also that thing's situation of our gaze in actual physical space. The event of this reciprocal informing constitutes 'sight', and any interior processing has to return to this surface if it is to 'see' at all. Hence no reconstruction of sight as internal event – whether in physical or phenomenological terms – is able to identify this experience as sight without reference to the irreducibility of the interactive and corporeal experience of vision.

It is true, as Henry contends, that the peculiar immediacy of subjective awareness cannot be reduced to reflection. But neither can it be prised apart from it, since every awareness is of something, and one cannot detach the awareness from this intending (including of self), even though the awareness is not reducible to intention. The consequence is that pure phenomenology is impossible, not just with respect to irreducible intentionality, but *also* with respect to the immediacy of the *cogito*. Because the mediation of intentionality is itself immediately experienced it can never be rounded upon as manifest. But because the immediacy

---

[135]   On 'affordances' see James Gibson, *The Senses Considered as Perceptual Systems* (Boston: Houghton Mifflin, 1965).

of self-apprehension can only ever be reflexively intended it, likewise, can never become manifest. If it is said to be manifest as 'saturated', then the excess of both intuition *and* intention involved here (since we have seen that the manifest can never be prised apart from the intended)[136] defeats both intuitional fulfilment of meaning and the intentional horizon of this significance.[137] That which appears only to blind has necessarily to be reflexively imaged through conjecture, else it turns into the didactic manifestation of a nihilistic abyss. Thus where phenomenology holds on to both its fundamental insights by insisting that everything is at once donated and intended, it must deny the adequacy of phenomenology to achieve its own ends both with respect to the knowledge of things and with respect to self-awareness. Its extension of the attempted fulfilment of a non-theological ontology as epistemology therefore negates itself, and points the way back to the unavoidability of metaphysical speculation.

8 Reason and the Incarnation of the *Logos*

From the reflections of the two preceding sections we can begin to understand how classical 'knowledge by identity', expanded to include the corporeal dimension, is required by an orthodox Christology (whose political significance we will eventually see), for which the Incarnation is appropriate, since humanity is inherently disclosive of God, and we can only be saved through the divine restoration of the *imago dei* in

---

[136] Jean-Luc Marion's supposition of an excess of intuited 'givenness' over intention would seem to assume a Scotist and Husserlian concept of intention as the fully if but formally 'mastered' mental object. But where it is allowed (with Heidegger and Merleau-Ponty) that the object of intention is corporeally and externally reached as real, then it follows that an agnostic experience of being overwhelmed is just as proper to the ecstatic reach of intention and the projection of a formal horizon of significance as it is to the blinding receptivity of fundamental intuition. Such realist intentionality is not replete in its intention of meaning, simply waiting to be exemplified by the adequate intuited object, which will never arrive. Instead, the more it receives new intuitions from without, the more its sense of a meaningful horizon is enriched and extended. Moreover, as I have already shown, to the degree that what is immediately manifest remains unknown as 'saturated', it must remain 'intended' if it is to be affirmed being, within intuition, yet in excess of any exhaustive intuitive seizure. Implicitly Marion concedes this, by substituting a sheerly arbitrary and fideistic willed 'decision' to acknowledge the otherness of donation (including onself as donated) instead of a measured intentionality. See Jean-Luc Marion, *Étant donné: Essai d'une phénoménologie de la donation* (Paris: PUF, 1997), esp. 251–342, 419–423.

[137] Marion, *Étant donné*, 321–323.

us – it being assumed that this image is substantively imitative of the divine *Logos* in terms of the shape of its thoughts and feelings, and not just formally possessed of a logical reason that differs from God's only in finite degree (as for Scotus and Ockham), or of a will that is identical when 'considered in its essential and strict sense' to God's (as for Descartes), since will is here defined only by indifferent openness.[138] 'Knowledge by representation', on the other hand, is compatible only with a thinned-out Christology that retains the formal shape but not the spirit of orthodoxy. For it must perforce understand the divine Incarnation as a matter of arbitrary decree, and not in terms of aesthetic suitability according to the intrinsic structures of the Creation. Within this perspective, the Creation, and humanity in particular within it, does not inherently reflect to a remote degree the very mind of God in its infinite expression in the *Logos*. It is instead but the result of a divine decision for this or that set of compossibles and is accordingly known by God in terms of a mere representation of what he has done or will do. The 'fittingness' of the Incarnation then reduces to some sort of economy of means or ease of rhetorical instruction of humanity. In consequence, even the reception of grace by Christ's humanity ceases to be, for Scotus, something inevitably following upon divine enhypostasisation and requires a special act of divine will.[139] For nothing, thanks to the formal distinction, 'intrinsically' goes together with anything else any more.

But in the Thomist account of Christology, God can only save us, according to *convenientia*, by transfiguring our understanding and corporeity – both individually and collectively. If Christ is indeed 'substituted' for us, in the face of our lack, then this is only in order to re-create us and indeed to re-create us by bringing about and disclosing a new yet eternal marvel: the God-Man who is both created and uncreated. For after the Fall humanity is only again possible through the 'more than humanity' of a man 'personalised' by the second hypostasis of the Trinity. Hence for Aquinas, while Christ (as Maximus the Confessor showed and the Byzantine intellectual era confirmed) had an entirely human will and so an entirely human, though sinless, history of interaction with others and encounter with contingent events and circumstances, this biography was realised as a human biography by becoming entirely fused with the eternal divine metahistory. Just as human

---

[138]   Descartes, *Meditations on First Philosophy:* 'Fourth Mediation', 57, p.40.
[139]   Duns Scotus, *Ordinatio* III, dist. 13 q. 4 n. 8. And see John Milbank, *Being Reconciled: Ontology and Pardon* (London: Routledge, 2003), 74–78.

created nature is only fulfilled through its self-surpassing by grace into a supernatural life, so, likewise, human fallen nature is only fulfilled through collective corporeal participation (the sacramental and social life of the Church) in the God-Man.[140] And thereby, astonishingly, to the wonderment of angels, even created deification is exceeded through its new identity with divine hominisation. This represents a still greater glory – contingent (in this specific mode) upon the entire drama of sin and redemption and yet also, since God has eternally foreknown all and responded to all, eternally conjoined to the immanent life of the Trinity. For this reason, while, on the one hand, we may partially indicate the reality of Christ through a 'stretching' of our usual ontological categories, on the other hand the human narrative of the events of Christ's life, and its continuation through his giving of the Spirit to the Church, through their combined conjoining to the Trinitarian metanarrative, now supplements our sense of the fundamental modes of being of all of reality. (How could the incarnation of the *Logos* mean any less?) Thus for the tradition consummated by Aquinas we can only 'represent' (in ontological terms) the reality of Christ, because in Christ God has fully 'identified' with us such that our knowledge of Christ is ceaselessly surpassed by the re-knowing of ourselves and all other realities in the context of the narrative of Christ and the continuous emergence of the Church.

But in the Scotist and later nominalist accounts, by contrast, a formal or real division between human and divine being in Christ (which effectively smuggles in a heterodox human personhood) will not allow that any reworking of the human essence in one man can (through cultural transmission) be contagious for the rest of us, but will only permit the legal transfer through grace of Christ's divine benefits to his human nature. In this way, the peculiar errors of Protestantism are already rendered possible: Christ in his incarnation and atonement becomes a 'mere' substitute for our deficiencies, in the sense that he extrinsically makes them good, without real, inward reworking of our nature. Because he is only a substitute, we can fully 'represent' what he means for us and forget about the narrative dimension of his life in favour of a neat set of propositions

I am immensely indebted in this paragraph to the work of Aaron Riches, who has developed the links between Henri de Lubac's 'natural desire for the supernatural' on the one hand and a Cyrilline and Maximian Christology on the other – a tradition elaborated by Aquinas, who already develops a greater mix of ontological and narrative elements in his Christology that reaches its consummation in Pierre de Bérulle's theory of Christ's *états* in which our true spiritual life is situated. See Riches, Ecce Homo: *On the Divine Unity of Christ* (Grand Rapids, Mich.: Eerdmans, 2013).

about his saving significance which in fact obliterates the saving *mystery*, or else in favour of a pietistic and *excessively* participatory Christological mysticism which tends to swallow up the believer in an eternal *stasis* of Christ's passionate anguish. For the divine *identification* with humanity is now reduced: either through a Calvinist weakening of the *communicatio idiomatum*,[141] or else through a Lutheran one-sided reading of this to mean God's kenotic 'enclosure' within a finite human space – which is one way to accommodate a nominalist suspicion of universal essences and constitutive relations.[142]

This 'substitution alone' is then of one synchronic piece with the substitution of image for reality in the theory of representation, since now the Incarnation and the Cross merely make up for our lack, such that their nocturnal travails yield to the literal day of our decreed restoration and there is no longer any devotion (abandoning the stress on this element in Scotus)[143] to the mystery of the God-Man as exceeding the occasion of his arrival (which Aquinas affirmed in his own way).[144] But just as the concept, *because* it is instrumentalised, becomes paradoxically a terminus in itself, so an instrumentalised Christology will also ensure a fetishistic, over-pious and too literally mimetic devotion to Christ's life and death, reduced to literal terms and shorn of its allegorical links with the intrinsic shape of every human destiny. An elusively sentimental 'personal relationship to Jesus' is eventually substituted for the partial disclosure of the mystery of the Trinity liturgically conveyed by the continued re-presentation of the God-Man in word, symbol and enactment.

---

[140]   Calvin reduces this to a rhetorical figure, not fully expounding the way in which the divine person, though not the divine nature, is fully the subject of all that Christ in his humanity undergoes, in such a way that divine and human properties have indeed here been more than metaphorically blended. See *Institutes of the Christian Religion* II. xiv.1–2.

[141]   See Thomas Torrance, *Space, Time and Incarnation* (Edinburgh: T. & T. Clark, 1997), and Graham White, *Luther as Nominalist* (Helsinki: Luther-Agricola Society, 1994).

[142]   In Scotus the idea that the Incarnation would have happened in any case, and not just as a remedy for the Fall, is linked with a denial of human deification. In consequence, the highest good of the joining of humanity to God can only come about through the Incarnation. For Aquinas, however, this highest good is already there, such that deification is a precondition for incarnation – even if he may also hold to the reverse (this remains somewhat unclear, though it is clearly the case in Maximus and other Byzantines whose Christology Aquinas essentially elaborates). So one is forced to say (going perhaps beyond Aquinas but in agreement with Eckhart) that insofar as incarnation is beyond deification, this is the eternally decreed conjoining of the event of human deification to the divine nature itself, which exceeds the mere accident of its being occasioned by sin.

[143]   See Milbank, *Being Reconciled*, 61–78.

9 The Passivity of Modern Reason

A merely 'substitutionary' Christology subordinates the theology of the God-Man to formal considerations regarding the divine *potentia absoluta*. But in a similar way, the 'substitutionary' character of knowledge by representation derives from the same formal insistencies concerning divinity, ensuring that theological considerations that are at once 'rational' (in the sense that the rational element in theology has now been reduced to the rationalistic which can only, without 'enlightened love', recognise the first cause as ultimate power) and also 'doctrinal' (in the sense that a particular mode of faith is privileging the divine will above all else), govern *both* the theological *and* the philosophical fields, with a secret depth of prior co-determination, at the outset of recognisably 'modern' thought.

For as has already been mentioned, it is the supposition that God *might* cause us to know an 'object' of understanding without it actually representing anything which ensures already in Ockham the dialectical turn from thinking of the concept as instrumental substitution to thinking of it as the sole *terminus* of the act of understanding, useful for pragmatically navigating our way through the world, but in principle subject to sceptical doubt, and useless as a foundation stone for the construction of any sort of metaphysical edifice. Thought at best, if it is reliable, gives us evidence as to the passing character of the world which we encounter and the items within it: it affords no clue as to the naturally necessary architectonic of this world, since there is no longer any reason to posit such a reality.

As de Muralt argues, this view effectively suggests, long before Kant, that we know only phenomena, handing over all noumenal certainty to the realm of faith.[145] He goes on to point out two crucial things about the philosophical trail which leads from the Venerable Inceptor to the sage of Königsberg. The first is that, if the conceptual object of understanding is merely the image of a thing that in principle might not be there, then the Aristotelian role of the active intellect becomes superfluous. This may appear highly ironic, in the light of the fact, already pointed out, that the initial Avicennian and then (to a considerable degree) Franciscan rejection of the intellectual *species* had partly to do with distaste for the idea of a passivity of spirit in relation to non-intellectual form. However, it can be argued that this refusal of an initial passivity condemns the mind to an all-pervading and double passivity: first of imaging and then of

---

[144] De Muralt, 'Kant, le dernier occamien'.

'auto-affection', wherein its self-elaboration is but a submission to a predetermined logical process in which judgement plays no real role.

By contrast, the Aristotelian and Thomist agency of the intellect was prompted precisely by a receptive engagement with the real world: an 'arriving' form had to be actively and judiciously abstracted. For the 'representation' model, however, a mirroring image just appears with certainty before the mind's awareness like a wilting rose before the eye's sight. This appearance must be accepted if it does not violate the principle of non-contradiction (now itself de-ontologised and apriorised) and if it is inseparable from our undeniable immediacy of self-awareness – the *cogito* already, as articulated by several of Ockham's contemporaries. So the 'turn to the subject', because it is a consequence of affirming the absolute power of God and his principled liability to override all secondary causes, is in fact correlated with the *utter passivity* of the human mind and not at all, as perhaps the majority of historical commentators suggest, with its active, creative capacity. If the Cartesian and Kantian mind 'constructs', this process is really the reception of an inexorably fated unfolding of intellection. It is, to the contrary, rather the Thomistic view which suggests that thought is an 'event', something which 'happens' to formal reality and something which involves our active and imaginative intervention.

This passivity is later clearly celebrated by Descartes, whose entire philosophy was in part motivated by a 'Counter-Renaissance' impulse to extirpate the role of immanent vital forces and of human innovative creativity, both being seen as dangerously paganising in character.[146] The mind for Descartes is doubly passive: once in relation to the geometry of the extended world with which it does not need to resonate (through identity or analogy) in order to understand, and twice through its reception of innate ideas from God. But just this double passivity opens up – with the most extreme irony – the prospect of a reduction of Renaissance *poesis* (both artistic and natural-magical) to modern classical *techne*: the measurable, mechanical world being revealed only to our clear, solitary grasp can become the object of endless manipulation according to prescribed and absolutely fixed mental standards. Modern Prometheanism therefore, is paradoxically linked to the *loss* of spontaneous mental activity and does *not* lie straightforwardly in continuity with the celebration of divinely human creativity by Nicholas of Cusa, Pico della Mirandola and others in the Renaissance period.[147]

---

[145]   See Henri Gouhier, *Les Premières Pensées de Descartes: Contribution à l'histoire de l'anti-Renaissance* (Paris: J. Vrin, 1979).

[146]   See Pico della Mirandola, *Oration on the Dignity of Man* (Cambridge: Cambridge University Press, 2012).

Later, in the case of Kant, there is a return to the sceptical horizon opened out by Ockham, and a fulfilment of it in terms of the theoretical bracketing of God which ensures a reigning agnosticism as to our knowledge of 'objects', now firmly confined to the screen of phenomena. Accordingly, Kant accentuates the role of the *a priori*, subjectivising even the frameworks of absolute, empty space and time. All that is received from the material world is atomistic items of sensory information, which are obscurely integrated by posited 'transcendental objects'. This extreme sceptical nominalism seems to open out a greater role for the constructive subject, who must impose and 'schematise' upon the sensory information with the help of the imagination and the *a priori* categories. However, passivity still rules, because this construction is not a *poesis* performed by the subject within and upon the real external world, but rather is something that happens in that virtual and internal space where the subject shapes for himself an object that can be satisfactorily known. He does so entirely under pre-given transcendental constraints, combined with his pure receptivity of empirical information. There is no real role here for an *intellectus agens*, nor for a reshaping *phantasia*. The latter is only allowed 'free play' within a deregulated interplay of reason and sensation in the aesthetic realm: but here the real beauty of the diverse objects thereby shaped is but the transcendental and formal truth of the most general and so 'free' co-ordination of the faculties. So originality is in fact discounted: every beautiful thing is differently beautiful only because, in reality, all beautiful things are but formally beautiful in forever the same, monotonous way.[148]

The role of the transcendental object in Kant remained unclear, and still more so that of the unknowable and yet underlying *noumena* which ultimately guaranteed a degree of real material 'externality' of the *phenomena* to the shaping mind. German idealism was an attempt to extirpate these obscurities, and in the case of Fichte this meant that the ego now 'posits' all of reality, while projecting matter as its own shadowy limit – both in a somewhat Plotinian fashion.[149] It would seem, then, that now, without either a transcendent God or an external reality, the Cartesian double passivity has finally been abolished. However, the auto-creating ego is at once wholly free and wholly determined, in its unravelling of the logic of a freedom understood still in entirely formal and neutral ('Ockhamist') terms. Here, as already with Kant's practical reason, to be free reduces to being utterly subject to freedom – every serious and so 'moral', not indifferent, act is only serious to the degree that it is

---

147   See Milbank, 'Sublimity: The Modern Transcendent'.

148   J.G. Fichte, *Introductions to the Wissenschaftslehre* (New York: Hackett, 1994).

auto-referring in re-receiving its own freedom – and by logical and utilitarian extension the freedom of others. (I cannot realistically be free myself, if others remain bound.) Therefore human passivity still rules, after all.

In comparison, Schelling and Hegel sought to recognise the independence of the natural world, in relation to the human mind. By acknowledging that thought is always the result of an interaction and an interchange between mind and nature they in part restored the Aristotelian perspective, along with many underground Renaissance influences, and abandoned knowledge by representation. *Just for this reason* they also now acknowledged to a degree (and in varying degrees in different writings) truth as an event, the mind as having a free and active shaping role according to its powers of judgement, and also, in the wake of Johann Gottfried Herder, started to realise that this implies the historicity of truth.[150] However, their agonistically dialectical understanding of the interaction between mind and nature severely impaired their reworking of a theory of knowledge by identity: this ensured that their perspective remained at bottom but a modification of Fichte. For Hegel mind in the end recovers nature within the power of its own self-constitution, which coincides with an abandoned material residue, while for the mid-period Schelling nature is reconciled with mind in terms of an immanent destiny at once disclosed and realised by aesthetic productions.[151]

So, in the end, the coincidence of freedom with necessity (in many different mutations) remains dominant. And therefore the same paradox of apparent pure activity still holds good as well: freedom which is auto-asserting and its own absolute horizon can only *suffer* itself. Hence for entirely rigorous reasons, in the case of all three great idealists our freedom is finally but a univocal fragment of the freedom of God who *also* must suffer this freedom – either as the doom of arbitrary positivity (the late Schelling) or else as the fate of a necessary becoming through the other in order fully to realise freedom's formality (Hegel). Because they construe the divine Trinity in these terms, and then understand history as the 'becoming' of the Trinitarian life, Hegel and Schelling both finally surrender their historicism to a logic of freedom as auto-determined. This precisely goes along with the fact that, for genuine providence standing as the ultimate eminent 'influence' above all secondary causes, they have substituted an immanent shaping logic or instinct, operating on the same univocal plane as other historical forces.

---

[149]   See Charles Taylor, *Hegel* (Cambridge: Cambridge University Press, 1975), 3–50.

[150]   See John Milbank, *Theology and Social Theory*, 2nd edn. (Oxford: Blackwell, 2006); 'The Double Glory'.

It can therefore be seen that throughout the course of modern philosophy, including much of phenomenology, except where it has drastically undergone the 'corporeal' turn, the passivity of the subject reigns as a direct implication of the theologically motivated turn to the subject itself – and it is this very passivity which is paradoxically to blame for the dominance of the technological paradigm. For this reason an entirely Protestant historicism, Protestant poetics or Protestant aesthetics has always been somewhat problematic. Where Protestant writers like Hamann, Herder, Novalis and the earlier Friedrich Schlegel offer us a genuine historicism, poetics and aesthetics, this is just to the measure that they have abandoned nominalism, voluntarism, univocity and a Protestant substitutionary Christology (the latter being still highly evident in Hegel).

Of course it should go almost without saying that the empiricism of Locke and Mill also elides the active subject. In theory a true empiricism would denote an openness to mystery that would require our free, active, interpretative response – to some degree this was the thesis of John Henry Newman.[152] But already with Francis Bacon the charitable orientation of knowledge was reduced to pragmatism, in alliance with the beginnings of a mechanisation of nature which now largely disallowed the vitalist and alchemical perspectives of Paracelsus, the earlier inaugurator of a more 'useful' and so more charitable philosophy of nature.[153] (Such an enterprise is in fact anticipated in several early Christian authors, for example Gregory of Nyssa and the Venerable Bede.) Once an atomist perspective had been adopted through the influence of Gassendi and Boyle, the empiricist tradition was in reality bound by the entirely *a priori* nominalist assumption that reality comes in discrete little bits and must at first be experienced piecemeal – synthesis being either logical tautology or else sheer whimsical artifice. So for this tradition the true learned gentleman, secure in his now commercially based pastiche of landed honour, proves his status by an ironically modest obeisance before the smallest facts, whenever he may chance upon them. Indeed, for a science-dominated society, the right to take an important part in pure social artifice is grounded upon one's submission to a pure ('non-revisionist') metaphysical passivity.[154] The type is of course still all too much with us in contemporary Britain.

---

[151]   See John Milbank, 'What Is Living and What Is Dead in Newman's *Grammar of Assent*', in *The Future of Love: Theological Interventions* (Eugene, Oreg.: Wipf & Stock, 2008).
[152]   See Charles Webster, *From Paracelsus to Newton* (Cambridge: Cambridge University Press, 1983).
[153]   See Steven Shapin, *A Social History of Truth: Civility and Science in Seventeenth-Century England* (Chicago: Chicago University Press, 1994).

10   The Baroque Simulation of Cosmic Order

The second important point made by de Muralt about the course which runs from Ockham to Kant is that the Kantian recovery and radicalisation of the Scotist-nominalist project was delayed by the phenomenon of a reworked Augustinianism. The latter intrudes already with Luther, but in the latter case Ockham's radicalism is really fully preserved, because the appeal to 'Augustinian' grace is a wholly fideistic one, against a background of metaphysical scepticism. Luther's theology mimics terminist philosophy, because just as, in the latter case, the knowing subject passively receives the object of understanding in independence from any intentionality, and just as the willing subject receives the divine legal command in independence from any teleology, so also, for (at least the later) Luther, the Christian self is 'justified' without any real infusion into the will of a supernatural habit of charity, and so in indifference to the works that she may or may not have performed.[155] This 'pure grace' is less gift than it is rather arbitrary election, which ensures the entire passivity of the saved every bit as much as the damned human subject.[156] This is surely (as de Muralt intimates) the bizarre conversion of faith itself into a kind of premature and entirely impenetrable *gnosis*.

In the case of Descartes, Malebranche and Leibniz, however, one encounters a more philosophical Augustinianism which is invoked to qualify the impact of the nominalist aftermath – including its Suarezian adumbration. One can even speak of a Baroque attempt to restore a high medieval synthesis of faith and grace under an overarching sense of the divine presence.[157] However, the continued dominance of univocity, nominalism and the *concursus* model of causality meant that this presence was not construed in a genuinely participatory way, but rather as a transcendentalist framework within created immanence, as a kind of overwhelming intrusion into our plane of reality, hovering over it like a perpetual dark but sunlit

---

154   See White, *Luther as Nominalist*.

155   For the more theological background to all this, see n. 104 above.

156   See Jean-Luc Marion, *Sur le prisme métaphysique de Descartes* (Paris: PUF, 1986). One can argue that there were also more successful and authentic (if philosophically incomplete) Baroque attempts at a new synthesis, for example that of Pierre de Bérulle in France and of many Anglican and even supposedly 'Puritan' thinkers – one can mention Richard Hooker, Thomas Browne, Robert Burton, Thomas and Henry Vaughan, Thomas Traherne and Peter Sterry.

cloud on a Baroque ceiling.[158] So this perspective remains essentially in accord with that 'modern passivity' already noted, and forms the other component of a 'classical outlook' which had its heart in France, but resonated elsewhere also.

With all three thinkers, one has a misreading of Augustinian illumination which imagines that this is once more a 'substitute' for the finite processes of cognition, including sensory reference, rather than its enabling light which operates at a higher, more removed level of causality (as Aquinas correctly realised). Thus for Descartes the divine infinity is present to us directly as a positive idea, while the continuity of corporeal and mental time is alienated to the divine *creatio continua*.[159] In the case of Malebranche the mind loses its control of its own body, and physical movements are 'occasionally' co-ordinated by God with mental ones. Meanwhile, for Malebranche's 'ontologism', the mind itself sees its ideas 'in' God, as literal parts of the divine spiritual extension. Finally, in the case of Leibniz, nominalist atoms have become vitalist monads which are, however, 'windowless', such that the apparent relations between things, including the relation between the knowing human subject and the known, are in reality the registrations of a divinely 'pre-established harmony'. In all three cases 'illumination' serves to alienate proper human powers and true human freedom.[160]

Nevertheless, the alien transcendental framework provides a regular order (even if for Descartes this is ultimately the result of an arbitrary divine choosing) which allows a Baroque equivalent for the medieval sense of a meaningful cosmos. One can read Berkeley's account of vision and knowing as a direct encounter with divine ideas as a similar alien-

---

[157]   For the presence of this outlook in seventeenth-century physical science, see Amos Funkenstein, *Theology and the Scientific Imagination* (Princeton: Princeton University Press, 1986). Although in the end he takes the normativity of seventeenth-century science far too much for granted (ignoring the counter-historical possibilities of more Neoplatonic and Hermetic medieval and Renaissance natural philosophies which sometimes seem to anticipate post-nineteenth-century physics and were left undeveloped), Funkenstein shows very well how univocity, precise representation, the voluntarist priority of the possible and causal concursus shaped modern natural philosophy (which became our 'science') every bit as much as philosophy in general. He is arguably wrong, however – for reasons which I have indicated in the main text – to see a real break with the seventeenth-century paradigm as occurring with Kant.

[158]   Descartes, *Meditations*, 'Third Meditation', 45–47, pp. 31–33; 'Objections and Replies', 'On Meditation Three', 109–111, pp. 88–89.

[159]   See Louis Dupré's excellent chapter 'The Faith of the Philosophers', in his *The Enlightenment and the Intellectual Foundations of Modern Culture* (New Haven, Conn.: Yale University Press, 2004), 269–311.

ation, although in his case it can be argued that there is an advance towards a more Patristic perspective in which what we see and know is truly a divine 'created language' whose beauty participates in the life of the Trinity.[161] But with David Hume it might appear (if one ignores, with most readers, his suggestions of a way to overcome post-Ockham scepticism by according a new revelatory role to feeling)[162] that one has truly a return to Ockham minus the invocation of God by faith. Every transcendental framework of 'natural necessity' now vanishes, and one is left only with the consistencies of logic and the constant passage of realities/impressions outside any anthropomorphic projection of causality. Kant inherits this perspective but tries unsuccessfully to fix and then to absolutise the 'human' framework for this passage of experience.

11   Deconstructed Representation and Beyond

In a sense, as Johann Heinrich Jacobi and, much later, Gilles Deleuze saw, Hume holds the balance between Spinoza and Kant. For if 'represented objects' are all that there is, then this would seem to suggest either absolute 'objectivity' (in the contemporary, not the Scotist, sense) — all that there is, is the flux of phenomena – or else absolute 'subjectivity' – all that we can be *sure of* is that there is the series of appearances that occur to our awareness. The latter position faces the problem of the mysterious absence of things in themselves, which might denote an ultimate nullity, while it must equally deal with the possible 'nihilistic' lack of any reliable connection between phenomena and noumena. But if the 'bracketed' real must shadow Kantianism as the spectre of nihilism, as Jacobi with genius saw, then equally, as he also saw, a philosophy of pure monistic immanence after Spinoza must be haunted by the question of the exact relation between the 'one' substance and the various finite modes in which it is 'expressed', including the mode of finite thought. If it is not transcendent to these modes, then its plenitude is in itself 'nothing'; but if the modes are not supported by any transcendence, and ultimately, from the mystical perspective of 'the third kind of knowledge', simply *are* the one substance, then their modal specificity is

[160]   See John Milbank, *The Word Made Strange: Theology, Language, Culture* (Oxford: Blackwell, 1997), 97–105.

[161]   See John Milbank, '"What lacks is feeling": Hume versus Kant and Habermas', in *Habermas and Religion*, ed. Craig Calhoun (Cambridge, MA: Harvard University Press, 2013), 322–346.

something almost illusory, again threatened by nullity – including the idiom of finite conscious mind.[163] In order to rescue the ultimacy of reason, Spinoza also had his own peculiar 'Augustinian' recourse: the one substance possesses the infinite attributes of extension and ideation which run in strict parallel and never interact.[164]

However, this cannot answer Jacobi's more fundamental point – which also runs against Leibniz – namely, that if one construes reason 'rationalistically' as a search for *exhaustive* explanation, for 'sufficient reason', then this will paradoxically destroy reason and issue in scepticism and nihilism. For an entirely rational reality must be 'one' reality (for this reason Jacobi thought Spinoza a more consistent rationalist than Leibniz), but (as Paul Franks helpfully explicates) this single auto-determination of reason faces the logical Hydra of the antique 'Agrippan trilemma': an adequate explanation must either presuppose something which it cannot explain, or else be viciously circular, or else again face an infinite regress, an infinite postponement of complete and therefore (for this paradigm) sufficient understanding.[165] So in the first case reason, which seeks to be all, must recognise that the foundation of the all is irrational; in the second it must recognise that the rationality of the all is only a tautology within the bounds of a unity that is irrationally and contingently 'just there', and so, once more, irrational; in the third case it must recognise that an irreducible infinity of the whole turns out to be a cognitively unsoundable void. At this point, as Jacobi reasoned, the options are either nihilism or else a new realist (and Augustinian) recognition 'by faith' that thought is inherently and inscrutably orientated towards an eminently rational being whose 'thereness' and mystery it cannot displace through exhaustive rational insight.

Yet Hume's deconstructed rationalism opens out a different prospect. It appears to point towards the *Sturm und Drang* ultimacy of rootless, character-exceeding passions which rule us like a thunderstorm, such that we can assume *no* rationally necessitated sequence of extension, while physical events are also 'impressions' of which the human brain is but the most complex site. In that case we have no 'objectivist' warrant to suppose a beautiful

---

[162] F.H. Jacobi, *The Main Philosophical Writings and the Novel* Allwill, trans. George di Giovanni (Montreal: McGill-Queen's University Press, 1994): 'Concerning the Doctrine of Spinoza in Letters to Herr Moses Mendelssohn' (1785), 173–251; 1789 version (excerpts), 339–378; 'David Hume on Faith, or Idealism and Realism: A Dialogue', 53–338; 1815 version, 537–590; 'Jacobi to Fichte', 497–536.

[163] See John Milbank, 'Knowledge: The Theological Critique of Philosophy in Hamann and Jacobi', in John Milbank, Catherine Pickstock and Graham Ward, eds., *Radical Orthodoxy: A New Theology* (London: Routledge, 1999), 21–37.

[164] Paul W. Franks, *All or Nothing: Systematicity, Transcendental Arguments, and Skepticism in German Idealism* (Cambridge, Mass.: Harvard, 2005), 146–200.

and mystical transcendentalist framework for immanence, after Spinoza. But equally we do not have any 'subjectivist' warrant to suppose anthropocentric privilege, after Kant, nor any contrast between appearances and things in themselves. There is only the totality of objective facts, or rather events, into which we have a limited and basically passionate insight: there are only occurrences, passionately apprehended according to human needs, while our ontological categories (like 'power' and 'cause') and ethical values (like 'honesty' and 'courage') are but the 'facts' of the way our passionate responses to reality work according to the force and vividness of habitual non-identically repeated impressions which yet give rise to an 'analogical' sense of resemblance – in a seemingly passive, given fashion which is natural and yet 'delirious', in no way according to any sort of *a priori* order, nor in accord with any given evidence.[166]

But in reality Hume's thinking already hovered between scepticism and a new, feeling-based fusion of cognitive faith with understanding.[167] For with respect to the empirical investigation of human understanding (which is Hume's 'philosophy'), all that is given is fictional association, and the only law which governs this givenness is 'the law of association'. But this means, as Deleuze noted, that our awareness of what governs our nature leaves us powerless to rectify this nature according to law, since the law denotes only the rule of a seemingly mad anarchy – which is the inevitable conclusion of pure enlightenment.[168] This is because apparently arbitrary and contingently mental associations, by a traceable associative path of analogy, give rise to fictions, including 'the fiction of a continu'd existence' (of supposed external objects and reflexively of a continuous self),[169] but our being aware of this can never cause us to give up fictioning, since this is the very substance of our human lives:

> The imagination tells us, that our resembling perceptions have a continu'd and uninterrupted existence, and are not annihilated by their absence. Reflection tells us, that even our resembling perceptions are interrupted in their existence and different from each other. The contradiction betwixt these opinions we elude by a new fiction, which is conformable to the hypothesis both of reflection and fancy, by ascribing these qualities to different existences; the *interruption* to perception and the *continuance* to objects.[170]

---

[165]   Hume, *A Treatise of Human Nature*, ed. E.C. Mossner (Harmondsworth: Penguin, 1985), I.II.xiv, pp. 205–223.
[166]   See Milbank, "'What lacks is feeling'".
[167]   Gilles Deleuze, *Empiricism and Subjectivity: An Essay on Hume's Theory of Human Nature*, trans. Constantin V. Boundas (New York: Columbia University Press, 1991), 77–84.
[168]   Hume, *A Treatise of Human Nature*, I.IV.ii, p. 259.
[169]   Hume, *A Treatise of Human Nature*, I.IV.ii, p. 265.

Even if one were properly to object to Hume that any nominalism of original 'punctilear' impressions is phenomenologically untenable, since we 'originally' hear a car arriving, not an assembly of sounds which we later synthesise, this would only *reinforce* the point that we must live within fictions. (Nor is it clear that Hume *does* espouse such nominalism – rather than recording our propensities to espouse it, as in the previous quotation – since for him the most 'basic' feelings can be empirically synthetic.)[171] These can then only be more than fictions if one subscribes to a theologically undergirded metaphysical realism, which Hume may not rule out and may even apophatically affirm. But if one does not do so, then once we have recognised the double fiction described above of imaginary combined with rational reflective products, their natural inevitability, together with the real but crazy sequences which underlie them, suggest no causal order in nature, but only insane regularities: designs which in no way point back clearly to a designing God. If, all the same, we can assume an ultimate divine ground which is the whole or the origin of the whole of nature, then it is the anarchy of meaningless patterns and their intensification as the human capacity to fiction which most discloses it – and we have, therefore, no warrant to assume that God is 'good'. This is the Baylean position, which Hume discusses in the *Dialogues Concerning Natural Religion*, but arguably himself in the end shies away from.[172]

[170] See Donald W. Livingston, *Philosophical Melancholy and Delirium: Hume's Pathology of Philosophy* (Chicago: Chicago University Press, 1998).

[171] David Hume, *Dialogues Concerning Natural Religion*, ed. H.D. Aiken (New York: Hafner, 1948), Part XI, pp. 71–81. Pierre Bayle's scepticism included the view that orthodox Christians cannot rationally answer with any plausible theodicy the Manichaean thesis as to an origin of evil independent of God. Whether he was sincere in his avowed Calvinist fideist stance in the face of this conclusion, or whether he remained secretly loyal to the Catharist ancestors of the Huguenots in his native Midi-Pyrénées, remains disputed. See the article 'Paulicians' from his notorious dictionary in Pierre Bayle, *Historical and Critical Dictionary: Selections*, trans. R.H. Popkin (Indianapolis: Hackett, 1991), 166–193. Hume's reference to Manichaeanism in the passage just cited most probably had this article of Bayle's in mind. One should certainly link this passage to that 'Caledonian antisysygy' or 'Scottish duality' which is a crucial aspect of Scottish literature from James Hogg and Walter Scot through R.L. Stevenson, John Buchan and Eric Linklater to James Robertson of Fife and Angus in our own time. It has complexly to do with factors all in play during Hume's day: a divided nationalist legacy between Gaelic-Pictish Highlander and Anglo-Brithonic lowlander, besides that between Presbyterian covenanter and Catholic-Episcopalian Jacobite, and in addition with Calvinist double predestination and finally the extraordinary modern coincidence of 'primitive' and 'progressive' culture (clans on the one hand, commerce on the other) within the bounds of one small country. John Robertson of Cambridge University has recently written illuminatingly concerning the analogies in this respect between the Scottish Enlightenment and the Neapolitan one – which also took place in the middle of a relatively remote, backward region of Europe. He in addition considers the relation of both Hume and

Hence, as Jacobi saw, Hume unveils the double spectre of the nullity of any ordered immanence and the nullity of any unified subject outside the general flux if we espouse a reason sundered from faith in reality (a faith which, on the most plausible reading, Hume himself upheld).[173] This 'nihilism' can then only be questioned within the inherited remit of empiricism (which I would contend Hume himself transcended)[174] if, like his more northerly Scottish successor Thomas Reid, one suggests that the passionate sensory responses are naturally and providentially ordered to the revelation of the real, albeit in a fashion that is to us entirely obscure and impenetrable.[175] Jacobi himself went further and exceeded this remit: the affirmation of a reliable real and of a coherent human subjectivity requires one to transmute Humean imaginary belief into a genuine 'faith' in true analogically sustained identities which is once more a Platonic erotic sense that what is seen participates in the divine order of the unseen.[176] Indeed, with Jacobi, the extreme Humean deconstruction of the paradigm of representation, which now elides things and impressions in the one flux, permits a certain new *recovery* of the paradigm of identity, albeit now much more explicitly under the auspices of a religious sense of reliance upon a reality grounded in God.

Here it must be noted that Hume's deconstructed representation is in reality closer to a retrieval of a Platonico-Aristotelian account of knowledge by identity than Thomas Reid's 'direct realism'. Reid himself negatively acknowledges this when he suggests that Humean ideas, now just as free from a location in substantive mind as they are from an anchorage in material substance, *could* be thought to be 'like the films of things in the Epicurean system' and yet could *also* be thought to 'resemble Aristotle's

the Neapolitan Giambattista Vico to Pierre Bayle – also the enlightened child of a 'wild' region – primarily with respect to the Baylean question of whether a society of idolaters would be more ethical than a society of atheists. See his *The Case for Enlightenment: Scotland and Naples, 1680–1760* (Cambridge: Cambridge University Press, 2005). However, my daughter Arabella Milbank has suggested to me that the 'antisysygy' is already traceable before the Reformation in the contrast between the embodied spiritual eroticism of James I of Scotland's humanist poetry on the one hand, and the bitter irony, exhibiting late scholastic influences, of the 'makar' Robert Henryson's poetry on the other.

172   See Galen Strawson, *The Secret Connexion: Causation, Realism and David Hume* (Oxford: Oxford University Press, 1992).

173   Again, see Milbank, '"What lacks is feeling"'.

174   Thomas Reid, *An Inquiry into the Human Mind on the Principles of Common Sense*, ed. D.R. Brookes (University Park, Pa.: Penn State University Press, 1997), ch. II, section V, p. 31; ch. VI, section XX, p. 170.

175   See Milbank, 'Knowledge: The Theological Critique of Philosophy in Hamann and Jacobi'.

intelligible species after they have shot forth from the object, and before they have yet struck upon the passive intellect'.[177]

This observation unwittingly exposes a specific superficiality in Reid's crucial and generally perceptive genealogy, according to which 'the ideal system' has eventuated inevitably in scepticism. The 'ideas' which Reid rejects are the Cartesian or Lockean ideas as 'representing' things, that always follow upon merely physically and efficiently caused sensory impressions, or else logical reflections concerning these impressions. In the course of this obscure process, they somehow modulate from being meaningless traces on the brain to being picturing traces within the mind itself – as if the mind were a kind of ethereal and reflexive physical organ.[178] But if what we primarily know are conscious sensations glimpsed on an inner screen which is taken to 'mirror' reality, then quickly we will come to suspect that this is sometimes a distorting mirror, if there is nothing that experimental science will confirm as corresponding to our experienced sensations in physical nature. Thus Locke came to conclude that whereas ideas of primary qualities like '*Solidity, Extension, Figure* and *Mobility*' are '*Resemblances*' of bodies, ideas of secondary qualities like 'Sweet, Blue and Warm' are only impressions in our mind, somehow produced in it by the 'Bulk, Figure and Motion of the insensible parts [the primary qualities] in the bodies themselves' but possessing no real objective correlate.[179] Berkeley, according to Reid, then extended this subjectivism to primary qualities also – all that we can know is our impressions of things and 'ideas' based upon these impressions, since we have no way of ever 'seeing round the back' of our mental mirror or exiting from the mental box of our *camera obscura*, as Reid himself put it. But if Berkeley left us with only spirits and ideas, Hume left us with only ideas, having denied the continuity and secure identity of the human mind.[180]

The upshot then, for Reid, is that philosophy has denied what 'common sense' knows as the impenetrable and unquestionable 'givens' of conscious sensation and its immediate recognition of other realities, including other intelligent minds through the senses, memory and the imagination. What Reid here recognises is something like the priority of the pre-reflective 'life-world' as eventually affirmed by Husserl. However, he generally speaks as if the upshot of 'the ideal system' was to lock us further and further into sceptical subjectivity, from which only a return to common

---

[176]   Thomas Reid, *An Inquiry into the Human Mind*, ch. II, section V, p. 34.
[177]   John Locke, *An Essay Concerning Human Understanding* (Oxford: Oxford University Press, 1979), Book II, chs. I–IV, pp. 104–132.
[178]   Locke, *An Essay Concerning Human Understanding*, paras. 10–15.
[179]   Reid, *An Inquiry into the Human Mind*, ch. I, pp. 11–24.

sense, supported by a belief in providence, will rescue us. Yet the sarcastic comparison of Hume to Aristotle just given, together with Reid's preceding comical and stylish passage about a Humean world in which impressions and ideas are the only realities and the only actors, shows that a deconstructed ideal system equally, or perhaps even more, tends to *remove* subjectivity, leaving us with only the objectivity of events as event-images (a perspective which indeed seems to anticipate Bergson, as Deleuze realised). And in actual fact this already began to be the case with Berkeley, Reid's erstwhile Anglican master whom he nonetheless misread (perhaps because his clerical Presbyterianism could not deal with the mystically Platonic and Trinitarian dimension in Berkeley's thought). For Berkeley *already* entertained a scepticism about mental identity (his solutions being to do with our participation in God) and concomitantly *already* saw ideas as 'external' to the mind, as real signs which were the created divine alphabet 'out there', and not the result of human mirroring.[181]

It follows that the more impressions and 'ideas' in Berkeley and Hume have become prior to the instance of an elusive mind or spirit, the more they cease to be the mere 'copies' of things and become the things themselves, or the infinitely various and fluctuating 'aspects' of these things. (It is clear that Husserl's aspectual phenomenology was in the first place a development from Berkeley and Hume – neither of whom was really an 'empiricist' in the Lockean sense.) So to this degree one could indeed say, following Reid, that Hume's 'ideas' have *reverted* to taking on some of the characteristics of Aristotle's *species* of understanding. Of course this reversion is clearly ambivalent and incomplete: on one reading (though it can be questioned), Hume leaves us with 'only simulacra', whereas for Aristotle the specific known *eide* retain a bond of identity with their material mode of instantiation and ineffably convey to the intending mind a reference to this formal-material existence. Reid, on the other hand, through his appeal to a kind of assumed 'life-world', retains this sense of purely given, non-analysable intention – yet he unnecessarily rejects a return to Aristotelian or Thomistic *species* which the Humean deconstruction potentially opens up.[182]

By rejecting this option, Reid remains *more* within the paradigm of representation than does Hume, and returns less to the paradigm of identity. This is because he actually augments scepticism about the resemblance between sensory impressions and external objects, opining for example that the sensation of hardness is nothing like the hardness of things as

---

[180]   Milbank, *The Word Made Strange*, 97–105.
[181]   Reid, *An Inquiry into the Human Mind*, Manuscripts: 'The Aberdeen Philosophical Society: Version I', pp. 297–315.

known by empirical science, and the experience of redness nothing like the redness of things which we must assume to have some unknown physical ground and so forth. (Yet can one really know?) So while this indeed denies all 'mirroring', it also suggests that we are stuck at the sensory (if not the cognitive) level, with mirror-like images that do not in reality do any mirroring at all. So no more than Locke does Reid think that the redness which we see is 'like' a red quality in reality, and he actually *agrees* with Locke that such a sensation (as opposed to a concept) can be referred to as an 'idea'. The difference is merely that, whereas Locke was inclined to see the experience of redness as a kind of illusion caused by a mechanical process, Reid thought that the 'real red', which for him we *rightly* ascribe to objects, is some sort of physically occult source (a hiddenness of origin which inconsistently refuses the hiddenness of resemblance) of our sensory experiences of redness – a 'certain power or virtue in bodies' as opposed to Locke's merely quantitative 'Powers'.[183]

In consequence, Reid affirms in the strongest manner possible the Ockhamist view that our sensations might be just what they are without being in any way connected to those realities which they do in fact convey to us – as the sensation of solidity to the touch conveys to us the reality of hardness. God, he says, could just as easily so have arranged it that we would smell or taste or hear hardness and indeed, as far as reason (as opposed to common sense) is concerned, all our sensations could be exactly as they are even if no real referential objects existed at all.[184] Again, as for Ockham, he sees this relation as immediate and as not involving any transition through an interior conceptual 'idea' or Augustinian *verbum mentis*, but rather as a direct relation between 'natural sign' and the reality signified.[185] This transition is so fundamental that it is cognitively inscrutable. We should, however, not trust it in the first place, like Descartes, because we believe in the infinite goodness of God, but simply because we

---

[182] Reid, *An Inquiry into the Human Mind*, ch. VI, section IV, pp. 85–87.
[183] Reid, *An Inquiry into the Human Mind*, ch. V, section II, p. 57: 'The firm cohesion of the parts of a body, is no more like that sensation by which I perceive it to be hard, than the vibration of a sonorous body is like the sound I hear: nor can I possibly perceive, by my reason, any connection between the one and the other. No man can give a reason why the vibration of a body might not have given the sensation of smelling, and the effluvia of bodies affected our hearing, if it had so pleased our maker. In like manner, no man can give a reason, why the sensations of smell, or taste, or sound, might not have indicated hardness, as well as that sensation, which, by our constitution, does indicate it. Indeed no man can conceive any sensation to resemble any known quality of bodies. Nor can any man show, by any good argument, that all our sensations might not have been as they are, though no body, nor quality of body, had ever existed.'
[184] Reid, *An Inquiry into the Human Mind*, ch. VI, section XXIV, p. 190.

are bound to do so, through our as it were transcendental confinement to 'common sense' (and there is a real resemblance to Kant here, even though Reid avoids the duality of conceptual scheme and empirical content). Yet a reflection which wishes to remain with common sense, and not abandon it for the Humean delirium of pure philosophy, will indeed attribute this relation to the arrangements of providence.

Without the Aristotelian *species*, this is surely once again tantamount to an 'Augustinian' fideistic evasion of a naturalistic scepticism: the inscrutable link between our perceiving and the real is very akin to a sort of pre-established harmony, involving a direct intervention of God in the world on the same univocal plane as us, according to the concurrence model of causality. Reid's view that our inference to a designing God is as immediate and non-reflective as our inference to other minds through the observation of articulate actions (whereas in truth the habitual human reception of both things and persons as divine gifts involves a more implicit, apophatic and questionable sort of immediacy) is part of this same intellectual perspective. He does indeed allow that an unknown immanent process may be at work here, but the fact that we can never have any scientific insight into this at all suggests again a causality that is equivocally 'other', although it acts within the scope of our world. Also, this same fact means that our knowledge cannot include in any measure the reflexive knowledge of the proportion that pertains between knowing and being – whereas for Aquinas knowledge *was* a 'return to self' of subjective perception that was also an attainment of self-reflection on the part of abstracted form.[186] By discounting, along with the *species*, this aspect of knowledge, Reid reveals that he does not see truth as what Heidegger would much later, long after the Greeks, once more describe as *aletheia*, 'unconcealedness'.[187] Instead, because he still regards truth as a 'substitute' for the real (and just for this reason fails to see the integrity of the moment of *species*), he regards sensation and knowledge as a divine providential and concurrent arrangement for ensuring our safe and pleasurable interaction with the physical world. This accords with the Newtonian programme of 'providential naturalism' of the Aberdonian school: the divinely appointed 'ends' of things can be empirically demonstrated, because ends are not implicit in the very means by which cognitive processes work, as they were for Aristotle.[188] Knowing, for the latter, was for the greater flourishing of knowing; for Reid, however, sensations, memories and imaginations (he scarcely treats of abstract

---

185   Thomas Aquinas, *De Veritate*, q. 1 a. 9. And see F.X. Putallaz, *Le Sens de la réflexion chez Thomas d'Aquin* (Paris: J. Vrin, 1991).
186   For example Heidegger, *On Time and Being*, 70.
187   See Derek R. Brookes, Introduction to Reid, *An Inquiry into the Human Mind*, xii–xxv.

reflection except as confirming the inscrutable operation of these faculties) are abolished in their dazzling blindness at the point where we recognise how they are crafted to guide us safely and pleasurably (on the whole) through mundane reality.

There is something 'homespun' about Reid's thinking here which has never failed to appeal to some Americans – whether one thinks of Alvin Plantinga's 'Reformed Epistemology' (which borrows the at once unbelievable and idolatrous claim about God as one more 'other mind') or Richard Rorty's neo-pragmatism, which takes 'direct realism' as the key to the rebuttal of the representation paradigm, following Reid – significantly in the long-term wake of the Franciscan Peter John Olivi[189] – in dismissing 'species' along with 'idea' as equally unnecessary specular third terms.[190] But I have just shown how, without *species*, sensations that do not mirror remain nonetheless like a continuous screen of felt apparitions into which we have no real judgemental insight – whereas if there are sensory as well as intellectual *species* (as for Aristotle) then even the eyes must already judge in order to see at all. Reid's sensations are too much still like images (or Lockean ideas), as he admits, but images now with only arbitrary relations to their originals, such that Reid above all rejects the role of 'analogy' (of thing to sensation, sensation to concept) in thinking about cognition. By comparison, the Aristotelian-Thomist sensations and concepts are transmuted forms and images, which analogically (by *convenientia*) resemble their originals and more inscrutably allow us to intend the originals through their own actuality. Why should it not be the case that when we see red we see something in the red thing that really is somewhat like our red – rather as with human beings it so often does seem to be the case that the red-haired tend to be fiery and passionate, whether they burn with an open or a concealed flame? At least in the case of Hume he does not think of imagistic impressions and ideas as a screen within our minds (whereas Reid, who does, is still confined in his *camera*

---

[188] Peter John Olivi, *Sentence Commentary*, qq. 58, 74. On Olivi in general, see Anne Ashley Davenport, *Measure of a Different Greatness: The Intensive Infinite, 1250–1650* (Leiden: Brill, 1999), 165–239, 251–301.

[189] Richard Rorty, *Philosophy and the Mirror of Nature* (Oxford: Blackwell, 1981), esp. 144–146. Rorty well describes here how Locke, by removing 'identity' from ideas, opens the way to scepticism. On the other hand, his acceptance of the Reidian view that Aristotle already too much modelled thought on sense impression seems too simple, and ignores the role of the *intellectus agens*, while being in a crucial sense *insufficiently* materialist. The point here surely is that 'sense impression' itself was very different for Aristotle; it already began the abstraction of form and the beginning of the release of the reflexive capacity of form itself – with which, for Aristotle, the intellect in act is identical.

obscura after all!) but as the one and only reality ('out there' or 'in here' through the folding back of the former) with which we have to deal.

All Reid-descended pragmatism is bound in the end to think that valid human cognitions promote and therefore surely 'represent', albeit blindly, physical and social achievements that are objectively measurable as such – as 'working' in some fashion or other. But all Hume-descended phenomenalism supposes that the images of things originally *belong* to the things and so are 'out there' rather than 'in here'. It also surmises that we inevitably inhabit 'fictions' whose plot is prior to any utilitarian purpose (even that of social consensus) and confines goals themselves to fictional projections. So because he retains *only* the middle of ideas-fictions – and accordingly suggests that we can *only* think analogically[191] – Hume's deconstructed representation is nearer to the identity paradigm than Reid's attempt to avoid representation altogether. For knowledge by identity involves the realisation of identity with the known thing through a certain (non-externally surveyable) analogical resemblance (for example of sensation of red – or better, 'red sensation' – to red thing, which we could never observe from an independent triangulated standpoint). This indeed, we must have belief in – and it is here that Reid's 'rational fideism' is right, and in this respect he was followed by both Jacobi and Hamann.[192] However, their new theologisation of philosophy was in reality (as they were aware) more after Hume than after Reid, since what they most proclaimed was the transmutation into religious faith of the Humean belief, which we are all bound to sustain, in fictions concerning the continuity and stable (though fluctuating) identity of events-images (which Hamann after Berkeley saw as the words of a divine created language) fully 'out there' in the world. For Jacobi this was once more a Platonic trust in the participation of these worldly partial identities in eternal ones.[193]

In the case of Reid, as we have just seen, a variant on 'modern Augustinian passivity' still remains. Rorty may claim that Reid released the intellectual capacity from being construed on the model of mirroring sensation, but in fact he confined it to our 'direct' attention to real things which the screen of sensations mysteriously permits. This attention is at once functional and wholly receptive in character. Equally, when Hume is

---

[190]   Hume, *A Treatise of Human Nature*, I.XII.192.
[191]   See George di Giovanni, Introduction to Jacobi, *The Main Philosophical Writings*, 28–30.
[192]   Jacobi, 'David Hume on Faith, or Idealism and Realism: A Dialogue' (1787), and 'David Hume on Faith . . . Preface' (1815), in *The Main Philosophical Writings*, 253–338 and 537–590 (esp. 549). See also, once more, Paul W. Franks's excellent post-analytic reading of Jacobi's intervention in his *All or Nothing*, 146–200.

read as he most usually has been, as a proponent of immanence, it is evident that once the divinely passive side of the representation paradigm is removed, empirical passivity still remains, or is even reinforced, because our shadowy spirit is entirely at the mercy of the 'actions' of events which are also images.

Only where Hume is read otherwise (as by Jacobi) as a proto-Romantic realist for whom feeling and faith give access to the real, is any activism returned to modern reason.

12 Passivity and *Concursus*

It must be stressed that this prevailing cognitive passivity, which denies the psychic realisation of being as truth, is also genealogically linked to the modern *concursus* model of causality, which involves the notion that God and creatures can contribute different shares to a causal upshot, like two horses pulling the same barge. It might seem, on the face of it, as if this model should ensure divine-human collaboration, but the point is that, when applied to human intelligence, the zero-sum game involved will tend to pan out wholly in favour of divine activity and human passivity, if one wishes to respect divine transcendence – once having compromised it by adoption of this model in the first place. Hence the acknowledgement of divine power can now *only* be made by an espousal of human passivity and not equally, or rather even more, by affirmation of human autonomous activity (at its own level), as it can in the case of the *influentia* model. Hence if one supposes that one most respects divine power by imagining it as overriding finite causes on the same univocal plane of being, then one *will* require some finite 'contribution' at the ultimate level (as one will not on the *influentia* model), but this will tend to be a merely passive and accepting contribution. In the case of human understanding, our obedient attention to divine ideas will indeed be 'all our own work' outside divine prompting, just as on the Molinist model of grace our choice passively to receive grace is entirely within our own control, 'outside' the will of God.[194]

One consequence of this conclusion is that late medieval and Renaissance advocates of the high dignity of the human soul and human active capacity, like Eckhart, Cusanus and Mirandola, may lie in far greater continuity with the high Middle Ages and stand far less unambiguously at the threshold of modernity than is usually supposed.

---

[193] See Henri de Lubac, *Augustinianism and Modern Theology* (New York: Crossroads, 2000).

So here it is important to mention a certain misunderstanding which some commentators, including André de Muralt, fall into.[195] One should not regard Meister Eckhart and Nicholas of Cusa's radicalisation of the Augustinian (and Thomist) view that creatures are of themselves substantively 'nothing' as yet another example of modern passivity and alienation of all positive activity to the divine side. It is in part strange that de Muralt makes this mistake, because he clearly sees that passivity is linked to causality by *concursus*, and not to reciprocal or hierarchically differentiated causality. Yet Eckhart and Cusa, in insisting that being and unity are so entirely from God that no creature 'is', or 'is unified' of itself (Cusa exposes the latter truth through the application of mathematical paradoxes), are clearly refusing the *concursus* model in the most drastic manner conceivable. Indeed, there are indications that Eckhart may well be criticising the Scotist univocal ontology which undergirds this causal vision, by insisting that initial, univocal being is divine *esse* alone.[196] If both he and Cusanus speak so paradoxically of the non-being of creation as such as if it were 'something', then this can be taken as their wish utterly to oppose any ontotheological notion that there can really be anything that exists literally alongside God.

Scotus had, in a sense, raised the stakes, by insisting that, in order to guarantee creation's real independence, it must have a being that is truly its own, which in logical and ontological terms can be seen as fully existing without reference to its createdness as the origin of its being from God. Aquinas's subtle point had been that it is *being* that is shared, and therefore that it is 'self-standing' existence that is paradoxically the thing that most participates.[197] But Scotus now suggested that the integrity of finite being can only be guaranteed if one allows that this being is fully its own reality outside participation; otherwise, he contended, what is most specific to finite being, namely existence itself, is also problematically the

[194] André de Muralt, *Néoplatonisme et Aristotélisme dans la métaphysique médiévale* (Paris: J. Vrin, 1995), 77–99.

[195] See Alain de Libera, *Le Problème de l'être chez Maître Eckhart: Logique et métaphysique de l'analogie* (Geneva: Cahiers de la Revue de Théologie et Philosophie 4, 1980); John Milbank, 'Preface to the Second Edition: Between Liberalism and Positivism', in *Theology and Social Theory*, ix–xxxii. See also Milbank, 'The Double Glory'.

[196] See Rudi te Velde, *Participation and Substantiality in Thomas Aquinas* (Leiden: Brill, 1995); *Aquinas on God: The 'Divine Science' of the* Summa Theologiae (Aldershot: Ashgate, 2006), 141 and 146 n. 49. Te Velde, however, perhaps tries to evade the aporetic quality of what Aquinas says about participation and to over-stress the 'independence' of creatures. He certainly gives an excellent account of participation in relation to an *influentia* model of causality which allows God to establish independent existence and fully 'autonomous' secondary causality while remaining the entire cause of the 'being' of all this. On the other hand, he does not quite allow

most alienated thing, and our integral action as creatures is compromised. So in defending a traditional perspective as most technically expressed by Aquinas, Eckhart and Cusa were forced more dramatically to concede that it indeed implies in a sense that 'God is all' in a way that seems to threaten either acosmism or pantheism. But at the same time they had not lost sight of the Thomist paradox that what God shares is being itself – in other words the 'self-standing' of existence as such. This then forces them to speak in more aporetic and arcane terms than are usually found

that this could logically permit one to speak of creation as at once 'divine' and yet 'not divine'. What prevents such a paradox arising for te Velde would seem to be his insistence that, for Aquinas, we do not participate in God himself, or the divine being or the divine essence. Yet Aquinas many times says that we participate in *esse*, and many times identifies God with *esse*, which has a perfect coincidence with *essentia*. When he says in his commentary on Dionysius, in a passage cited by te Velde (*In Div. Nom.* c. 2 lect. 4, n. 178), that the essence of God itself is imparticipable, he certainly does not mean that we only participate, in Palamite fashion, the divine uncreated 'energies' or actions towards us, as this would compromise the divine simplicity: for Aquinas the divine omnipresence simply *is* God. So what Aquinas must mean here is that God does not hand over the entirety of his essential being: he does not make 'other Gods' entirely like himself. What he gives is rather 'similitudes' of his 'essence' through which creatures are 'propagated'. But he does not say that we participate only in a 'similitude' of God that is secondary to the divine essence: rather, the similitudes are likenesses of the essence and these likenesses *are* the created beings. Te Velde's Utrecht colleague, Harm Goris, likewise translates a certain passage in the *Tertia Pars* as a participation 'in a certain similitude of the divine being'. (See Harm Goris, 'Steering Clear of Charybdis: Some Directions for Avoiding "Grace Extrinsicism" in Aquinas', *Nova et Vetera*, 5/1 (2007), 67–80.) Translated thus, it is very unclear exactly what the participation could be in at all, and in fact Goris is offering an eccentric reading of the entire phrase, *gratia, secundum se considerata, perficit essentiam animae, inquantum participat quandum similitudinem divini esse*. Despite the word order, it is surely more plausibly translated as 'grace, considered in itself, perfects the essence of the soul, insofar as it participates of the divine essence [through] a certain similitude'. The old 'literal' English Dominican translation has 'grace, considered in itself, perfects the essence of the soul, insofar as it is a certain participated likeness of the divine nature'. It is possible that this phrase has in reality been mistranscribed, giving rise to the ambiguity. But te Velde himself declares that the contrast between 'essence' and the supposed divine 'similitude' is no simple opposition, as if these things stood alongside each other, but rather that in the similitude there lies an 'immediate relationship to God himself who is self-subsistent being' (*Participation*, 146 n. 49). Yet this phrase must surely imply the paradox that what creatures participate *is* 'the imparticipable' divine essence itself. The entire point of the Neoplatonic idea of participation, which Aquinas fully perpetuates, is that the ultimate shares itself without reserve, while nonetheless entirely reserving itself in its unsoundable mystery. What it gives in a measure is the ungivable, and it is only the ungivable that can be given. Hence it is precisely the imparticipable that can be participated and actually *because* it is imparticipable, an inexhaustible fountain: as Nicholas of Cusa puts it with regard to a mathematical paradigm, 'although the circle does not impart itself otherwise than as it is, nevertheless it can be partaken by another only otherwise' (*De Coniecturis*, I.11). Te Velde suggests that Aquinas's model of participation in *esse* qualifies the Neoplatonic notion that 'the creature

in Aquinas (although they can be found in certain places):[198] thus Nicholas declared that 'God's being in the world is nothing other than the world's being in God'.[199] For the most interior reality of created things simply *is* God, and humans as reflective have conscious access to this interiority; creation is the 'laying out' (*explicatio*) of God; God in his inner 'complicated' Trinitarian life is the going out towards creation and the return of creation to himself.[200]

But to see this newly aporetic rendering of the creator/created difference, in the case of Nicholas of Cusa, as a further mutation of Scotist *concursus*, as de Muralt does, is surely perverse: nothing in Nicholas's intellectual lineage suggests this, and nor does his overwhelmingly participatory framework. His God is infinite but simple, not formally divided, while the distinctions of creatures somehow consequent upon the *nihil* are real and not formal. Nor does the *nihil* really contribute anything, like a concurrent cause (as de Muralt quite bizarrely suggests): it is God who wholly gives finite things and yet their privative limitation is alone 'proper' to them – Aquinas thought no differently. Finally, Cusa does not contrast (as de Muralt avers, stretching his analogical historical method to breaking point) a negative 'comprehension' of the coincidence of opposites with their application to the real, unsoundable

is nothing other than a dependent "manifestation" of the divine subsistent being without having a proper substantial mode of being' (*Participation*, 141). However, Proclean Neoplatonism already allowed a certain subsistence to finite beings. And while one can fully agree with te Velde that a doctrine of creation *ex nihilo* as expounded by Aquinas in terms of a sharing of being increases this sense of independent substantial existence, it *also* increases the sense that creatures are, indeed, but 'dependent manifestations', precisely because of the idea that alongside God, apart from his creative act and omnipresence, there is only 'nothing'. So while, certainly, I would wish to stress a qualitative difference between Christianity and Neoplatonism, the point is that an over-apologetic approach here can miss the truth that Christianity, as it were, renders Neoplatonism 'still more Neoplatonic' and not less (rather in the way that the New Testament accentuates as much as it qualifies the message of the Old). Te Velde also ignores or plays down those 'proto-Eckhartian' passages in Aquinas which suggest that at the deepest level creatures are more accidental than they are substantial: indicating that they are only relatively substantial in a participated sense (while God is actually 'hyper-substantial' since nothing underlies him and he is only entirely self-standing as infinite, not as circumscribed; there is a real sense in which substance is found to be 'nowhere' in Aquinas). See Milbank and Pickstock, *Truth in Aquinas*, 33–35; Jean-Luc Marion, *Étant donné: Éssai d'une phénomenologie de la donation* (Paris: PUF, 1997), 17–21, and Aquinas, *De Potentia Dei*, q. 5 a. 4 ad. 3.

[197]   See Rosemann, *Omne ens est aliquid*, 191–210.

[198]   Nicholas of Cusa, *De Coniecturis*, II.7: 107; Johannes Hoff, *Kontingenz, Berührung, Uberschreitung: Zur philosophischen Propädeutik christlicher Mystik nach Nikolaus von Kues* (Frankfurt am Main: Albert Karl, 2007).

[199]   See Burkhard Mojsisch, *Meister Eckhart: Analogy, Univocity and Unity* (Amsterdam: B.R. Grüner, 2001).

divine mystery, on the model of the Scotist conceptual *esse objectivum*, which stands for a reality that is in itself entirely obscure. Rather, based upon mathematical examples, we have a partial positive insight into the way finite opposites can converge at an infinite vanishing point, and through mystical contemplation we can gradually advance along this path.[201]

The reason for de Muralt's mistake here is really his rejection of the Neoplatonic dimension within Aquinas – despite the fact that this alone fully upholds the latter's accounts of analogy, of *influentia*, the prior exemplary plenitude of the *actus purus* and of intentionality. Hence de Muralt denies that the dominant hold of analogy of attribution – where a lower thing is only 'like' a higher thing by borrowing from it – in Eckhart is in continuity with Aquinas, and argues that, for the angelic doctor, the analogy of proportion – for which God and creatures can exhibit the same ratio in different degrees – carries equal weight.[202] But this is surely to perpetuate an anachronistically Cajetanian reading of Aquinas that is itself too contaminated by the univocity of being: Aquinas does not really allow one to say that a creature 'exists', independently of God, even in its own proper degree. To the contrary, being is that alien, eminent height by which our natures are actualised through participation alone.

This issue is not a trivial one. For to adopt de Muralt's position on Eckhart and Cusanus is to suggest that all we need to do is to return to the perspectives of Aquinas, as if, for all their dubiety, the intellectual moves of Scotus and Ockham posed no new questions which the heirs of the *via antiqua* must now perforce answer in somewhat novel ways.

These questions concerned:

1   The nature of creatures' integral standing 'outside' God.
2   The apparent violation of the principle of non-contradiction equally by the notion of analogy whereby two things are simultaneously *in toto* same and different (and not just in different respects); by that of realist and not nominal essence, where the *eidos* of a thing is coincidingly particular and universal; and of real relation where something is seemingly defined as also something else, since it depends on a constitutive contrast.
3   The possibility that God has communicated in some measure his creative power to creatures, which, as we have seen, Duns Scotus already regarded as an implication of concursive causality. (Even though, as we have also seen, such co-creativity can only

200   Nicholas of Cusa, *De Docta Ignorantia*, I.11: 30–21: 66.
201   De Muralt, *Néoplatonisme et Aristotélisme*, 100–156.

really operate as a passive fatality, rather than as a matter of active participatory engagement, on the *concursus* model.)

4   The idea that the active element in understanding, since it is essentially arbitrary, is dependent upon linguistic construction.

The nominalists answered these questions respectively in terms of:

1   Full finite standing in being.
2   Univocalist/equivocalist denial of analogy, universals and real relations.
3   The arbitrary power of God to transfer all of his own powers, including creative power.
4   The consequent arbitrariness of our cognitive generalisations or even claimed intuitions on account of their linguistic constructedness.

But Eckhart, Cusa, Mirandola and some other Renaissance thinkers tended to answer them in 'post-nominalist' rather than simply ancient realist terms, to give respectively:

1   A paradoxical reading of the creation as equally inside and outside the Godhead.[203]
2   A new thinking of analogy, universal and real relation as exceeding the terms of non-contradiction, by virtue of the character of the infinite and its impinging on the finite.
3   The idea that human creative activity is itself a participation in the inner-Trinitarian generation of the *Logos* and therefore that our making is teleologically constrained, not arbitrary, since (as supremely in God himself) *facere* fully coincides with *intellegere*.[204]
4   A greater association of the reasoning process with word, image and emblem. This involves, as Johannes Hoff has shown with respect to Nicholas of Cusa, a drastic effort to restore and renew high medieval symbolic realism by now showing that the most seemingly ordinary and also artificial objects – a spoon, a triangle, a map, a ball game, an astrolabe etc. – can be made to yield the full height of mystical significance.[205] The consequence of this is a more 'figured' and exotic

---

[202]   On Meister Eckhart in this respect, see Milbank, 'The Double Glory'.

[203]   See John Milbank, 'The Grandeur of Reason and the Perversity of Rationalism: Radical Orthodoxy's First Decade', in John Milbank and Simon Oliver, eds., *The Radical Orthodoxy Reader* (London: Routledge, 2009), 367–404.

[204]   Johannes Hoff, *The Analogical Turn: Rethinking Modernity with Nicholas of Cusa* (Grand Rapids, Mich.: Eerdmans, 2013).

discourse that is sustained by the Baroque and especially the later Anglican Baroque, as is most familiar from so-called 'metaphysical' poetry and was already promoted against the stripped-down logic and grammar of the Puritan Ramists by the Cambridge and East Anglican renegade Thomas Nashe.[205] Against an already arriving 'dissociation of sensibility' (of reasoning from embodiment and sensation), the post-Cusan writers reasserted association in a hyperbolic and pan-sacramental fashion.[207]

In the long term this post-nominalism suggested a saving of participatory reason and of symbolic realism by a greater invocation of the transrational: of the emotively led, the aesthetic, the imaginative and the poetic. Thus this current eventually helped to give rise to the proto-Romantic and Romantic revisionarily realist critiques of the *via moderna*, as seen in Jacobi, Hamann, Friedrich Schlegel and others.[208]

---

[205] See Marshall McLuhan, *The Classical Trivium: The Place of Thomas Nashe in the Learning of his Time* (Corte Madere, Calif.: Gingko Press, 2006).

[206] This hyperbole could also invite atrophy due to an excess of artifice that could lose sight of any realist import altogether, as occurred with continental 'conceptism' or 'Gongorism' in poetry, where the use of conceit lacked the English restraint and ludic seriousness. In consequence there occurred, with Nicolas Boileau, in late seventeenth-century France, a reaction in favour of simpler and more 'sublime' poetic imagery, which had a strong influence in Britain also. It can often be overlooked that this reaction (and this point may well affect assessment of Milton's poetic style) is by no means a 'secularisation' or a 'classicising' and post-Cartesian disenchantment, but in many ways the opposite. In consequence, some English eighteenth-century poetry, that of Christopher Smart supremely, is at once 'sublime' and yet in continuity with the earlier 'metaphysical' impulse. The phrase 'dissociation of sensibility' is T.S. Eliot's: see his essay 'The Metaphysical Poets' (1921). And see also in this respect Michel Foucault, 'The Prose of the World', in *The Order of Things: An Archaeology of the Human Sciences* (London: Routledge, 2001), Part I, ch. 2, pp. 17–45. Although Eliot spoke of the metaphysicals as if they still naturally 'felt their thought as immediately as the odour of a rose', his eventual preference for Dante's greater ease and restraint of expression as compared both with the metaphysicals and with Shakespeare implicitly acknowledged that there was already something 'forced' in their poetics. This brought him also a greater appreciation of Milton in his later years, and, again by implication, of the turn to 'sublimity'. However, one could say that this later preference failed to acknowledge both the *need* for 'forcing' in the face of an already commenced dissociation which Eliot perhaps did not fully recognise, and the way in which this Baroque hyperbole actually attained a more adequate emphasis upon the incarnation of reason which Christianity had always implied but never sufficiently thought through or enacted.

[207] See John Milbank, 'The New Divide: Romantic versus Classical Orthodoxy', *Modern Theology* (Jan.–Feb. 2010), 26–38; Manfred Frank, *The Philosophical Foundations of Early German Romanticism*, trans. Elizabeth Millain-Zaibert (New York: SUNY, 2008).

13   Representation in Philosophy

From a 'philosophical' point of view (even if that can be but problematically distinguished from the 'theological') a theory of knowledge by representation is also questionable – as we have already seen, to some degree. Its paradigm is that of vision, but even this paradigm has a genealogy. Arabic optics, as inherited by Roger Bacon in the twelfth century, tended to encourage the view that the eye 'copies' the thing seen by forming an image of it, as if the idea were already conceived as a 'camera'.[209] Traditionally, since Plato, Euclid, Galen and the Stoics, the idea of the eye as chamber of received images had been qualified by the notion that the eye emits its own answering beam of light in response to the light received from the thing seen: this notion was repeated by Augustine but rejected by Ibn Sina, following the lead of Aristotle.[210] Now even if the physics of this older notion be considered obsolete (and even that may be debatable), it retains its phenomenological pertinence, and indeed it is one of the paradigms for 'intentionality' itself in Augustine, which, via the scholastic development of this concept, helped to shape the very enterprise of modern phenomenology.[211]

For how is it that, standing consciously 'at the back' of our camera, we are able to see through its impressions, as though through a viewfinder? We never, as a seeing subject, *do* see the image at the back of the retina, whatever may be the case (metaphorically) for the brain. Rather, this image somehow permits us really and intentionally to 'look out' upon things, to throw a beam of invisible sensory light upon them. While Aristotle rejected the 'ocular beam' theory, he still thought of the eye as very remotely touching the object, just as the object remotely touched the eye, by way of the medium of irradiated air.[212]

---

[208]   See Boulnois, *Être et représentation*, 56–67.
[209]   Augustine, Sermon CCLXVII, 10; *De Genesi ad Litteram* I.31 and VII.20, and see also XII.6.15–12.26; Aristotle, *Parva Naturalia*, 'On Sense and Sensible Objects', 438a26–438b15.
[210]   See n. 93 above.
[211]   Aristotle, *De Anima* 435a15–25: 'the other senses [besides touch] perceive by contact too, but through a medium'. (Conversely he thought that there is always an infinitesimal physical medium in the case of touch, even if this is not enough to explain why the necessary proximity involved in touch does not 'blind' our sensibility, as it does in the case of an object brought too close to the eye. Here he thought that one needs to understand that the body itself is the medium between the soul and material reality. To complete the circle, this fleshly medium is required to ensure the conscious contact achieved by all the senses, since the soul must be 'distanced' even from the material point where the sensation reaches its body, if it is not to be psychically 'blinded'. See the entire argument of the *De Anima*.)

Thus, phenomenologically considered (and sight cannot be reduced to a sheerly physical process without destroying its reality, which *is*, through and through, phenomenal),[213] the relevantly paradigmatic instance of sight is itself not one of passive representation: rather, it involves both an active beaming and a reciprocal touching.

So if seeing itself is not simply the regarding of images upon a screen within an ocular chamber, then neither need the mind plausibly be seen as a psychic chamber. Certainly information passes within the brain, but, when we think, we are not really 'inside' our brains any more than we are inside anywhere else. Rather, we are in a placeless psychic realm that enables us to be 'anywhere', exactly where the things are that are known by us (as Hume understood even better than Reid) or indeed 'to be all things' (as Aristotle put it).[214] Thus when we move about in the world we deal with things simultaneously in the concrete though bodily encounter and sensation, and in the abstract through mental modification which our hands' shaping of things has already commenced. We move always through the day as if in a dream and must dream in order to move at all.

If we *do* imagine that the mind is a psychic chamber upon which we watch the passing of images as 'ideas', then a number of problems ensue. Were images all we had to go upon, then how would we be able to check that the images correspond to the originals? So only knowledge by identity guarantees a strong realism, whereas knowledge by representation remains chronically subject to scepticism. Any supposed ability to check the veracity of 'ideas' must propose that there is some way of distinguishing between the contribution of our mind and the contribution of reality, and must further propose criteria for ensuring the purity of both. However, since our only access to things is through words and strings of coherent images, according to cultural codings, everything we consider has been already synthesised and schematised in spatial and temporal relativity alongside other things. There *are no* isolatable facts which we can be sure of having received in their purity: only relatively reliable facts which fall under a certain description for certain purposes, like fragments of evidence used in a courtroom. In short, there is no *pre-given* reality which we can first consider apart from our engagement with it. Inversely, there is no

---

[212]   Equally, if thinking is not dualistically divorced from material process, we cannot dismiss the idea that, even in some physical sense, our eyes 'throw light' upon things. For it might be asked whether in general modern physics has too easily dismissed the idea that reflective surfaces contribute some emanative effect of light on their own account – as the medieval use of coloration so evidently assumed. After all it is dense material realities – the stars – that in the first place cause the effects of both fire and light.

[213]   Aristotle, *De Anima* 431b20–25.

decent standard for the purity of our cognitive *schemata*, as Kant supposed: the more boring nuances of our everyday language (ignoring all poetic turns) beloved once of Oxford philosophers, do not disclose any eternal subtleties of the cognitive universe, but only features, in one aspect factual, of the way humans in general (or sometimes Oxonians in particular) tend symbolically to inhabit their world.[215]

The model of representation, then, if seriously adopted, will lead inexorably to the post-Humean view (as articulated by Deleuze, for example), that there are only sequences of self-replicating movement-images, coiled in greatest intensity to shape those material *simulacra* of *simulacra* known to themselves as 'human beings'. But then it follows that our 'representing' lies entirely on the folding and unfolding surface of things and does not occur within a hidden chamber. Such motions and images at once perpetuate and betray, continue and discontinue, univocally and equivocally, the flux of the real as a series of local and indeed some-what illusory specular echo-chambers. As befits, then, its initial link with a reserved lawless power of God, postmodern deconstructed representation can only in the end represent – in terms of the entire meaningless 'process' of eventuation-imaging – either chaos or nullity.

One can elect instead to adopt the model of knowledge by identity – but its links with a participatory theology, as we have seen, are not at all incidental.

14 Actualism versus Possibilism

The third assumption of modern philosophy – the priority of possibility – denies the traditional theological sense that there can be a kind of necessity in actuality as such which is a beautiful, harmonious, grace-imbued good order, recognisable by wise, rightly ordered judgement. It also tends, when applied to the human sphere, unrealistically to think of choices in terms of pure logical availability, whereas in practice certain initial choices drastically preclude later ones, whether for pragmatic reasons or for reasons of the formation of a habit.[216] The same theory also leaves mysterious the question of what sways any choice: in reality there is no 'pure will', but only the persuading of desire by some reason or lure that appears to a subject as more convincing or persuasive.

---

[214] Rorty, *Philosophy and the Mirror of Nature*, 167–212.
[215] See David Burrell, 'Al Ghazali on Created Freedom' and 'Creation, Will and Knowledge in Aquinas and Duns Scotus', in *Faith and Freedom*, 156–189.

Possibilism, since in this way it neglects the lure of desire, can also be described as a 'cold' rendering of reality. It fails truly to provide an answer to the question 'Why being?' and confines itself in effect to the 'how' of being's constitution, whether as infinite or finite. Nothing in neutral reason really justifies this perspective: instead it rests upon a mere decision to read reality in 'cold' terms as doubly 'given' – once as possibility, secondly as existentiality – rather than in 'warm' terms as the receiving of a gift, such that only the arriving actuality of a thing entirely defines it as what it is, since here existence is taken as fully particularising and defining a general form or essence.

The cold reading of reality effectively construes *all* of being as merely like instances *within* being. So, for example, within the bounds of finite existence, a bicycle in a shop window might present to the spectator the possibility of a gift to be given, whereas its later handing over to a child (after purchase) is the actuality of donation. At first the potential gift is just a spectacular 'given' in the window, while its later becoming a gift is a second 'given' fact of actu-alisation, once one has decided to intervene in the proffered drama by entering the shop door to act first upon the stage of commerce and then later upon the interpersonal stage of gratuity. In a similar fashion, a univocalist transcendental ontology comprehends finite existences as simply the 'matter of fact' given instantiations of previously 'given' (and not in any sense donated) possibilities of finite being. The same dual givenness applies to the specific general arrangements of the world which we happen to inhabit.

But surely the religious sensibility tends to read existence as such as only *definable* in terms of gift – as if the bicycle had never first appeared in the window and never had to be bought, but was miraculously conjured up only in that instance when it first appeared to the child on the morning of its birthday. As if we could only receive and ride bicycles which were pres-ents and the theatre of gratuity were never preceded by the theatre of commercial transfer.

Yet despite this truth, as we have seen, the shift from interpreting being as created gift to interpreting it as the elective instantiation of uncreated possibility did not first occur mainly in terms of an exercise of purely philosophical and secular reason. Instead, certain modes of reasoning were adopted in terms of a religious attitude which wished to protect absolute divine freedom beyond even the scope of its generosity, by insisting that God, in relation to the world, mainly considers a range of 'given' possibil-ities, and then, 'as a matter of fact', makes a certain decision as to which ones will be actualised. Here, Aquinas's alternative religious vision, according to which God is himself 'compelled' in creating by the aesthetic glory of his own intellect in the Paternal uttering of the *Verbum*, and the discriminating 'aesthetic' judgements which he makes as to the contents of the created world, is dogmatically, not critically, abandoned.

Philosophically speaking, it would seem that there are at least equally good reasons in favour of the priority of the actual as the priority of the possible. Does not this principle alone conserve a strong realism, and indeed a kind of radical empiricism, as G.K. Chesterton divulged? For if we do not first know the fundamental patterns of the world and the kinds of things that are in it by encountering them in existence, then we can never encounter anything radically new, which seems counter-intuitive. All that we could meet with would be instantiations of essences that we already knew about, or could in principle imagine, trivially varied. Of course there is the problem of how we can recognise radically new things or search for unknown ones, but Plato (the *Meno* problematic) and Augustine (the theory of illumination) recognised that our strange anticipation of the unknown is radically aporetic, and requires an appeal to transcendence (in terms of recollection or illumination), on pain of denying the arrival of something new as something still rationally coherent.

Here again it can be seen how Aquinas's legacy, this time in terms of its actualism, supports historicisation in a way that is not usually acknowledged. And that just as the 'turn to the subject' (linked to representation and *concursus*) does not after all favour any taking into account of the real contingent freedoms of history, so likewise the priority of the possible (which still dominated the horizon of Schelling and Hegel) must reduce history either to necessity or to the exercise of freedom without any teleological meaning and so without any meaning relevant for truth whatsoever. This is precisely why Vico, who sustains both Thomist actualism and Renaissance 'external', non-technologically reduced *poesis*, was a far more genuinely historicist thinker than the German Protestant idealists. (The same goes for those later Catholics Pierre-Simon Ballanche, Charles Péguy and Christopher Dawson.)[217]

The saving of the appearance of arriving novelty is the first, positive philosophical argument for the priority of the actual. The second, negative argument is that, just as we can ask the idealist, 'But what is the reality of your thinking?' so also we can ask the possibilist, 'But what is the actuality of your pre-given range of possibilities?' Surely they are only the possibilities that we have abstracted by affirmation or else by counter-factual contrast from this actual world, such that fully to sustain possibilism one would have to argue, in a speculative fashion, that there are a myriad unknown possibilities, which the limited structure of our mind fails to grasp. As with the

[216]   See further below in the second sequence, section 10.

Kantian contrast of phenomena and noumena, a somewhat nihilistic prospect would thereby be opened out of meta-possibilities in excess of a notion of 'possibility' that would seem to be *defined* in part by mental graspability. Meanwhile nihilism itself is forced to speak of the void (just as modern mathematics speaks of zero) or the repertoire of the sheerly aleatory as if this also were 'actual'.

If possibility is predatory upon actuality rather than vice versa, then this would favour the view that all 'possible worlds' are in a weak degree 'actual'. Here it is relevant that modern philosophy sometimes describes a possibility that is non-actualised as 'fictional', because fictions, especially novels, reveal that thickly imagined alternative possibilities possess some degree of actuality of their own, since one can only grasp, say, the 'logic' of *Bleak House* by treating its world *as* a complex actuality and not at all as mixture of atomistic items of 'possibility' blended together in varying combinations with certain diverting but inessential variations. Such a formalistic reduction of the book to predictable manipulations of narrative structure would simply lose the specificity of the novel and its precondition of narrative genius. This is partly why Chesterton thought that the 'other realities' of fictions, especially fairy-tales, revealed by indirection the 'magical' and unfathomable curious necessities ('limitations') of our own world which are inseparable from its actuality, yet which can now, through this indirection, be seen as more than arbitrary, but rather as strangely crucial for the achievement of a life that bears aesthetic weight and moral solemnity.[218]

In these ways the bias of common sense runs towards the priority of the actual. However, the counter-intuition of possibilism cannot readily be refused by pure reason – even though, in its atheist guise, it is bound to evolve into nihilism. By contrast, the bent of the natural mind within this world can only be confirmed by resort to the theological. For if a purely immanent actuality were self-sustaining, it would still divide between that virtual aspect which propels it along with all other actualities, and the surface of its actual appearing, since there is nothing in any specific actuality in itself which necessitates its being: 'There are others, it seems to me, who have at best to live / In two worlds – each a kind of make-believe', as T.S. Eliot expressed it in *The Confidential Clerk*.[219] The actual can only sustain

[217] Chesterton, *Orthodoxy*, 66–102.

[218] These 'others' are those who are neither geniuses nor untalented nor yet again religious, whose lives are split between a private artistic imagination and a public life which is itself a collective fantasy. Eliot implies that it is only religion that can integrate both, and ground both in a secure reality beyond our fantasising, even if we only have access to this reality through the imagination. See T.S. Eliot, *The Confidential Clerk: A Play* (London: Faber & Faber, 1954), 36–37, 40–42.

itself as irreducibly self-caused on the surface of the world if it is suspended from an infinite plenitude of the actual. And only as simply infinite – where there is no before and after, no conditioning and conditioned – can the actual be entirely self-sustaining without any self-division, or any subordination to virtual propulsion.[220]

15   Influence versus Concurrence

Finally, the theory of causal concurrence idolatrously reduces divine power to being merely a supremely big instance of the kinds of power that we know about, and denies the eminent capacity of divine power fully to determine even created freedom, while leaving the latter as free in its own terms and on its own level.

Even in philosophical terms this theory makes little sense. One can no longer take seriously the notion of an 'almighty' factor within the ontic realm who is either an overwhelming yet partial influence (in the reduced sense) upon us, or a kind of supreme headmaster who is giving us a fair bash at playing some rather risky games and not often intervening even when the going gets rough in the playground, as this freedom and enterprise is ultimately good for us. Neither the slightly preposterous God of Leibniz nor a cosmic less-than-Dumbledore can today be taken seriously.

When it comes to *concursus* within the structures of the finite world, this does less than justice to the way in which some 'higher' and often elusive causal (or better, 'emanative') processes operate as a holistic, integrating element – like the covering forces across the whole field of microbiology, for example – that does not simply 'interact' as one more factor with other causes at a more basic, intimate level. Nor, as we have seen, can the notion of 'matter as quasi-act' hold, without problematically abolishing matter altogether.

---

[219]   This would be my response to John Mullarkey's view that it is a philosophy of pure *immanence* which requires an undiluted actualism, in his *Postcontinental Philosophy: An Outline* (London: Continuum, 2006). This is an entirely logical position, since any dominance of the possible or the virtual would seem to be the shadow of transcendence. However, as I try to indicate above, only transcendence allows a notion of *actus purus* and then the idea that all finite things limit this pure actuality by degrees of potential. This scheme one might regard indeed as somewhat 'dualistic', but it is *the nearest one can get* to non-dualism. Immanentist monism, by comparison (for reasons Mullarkey much of the time sees), is always deconstructible into a much more rabid dualism of a 'basic' virtual whole over against semi-illusory actualised parts.

So it remains highly coherent to assume that an embedded series of qualitatively differentiated causes points always upwards, to the ultimate, self-abiding 'influence'.

16 Transition

In this sequence it has been shown how modern philosophy as an 'autonomous' discipline was paradoxically generated by a certain style of theology. This same style has fundamentally shaped its most fundamental presuppositions of univocity, representation, possibilism and concurrence. So, insofar as these presuppositions are theologically questionable, they tend to remain philosophically questionable also. The conversion of a certain theology into secular immanence fails to purge this questionability but rather increases it – at least in existentially humanist terms – insofar as the assumptions are thereby exposed as tending to have a nihilistic drift.

But as was said in the Preface, ontology does not govern performance so much as coincide with it, insofar as essence is *ergon* and metaphysics is also divine governance. Thus the manifold works of modernity implicitly assume ontological categories, but they equally construct these assumptions which they manifest. The discourse of political theory tends to summarise in a condensed theoretical way – if both thin and veiled – this coincidence of the ontological with the pragmatic in terms of an assumed or articulated anthropology. Hence its translations of the ontological categories which I have outlined into anthropological and political terms equally show us in a more adequate way just how these categories were practically shaped in the course of western civilisation.

Hence having now explained the vision assumed by modern western works, we will now examine the coincidence of that vision with the theoretical traces of the works by which that vision was performed, and in this performance further constructed as an anthropology, and so the more confirmed as secular assumption.

Sequence on Political Ontology

1 Cosmos, Law and Morality

One reflection which the first sequence points towards is that there is an inherited yet semi-concealed division within Christian thought which today is increasingly resurfacing and which may even be more important for the future of the world than the question of the inter-relations between the three great monotheistic faiths, or the relationship of Christianity to the Enlightenment legacy.

With respect to the first circumstance, it is impossible to prophesy the future power of Islam, since it could yet benefit from a decadent implosion of the west. Yet it remains itself decadent in terms of a gradual loss of its mystical, gnostic and philosophical traditions, and increasing capture by a politicised ideology (Wahabism etc.) which ironically mimics western Protestant iconoclasm, textual literalism and focus upon the sovereign state (even if the latter has certain earlier origins within the Islamic focus upon the 'One'). Equally, it remains more culturally specific and geopolitically confined than Christianity, while the more it escapes these conditions, the more perforce it must take on what is in reality a more 'Christian' profile – in terms of its understanding of the relation of the religious to the secular, for example, or of the place of the sciences and the arts within human culture.

With respect to the second circumstance, it is certainly the case that the twenty-first century is likely to be shaped by interactions between the one truly global religion, namely Christianity, and the only seriously rival global world-view, which is scientistic rationalism (arguably more the child of nineteenth-century utilitarianism and positivism than of earlier

Beyond Secular Order: The Representation of Being and the Representation of the People, First Edition. John Milbank.
© 2013 John Wiley & Sons, Ltd. Published 2013 by John Wiley & Sons, Ltd.

'enlightenment'). However, for many reasons (some of which I have indicated in the first sequence) the latter is always likely to exhibit a palpable slide into scepticism, relativism and nihilism. This poses at once a psychological and a political threat: nihilism is not really liveable. For just this reason, the theological phase of modernity – Scotist, nominalist, Protestant, Baroque Catholic – is never likely to be simply superseded by the secular which, as we have seen, this phase itself invented in its modern guise. Instead, what should be dubbed (following John Bossy's terminology) 'modern Christianity' is likely to make a constant return in order to ensure a more stable modernity that is restrained by a morality confined mostly to the private sphere which ensures discipline, docility and a 'charismatic' channelling of the ecstatic (a function of religion which has become more and more important in modern times). This, arguably, is why the neoliberal advance of capitalism into a new phase of deregulation has been accompanied not just by a neo-conservative policing of behaviour which substitutes formal control for individual and social self-restraint (which capitalism tends to abolish), but also by a new wave of Protestant evangelical religiosity and revived Catholic neo-scholasticism. Even if these religious trends directly affect only a minority, they may still indirectly have a considerable restraining impact upon social norms at large. The most secular minds remain characteristically haunted by the sense that there is a 'stricter' religious standard which others are adhering to and which remotely guides even their own more lax conduct. One sees this particularly in people's approach to sexual relations and even more in their aspirations for their children's education.

But at more elevated levels also we see recuperations of what are in reality the Scotistic, Protestant and seventeenth-century 'Classical Augustinian' legacies which allow Christians to argue that 'the reign of the formal distinction' is an authentic upshot of the Christian legacy. Thus the modern separations of science, philosophy, politics, economics and ethics from an overarching religious vision are seen as the result of the Christian separation of divinity from law and from cosmic mediation, even by some thinkers otherwise acutely and perceptively critical of modernity.[1] From this point of view, the Enlightenment and the French Revolution are guilty of the merely venial fault of not realising that the

---

[1] See in particular Rémi Brague's sometimes questionable but always fascinating and signficant tomes, *The Law of God: The Philosophical History of an Idea*, trans. Lydia G. Cochrane (Chicago: Chicago University Press, 2007) and *The Wisdom of the World: The Human Experience of the Cosmos in Western Thought*, trans. Teresa Lavender Fagan (Chicago: Chicago University Press, 2003).

affirmation of the secular did not really require 'emancipation' from the religious, since this affirmation had already been made by Christianity, in such a way that modernity, at its best, when it respects the sphere of religious freedom, is but a more emphatic drawing out of the implications of this affirmation. It then becomes possible neatly to align one's loyalties both to modern liberalism and to Christianity – or to both the American and the French republics and the Pope. The modern differentiation of spheres is regarded as a natural outcome of the evolution of rational society such that the autonomy of reason and distinction of 'reasonings' (ethical, economic, aesthetic etc.) are seen as occurring under the aegis of a further differentiated faith which guards against nihilism, motivates ethical behaviour (that is not seen as being of itself, however, intrinsically religious) and hints at the providential purpose of the diverse immanent orderings. Without the continued discrete hegemony of the Christian outlook (as opposed to the Jewish and Islamic ones, which are regarded as not having so clearly attained the emancipation of the content of practice from religion) the secular post-Enlightenment settlement would be fragile.[2]

However, in the previous section I tried to suggest reasons why post-Scotist Christianity is a thinned-out version of the Catholic faith. If, indeed, 'modern Christianity' often no longer sees the cosmos as sacred, nor regards our human moral nature as continuous with our biology and with cosmic order in general, then this is a result of the late medieval collapse of a participatory, analogical or 'symbolically realist' world-view rooted in a more authentic tradition, which eastern Christians continue to maintain. It is certainly not – as so often thought – rooted in the Bible itself, nor in Philo's writings (the first synthesis of the biblical with the philosophical outlook) which both sustain a cosmic aspect to law and a cosmic aspect to the understanding of liturgy: all creatures obey the law; human beings have a responsibility to conserve natural bounds for all creatures; through humanity a cosmic worship is fulfilled.

This should be said in qualification of Rémi Brague's reading of Philo, in his absorbing and highly insightful *The Wisdom of the World*, as expressing a

---

[2]   For elements of this view, adopted in a specifically Scotist idiom, see Orlando Todisco OFM CONV, 'L'univocità Scotistica dell'ente e la svolta moderna', *Antonianum*, 76/1 (Jan.–Mar. 2001), 79–110, and Isiduro Manzano OFM, 'Individuo y sociedad en Duns Escoto' in the same issue, 43–78. On the more specifically legal aspect of such a position, and the privileging of Christianity's relationship to modernity, see Brague, *The Law of God*, 256–264.

supposed Hebraic 'desacralisation' of the cosmos.[3] Such a reading tends to overlook Philo's interest in the idea that man is in the cosmos like a priest in a temple and the fact that the high priest bears on his robe an image of the cosmos because humans are enjoined to make their lives worthy of the nature of the universe.[4] If contemplation of the latter is indeed here surpassed, then this is because active worship of God by man, but also of God by the cosmos *through* man, now counts higher than a merely contemplative response as hitherto advocated by philosophy. One could also variously point out in criticism of Brague the interest of the Torah in 'just' arrangements of non-human animal life (e.g. Leviticus 19:19, 23); the influence upon Christian thinking of the reworking of cosmic exemplarity by Plato in the *Timaeus* and later in his wake by Proclus; the sustaining of a sacred cosmos even by those, like Eriugena, who denied the 'ethereal matter' of the realm above the moon, and finally new renderings of cosmic sacrality by Nicholas of Cusa, Pierre de Bérulle and others *after* the collapse of the Ptolemaic picture and geocentrism (which Brague rightly points out, in the wake of C.S. Lewis, did not at all support anthropocentrism, but rather the idea that we occupy a very lowly position in the cosmos).

So while Brague's book is excitingly and indispensably innovative in exploring just how the cosmos was a source of ethical norms, it is in the end perhaps too conventionally modern in suggesting that we have now outgrown this idea, which was in any case, as he (questionably)[5] claims, already at best marginal for the biblical and Socratic visions. Therefore he

---

[3] See Brague, *The Wisdom of the World*, 78–84; Philo of Alexandria, *De Plantatione*, 126–132; *De Vita Moysis* I.134; II.127–134; *De Specialibus Legibus* I.95–96; *Quis Rerum Divinarum Heres* I.95–99; *De Somniis* I.58, 98, 134, 139, 142–143, 215. See also, for a better account of Philo in this respect, J.-L. Chrétien, 'The Offering of the World', in *The Ark of Speech*, trans. Andrew Brown (London: Routledge, 2004), 111–149, and, for the Old Testament, Robert Murray SJ's brilliant book, *The Cosmic Covenant* (London: Sheed & Ward, 1992), and Margaret Barker's equally remarkable *The Gate of Heaven: The History and Symbolism of the Temple in Jerusalem* (Sheffield: Sheffield Phoenix Press, 2008). Mary Douglas's *In the Wilderness: The Doctrine of Defilement in the Book of Numbers* (Oxford: Oxford University Press, 1993) is also relevant here. For a critique of necessary correlations of belief in transcendence with the instrumentalisation of nature, see the work of my erstwhile Lancaster pupil Bronislaw Szerszynski, *Nature, Technology and the Sacred* (Oxford: Blackwell, 2005).

[4] Philo, *De Specialibus Legibus* I.95–96.

[5] The reading of the Old Testament/Hebrew Bible as 'disenchanted' in a German Protestant trajectory has now been heavily questioned by British Catholic and Anglican scholars. See Murray, *The Cosmic Covenant*; Douglas, *In the Wilderness*; Mary Douglas, *Leviticus as Literature* (Oxford: Oxford University Press, 1999); Barker, *The Gate of Heaven*. Likewise many would now argue that the cosmic and theurgic stresses of later Neoplatonism are true to the original impulses of Plato's writings (especially in view of its Pythagorean influences) and possibly the vision of Socrates himself.

sustains the usual views that the more one invokes transcendence the more the cosmos is desacralised, and that the collapse of the sacral cosmos can be ascribed to scientific developments which removed the duality between the supralunar and the sublunar spheres. In reality one can suggest that it was rather due to the eventually predominant, but by no means inevitable, philosophical influence of nominalism-voluntarism, while authentic Christianity requires a re-enchantment of the cosmos and a recovery of the way in which it mediates to us the divine pattern of goodness. As Philo wrote: 'God intends in the first place that the high priest should have a representation of the universe about him, in order that from the continual sight of it he may be reminded to make his own life worthy of the nature of the universe, and secondly, in order that the whole world may co-operate with him in the performance of his sacred rites.'[6]

Equally, and again in qualification of Brague, Christianity only removes divinity from law when, with the nominalists, divine grace gets formally detached from the shaping of merit within us, and both the ethical and the political, in terms of their substantive content and obligatory character, become subordinate to the capricious will of 'The One' (God or earthly potentate) entitled to issue binding decrees. These were seen as implementing certain rational possibilities and compossibilities, rather than as offering organic human institutions a modicum of participation in the 'actual necessities' of the divine nature, which is free as willing the absolutely good.

Of course it is true that St Paul had declared that law in general – by which he meant *all* ethical and political law-codes – cannot save us, because it cannot transform our bad desires and even colludes with them.[7] But this was simply to subordinate the role of 'reactive law': that is to say, law which assumes the overwhelming presence of evil and so concentrates upon negative prohibitions and rigid positive prescriptions. Most certainly this subordination was a revolutionary move which distinguishes Christianity from both Judaism and Islam (although there are antinomian parallels within both traditions which are less eccentric than is sometimes thought).[8] Diversely it was to do with an enhanced

---

[6]   *De Specialibus Legibus* I.96.

[7]   See my article, 'Paul versus Biopolitics', *Theory, Culture and Society*, 25/7–8 (2008), 125–172. Brague is right to argue that for Paul God is no longer the direct legitimate source of specifically coercive law – which he associates with the 'bondswoman' and with the mediation of *daemons*. See Brague, *The Law of God*, 86–93.

[8]   See Jacob Taubes, *The Political Theology of St Paul* (Stanford, Calif.: Stanford University Press, 2003); Brague, *The Law of God*, 178–181.

role for equity; a belief that pre-legal 'trust' (*pistis*) enables both religion and society more basically than commandment (Abraham before Moses); the view that, even in countering evil one should not 'resist' it but rather 'overcome' it (as Christ recommended) out of the sources of a good ontologically prior to evil, and finally a perfectionism which considers that a rightly directed desire will not require the banning of evil. A concomitant of this perfectionism is that human society should always aim beyond the negative peace of punishment and containment towards the true harmony of reconciliation.[9]

However, Paul still speaks of this new gospel path as '*the law* of the spirit of life in Christ Jesus' (Romans 8:2) which, unlike the old law (the work of daemons), derives directly and legitimately from God the Father.[10] Likewise, for the Church Fathers and for Aquinas, 'the law of Charity' expressed the highest aspect of the 'eternal law' of God. The 'natural law' obeyed by all creatures and by rational creatures in their own appropriate way was fulfilled in the law of charity, and human positive law, while it had a relative, circumstantial aspect, had both to retain an equitable unity with natural law and to seek ultimately to promote the reign of charity.[11] The latter could even be partially and yet appropriately expressed in the compendium of principles, precepts and precedents which was 'canon law', concerned with the practical conduct of all ecclesiastical matters. If, in the west, the behaviour of the clergy came more and more to be dealt with by this Church law, then this was in part because the clergy, as the more 'spiritual' order, aspired more to non-coercive or more mitigatedly coercive ideals than secular Christians (by their removal from the sphere of warfare and violent punishment). Yet secular law had to be ultimately consistent with canon law and often appropriately borrowed from it, while canons could extend their reach to protecting the laity when it came to matters like criminal sanctuary or the regulation of lay fraternities – and here they impinged upon the economic and social sphere. (Of course this inserting of love into law was ambivalent insofar as it risked the diluting of love by legalism.)[12]

It follows that one can scarcely say, with Rémi Brague, that by separating divinity from law, Christianity separated the *practical as such* from divinity with respect to the content of human behaviour, reserving the religious

---

9   See again Milbank, 'Paul versus Biopolitics', and Bruno Blumenfeld, *The Political Paul* (London: Continuum, 2001).
10   See again Milbank, 'Paul versus Biopolitics'.
11   More will be said about natural law in *On Divine Government*.
12   Again, *On Divine Government* will further explore this ambivalence.

aspect to merely providing inspiration for this behaviour.[13] First of all, the supreme Christian religious 'obligation' to love may be a strange sort of obligation because love as an ontological bond (which is how the high Middle Ages saw charity)[14] cannot exactly be commanded, and is indeed for Christian theology a gift of grace. Nevertheless, if one considers that being is such that it is more hospitable to love than anything else because it is fundamentally relational, and all relations in some degree instantiate love, then faith in this reality will understand that love can properly be commanded because love can always be discovered as newly granted or newly affordable in any arising situation. Hence love, for Christianity, is not simply an optional attitude of mind, but the supreme practical mode in which new temporal realities are imperatively to be brought into being. Love is categorical because is it also an ontological category coincident with being itself.

Moreover, according to Augustine there is an *ordo amoris*, requiring that love be established in varying degrees according to an 'unprejudiced estimate of things', which ensures that *love itself* is always a matter of distributive justice and hence of a series of decisions about practical priorities. Supremely, all things can only be properly loved if they are loved for the sake of God who can alone be loved purely for his own sake. This principle requires a hierarchy within earthly loves on pain of their remaining genuine loves at all. Thus, for example, in loving human beings for the sake of the love of God we are to love sinners but not their sins, and other people more than our own bodies. But supremely, in fulfilment of the evangelical link between love of God and love of neighbour, we are to love those to whom we are naturally closest – including angels and the human stranger, who have happened to draw near us.

We can gloss this by saying that since God is always for Augustine 'closer to us than we are to ourselves', we most of all love other things for God's sake when we love that which is the nearest. But there is also a more pragmatic consideration. To cite his *De Doctrina Christiana*: 'further, all men are to be loved equally. But since you cannot do good to all, you are to pay special attention to those who, by the accidents of time, place,

---

[13]   Brague, *The Law of God*, 1–18, 256–264. This book is a very fine work of scholarly synthesis, full of novel and helpful aperçus, and it often helps to clarify the differences between the three monotheistic traditions concerning law. However, as with the companion 'cosmonomy' book, *The Wisdom of the World*, in the end it seems still to tell a 'Whiggish' and even Durkheimian or Weberian tale about how Christianity has been the nursemaid to a desirable social and intellectual distinction of human realms of interest.

[14]   See John Bossy, *Christianity in the West 1400–1700* (Oxford: Oxford University Press, 1975), 57–64, 140–152.

or circumstance, are brought into closer connection with you … since you cannot consult for the good of them all, you must take the matter as decided for you by a sort of lot, according as each man happens for the time to be more closely connected with you'.[15] Since we are not God, we cannot be friends with all equally, and if God commands for humans the exercise of perfect love, then we have to trust that behind the apparent 'lottery' lies a providence that is simultaneously putting others in the way of others.

Thus the pragmatic point of view confirms the ontological priority of proximity. Yet this is not properly to be considered a mere allowance for our finitude, a rendering which at times in the past encouraged the aspiration of a misconstrued love to transcend our limitations altogether. Instead, proximity itself is only possible for finite creatures to a restricted degree, whereas the infinite God is equally close to everything, while as Trinitarian he is infinitely close to himself in his interior differences. So proximity is not just a function of restriction; indeed it is rather that creatures are confined to distance. Only the Samaritan – not God – arrives from afar. But he is shown as God when he acts as the neighbour, thereby (as the Fathers construed the parable) figuratively revealing his journey as the infinite non-distance travelled by the divine Son from heaven to earth.

But one can go further than this. If the command to love is a command that is heard within the Church as the body of Christ (since where there is charity we are within this body), which for Paul is an exchange of gifts,[16] then we are able to understand that this is also a social command, a command to establish a true polity of friendship, where we can more safely with a good conscience love most the near, with a certain amount of trust that those more removed from us are also being loved by their neighbours in turn, through the workings of a shared ecclesial practice.

In all these ways love, though it lies beyond the law in one sense, is still a matter of 'order' and therefore of justice, of 'economics' and of 'politics'.[17]

---

[15]   *De Doctrina Christiana* I, chs. 27–30; Robert Spaemann, '*Ordo Amoris*', in *Happiness and Benevolence*, trans. Jeremiah Alberg SJ (Notre Dame, Ind.: Notre Dame University Press, 2000), 119–131.

[16]   See Milbank, 'Paul versus Biopolitics'.

[17]   Brague's perspective perhaps accords with that of many today for whom love cannot be in any sense a matter of economic calculation. But the citation from Augustine shows that Christian theology has tended to believe that love does belong to an order of divinely economic distribution, which is quite different from a modern self-interested calculation of possible profits and losses, although it does famously include a 'self-love' also in due proportion. This issue of *economia* will be further explored in *On Divine Government*.

For this reason it is not true that Christianity emancipates the content of the practical from religious considerations. Brague's account of divine law, while appearing to wish to historicise the entire question, curiously leaves a certain contemporary framework of understanding unhistoricised, in a way which would, on the face of it, appear to collude with political liberalism and an apologetic desire to show that liberalism is the natural upshot of Christian theology – understood as reflection on God's showing himself as a speaking person in time, in contrast with 'theonomy' – understood as reflection on God commanding a law – which is the dominant discourse of both Judaism and Islam.

This current framework of the normative understanding of the relationship of the political to the religious involves:

1   A strong distinction between the theoretical and the practical.
2   A clear demarcation between the religious and the political realms.
3   A sub-division of the sphere of the practical into the ethical, the political and the economic.
4   An equation of political with state activity.

In each case these distinctions and assumptions can be questioned in the following ways:

1   With respect to the theoretical versus the practical it is clear that Aristotle proffered such a duality in a way that Plato did not, and that the Church Fathers and Aquinas followed Plato and not Aristotle in this respect.
2   There is no clear division, contrary to what Brague seems to suggest, between the religious and the political in any of the three monotheistic traditions. The very constitution of these categories and their relation is historically situated and contingent. As Georges Dumézil discovered, the Indo-European tradition (but not *all* human traditions) knows of a distinction between ruling and priestly functions, but still within an overarching unity of both – even if the intensity of the fusion of these two aspects could vary: in ancient Rome, for example, this fusion was particularly strong.[18] But the notion of a practice of a 'politics' whose procedures become more independent of religion derives from the Greek *polis*, and that of the practice of religion as wholly separable from the practice of politics in part from the diaspora of the Jews amongst an alien polity, and in part from the invention by Christianity of a different

---

[18]   For my understanding of the Dumézil thesis, see John Milbank, 'From Sovereignty to Gift: Augustine's Critique of Interiority', *Polygraph*, 19/20 (2008), 177–199.

sort of religious society which is *itself* a *politeia*, namely the Church (the word *ecclesia* being derived from the contemporary Greek and Jewish-Greek name for the governing assembly of a city). In the case of Islam, a gradual secularisation of the political sphere was to do with the increasing capture of the whole field of divine law by Shi'ite *imams* and Sunni teachers, as Brague himself well details,[19] besides the tension as well as association between law and free will which permitted the caliph, ruling by divine right, to be a legislative innovator. Yet Brague occasionally makes it sound as if these three religions are making different applications of *a priori* categories of the political and the religious. At times he even does the same with the terms 'Church' and 'State' (notably in the conclusion to the book),[20] despite other strong notes of caution.[21] Yet it is clearly not the case that the early to high Latin Middle Ages had already distinguished these two when, to the contrary, the period mostly identified merely two aspects of 'Christendom' (and it knew of no '*Christianisme*') as *sacerdotium* and *regnum*. Where it *did* place the latter *somewhat* outside Christendom or 'Christianity' (they meant the same thing – the body of Christians, not a system of 'belief'), then this was either because, after Augustine, it saw the *regnum* as containing a trace of the pagan city, albeit a providential trace, or because of the influence of Aquinas and others which recuperated both the ancient Greek academic-peripatetic *and* the Greek Patristic sense that political rule would have existed even despite the fact of sin.[22]

3   The sub-division of the sphere of the practical into the ethical, the political and the economic is often today spoken of as if this categorisation were a timeless division.[23] However, for Aristotle the ethical was a sub-division of the political,[24] as it is not, usually in modernity, while what we now think of as 'the economic' was more Aristotle's *chrematistike*, the process of money-making, than his *oikonomia*, which meant literally household economy. In continuity with Aristotle, questions of property right and the processes of trade came under ideas of distributive and rectificatory justice, and so remained within general norms of morality in the Middle Ages, but were 'emancipated' from ethical concerns

---

[19]   Brague, *The Law of God*, 146–156.

[20]   *The Law of God*, 258–259, 263.

[21]   *The Law of God*, 9, 15, 257.

[22]   See below in this sequence, section 23.

[23]   *The Law of God*, 6–7, 258–259, 263.

[24]   In Book V of the *Nicomachean Ethics*, Aristotle makes it clear that 'complete' virtue must include a concern for the virtue of other people, and therefore coincides with justice, and, in consequence, politics.

during the Enlightenment, or rather 'the long Reformation and Counter-Reformation', since overwhelmingly the reasons for this momentous shift had to do with Calvinist and even more Jansenist belief that humans since the Fall were totally depraved in their natural will, and that in consequence a purely secular and instrumentally useful order had to be paradoxically distilled from human selfishness and even inclination to vice.[25] Yet despite this deviation, eventually, in the wake of the horrors perpetrated by capitalist industrialisation and 'free trade', both Catholicism and the Protestant denominations have mainly backed away from such a theology, and today at least most of their official spokespersons (if not large numbers of their articulate followers) refuse the idea of a 'disembedded' and amoral economic sphere. In this respect genuine Christian theology delivers the same verdict as does the theonomy of the two other major monotheistic traditions.

4   Finally an equation of 'political' with 'state' activity surely underestimates the degree to which medieval Jews, even without states, were 'self-governing' within the ghettoes or other assigned terrains, while it ignores the 'socialising' (after Augustine) and 'pluralising' of political association within Christianity (whose corporatism has spawned thousands of non-state free associations which have still helped to compose the overall political fabric).[26]

Therefore one should reject the dubious idea that authentic Christianity 'secularised the practical', meaning the ethical and the political in every sense – though there is indeed crucial validity in saying that Christianity secularised the political in the guise of state coercive power. Instead one should say that Christianity reconceived the practical within a more perfectionist and universal horizon: 'Touched by the lodestone of thy love, / let all our hearts agree, / and ever toward each other move, / and ever move toward thee ... This is the bond of perfectness, / thy spotless charity'.[27] It is the Church itself which projects this horizon, and the Church in one dimension is a practical operation, which seeks to establish an international, harmonious *cosmopolis*. So while one should not exaggerate the difference between the moral perspectives of different human societies, and it is easy to identify many shared values (generosity, hospitality,

---

[25]   See Serge Latouche, *L'Invention de l'économie* (Paris: Albin Michel, 2005), 117–164, and Jean-Claude Michéa, *The Realm of Lesser Evil: An Essay on Liberal Civilisation*, trans. David Fernbach (Cambridge: Polity, 2009). And see section 27 of this sequence below.

[26]   *The Law of God*, 123–127.

[27]   Lines quoted from Charles Wesley's hymn, 'Jesus united by thy grace' (1749).

bravery, honesty, sexual fidelity, temperance and compassion, for example) it remains the case that Christianity, by privileging the exercise of certain virtues above others – charity, trust, hope, patience, humility, mercy, forgiveness – does not simply tilt 'common morality' according to a certain bias (as Brague has it), but rather transvalues all morality in terms of an all-embracing final end of unlimited perfection predicated on a notion of original divine innocence which ensures that the good is prior to any legal 'reaction' to evil.[28] Here it is crucial, following Alasdair MacIntyre, to point out that the content of morality traditionally did not only, or even primarily, concern legal commands to do this or avoid that, but rather the promotion of a certain desirable *telos* which is a state of actual being rather than simply an instance of 'valuation' that is imposed or preserved by a moral edict.[29] This state concerns the flourishing of the virtues in unison, while the way to achieve this state is also primarily the cultivation of the virtues. It follows that if one is looking for a Christian 'difference' in ethics, that one should look first at Christianity's account of the virtues and only secondarily its account of moral law.

By implying that the latter is the prime content of the ethical, Brague would appear to treat post-Kantian assumptions as if they were ahistorical universals. He can even say baldly 'there is no theological morality' (and never has been, so that secular ethics had no need to 'emancipate' itself from it), while remaining silent about the medieval doctrine of the 'theological virtues' of 'faith, hope and charity' which were certainly not just matters of 'inspiration' for doing the good deeds of the law, but concerned a new way of doing them and of going beyond them according to a 'counsel of perfection' which was now newly 'required' within the Church order.[30] To deny with Brague that the Christian God says '*what* should be done'

---

[28] Brague, *The Law of God*, 259–262. I am implying here that Christianity had already performed a 'transvaluation' of the ethical in a way both like and unlike that carried through by Nietzsche. See John Milbank, 'Can Morality be Christian?', in *The Word Made Strange: Theology, Language, Culture* (Oxford: Blackwell, 1997), 219–232.

[29] Alasdair MacIntyre, *After Virtue* (London: Duckworth, 1981); *Whose Justice? Which Rationality?* (London: Duckworth, 1988).

[30] Brague is nonetheless good on the topic of the relation between law and counsel. He rightly points out that, in the modern age, beginning with Francisco Suárez, law became entirely separate from counsel, both as the nurturing precondition of command (rather like 'trust' in Paul) which built upon a sense of one's real happiness as lying in the pursuit of virtue, and as the equitable refinement of law 'beyond law'. Hence for Suárez law becomes entirely a matter of positively commanded *praeceptum*, and a similar notion is found in Jean Bodin. The more lowly traditional 'preceding' counsel, Brague suggests, then becomes a purely egotistic 'self-interest' in the Enlightenment era, while the traditional higher 'modifying' counsel becomes the ruthless licence to override all common morality of the revolutionary and the partisan. But it is surely just these sorts of conceptual shifts which, for the first time, 'secularise' the practical sphere in its legal guise.

would be to ignore, for example, Christ's command to forgive without limit, and Brague indeed only mentions 'pardon' as the prerogative of God in releasing from legal demands not as the positive task of reconciliation.[31]

And all this is in addition to the issue of the connection made by the Middle Ages between the content of *natural* morality and divine goodness. At least up until roughly Duns Scotus, the discernment of the former involved a discernment of the latter, and Brague himself notes that an earlier conception of divine law as 'the impression of divine wisdom on the very nature of the created' was later changed to one of 'the expression of the will of God imposed on things already created',[32] in accordance with the 'concurrence' model. He again rightly observes that the latter model bypasses our human mediation altogether, since God's will might just as well have been revealed to an angelic rational nature, lying outside our reaches of the cosmos. It was in reaction to this *purely* divine law, as he says, that one got for the first time the notion of a purely *human* law. But surely this genealogy of 'secularisation' implies that the earlier model of divine law involved a human-cosmic-divine synergy such that, within earlier Christianity, all morality was theological in the broadest sense of the latter term.[33]

Hence the 'interpretation of common morality' (in Brague's terminology) does not occur only at a reflective meta-level, but inflects the final direction of the exercise of the moral virtues.[34] This final direction is, in the broadest sense, 'politico-religious', and to deny altogether cultural moral relativity is in effect to ignore this human historical circumstance. Thus as Nietzsche, or most recently Bernard Williams, have observed, pre-Socratic cultures valued most of all the control of the passions by *thumos*: hence the sustaining of heroic attitudes which invite public honour rather than the inward self-satisfying of conscience.[35] Or again, while certain classical Hindu civilisations might have recommended many of the same everyday virtues and duties that we would today, this was often in the ultimate interests of a mystically pragmatic sustaining of power and freedom which was consummated 'beyond good and evil' in the maintenance of indifference to good or bad fortune, and violent or non-violent actions, as the *Bhagavad-Gita* reveals.

Far from it being the case that Christianity helps to sunder the ethical (in terms of the content of valuation) from the religious, it rather inherits

---

[31]   Brague, *The Law of God*, 259–261.
[32]   Brague, *The Law of God*, 237.
[33]   Brague, *The Law of God*, 237.
[34]   Brague, *The Law of God*, 259–260.
[35]   Bernard Williams, *Shame and Necessity* (Berkeley: University of California Press, 1993).

the quite peculiar Jewish-Platonic association of 'the Good' with the ultimate understanding of this 'Good' as an entirely ethical good, since it is concerned (beyond the dominant monisms and dualisms of other cultures) with the *relationality* of both justice and friendship. This understanding of the Good is inseparable within Christianity from belief in a God who is internally relational and who has established the creation in an entire relational dependence upon himself. Brague seems to read this dependency only 'religiously'. God demands no more than gratitude in return for the gifts which he has given us freely, independent of our deserts and what we may choose to do. Such gratitude may indeed shape our ethical formations, but it does not form their intrinsic basis, and God demands from us in return nothing save 'ourselves' in terms of an account of these selves that can be given in entirely secular terms. (For reasons that we have seen this would appear to affirm the univocity of being.)[36] Such a rendering of the nature of the divine gift ignores the fact that gratitude, in order to show itself as genuine, must always take the form of an appropriate expression which is already an appropriate counter-gift.[37] Hence the liturgical worship of God, as understood by the Church Fathers, is, in its full reality, a work which involves a generous approach to others which further transmits the divine gift and a use of all created things which respects their given and valuable nature as signed with the character of the divine giver. As Luigi Giussani insisted, faith is inseparable from 'following' – from an unpredictable and yet always specific reshaping of human culture.[38]

---

[36] Brague, *The Law of God*, 262: 'The divine shows itself, or rather, gives itself, before asking anything of us and *instead* of asking.' Here Brague indicates a perspective that seems like that of Jean-Luc Marion's phenomenological understanding of God in terms of pure one-way donation. But the extreme vision of human passivity which this implies is surely not borne out by the New Testament. For the latter we *only* see Christ correctly when we respond with true worship (which is something we must 'shape') and true virtuous practice, while in the paradigmatic instance of the Incarnation, the very possibility of divine action depends upon free human reception, however much that receptivity was itself granted by divine grace. It is less that God demands a response from us as his right than that in showing us himself he shows us also that good practice consists in non-bloody eucharistic worship and the life of charity. But apparently to deny that a practical response, including a moral response, is involved from the outset in apprehending the divine phenomenon would appear to confine God to an ontically 'religious' category, and to implausibly imply that the vision of God, like the vision of objective realities in science, is independent of our emotional response, subjective interpretation and practical orientation of our will. See Jean-Luc Marion, *God Without Being*, trans. Thomas A. Carlson (Chicago: Chicago University Press, 1991).

[37] See Antonio López, FSCB, *Gift and the Unity of Being*, (Washington DC: CUA Press, 2013).

[38] Luigi Giussani, *The Religious Sense*, trans. John Zucchi (Montreal and Kingston: McGill-Queen's University Press, 1997); *The Risk of Education: Discovering our Ultimate Destiny* (New York: Crossroads, 1996).

2   Metaphysics and Modern Politics

For these reasons, then, it is historically implausible to say that the secularisation of the ethical, the economic and the political was always covertly on the Christian agenda. These things are, indeed, the upshot of theology, but of a particular type of theology: one which distinguishes a natural from a supernatural end; which treats abstractable domains as if they were really separable (following the Scotist formal distinction), and which abandons the teleology of the will in favour of extrinsically imposed norms which are either arbitrary or else concern a formal framework for conserving pre-moral happiness and pre-moral freedom. Accordingly, the ethical ceases to have reference to a natural end, still less a supernatural one, and is confined to a finite realm, univocally complete in itself. Likewise, the economic becomes the technical science of wealth production which requires fidelity to contract, but can dispense with the traditional Christian opposition to the systematic practice of buying as cheaply as possible in order to sell as dearly as possible, besides the ban upon the 'usurious' selling of a phenomenon, namely money, which consists only in its use as a means of measure between diverse items and exchange between different human needs. Finally, politics and jurisprudence become the arts of achieving maximal power and order, permitting one to rule purely according to precedent without equity (as in much of the modern tradition of English common law), and to impose punishment for utilitarian reasons of deterrence rather than as economic redress and psychic medicine (as for Aristotle).

It follows that the alliance of many Christians today with neoliberalism amounts to an explicit or implicit adherence to Scotism, or the *via moderna*, or else again Baroque scholasticism (the latter two building on the first, as we have seen in the first sequence). The practical temptation to this alliance often takes the form of being offered, by the secular political and economic powers, in return for tacit support of capitalist norms, an increased role in the sphere of education, since this sphere is now increasingly open to a free market, while society tends to desire the moral discipline which religious schools are though to instil. However, if post-Scotist Christianity is theologically a deviation, for the reasons which I have tried to give, then can be this a devil's pact in which educational influence (which I am not as such eschewing, since the state monopoly and control of education is but another aspect of liberal, modern tyranny) is bought at the expense of resignation to the totally non-Christian reality of contemporary economic, bureaucratic, spectacular and military power.

However, there might also be a less committed reason for questioning any future hegemony for a post-Scotist, neoliberal Christianity. In however subtle ways, it tends towards fideism, and to an 'anti-metaphysical' stance which denies the role of those discourses of reason which tend to mediate between reason and faith. Sometimes, indeed, these are replaced with phenomenological discourses, but where these eschew ontology they tend to see only the subjective sphere as a threshold for religion, and to bypass the cosmic, the ethical (in any substantive sense) and the social altogether. William of Ockham had already in effect dispensed with the metaphysical by reducing all ontology to the assumptions involved in the logic and grammar of 'supposition'. We have already seen the sceptical and fideistic consequences which ensued, and which persist all the way down to certain manifestations of phenomenology and of analytic philosophy. But human individuals and human societies have a psychological and functional need for all-embracing world-views – hence, as both the materialist philosopher Quentin Meillassoux *and* Pope Emeritus Benedict have noted, the lack of a metaphysical discourse of reason in the twentieth century and of a bridge between reason and faith (as the Pope adds) has surely helped to foment the 'return of religion' in an unfortunately fanatical guise.[39] There is, then, as Meillassoux argues, a link between the sophisticated fideism of a Wittgenstein, whose mysticism floated free of any transformation of the world (and encouraged rather resignation to transcendental boundaries whose reality can be contested) on the one hand, and the rabid, dangerous fideism of the religious fanatic whose social alienation and lack of detached intellectual reflection ensure that his faith must translate much more directly into a positive and rigid world-view.

It follows that 'religious terror' is not, most fundamentally, a reaction against modernity. Rather, it is part and parcel of modernity in just the way that fideism and an over-pious passivity in the face of the will of God (as in Ockham, Luther, Descartes and Jansenius) are part and parcel of modernity. Already, in the eighteenth century, it had been observed that there was an oscillation between 'fanaticism' and 'libertinism' and a kind of agonistic collusion between the two, which is perhaps most marked in French, Dutch, Scottish and Irish culture which are all strongly marked by Calvinist and Jansenist influence, where strong doctrines of election detach religion from morality and encourage a kind of demonic antinomianism:

---

[39]   Quentin Meillassoux, *Après la finitude: Essai sur la nécessité de la contingence* (Paris: Éditions du Seuil, 2006); Joseph Ratzinger, Pope Benedict XVI, 'Faith, Reason and the University: Memories and Reflections', lecture given in the Aula Magna of the University of Regensburg, 12 Sept. 2006, at <cwnews.com/news/viewstory.cfm?recnum=46474>.

hence the literatures of 'the double' and of prurient puritanical fascination with the mechanisms of debauchery.[40]

Here the important thing to realise is that 'the fanatic' is just as much a modern figure as the *libertin érudit*, even though modernity casts the former in the 'conservative' and the latter in the 'radical' role – though by no means always: think of gothic novels where the amoral aristocrat is the 'antique' villain, or *The Marriage of Figaro*, where democratic purity must free itself from the perversions of traditional privilege. Modernity is *both* individualist-liberationist and sectarian or (sometimes) populist-puritanical – the trouble with both perspectives being that they fail to see sexuality as something integrally natural and cultural. 'Radicals' either see it as an animal phenomenon to be set free or else as an affair of sheer cultural contrivance *ad libitum*. 'Conservatives' see it also as something natural, but culturally threatening, while they accordingly view cultural restrictions as mainly an artificial, disciplinary contrivance. An integral account of marriage as respecting the different given biological-cultural characters of men and women, and the given biological link of sexual attraction to procreation, while fulfilling our specifically human desires to link love and nurture, to protect women and children and to anchor men in the domestic (by tempering their ambitions while allowing for their pride), becomes then almost impossible. (And this is not to deny that pre-modern practices of marriage did not sufficiently allow it to emerge as that free association which Christianity – to an unprecedented degree – already in principle envisaged it to be.)

This same structure – opposition between the conservative (or 'the ancient') and the progressive (or 'the modern') when both are secretly equally modern – turns out to be, as I will now show, the main clue to approaching contemporary politics and contemporary theologico-political dilemmas. A research programme committed to exposing the theological roots of modern philosophy, and probing the theoretical implications of this, must include a consideration of the theological roots of modern political theory and practice. And just as the former aspect tends to conclude that modern secular philosophy is only reacting against *modern* theology and *modern* metaphysics, while imagining that it is rejecting the legacy of the ancients, so also the latter aspect will tend to conclude that what is considered socially 'progressive' in modernity is in reality only constituted in

---

[40]   See André de Muralt, *L'Unité de la philosophie politique: De Scot, Occam et Suarez au libéralisme contemporain* (Paris: J. Vrin, 2002), 57–59, and also the Scottish borders writer James Hogg's 1824 novel, *The Private Memoirs and Confessions of a Justified Sinner* (London: Everyman, 1998).

opposition to an often theological 'conservatism' which has every bit as valid a title to be considered 'modern'. But here again, progressives imagine that what they are opposing in conservatism is a kind of antique feudal survival, while equally conservatives imagine that they are the guardians of long-term tradition. Or more precisely, conservatives are always involved in a double-think: they are traditionalists, yes, but of a modern sort; hence sometimes they fight rearguard actions which their heirs are bound to betray (in support of slavery, or against female suffrage, for example) while at other times they themselves take the lead in the modernisation process (the Peelite Tories; Thatcher and Reagan).

One can put this even more drastically: modernity, as the process of ceaseless transgression of given bounds, seen as a constraint upon freedom, constantly produces new traditions which it must later oppose – practices of slavery and racism, for example.[41] Since the modern is based upon the promotion of a non-teleological freedom, the entire series of its positive acts of freedom tends eventually to count as 'conservative', because for metaphysically the same reason that these acts were first performed, they must now be called into question. Thus in our own day the state control of the economy and of welfare was once seen as 'advanced' but has now come to be seen as 'retrograde'. Or, further back, the Victorians saw their puritanism as an advance upon eighteenth-century old-fashioned aristocratic and rural laxity; the twentieth century gradually reversed this verdict, so that today it is considered that sexual freedom is 'advanced', while the failure to keep healthy or to work in a constant routinised manner is a sign of recidivism.

Given these considerations, one should resist two common accounts of modernity in relation to religion and tradition. The first is associated with the 'Christian neoliberal' outlook already described. Here the conflict of the ancients and the moderns is correctly viewed as shadow-boxing,

---

[41] See Pierre Manent, *An Intellectual History of Liberalism*, trans. Rebecca Balinski (Princeton, NJ: Princeton University Press, 1995); *The City of Man*, trans. Marc A. LePain (Princeton, NJ: Princeton University Press, 1998). Quite quickly there were 'left' *philosophes* who opposed both racism and slavery, but the fact remains that Enlightenment scientific classification first encouraged racism, which had previously had but a shadowy existence, while the moral neutrality of political economy and the enlightened grounding of ethics in self-interest (which only with strain gets extended to always respecting the self-interest of all others) helped to encourage a new western extension of the ancient African slave-trade. On all this see the crucial work by my erstwhile pupils from Cambridge and Virginia respectively: Michael Mack, *German Idealism and the Jew: The Inner Anti-Semitism of Philosophy and German-Jewish Responses* (Chicago: Chicago University Press, 2003); J. Kameron Carter, *Race: A Theological Account* (New York: Oxford University Press, 2008).

but for the wrong reasons. Basically, for this outlook, Baroque Christianity continued to try to reinstall Christendom, failing to realise that the Church better fulfilled its mission by confining itself to the religious sphere. In over-reaction to this, 'enlightened' forces imagined that they must necessarily win the emancipation of science, economics, politics and morality *from* religion, rather than in its name. In contemporary retrospect a grand Christian-secular *concordat* becomes possible.

We have adequately seen how this scheme downplays the importance of 'the rupture of 1300' and falsely projects back into the far past a Christian favouring of secularisation in the modern sense.

The second common account sees modernity as essentially a reaction against Church Christianity in particular and perhaps religion in general. This logically requires that one sees the 'radical Enlightenment', which followed Spinoza, as 'the real Enlightenment', covertly driving all the debates in the background, as argued by Jonathan I. Israel.[42] Hence on this view modernity is in its very essence to do with the emancipation of forces deemed metaphorically (be it noted, for this is one of the metaphors which modernity 'lives by') to be 'from below': forces of matter, of life, of sexuality, of hedonism and (supposedly) spontaneous freedom. However, for the genealogy which I have been outlining, this 'freeing of the material' would be but one possible development of a more fundamental paradigm: namely the 'concurrent' causal operation of matter and form, combined with the Scotist 'real distinction' of the two, which rendered matter a 'quasi-act' rather than pure potentiality. Within a Thomistic outlook, by contrast, there would *be* no material sphere to be released: metaphysically, physically, sexually or politically. So here a 'materialist Enlightenment' presupposes a prior theological work of a virtual prising apart of form from matter and vice versa.

And seventeenth-century intellectual history confirms this: Spinozism might well have been pitted against the 'Aristotelianism' favoured by princes and prelates, and the latter was not counted as 'enlightened'; but nevertheless it was an entirely modern derivation from Suárez's clever blend of Thomism, Scotism and nominalism which shaped the main philosophical agendas of Protestant as well as Catholic universities.

---

[42]   Jonathan I. Israel, *Radical Enlightenment: Philosophy and the Making of Modernity 1650–1750* (Oxford: Oxford University Press, 2001); *Enlightenment Contested: Philosophy, Modernity and the Emancipation of Man 1670–1752* (Oxford: Oxford University Press, 2006). Israel also tends without argument to see the advocacy of sexual liberation as the 'real' Enlightenment and not to realise, with Foucault, that it could also sustain an equally modern disciplinary codification of the sexual field. See my earlier remarks in the main text above.

Indeed, via the work of Descartes and other sources, its influence was most certainly important for Spinoza himself, who develops in his own way the paradigms of univocity, representation, possibilism and concurrence. But as we saw in the previous section, these paradigms were equally well developed in terms of a more spiritual rationalism, subjective *a priorism* and later idealism.

Nor was Spinoza in every way obviously the most 'radical', for his conception of rational fate and *conatus* demands social collaboration but individual resignation, while his account of the popular need for imagination suggests that democracy is more concession than ideal, and that rulers will always have to deploy the guidance of 'imaginary' religion. Most people for Spinoza are made by nature to be governed by their passions and not by reason, which is alone able to take the standpoint of universal 'substance'.[43] The political order contrives a kind of simulacrum of rational cosmic unity, because the predominance of fear and insecurity over all the other passions causes people contractually to hand all their power over to a legal sovereign who then acts in their name, making decisions rather more on the basis of reason, while convincing the people of their validity through an appeal to their imaginative religious sensibilities. Thus Spinoza defines the ideal constitution, 'democracy', as 'a society which wields all its power as a whole'.[44] So the initial alienation of power by all to a sovereign centre, in the interests of the triumph of reason over 'mass' passions through their mutual cancelling out is the crucial thing, even if Spinoza believed (uniquely, before Rousseau) that this initial mass expression of will could be constantly renewed and sustained by the right of all to 'vote in the supreme council' or to occupy public office should they so wish. (He realised that more representative forms of democracy, involving a measure of oligarchy, were to be distinguished from pure aristocracies where the sovereignty is permanently alienated to a few.)[45] This corresponds politically to the way in which his parallelism of mind and extension is still a mode of extrinsic divine co-ordination on the 'Augustinian' model (as we saw in the first sequence), while his 'third kind of knowledge', which is the highest wisdom of identification with the whole, involves an apolitical, consoling

---

[43]   See Adrian Pabst, *Metaphysics: The Creation of Hierarchy* (Grand Rapids, Mich.: Eerdmans, 2012), 341–382.

[44]   Benedict de Spinoza, *A Theologico-Political Treatise*, trans. R.H.M. Elwes (New York: Dover, 1951), ch. XVI, p. 205; see also ch. XVI in general, besides chs. XV and XIX, and also *A Political Treatise* in the same edition, pp. 287–387.

[45]   Spinoza, *A Political Treatise*, ch. XI, pp. 385–387.

religious beatitude.[46] In the case of both his politics and his metaphysics, a higher abstraction exactly traces the path of a lower material connectivity, yet subsumes and trumps it in the name of a totality which is either 'God' or the state.

It was partly because of these more elitist aspects that many more conservative thinkers covertly made use of Spinoza's notions: thus, for example, Vico developed aspects of Spinoza's account of the sensory and poetic character of religion (yet with far more humanist respect for poetry) precisely in order to rebut Pierre Bayle's in one sense yet more radical suggestion that there could be a society of atheists, or that they would be more moral than a society of pagans. For Israel to suggest that the use of Spinoza by Vico and his equally Platonising friend Paulo Mattia Doria is a sign of their hidden, quasi-Spinozistic 'radicalism' is therefore too simplisitic.[47]

As we saw in the first sequence, it can be argued that David Hume was in fact the more philosophically 'radical' in eschewing either a basic cosmic monism or a basic subjective perspectivalism. The fact that he, like Hobbes, was politically conservative is not to the point, but rather alerts us to the

---

[46]   Benedict de Spinoza, *The Ethics*, trans. R.H.M. Elwes (New York: Dover, 1955), *passim*.
[47]   Israel, *Radical Enlightenment*, 664–674; *The Enlightenment Contested*, 513–542. The arguments over this issue however, are far too complex to be properly gone into here. Suffice it to say that Israel ignores Vico's frequent support for a by his day somewhat archaic humanism linked to civic virtue (although aspects of 'the Enlightenment' itself were soon partially to revive this) in contrast to the new 'objective' textual scholarship, and that he also too readily assumes that caution about the local Inquisition implies doctrinal unorthodoxy, rather than simply pessimism about its intelligence in the face of novel but perfectly orthodox intellectual strategies. The remarkable depth of Vico's engagement with traditional theological doctrine, especially Augustinian doctrine, at certain crucial points, supports the view that he is already deploying modern critical methods against modernity itself and truly does anticipate a 'Counter-Enlightenment' built upon a positive rather than sceptical approach to the primacy of the human imagination that reworks many humanist aesthetic and metaphysical thematics. My own contentions to this effect in my published doctoral work (which would now be in need of considerable revision) have more recently been developed by my former pupil Robert C. Miner in his *Vico: Genealogist of Modernity* (Notre Dame, Ind.: Notre Dame University Press, 2002) and by Antonio Sabetta in his *I 'Lumi' del Cristianismo: Fonti teologiche nell'opera di Giambattista Vico* (Vatican City: Lateran University Press, 2006). What is more, the most sophisticated contemporary Hume scholar, Donald Livingston, far from 'reducing' Vico to Hume read as an atheist positivist, instead reads Hume himself in an explicitly Vichian way as a philosopher defending the often religious human feelings and imagination against the anti-political tendencies of pure reason, in a way which brings out Counter-Enlightenment and proto-Romantic tendencies at the heart of the Scottish Enlightenment (or arguably pre-Enlightenment, if one takes the Enlightenment to coincide with the full birth of 'political economy') itself. See, once more, Livingston, *Philosophical Melancholy and Delirium: Hume's Pathology of Philosophy*, and *Hume's Philosophy of Common Life* (Chicago: Chicago University Press, 1986).

fact that, as later with Friedrich Nietzsche, some of the most hypercritical modern thinkers transcend the usual atheist/materialist-left versus religious/ spiritualist-right division, by arguing that an ontological reality of pure power scarcely favours any sort of sentimental equality of treatment amongst human beings – save that, perhaps, which for Hume flows unstoppably from the operation of sentiment as sympathy itself. Hence Hume's more 'Thatcherite' views (though he also, and contradictorily, held to much more 'High Tory' ones) that we should always promote luxury, never encourage indigence through welfare and never defend tyrannicide, belong every bit as much to 'Enlightenment' (or arguably more so) than the opposite views which the Enlightenment also gave rise to.[48]

For that reason we need to recognise 'the equal modernity of the ancients and the moderns' with respect to these categories that were initially ones of seventeenth- to eighteenth-century aesthetic dispute. This translates in the first place as the equal modernity of 'modern Christianity' and 'the modern reaction against Christianity' – an oscillation which, it must be anticipated, is likely to be perpetuated far into the future. It also translates as 'the equal modernity of Right and Left' (while stipulating that 'socialism' does not really belong on this spectrum).[49] This hypothesis should be initially entertained by a hypercritical outlook, while suspending for the while the question of precisely what political stance the Christian should take in the present day – supposing that this question admits of an answer.

For the rest of this sequence I wish to test this hypothesis. I will argue that pre-modern politics was neither progressive nor reactionary, neither left nor right, but rather focused, in the Middle Ages, round a quadruple anthropology, linked to a 'symbolically realist' metaphysics. This comprised: (1) the *animal rationale*; (2) the *animal sociale* (Aristotle's *zoon politikon*); (3) *homo faber* or 'the fabricating animal', who is also the cultural and historical animal; and (4) Pascal's *Bête-Ange*: humanity as naturally orientated to the supernatural.

What is crucial to note is that, in every case, we are talking about a *hybrid*, which Victor Hugo in the Romantic period was correctly able to link with the 'grotesque' and with the manifest gothic fascination for this category.[50] Nonetheless, we are also talking about an *integral hybrid*, a unity which cannot be undone without destroying its parts – so disallowing

---

[48] David Hume, *An Enquiry Concerning the Principles of Morals*, ed. L.A. Selby-Bigge and P.H. Nidditch (Oxford: Oxford University Press, 1982), Section II, Part II, 143–144, pp. 180–182.

[49] See Michéa, *The Realm of Lesser Evil*, and section 27 below.

[50] I am indebted for this point to Alison Milbank. And see Victor Hugo, *Préface de Cromwell* (Paris: Larousse, 2009).

even a Scotist, virtual division. The 'rational animal' is only animal *as* rational, and yet the mode taken by animality here is essential to reason. The 'social animal' is only animal *as* social, yet this sociality is an entirely natural phenomenon. *Homo faber* is only human *through* making things and 'making things up', yet this 'artificial' character which belongs to the individual through artefacting *is* an aspect of that individual's integral nature. Finally, human nature paradoxically *is* that which exceeds itself in receiving the gift of the supernatural end; yet this 'deification' is only possible as the fulfilment of human created nature, and not as its destruction.

In all four cases, what political modernity does (and likewise ethical, social and economic modernity) is to destroy the grotesque in its aspect of unusual, aspiring and yet kenotic beauty. It questionably deconstructs a peculiar 'trans-organism', an oddly ruptured and yet healed human integrity. Instead of an 'integral' politics (in a certain sense which we should carefully distinguish from positivistic *intégrisme*)[51] it enters on a politics

---

[51]   The phrase 'integral humanism' was validly used by Jacques Maritain to describe his project of a 'new Christendom' which refuses the modern view that natural political goals can be adequately fulfilled without any influence of supernatural grace. Other writers, like Henri de Lubac, advocated even more strongly a Christian humanist 'integration' of the natural with the supernatural, denying the existence of a 'pure nature' in the concrete altogether. Yet clearly both writers utterly rejected the *intégrisme* of the Action Française (and indeed just this rejection was a crucial driving force for their intellectual and cultural activities in either case) which wanted seamlessly to fuse secular power and ecclesiastical authority and which was eventually condemned by the papacy. In fact one can rigorously argue that the project of the atheist and opportunistically 'Catholic' Charles Maurras was in truth not integralist enough, insofar as it was based upon a positivistic conception of political order and a naturalisation and politicisation of the Church's presence in the secular sphere. Without Maritain's sense of 'the primacy of the spiritual', one cannot have a true integration of the natural with the supernatural, because the real place of the latter has been denied along with the real character of its influence, which must be basically suasive in kind, not based on coercion or absolute institutional rights to overrule other power blocs. Moreover, this true integration has to sustain an element of hybridity which allows that supernatural concerns cannot be politically administered, while also allowing that sheerly political matters involve temporary compromises with human disagreement and imperfection which the Church as such must eschatologically refuse – in this sense true integration is *never* 'perfect' integration and this imperfection even helps to define its 'integrity'. Nevertheless, the supernatural virtues should inform the natural ones in the political domain and the endeavours of the latter must finally be measured by the assistance which they give to the supernatural society which is the Church. Maritain's vision here, following Charles Péguy, was in the end grounded in a Thomistic Christology, stressing strongly (following the Byzantines) the personally mediated 'communication' of divine and natural natures in the God-Man. After the Incarnation God is only mediated to us through the total inter-communication of the mystically divine with the human in all its aspects, including the political. See Yves Floucat, *Pour une restauration de la politique: Maritain l'intransigeant de la contre-révolution à la démocratie* (Paris: Pierre Téqui, 2004), 15–121. Also Aaron Riches, *Ecce Homo: On the Divine Unity of Christ* (Grand Rapids, Mich.: Eerdmans, 2013).

which is dualistic and so sundered between animality and reason, nature and culture (or the individual and the state), fact and fiction (or reason and the imagination) and finally the political and the ecclesial. Instead of the trans-organism, it posits a ruptured organism which it brutally reconstitutes as a single totality that is indeterminately and problematically 'purely' animal and yet 'purely' rational. It is both at once, and yet without any integration or any resignation in the face of this lack of integration, which remains inevitably a theoretical requisite. So everything now proceeds as if we had a perfect Spinozistic parallelism, yet without any *rationale*, and in such a way that, turn by turn, one track or another claims a monistic sway in its own dimension alone.

3   The Fate of the Rational Animal

As has just been indicated, the Aristotelian notion of a 'rational animal' concerns a manifestation of animality *as* rationality, or as a 'kind of life' in Augustine's phrase, later deployed by Aquinas.[52] It does not involve a Cartesian hybrid between the merely animal on the one hand and the independently spiritual on the other. This is especially shown by the way in which Aristotle and Aquinas link the human capacity for reason to upright bodily posture, possession of hands which are mainly redundant organs in terms of self-transport, and also of hairless skin which renders human touch supremely sensitive. For this outlook – as later still more intensely in the twentieth century for Merleau-Ponty, building on Husserl's ideas in this respect (as described in the first sequence, section 6) – the specifically human animal body is a threshold for thought: all its external movements, whether conscious or not, are intelligent movements and all its sensations are intelligent sensations. Inversely, the human being is intelligent in terms of the co-operation between its brain and a body finely attuned both to the capacities of its brain and the nature of its physical environment.[53]

One can speak here of an integral yet discontinuous unity, or 'trans-organicity', meaning an integrity sustained despite an interruptive leap: a continuity of transcendence with the biological ground that it exceeds, and a continued biological enfolding of a vertical *ecstasis* beyond the merely

[52]   Augustine, *De Trinitate* IX.1.4: 'knowledge is a kind of life in the reason of the knower'; and X.2.6: 'just as the whole mind is, in the same way the whole mind lives'.
[53]   See John Milbank, 'The Soul of Reciprocity Part Two: Reciprocity Granted', *Modern Theology*, 17/4 (Oct. 2001), 485–507.

biological – beyond 'life' towards 'reason' (as also towards the social, the cultural and the artificial) yet in such a way that reason constitutes a more elevated kind of life. Scotism and nominalism, however, began subtly to prise apart this curiously supplemented monad in two decisive ways.

First of all, as we saw in the first sequence (section 4), Scotus declared, in an Avicennian line of descent, that *by nature* the first object of human understanding was being, rather than material being. This already suggested, long before Descartes, that the human mind, even when conjoined to the body, has a more fundamental kinship with the abstract than with the sensorily concrete. The *necessarily* mediating role (even for Adam, in the garden of Eden according to Aquinas) of the *conversio ad phantasmata* is here abandoned. Accordingly, a proto-intellectual integration of thought with sensation through the workings of the imagination is here deemed to be an aberrant result of the Fall.[54]

In political terms this suggests an absolute primacy for abstract and univocal conceptions of legal and political order, with imaginary conceptions reduced to the status of convenient fictions. This is especially true with ideas of collective embodiment, for which, increasingly, humanly invented 'corporations' cease to be thought of as having any organic integrity that exceeds the sum of their parts and a 'mystical body' becomes more or less cognate with a 'pretended' body, a group of individuals treated 'as if', for convenience, it really composed a whole (clearly nominalism later greatly augmented this tendency).[55]

Eventually, in the case of Spinoza, the same outlook leads to an intrusion into the Christian west of the Islamic and then Jewish scholastic philosophical (rather than theological or theonomic) view that the imaginative and historical level of religious discourse is essentially irrational, and that its true purpose is to serve as a tool for the communication with, and manipulation of, the intellectually deficient mass of the population. What is now generally viewed by scholars in Spinoza's sceptical reading of the Bible as a 'critical' hermeneutic advance, could rather be viewed metacritically as an expression of a characteristically Jewish-Islamic philosophic duality of thought and image, and also of legal command and image (which is bound in either case in reality to over-elevate the *abstract* image) that was sustained as much

---

[54]   See Catherine Pickstock, 'Duns Scotus: His Historical and Contemporary Significance', *Modern Theology*, 21/4 (Oct. 2005), 543–575.
[55]   See Henri de Lubac, *Corpus Mysticum: The Eucharist and the Church in the Middle Ages*, trans. Gemma Simmonds (London: SCM, 2006); Ernst H. Kantorowicz, *The King's Two Bodies: A Study in Medieval Political Theology* (Princeton, NJ: Princeton University Press, 1993); Michel de Certeau, *The Mystic Fable: The Sixteenth and Seventeenth Centuries*, trans. Michael B. Smith (Chicago: Chicago University Press, 1995), 79–93.

by their extreme suspicion of figurative depiction (though this is heavily resisted by more mystical traditions, which in the Islamic case put the imagination at the centre of their thought) as by their difficulties of integrating philosophical with religious discourse.[56]

Christian theology, by contrast, is an exposition of a revelation which indissolubly links the rational *Logos* of God to a human figure who can only be imaginatively and narratively conceived. It therefore assumes, because it is credally bound to read the Bible Christologically, that the mysterious blending of idea, imaginative resonance and historical event in the Bible is likewise indissoluble, and constitutive of the very character of 'revelation'. Hence the 'literal word' of biblical narrative retained within Christendom, as Hans Frei argued, an authority above that of univocal legal prescription, legal commentary or philosophical reason.[57]

It follows that to propose instead, with Spinoza and the hyper-Protestant iconoclast Hobbes, a 'rational' reading of the Bible which confined its less clear and most contingent, seemingly fantastic and imaginative elements to purposes of human political and cultural manipulation, was basically to deny that an imaginatively apprehended past *figura* – the God-Man Christ – could still be ascribed in the present an ultimate political and social authority. Their 'critical' approach to the Bible in the end only works as a *theological* denial of the principle of Christocentric hermeneutics (which of itself demands that blend of 'philosophy' with 'theology' that Spinoza, with his Marrano background, deemed to be 'false subtlety'), and so of the very authority of Christian theology as a logic which implicitly insists that the imaginative integration of the ideal and the sensory cannot, by human beings, be surpassed.

In effect, one can deconstruct Spinoza and Hobbes's 'critique' of the sacred texts as but a power ruse which removes legitimacy from a social organisation, namely the Church, that can challenge the unqualified sovereignty of the modern state, which is based upon an entirely formal non-teleological reason and an absolute concentration of *de facto* power. The Church can do so by appeal to its own 'imaginative' unity as the body of Christ and to the overriding authority of a narrative which seamlessly blends the instructively 'fictional' (or the 'allegorical') with historical factuality.[58]

---

[56] On all this see Henri Corbin, *Histoire de la philosophie islamique* (Paris: Gallimard, 1986).

[57] Hans W. Frei, *The Eclipse of Biblical Narrative: A Study in 18th and 19th Century Hermeneutics* (New Haven, Conn.: Yale University Press, 1980).

[58] See John Milbank, *Theology and Social Theory*, 2nd edn. (Oxford: Blackwell, 2006), 18–22. And for more on this 'blending' see sections 9 to 12 below.

Secondly, the Scotist-derived notion of *esse objectivum* also tended to loosen the sinews of animal rationality. If, as for Aquinas, the mental concept of its very nature intends a real material thing, then the operation of the mind is at one with the directedness of sight and of the other senses, as we saw in section 6 of the first sequence. But if the mind knows first of all a mental 'object' with no necessarily faithful indication of what it appears to 'represent', then the link between spiritual thought and animal sensation has been somewhat loosened.

The political correlate of the notion of the 'representing concept' is the idea of the sovereign government as 'representing' the people. And here also one has an equivalent to the *paradox* of the epistemological paradigm. In the latter case, representative imaging suggests an accurate and reliable copying – but, as we have seen, without an assumption of continued identity of form, there is no guarantee of the reliability of the copy, because there cannot, in principle, be any way of comparing copy with original if we are doomed to know the original only through the copy. In this way the merely *substitutionary* character of the concept migrates from being a sign of humility to being a ground for the liberation of thought from the tyranny of the real. By parallel, modern representative government, and especially representative democracy, presents itself as a humble substitute for the will of the people, but, in reality, the notion of representation is a charter for the alienation of the popular will, once the polling booths have closed on every election day. Moreover if, in a pure democracy, only what the people happens to will is validly to be represented, then the problem ensues as to how the people are to decide what to will and what they will be deemed to have willed. They cannot *really* be deemed to have willed all the irrational and selfish things that they might will as mere animals, since these desires have been already excluded from the political game by the imagined 'original contract' which suspended natural anarchy. Nor will these desires help the people to make up their mind – yet what other resources do they have, since the political supplement to their animality will have been constructed only *after* the representative process of democracy has been completed?

Thus while it might appear that politics is a mere artifice which 'represents' sheerly natural persons, in reality only severely denatured 'citizens' can be represented at all, even if this denaturing is taken to be at bottom naturally motivated through the outrunning of our ambitions by our fears. Nor can the people politically will what the wise present to them as the intrinsically just and true, because these things have already been relegated to the realm of mere subjective opinion or 'value', for a democratic sphere in which only the will of the majority has validity.[59] In this way both 'lower animal' and 'higher angelic' goals have been always already discounted by democracy. It remains, therefore, as Alexis de Tocqueville realised after he had toured the United States, that in a pure representative democracy the people will tend to will precisely *what they are generally represented as willing*,[60] through the operation of their artificially qualified desires that the contracted polity alone recognises as privately authentic and politically valid. So when the principle of representation triumphs, in the political as in the gnoseological sphere, representation always degenerates into a representation only of itself as representing. In the political sphere this means the inevitable self-subversion of democracy by propaganda. The will of the represented people is alienated to their representatives who, the more they pose *only* as such and not also as leaders, become mainly 'spin doctors' who constantly concoct the spectacle of 'public opinion' and 'prevailing trends'.[61]

This parallel can be historically confirmed as more than fortuitous, because Franciscan and Franciscan-linked thought tended, from Bonaventure through Scotus to the nominalists, to abandon notions of the 'common good' or the conviction that the test of political legiti-macy is adherence to natural equity, in favour of a formal derivation of entitlement to rule which necessarily concerned issues of the representa-tion of will, whether that of God or of the people.[62] This combination of formalism with voluntarism precisely parallels the way in which the representation paradigm for cognition tends, as we saw, dubiously to approximate the order of knowing the truth to the order of willing the good, since the moment of conceptual understanding is now seen as a mere means, and no longer as in itself a contemplative fulfilment. And the same combination can, of course, be seen in the way in which, in the case of the economy, wealth is increasingly measured by the monetary or capital 'representation' of the useful or the pleasurable insofar as these things are willed and desired, and no longer insofar as they are taken to be objectively desirable.

---

[59]   See Eric Voegelin, *The New Science of Politics: An Introduction* (Chicago: Chicago University Press, 1987), 1–26.
[60]   Alexis de Tocqueville, *Democracy in America*, trans. Harvey C. Mansfield and Debra Winthrop (Chicago: Chicago University Press, 2000), 172–180, 239–250.
[61]   See John Milbank, '*The Gift of Ruling*', *New Blackfriars*, 85/996 (Mar. 2004), 212–238.
[62]   Pickstock, 'Duns Scotus'; John Milbank, '*Against Human Rights*', *The Oxford Journal of Law and Religion* (Jan. 2012), 1–32; Michel Villey, *La Formation de la pensée juridique moderne* (Paris: PUF, 2006); Georges de Lagarde, *La Naissance de l'ésprit laïque à déclin du Moyen Âge, III: Secteur social de la scolastique* (Paris: Éditions Beatrice, 1942), 116–145.

4   The Irony of Representation

In either case, one can also speak of a certain later early modern 'aestheticisation' of the social order, in parallel with a new, post-mannerist Baroque sense of beauty in rhetoric, poetry and painting which has further, in the wake of mannerism, stressed the originality of the artistic *concetto* or *disegno* (in the mind of the artist and then in the work produced), but weakened its links with the Good and the True.[63] Just as a remarkable poem or fine picture can increasingly be deemed successful merely through 'realising' a novel conception or, for later artistic realism, in 'representing' a natural or human reality, and not through inculcating some sort of intellectual or moral lesson (although this development was slow and never became complete), so also the test of a successful market or a successful government initially becomes its ability to 'reflect' and to 'respond to' the dominant social tendencies of the day.

And here also the paradox of representation holds good: *mere mimesis* is latently pictorial abstraction, because a new subjective insight into any reality can implicitly stand on its own. Since the charm of an invoked reality must be charming in its own terms and not merely by virtue of its reference (which quickly seems banal), the invocation can eventually be dispensed with. Hence just as figural *mimesis* of either concept or nature gives way first of all to a classicism which holds its rule-governed forms to be independent of either specific transcendent derivation or of pure 'truth to nature',[64] and then further to abstraction (which is often like a kind of hyper-classicism) in art, so also economic and governmental structures tend increasingly to control and 'idealise' through abstract procedures the very realities they claim to represent, until the manipulation of imposed capitalist and bureaucratic abstractions takes up most of the business of actual everyday life – instilling an all-pervasive fatigue, sterility, irritability and frustration amongst most modern people for most of the time.

By contrast, the older 'abstraction' of form and yet continuity with the represented thing through identity (which reigned in many mutations all

---

[63]   See Walter J. Ong, *Method and the Decay of Dialogue* (Cambridge, Mass.: Harvard University Press, 1958), 92–313; Guido Morpurgo Tagliabue, 'Aristotelismo e Barocco', in E. Castelli, ed., *Retorica e Barocco* (Rome, 1955) 119–195; John Milbank, *The Religious Dimension in the Thought of Giambattista Vico 1668–1744*, vol. 1: *The Early Metaphysics* (New York: Edwin Mellen, 1991), 261–325; Erwin Panofsky, *Idea: A Concept in Art Theory*, trans. Joseph J.S. Peake (New York: Harper & Row, 1960), 71–99. The new mid-seventeenth-century 'classicism' could also tend to weaken the link of aesthetics with the ethical by promoting an 'idealisation' of natural form which no longer made reference to any transcendent 'idea' in which notions of the good, the true and the beautiful were fused.

[64]   Panofsky, *Idea*, 103–111.

the way from Byzantine to mannerist painting and beyond) implies an integral art in which one necessarily abstracts in order to fulfil and yet thereby all the better to imitate and remain faithful to nature. Here abstraction and imitation are not only always involved (as they must be, in every work of art) but they also integrally reinforce each other rather than pulling in opposite directions. Similarly, for an older politics, government was not a pragmatically necessary 'substitution' for the will of the people, but rather the role of the ruling 'one' or advising 'few' was symbolically necessary to the very constitution of the people as a people, just as the intellectual concept, for the older view, was part of the perfection of the cosmos and even necessary for its sustaining.

Representation claims aesthetically to image the people, but in reality it substitutes for the people the body of citizens, such that each person can only enter into economic, political and even social life – now defined by the abstract currency of manners, which lack any ritual import or respect for different social roles – under the guise of a uniform civil mask, which considers each individual only with respect to their inter-substitutionability and the 'general' relevance of what they have done, for which an exact equivalent can always be found.[65] In this way they are considered only from the point of view of 'social reason', while all their incongruities and elective preferences are relegated to the realm of the 'natural' which is indifferent and irrelevant, so long as it does not violate any of the codes of formal urbanity, guaranteed contract and administrative regularity. What is collectively rational has now therefore become wholly conventional and artificial, while what is collectively animal is strictly split between, on the one hand, the 'wild' desires of the individual that inhibit the desires of others or the strength of the state and must be controlled and, on the other, 'tame' but still natural desires whose harmless zoological variety can be benignly encouraged – though sustaining this boundary becomes increasingly problematic, as some writers and film-makers have realised.[66] The animality of the collective body as such is exemplified either as fashion or hysteria, the latter being the disease to which the former is subject. In either case we are speaking about a contagion of individual influence and not about desirable properties intrinsic to the social body as a total organism.

---

[65]   For the mathematics of this, see Alain Badiou, *Being and Event*, trans. Oliver Feltham (London: Continuum, 2005), 327–391. But the inferences I have drawn here are very different from his own.

[66]   See the late J.G. Ballard's novel *Super-Cannes* (London: Harper, 2006). David Fincher's film adaptation of Chuck Palahniuk's *Fight Club* is also highly relevant.

Is this, then, an argument against all forms of representative democracy and in favour of either direct democracy or paternalistic control? Or else a combination of the two, which is generally the advocated alternative, all the way from Jean-Jacques Rousseau to Carl Schmitt – since for anything beyond the size of the Athenian *polis* one has to propose the figure (in the singular or the plural) of 'the legislator' who directly puts into effect the 'general will', either as it appears to be or else as it 'objectively is', in terms of its own real interests?

Such a consequence does not follow, because this alternative model lies itself firmly within the modern paradigm and is in fact at once a degree maximum and a degree zero of the notion of representation. The most common version of the latter, as Karl Ankersmit argues, is 'mimetic representation' where, by analogy with high Renaissance or later more outrightly realist art, the democratic ruling power seeks fundamentally to 'imitate' the will of the people, even if this is seen as subject to expert interpretation as regards the implementation of details.[67] The Rousseauian position is then like this version carried to the most extreme degree: here the 'picture' of popular reality that is government is so exact a representation that it becomes more like a mirror-image or even a glass that one 'sees right through' such that it is supposed that the people can act with unmediated directness.[68] The guiding assumption here is really the 'left' one of the sovereignty of the many, even if this is slanted in a 'modern republican' (post-Machiavellian) rather than liberal individualist direction – such that, in the wake of the mythical 'social contract', all individual freedoms are now forever only to be realised through a patriotic devotion to the liberty of the state as such. The guidance exercised by the state can then notoriously start to take more or less totalitarian forms as revolution drifts logically towards empire.

It follows that there is no real 'identity' here in the pre-modern sense of an identity between the many, the few and the one that is based on common subscription to a teleological aim grounded in a transcendent reality that exceeds these numerical divisions, and allows for mediation between them. The identity achieved on the Rousseauian model is, rather, one of the (supposed) absolute imposition of the rule of the many on the political whole, whereby its original ferality is alchemically transmuted

---

[67] Karl Ankersmit, *Aesthetic Politics: Political Philosophy Beyond Fact and Value* (Stanford, Calif.: Stanford University Press, 1996), 21–115. I am grateful to Anthony Paul Smith for pointing this work out to me.

[68] Jean-Jacques Rousseau, *The Social Contract*, trans. Maurice Cranston (Harmondsworth: Penguin, 1968).

into pure artificial civility – this unmediated transition being something that was constantly staged on the streets of Paris during the French Revolution.

But how did the pre-modern mediation work? Here it must be recognised that there was, at least in the post-Christian era, a specifically pre-modern, alternative notion of political representation. Just as the *species* is identical with the materialised form and yet also 'stands for', 'depicts' or 'intends' this materialised form in the realm of knowledge, so also the few or the one are 'identical' with the many since they are all involved in a common participation – for the Middle Ages in the body of Christ under the governance of an invisible head – and yet the one and the few also 'represent' by consent or acclamation the needs and even the will of the many. However, because this 'corporatism' is a mode of representation based upon participatory identity and not a mere external and perspectively realist 'picturing', the representative *as such* is here expected to act also in terms of his own judgement and his own personal devotion to truth and justice. The modern contradictory tension between being a 'representative' or a 'delegate' was absent in the Middle Ages because, as Karl Ankersmit puts it, it was supposed that there was a *tertium comparationis* between the people on the one hand and the ruler plus the aristocracy on the other. This was something like 'social reason' or a sense of the 'common good', in parallel to the 'third term' of reason which, for a traditional metaphysics, united the created natural world with the operation of human intelligence.[69]

Ankersmit, however, oddly associates this notion exclusively with post-Renaissance Stoicism, whereas it was the common currency of most inherited philosophy and theology: supremely present in the Aristotelian idea that *eidos* is common both to material nature and to the rational mind. If anything, Stoicism started to introduce a bifurcation and an alienation between mind regarded as simply an aspect of the operation of material nature on the one hand, and mind that is locked within its own private chamber on the other. Hence in Descartes our ideas of material extension are the (Scotistic) 'objective' presence of the formality of real space itself (which is identical with materiality) as mirrored by the mind, while our self-awareness cannot be linked with this real space in any way whatsoever.[70] The notion of a 'mirroring' of the latter by the former arises *from* this separation, upholding the extrinsicist aesthetic model of 'representation by copying', whereas

---

[69] Ankersmit, *Aesthetic Politics*, 64–114.
[70] Descartes, *Meditations on First Philosophy*, 'Third Meditation', 40–41, pp. 28–29, and 'Sixth Meditation', 79, p. 55.

Ankersmit wrongly links this modern idea (in epistemology, aesthetics and politics) to the operation of a *tertium comparationis.*

He does, all the same, offer a subtle account of the ways in which the modern political model of representation as *mimesis* does not work in practice and does not really describe the workings of modern constitutions.[71] What this analysis shows is that the modern state is always *haunted* by the workings of pre-modern socio-political realities and produces in the end less a genuine alternative to them than a simulacrum of them. Ankersmit wants us to be more honest about this simulacrum, and so he proposes a new postmodern model for liberal democracy which he thinks is both more accurate and will work more successfully, since the disguised realities turn out for him not to be things that we should be ashamed of after all. At this point I diverge from his conclusions: nevertheless there is much to be learnt from him, and he is even astonishingly candid about the possible future limitations of what he proposes.

The reason why representative democracy fails to be mimetic, even in its anchorage, is twofold. First of all, in terms of a logic already described, it involves inevitably an alienation of power from the many to the sovereign one, and in the absence of normative standards which transcend the democratic, the supposedly represented are bound to finish up by responding to the spectacle of the representing process rather than the other way around.[72] On top of this, as Ankersmit points out, since the 'position' of sovereign oneness is not *itself* elected, but from the outset assumed, elective alienation constantly reinforces the power of this position which increasingly sustains itself as a self-maintaining bureaucracy that acquires its own power-interests as the function of executive 'administration', which have little to do with the interests of society as a whole and are distinct from the interests of any sectional social faction.[73]

As Ankersmit puts it: democracy is entirely reflexive in that here the people are sovereign over themselves, yet the state-function escapes this reflexivity and is not itself represented as an interest group, but rather disguises this interest behind the representing function. Indeed the elected rulers themselves are frequently unaware of this disguise: they think in terms of 'representation of the people' or manoeuvring to ensure their

---

[71]   Ankersmit, *Aesthetic Politics*, 115–254, 345–372.
[72]   See Guy Debord, *The Society of the Spectacle*, trans. Donald Nicholson-Smith (New York: Zone, 1992).
[73]   See Giorgio Agamben, *State of Exception: Homo Sacer 2*, trans. Kevin Attell (Chicago: Chicago University Press, 2005).

own re-election. Only the people themselves perceive clearly that there is a hidden state-power over against them, and this may be why, as Ankersmit suggests, Machiavelli wrote that only the people can 'know well the nature of Princes', just as 'those who sketch landscapes place themselves down in the plain to consider the nature of mountains and high places' – while equally only the Prince knows the people as a whole, just as a painter would sketch a plain from the perspective of a mountain-top.[74] But this double dictum only holds because a detached 'representing' ruler (as Machiavelli's calculating Prince already was) is a *rentier* of the hidden but continuous state, whereas the pre-modern king *was* mystically his realm, such that his power resided in his constantly renewed manifest symbolic penetration of that realm and not primarily in a 'reserve' treasury of inherited administrative machinery.[75] This is exactly why the transition from king to king, besides the legitimation of the living king's personal power to innovate (not as yet guaranteed by the function of an impersonal sovereign state), required in the Middle Ages the fictional notion of the king's second, mystical body, as Ernst Kantorowicz famously described.[76]

The second reason why modern democracy cannot adequately be described as mimetic is that not only are the popular will of the many and the sovereign authority of the one combined through alienation, but their endemic conflict is also incorporated through an overarching pure neutrality. As Ankersmit lucidly argues, we should not delude ourselves into supposing that democracy is today dominant as the result of a progressive evolution. To the contrary, it has come about in every instance as the result of a compromise. Ankersmit tends (rather confusingly) to confine this notion only to Continental European democracy, but we can surely say that in England the Glorious Revolution ensured a permanent dynamic deadlock (up till the present day) to be played out through party politics, between erstwhile revolutionary factions proposing extensions of private economic and religious freedom and sometimes of property ownership and franchise on the one hand, and devotees of a more authoritative monarchy, the established Church and local patriarchal rule (still blending in a quasi-feudal manner economic wardenship and political-legal authority)

[74] Niccolò Machiavelli, *The Prince*, trans. Harvey C. Mansfield (Chicago: Chicago University Press, 1998), 'Dedicatory Letter', p. 4. Cited by Ankersmit, *Aesthetic Politics*, 119; see also 197–211.

[75] On this matter see Hans-Hermann Hoppe, *Democracy: The God that Failed. The Economics and Politics of Monarchy, Democracy and Natural Order* (New Brunswick NJ: Transaction, 2007), 45–95.

[76] Kantorowicz, *The King's Two Bodies*.

on the other: the Whigs versus the Tories (and later the Liberals and then Labour against the Tories).[77] This means that party politics is not the stability of normal rule as guaranteed by representative democracy, but a highly unstable agonistic truce that is not necessarily destined to last. It does not 'conclude' the historical process, but only suspends hostilities that are always likely to break out again, sooner or later.

Somewhat similarly, the American Constitution entrenched an oscillating balance between oligarchic and wealthy forces on the one hand and mass direct democracy on the other. In this case, however, because of the separation of powers, and the further separation between Senate and Congress, one can argue that the balance has proved both a more stable and a more sterile one than in the case of England, and one which has somewhat less permitted the vagaries of oscillation. Ankersmit is indeed right to see this contrast as still more marked between American and Continental parliamentary democracy – which is far more open to either radical forces speaking for the many or right-wing forces seizing absolute control and undemocratically not relinquishing it, just to the measure that it is also more genuinely democratically responsive. Yet even if the United States democracy is, as he says, more 'metaphysical' and less opportunist, it *was* nevertheless still founded on compromise, and so in consequence the 'metaphysics' which it instantiates is not only that of sheer mimetic representation (as Ankersmit implies) but also one of ensuring a permanent balance between a moneyed oligarchy on the one hand and mass opinion on the other.

In the case of the Continental democracies, they were, as Ankersmit recounts, the product of the attempt of the French Restoration to produce order out of chronic and unmediable socio-political division between revolutionaries and legitimists. He argues (more than debatably in the former case) that both the German Romantic ironists (mainly Friedrich Schlegel and Adam Müller) and the French 'doctrinary liberals' of the 1830s (supremely Victor Cousin) can be seen as already 'political post-moderns' insofar as they advocated (and in France brought about) the establishment of a neutral, impartial 'void' at the heart of the governmental regime, and even dialectically ironised the differences between left and right – thus Alexis de Tocqueville famously showed how the extreme centralisation of the *ancien régime* was the real cause of its own downfall, while this very centralisation project was the thing which the revolution

---

[77]   However, in the twentieth century the Tories became progressively more liberal, while the Labour movement has always had a High Tory element in its legacy – via both popular Methodism and the influence of John Ruskin, besides the influence of a Tory background on many of its leaders.

most successfully promoted. Whether the people had benefited from the revolution was a moot point: unquestionable was the fact that, once the king's head had been removed, state bureaucracy expanded, according to a logic which I have just described.[78]

In the tradition of the Romantics as he debatably understands them (following the lead of Carl Schmitt),[79] Ankersmit argues for an ironising politics which now brings to the fore the latent aestheticised and amoral character of the modern representation paradigm as such. Since representation as mimesis (which Ankersmit wrongly confuses with older representation as identity) is impossible, it needs to be thought of in terms of representation as 'substitution' – and we have already abundantly seen how the one is bound to turn into the other. Since he eschews all participatory identity, Ankersmit openly embraces and celebrates a naked gulf of alienation between rulers and ruled based upon an artistic paradigm borrowed from Arthur C. Danto and Ernst Gombrich, according to which art cannot possibly involve any *tertium comparationis* between representation and represented, since the represented thing is only there for us as an 'independent reality' (redundant for the pragmatic tests of natural science) when it is freely and arbitrarily represented by some sort of symbolic depiction.[80] Similarly, the represented people are only first politically 'there' when they are represented, such that politics springs up within this 'between' as Ankersmit puts it – though we can add that this is a false between, as it is a merely external relation that in no way constitutes its two poles through the intrinsic binding of both in friendship confessing a shared teleology. Ankersmit also fails to see that on this model both the people and the ruler are always latently abjected in the manner of Giorgio Agamben's 'reduction to bare life', since their respective independent realties are at once recognised (this is not, as Ankersmit insists, an idealism) and yet discounted as irrelevant to the political.[81] Thus a merely nominal contractual bond forming the representing/represented of the 'between' could potentially at any time be deemed inapplicable – leaving either a private citizen or a disgraced ruler entirely outside the social fictions in which forms of subjective 'right' can possibly be recognised.

---

[78] Ankersmit, *Aesthetic Politics*, 115–162; Alexis de Tocqueville, *The Ancien Regime and the French Revolution*, trans. Stuart Gilbert (London: Collins, 1969), 61–70, 84–103, 211–221.
[79] Carl Schmitt, *Political Romanticism*, trans. Guy Oakes (Boston, Mass.: MIT Press, 1991). But I eventually hope to contest this reading of the political thought of Novalis et al.
[80] Ankersmit, *Aesthetic Politics*, 45–61.
[81] See Giorgio Agamben, *Homo Sacer: Sovereign Power and Bare Life* (Stanford, Calif.: Stanford University Press, 1998).

Within Ankersmit's Gombrich-derived model of 'substitutionary' representation, politicians must act like truly creative artists, developing their own style in an endeavour to resolve conflicts by distracting attention towards that diverting spectacle which they encourage and develop. They should not pretend only to mirror the social facts, nor to mirror or erect ethical values, since there are no foundations for these on which all can agree – as modern mimetic liberalism already effectively presumed. In this way they will be more able to link themselves to the independent state function, luring the bureaucrats into their own stylistic project and thereby ensuring the greater visibility of the state function to the people. Paradoxically, *less* participation and *more* representation will ensure the only attainable measure of democratic accountability.

The problem with this proposal is that such a liberal 'aesthetic state' is surely a mode of novel 'liberal fascism' (as, arguably, we already have in the early twenty-first century). The state will only be more visible because of the yet greater engulfing of all in the propagandistic spectacle. It cannot thereby become more accountable. But the interest of Ankersmit's candour is that he exposes to just what degree the modern state is a pastiche of a pre-modern polity and of its ideal of a 'mixed regime' (blending, in various degrees according to circumstance, the democratic with the aristocratic and the monarchic). The role of the sovereign one beyond representation has not really vanished: it has merely been both bureaucratised and aestheticised. It still *has* to judge for itself beyond its popular mandate, but it no longer supposes that this judging takes place within the orbit of a belief in an objectively good *telos* for the human social animal. Instead, an abjected animal side of our humanity is policed in the 'rational' interests of state power itself, while supposedly animal desires are lured by the spectacle of a purely artificial glamour, without any intrinsic meaning. But the mark of the lack of any mediation between our animality and our cultural reason is the absence even from Ankersmit's *pastiche* of the pre-modern of the crucial mediating aristocratic few (in whatever guise) who might integrate the gaze of the rulers with the return gaze of the ruled.[82] We remain thereby trapped in an aesthetic or dramatic model of spectatorship or 'double passivity', where the two parties cannot really interact, as they would within a more ritualised politics, for which style and

---

[82]   He can only recruit Tocqueville for the cause of postmodern irony by neglecting to discuss the French writer's desire to find modern equivalents for the aristocratic mediating role – in the case of the United States he located this in the churches, though admittedly his attitude to this phenomenon was complex and by no means as entirely optimistic as American redactors often like to claim.

living performance are blended in terms of shared vision. Within such an older outlook, elements of direct democracy become possible at a local level to which as much as is appropriate should be assigned (according to the principle of subsidiarity), while the necessity for representation at a higher level (where direct democracy must, indeed, degenerate into a sham, for reasons which we have seen), has to include aspects *both* of identity with the many *and* of independent creative style pursued by the one and the few – but within the horizon of the search for the objectively good fulfilment of all.

Contra Ankersmit, art itself, which is his operative paradigm, *was* once thought (up to and beyond the eighteenth century) to depend upon a *tertium comparationis*: this, as Panofsky described, was 'the idea' common at once to transcendent reality, to the artist's *concetto* or *disegno* and to the work which then comes to embody a 'design' in itself.[83] Ultimately Ankersmit assumes such mediation to be impossible in the political sphere, because he accepts that the function of the dispersed populace is purely economic in the sense of a kind of feral anarchy, while he equally sees the function of the representing and artistic sovereign as purely political in the sense of a sheer artifice. In this way, the political possibility of 'animal rationality' goes unconsidered, as the possibility of a material striving that intrinsically seeks a 'self-government' as the intuition of a more than human order which it must presuppose, else it resigns itself to anarchy and the rule of the strong, even if this be the aesthetically strong who (to allude to the 1960s) have 'revolted into style' – neither a high one nor a low one, but instead that of an avant-garde turned inexorably middle-brow.

In advocating this stylistic turn, Ankersmit is not able to explain how it can be other than a new mode of fascism and nihilism. Yet his acute powers of analysis are instructive, and almost in self-criticism he points out how bad *any* form of modern representative democracy is in dealing with problems that are not to do with social or ideological conflict but rather with external or structural threats facing the *whole* of society: he cites eco-logical crisis, traffic jams (which all hate but all contribute to) and crime (where the democratic state, unlike the monarch, can be largely indifferent to private victimage, since its own very secure authority is not thereby really impugned, even though in not 'personally' associating with the victim – like the monarch – it tends to insist all the more that a crime is really a crime against the law and not against other human beings).[84] To this one could also add poverty, plus extreme economic inequality

---

[83] Panofsky, *Idea*, 33–99.
[84] Ankersmit, *Aesthetic Politics*, 195–205.

(where there is now no one clear 'class' to take this up as a sectional cause), the increasing absence of any interpersonal loyalty,[85] as opposed to enforced respect for law and work rules, which results in ever more amoral behaviour in people's leisure time,[86] and the decline of deference towards genuine excellence, achievement and wisdom – which leaves most in the double of bind of supposing that they are 'as good as anyone else', yet also knowing that, without the benefit of any real education or guidance, they are impotent to realise this potential, resulting in a permanent idiom of sulky irritation.

These problems cannot be dealt with by democracy as we know it, because they require that the entire community, through the mediation of the state, exercise an 'animal rationality' in the sense of judging what is best for us in the future as a whole. Nor do these problems only exist as ironic 'unintended outcomes', as Ankersmit claims. That is only true to a degree, because, for example, traffic jams are an all too predictable result of certain priorities whose bad consequences we have indeed objectively 'intended', even if we like to pretend otherwise. Driving too much and too needlessly in-tends – 'tends towards' – the traffic jam. No: irony is often the rebound of the denial of teleology, and the sheerly reserved, ironic sovereign state based upon supposed procedural neutrality (between ideologies and between religions) cannot deal with deservedly ironic upshots that cause all too real suffering. What is rather required – as I shall later contend – is some sort of more democratic and freely creative variant on the *genuine* 'mixed regime' of pre-modernity.

5   On Legal Concurrence

In addition to political univocity, political nominalism and political substitution, there is a third respect in which Scotism and the *via moderna* tended to undermine trans-organicity

This is the way in which they simultaneously de-biologised and biologised the will, newly sundering it between rationality and animality. For an older view, the will was in continuity with an organic tending towards an end because it was only moved if it was informed by reason, while reason had to be reciprocally moved by right desire. But now, if will concerns primarily a purely unmotivated choice, it is apparently elevated above animal desires,

---

[85]   In Christian terms this means an increasing state of 'sin' which is the absence of charity, understood in the traditions of Augustine and Aquinas as reciprocity and friendship.
[86]   See n. 30 above.

so much so in Descartes's philosophy that the human will in principle enjoys univocally the same scope as that of God.[87] This spiritualised will can then be considered by Kant as exhibiting the highest sort of reason, which is practical reason, because it is the most autonomous: concerned simply with reproducing the conditions for its own freedom as self-governance.[88] On the other hand, will which wills itself must always incidentally will also something (as Kant recognised) in order to be able to will itself. Therefore, a will defined formally and no longer teleologically, as simply the will to will, must also be a will which wills *aliquid*, some sort of indifferent content. This aspect to willing is therefore purely natural and can only be considered to be what Nietzsche would later term a 'will to power'.

Such a double tendency had implications for the conception of law, both in ethics and in politics. For later medieval and early modern scholasticism, the cause of a moral act had been likewise typically twofold. On the one hand, there was the 'form' of law as derived from divine command and so rendered valid by the decision of the divine will. On the other hand there was the human 'act' of judgement as to what falls under this law and what should be considered 'right' from a purely natural point of view. Only the imposition of the form of divine law, however, rendered the action fully moral or just.[89] Here one sees a causal 'concurrence' at work between two collaborating elements, albeit that one is higher and more decisive than the other. No longer is the divine law regarded as primarily something rational which intrinsically 'influences' the human act, moulding it from within, such that it only registers legality *through* judgement and *through* the prudential application of a historically inherited general maxim to the specific instance which confronts it.

So in the political case also, will conceived as 'sheer choice' destroys the way in which will as desire lured by right reason conserved rational animality through an aspect of 'rational drive'. The new notion promotes legal rationalism as a legal positivism which reduces jurisprudence to a system of repeatable procedures and rules for handling precedent. Modern law conceived in this manner no longer thinks of a code of laws as primarily offering a rough guide to the way a society should be, as both the ancient law codes of Israel, Athens, Sparta and Rome, and the medieval law codes of Christendom and Islam undoubtedly did.[90] Instead, it is newly and

---

[87]   Descartes, *Meditations*, 'Fourth Meditation', 57, p. 40.

[88]   Immanuel Kant, *Groundwork of the Metaphysics of Morals*, trans. Mary Gregor (Cambridge: Cambridge University Press, 2012).

[89]   See de Muralt, *L'Unité de la philosophie politique*, 35.

[90]   I am indebted to discussions with Dr Caroline Humfress of Birkbeck College London on this point.

primarily concerned with rigorous implementation of the letter of the law, in a way which the ancient codes never envisaged, or was for them in practical terms impossible. So as to the spirit and content of the political law, this derives from the divine freedom, mediated through the freedom of the ruler or the collective wills of the individual citizens. *Ius* respects first and last *libertas* and so is based upon *voluntas*, which sundered from reason has nothing left to express except natural *potestas*. A modern politics that despairs of the promotion of virtue must therefore confine itself to the rational inhibition of human animality, yet at the empty heart of its reasonings a more cunning animality sits enthroned, and can even be hypostasised as the almighty deity. It is perhaps at this point that secular liberal modernity and the most radically disenchanted modes of Islam both confront each other and yet converge.

6   The Fate of the Social Animal

Just as, for Aristotle, Aquinas and John Fortescue, human reason was not a kind of 'add-on' to human animality, so, likewise, human sociality was no such 'add-on' either. Unlike the Stoics, and the Latin Church Fathers (to some degree), these three authors did not think of social and political institutions as only necessary to restrain human individuals after the lapse of the golden age or the expulsion from Eden. They did not therefore regard them as a kind of 'substitute' for a spontaneous lost anarchic peaceableness. Rather, they saw the architectonic dimension of human association as crucial to the ordering of positive activities like sexual love, childbearing, education, agriculture, manufacture and trade.

Thus the idea of asocial or apolitical human beings, which also means the idea of acultural human animals, was for these thinkers a fantasy. Social structures are not to be taken as inhibiting or redirecting our specific mode of animality, but as expressing it. All the same, Aristotle already identified a certain artistic or 'architectonic' factor as predominant in the political organisation of human society,[91] and Aquinas, who recognised, following Augustine, a greater range of legitimate human institutions, and

---

[91]   Aristotle, *Ethics* 1141b20–27: 'Political science and prudence are the same state of mind, but their essence is not the same. Prudence concerning the state has two aspects: one which is controlling and directive [i.e. a kind of *techne* or *poesis*], is legislative science; the other, which deals with particular circumstances, bears the name which properly belongs to both, viz political science.'

had direct experience of the ecclesial promotion of new, constitutionally governed voluntary associations, accentuated this artificial and consensual dimension – even if he was by no means, as Lord Acton (Whiggishly) supposed, 'the first Whig'. So once again we are talking about a strange kind of 'trans-organism', an animality inclined to social artifice from the very depths of its animality and an architectonic law-shaping power that still expresses – and in a sense only expresses – the impulses of the herd or the pack.

As André de Muralt argues, this conception is far truer to the *historical* character of humanity than early modern and later obsessions with either the state of pure human nature or dreams of ideal utopia.[92] This should give us pause for thought when considering the common view that the Middle Ages had little 'historical sense'. Perhaps this begs too many questions (especially about the continuity of Renaissance proto-historicism in writers like Francisco Patrizi with medieval thought), and it should also be noted that, when the Romantic era recovered a sense of historicity as not subordinate to enlightened 'progress', it also recovered a sense of the importance of the organic and a renewed resonance with 'gothic' phenomena.[93]

Human beings are found always already within family structures (which are far more similar from culture to culture than intellectual fashion once allowed),[94] within local economies, within cities and vestigial states, as well as within multiple forms of brotherhoods and sisterhoods (esoteric or open) that are as old as the existence of more encompassing tribal formations. Human history, one might say, has always been biological – it has involved the surprisingly regular unfolding of the human organism. Yet equally, human biology has always been historical: the peculiarity of *human* organicity is its resort to endlessly original artifice and its invention of variations sometimes so astonishing that they equal or exceed in significance the import of the generic organic categories. For example, 'Rome' is a reality greater than 'empire' in general; *ecclesia* than religious body in general; 'Greek theatre' than ritual performance in general; the *polis* than urban settlement in general; cinema (which makes images and even scenes 'sing' in conjunction, like music) than modes of artistic representation in general.

---

[92] De Muralt, *L'Unité de la philosophie politique*, 64–65, 87.
[93] By comparison, strictly Enlightenment interest in historicity tends to be fixated on the difference of the supposedly 'primitive' and the logical social processes by which this evolved into the 'civilised'. See section 10 of this sequence below.
[94] See Adam Kuper, *The Invention of Primitive Society: Transformations of an Illusion* (London: Routledge, 1988), 17–41, 190–230.

But what it is above all important to realise here is that, while indeed the highest level of social unity which is the political (the tribe, the city, the state, the empire etc.) is necessary for the existence of human sociality as such – without this there would be no unified language and set of shared customary practices, even amongst hunter-gatherers – nonetheless human sociality does not reside only at this centralised and overarching level. Modernity likes to fantasise that it does, by deciding that only the abstracted individual is of political or even social relevance – it is he or she who must be educated, disciplined, recorded, taxed and so forth. The family, local economies, even the economy as a whole, along with voluntary associations, are treated as if they were politically incidental, save as legitimate expressions of freedom, while inversely these organisations are no longer considered to be themselves mediators of political power, in contrast to the traditional paternal family (however much we may regret the inherited undervaluation of maternal authority), the 'feudal' manor, the Church itself and the various religious orders and organisations.

This creates a very strange situation. For on the one hand political society *really* starts to conform to this shape, and with dire results. For as Edmund Burke put it, it is now the case that 'laws are to be supported only by their own terrors, and by the concern, which each individual may find in them, from his own private speculations, or can spare to them from his own private interests. In the groves of *their* academy at the end of every visto, you see nothing but the gallows'.[95] (Burke is here speaking of the enlightened revolutionaries in France.)

Yet on the other hand, this shape is objectively a distortion, because in reality individuals only exist, even now, through participation in groups below the level of the state, and all these groups perforce *do* take on certain quasi-political functions. Indeed, one of the most complex ironies of modern economic history is the way in which it commences with the abolition of guilds and corporations that included political functions (defined at least originally in terms of the promotion of public and private virtue) and yet of itself, by the exaltation of abstract wealth and the sole reign of the profit motive, tends to engender monopolies that are protected by law and finally attain to the quasi-political standing of *modern corporations*, even though they remain formally only economic in their *raison d'être*, and are often protected from the full public (economic, social and political) consequences of their actions by the 'limited liability' norms under which they operate. Surely Catholic political thought has been right

95   Edmund Burke, *Reflections on the Revolution in France*, ed. Conor Cruise O'Brien (Harmondsworth: Penguin, 1982), 171–172.

to suppose that social justice will only be achievable in any measure when we have once again re-politicised these corporate bodies and subjected them to appropriate levels of dispersed control, within a new social and political understanding of what their aims must be, strictly subordinating the pursuit of profit to the attainment of socially and naturally desirable ends?[96]

By contrast, the pre-modern polity saw itself explicitly as a *societas societarum*. There was no idea here of a centrist rational regulation of atomic 'natural' individuals, because all individuals were already socialised and politicised in institutions below the level of the state. This was not, of course, to fall into another modern trap of supposing that therefore the ultimate 'state' authority is comparatively artificial and only regrettably necessary, like a sort of unfortunate substitution for the intrinsically better reality of local rule (many misreadings of the Catholic principle of subsidiarity make this mistake).[97] On the contrary, the overarching state function is necessary to preserve within an overarching legal framework the very existence of the lesser corporate realities. Moreover, it is not 'neutral' with respect to the economic and the familial, as the modern state is in theory, and as modern 'conservatism' (which, like Christopher Tietjens in Ford Madox Ford's novel *Parade's End*, never looks back before the already ambivalently modern eighteenth century) tends to recommend.

---

[96] For contemporary Catholic proposals for a neo-corporatism, see John Médaille, *The Vocation of Business: Social Justice in the Marketplace* (London: Continuum, 2007). Also very suggestive, if insufficiently critical of capitalism, is Jonathan Boswell's *Community and the Economy: The Theory of Public Co-operation* (London: Routledge, 1990). In general the fault of 1930s corporatism was often to treat capital interests as if they were authentic 'organic' ones like manorial overlordship in the past. Precisely because capital is based upon unjust appropriation and the amoral pursuit of power, this mistake carried the seed of a fascistic corruption of the corporatist ideal. On the question of the hazy boundary between Catholic corporatism and fascism in the Portuguese case, see the 1937 manifesto of António de Oliveira Salazar, *Como se reergue um estado* [*Comment on relève un État*] (Lisbon: Esfera do Caos, 2007). After the Second World War, the European Christian Democratic parties for a short time tried to pursue a more liberal version of corporatist and personalist ideals, but again the confused compromise with capitalism ensured that they were quickly overtaken by Adenauer and de Gaulle's commencement of the long-term switch towards economic liberalism. Nevertheless, humanity needs in the future – as indeed the early British Labour party already realised – a blend of corporatism with co-operativism, because worker co-operatives are not appropriate to every level of economic organisation. But larger, more hierarchical firms serving social and political as well as economic purposes should still subordinate the pursuit of profit to socially and politically beneficial purposes and the levels of profits and salaries require collective determining by regulatory bodies concerned with issues of substantive justice.

[97] This has been pointed out to me by Russell Hittenger of the University of Tulsa.

Rather, since it is not really a 'state' function in the modern sense at all, it rules through its ownership of 'eminent domain', its elevated concern with economic flourishing and with the upholding of family honour. Hence kings in the Middle Ages concerned themselves with the granting of economic 'liberties' and licences, including the minting of money, and with the sustaining of patriarchal order.

It follows that traditional (ancient and medieval) political thought and practice laid much stress upon the role of intermediary associations between the 'one' centre on the one hand, and the 'many' dispersed individuals on the other. These were seen as the sites for the formation of virtuous practices which central rule must then co-ordinate and redirect. However, the number of these associations was greatly augmented by the presence of the Church, and its problematic doubling of central authority. This meant that, *within* the secular (time-bound) domain of practices like agriculture, education, law, medicine, manufacture, building, trade, banking and warfare, there emerged monastic, mendicant, university and guild organisations which, to use set-theoretical parlance, 'diagonalised out' of this domain altogether, by subordinating aspects of secular practice to the supernatural ends of the Church which lay beyond those of this-worldly legal concern – if not, however, beyond those of the king, who, as himself anointed, was supposed to have an ultimate onlook to just this subordination.

The upshot of this phenomenon was considerably to augment the role of those intermediary associations which were constitutional, voluntary bodies or 'corporations' dedicated to considered ritual practices, ideal modes of organisation and the furtherance of inspired rational reflection. And this meant in turn that gothic vertical organic hierarchy was much complicated by an equally gothic horizontal elaboration of overlapping and often competing jurisdictions and ideals.[98] Eventually, this perhaps proved too much to contain with any semblance of order, but while it lasted it emphasised to a unique new degree the interfusion in 'the middle' of society of familial with economic, craft, contemplative and religious functions. These voluntary intermediate bodies most of all guaranteed the integralism of the trans-organic, and they even made this sphere of the 'between', like a kind of foretaste of resurrection (as seen in the rambling yet aspiring gothic cathedral, in contrast to the sepulchral womb-fortress of the Romanesque edifice),[99] paradoxically exceed the secular totality and the secular height of rational governance. Both the recognised human

---

[98]   See John Milbank, 'On Complex Space', in *The Word Made Strange*, 268–292.
[99]   See Victor Hugo's novel *Notre Dame de Paris*, trans. Alban Krailsheimer (Oxford: Oxford University Press, 1993), Book III, 119–152.

fragility of free constitutions acknowledged to be imperfect, and the aspiration to modes of reconciliation in excess of an uneasy secular truce, tended to qualify the power-claims of secular rulers and helped to ensure that medieval kingship remained on the whole within constitutional bounds.

One could say that, by further developing the role of the independent corporation (a development which has fragmentarily continued well beyond the medieval epoch – providing another crucial sense in which 'we are still medieval'),[100] the Middle Ages augmented the role of 'the few', understood as those who are virtuous and able to guide others in the path of virtue, in traditional political thought. It would seem appropriate here to speak of a novel 'extended few', resulting from a kind of Christian dispersal, diversification and democratisation of the ancient 'aristocratic' principle, understood as both the political rule of virtue, and rule taken to have the inculcation of virtue as its proper goal.

In this respect the medieval period exhibits just the opposite tendency to modern political theory, if not so obviously to modern political practice – remembering here that, in reality, even eighteenth-century Whigs (or at least one faction amongst them[101]) appealed against modern absolutism far less to Locke than they did to 'gothick' constitutionalism (as the landscaped grounds of a Whig magnate at Stowe in Buckinghamshire so clearly reveal), even if their understanding of its theoretical underpinnings in the promotion of public and Christian virtue was somewhat inadequate.[102]

But modern political theory, which is always *liberal* political theory, and which has continued to grow more and more influential up to and including our own day, is characterised by an attempt to excoriate and remove the role of the few, regarded as the seat of privilege, of non-consensual power, of debatable claims to ethical value and as a threat alike to overall unity and individual liberty. Cogent as these objections may appear, they have often

---

[100] For example, the tremendous growth in legal 'societies' of all kinds in Victorian Britain gave women a new experience of participation in public debate and organisation which significantly fuelled the later demand for female suffrage. This factor was arguably more causally important than the liberal argument for the equal 'right' of women to vote, taken one by one, just as the gradual increase in the social and political participation of women is of greater moment and worth than their acceding to formal representation.

[101] These were the 'patriot Whigs' like Bolingbroke, in the current that eventually led to the thought of Edmund Burke, who remained a Whig, for all his later fêting by Tories. The patriot Whigs were less Lockean and contractualist in their approach to constitutionalism, and tended to see this as rather a matter of organic evolution, with strong medieval roots. I am grateful to discussions with Alison Milbank on this matter.

[102] See J.C.D. Clarke, *English Society 1688–1832* (Cambridge: Cambridge University Press, 1985), 42–64.

been countered within liberalism itself from Althusius through Burke and Tocqueville to late nineteenth-/early twentieth-century 'pluralists' who have pointed out that, since the isolated individual is a fiction, no individual possesses any real liberties unless he can express these through the relative freedom of the local corporate body – the school, the club, the hospital, the trade union, the co-operative association and so forth.

Nevertheless, the main line of liberal theory, which has ceaselessly tended to radicalise itself, has always sundered the body of the social animal by removing the integrating role of intermediary associations in general and that of the 'virtuous few' in particular.

By contrast, classical political thought considered that every political constitution was a matter of a balance between the one, the few and the many or the ruler (king or emperor), the aristocracy (of land or virtue) and the working populace at large.[103] From a modern point of view it was totally 'non-ideological', for two reasons. First of all, it usually considered that all these three elements would be present in any political order and had no *a priori* interest in extirpating the political role of any one of these three elements in favour of any one of the others. Secondly, although there were divergent theories as to the most 'perfect' political order (monarchic, aristocratic or democratic), antique and medieval political theory generally

---

[103]   See Plato, *Republic* 543a1–569b5; Aristotle, *Politics* 1279b–1288b; 1325a17–1325b33. Unacceptable forms of political rule were in classical times generally considered to be degenerations of the three acceptable types: tyranny of monarchy, oligarchy of aristocracy (or 'timocracy'), ochlocracy (or 'demagoguery') of democracy. It was also thought that the three good forms, followed by their respective degenerations, succeeded each other in a process of 'anacyclocis' beginning with monarchy and ending in ochlocracy, before a new cycle began with the emergence of one strong and virtuous individual. This was extensively expounded by the Greek historian Polybius in his history of Rome: Polybius, *Histories*, Book VI. The Islamic philosopher Ibn Khaldun later 'sociologised' this theory, by arguing that an excessively urban life had to be periodically renewed by rural purity and energy; since the eighteenth century such notions have generally been incorporated into European versions of Polybian theory. One could validly say that, following the Enlightenment, modern substantive philosophy of history remains a battle between those advocates of progress who imagine that, with the advent of the modern state, we have now escaped cylicity in favour of endless progress towards an 'end' of history (Adam Smith, G.W.F. Hegel, Karl Marx) – which secularises the heterodox Joachite notion of an 'age of the Spirit' after that of the Son, and those who think that modernity is an illusion and that we remain within the eternal antique cycles (Adam Ferguson, Oswald Spengler and, to a degree, Leo Strauss). One can also argue that Christian (specifically Catholic, Anglican and Orthodox) philosophical historians provide, after the example of Augustine, a synthesis: cyclically interruptive progress is only by virtue of grace: otherwise civilisational political cycles will ineluctably reassert themselves (Giambattista Vico, Christopher Dawson, the earlier Arnold Toynbee, Nicolas Berdyaev). This issue of metahistory will be much further developed in *On Divine Government*.

subordinated such preferences to the more relative and pragmatic question of the most suitable constitution given particular geographical, social and historical circumstances. And amongst these circumstances, the most crucial was that of the relative prevalence of ethical virtue. In Aristotelian terms, this meant that an 'aristocratic' polity remained the guiding lodestar for any regime whatsoever. For such a polity was defined as governance by virtuous rulers, intended to promote virtue in the ruled, though these roles are in principle reversible and reciprocal. Nevertheless, for Aristotle and many others this gold standard was not a utopia to be imposed, but something only achievable in certain specific historical circumstances. In other circumstances the rule of virtue might have to be much more distantly approximated.

So where one man was obviously outstanding, it was considered that he should rule, although this notion was generally viewed with sensible ambivalence.[104] On the other hand, if there was an elite body exemplifying the right virtues relevant to politics, then this body should rule. Democracy, or rather 'polity' for Aristotle ('democracy' being defined by him as its debased form of mob rule),[105] was appropriate either if a modicum of virtue was widely distributed, or if virtue was totally lacking and the balance of vice with vice was the best that one could aspire to. Aristotle regarded true 'aristocracy' as a balance between the rule of the virtuous few with 'political' rule of all in the interests of all, but with a bias to the judgements of the former (as in Plato's *Laws*), while he regarded 'polity', which is most often the best resort in middling circumstances, as embodying the same mixture but with a bias towards popular governance.[106]

It should therefore be obvious that there was no question of 'conservative' versus 'progressive' politics within this ancient outlook, much less of 'right' versus 'left' – a division which descends to us only from the aftermath of the French Revolution, which has already been discussed. Of course both right and left factions have conspired since then to understand the pre-modern as 'conservative'. But in all critical rigour we must reject this as anachronistic. The meaning of the pre-modern for us today is not that of the 'conservative' or the 'traditional' – rather, it confronts us as an enigma which challenges all our modern preconceptions. It requires

---

[104]   See Aristotle, *Politics* 1285b33.
[105]   This is 'ochlocracy' or 'demagoguery' for other writers.
[106]   Aristotle, *Politics* 1294b14–18. See also John Milbank, 'Dignity Rather Than Rights', in Christopher McCrudden, ed., *Understanding Human Dignity* (Oxford: Oxford University Press, 2013).

us also to see that these preconceptions rest upon a new theological idiom born in the Middle Ages themselves – an idiom by no means obviously more 'progressive' than the *via antiqua*, but simply different. Indeed the philosophical *via moderna* is not named modern because of its 'modernity' in our sense; rather, our sense of 'the modern' is derived both from this philosophical 'way' as well as from the new aesthetic path shaped in seventeenth-century France after the intervention of Descartes.[107]

How exactly did modern political thought remove the role of the few? Here we need to advert to two metaphysical *topoi*, the one nominalist and the other Scotist. First of all, there is the central claim of nominalism itself: there are no real universal essences, even existing within our minds. This had a direct political correlate, as has long been known by historical scholars and has been more recently confirmed against some attempts at denial: if there are no universal essences, then neither is there any real 'common good', nor any reality to ideas of 'justice in general'.[108] There are only the claim rights of individuals, grounded upon *de facto* use and possession and the formal co-ordination of these claims. Society cannot be

---

[107]   See John Milbank, 'Sublimity: The Modern Transcendent', in Regina Schwartz, ed., *Transcendence: Philosophy, Literature and Theology Approach the Beyond* (London: Routledge, 2004), 211–234.

[108]   See de Muralt, *L'Unité de la philosophie politique*; Villey, *La Formation de la pensée juridique moderne*; Pierre Mesnard, *L'Essor de la philosophie politique au XVe siècle* (Paris: J. Vrin, 1969); Michel Bastit, *Naissance de la loi moderne: La Pensée de la loi de Saint Thomas à Suarez* (Paris: PUF, 1990); J.-F. Courtine, *Nature et empire de la loi: Études suaréziennes* (Paris: J. Vrin, 1999). For an (inevitably American Catholic) attempted rebuttal of the 'Villey thesis' which derives modern liberalism from nominalism see Brian Tierney, *The Idea of Natural Rights* (Atlanta: Scholars Press, 1997). One can argue that, while Tierney makes some important points (for example that there is no real distinction of *lex* and *ius* in this period, as Villey suggested) his critique fails in four respects: (1) he ignores the strongest evidence in Ockham of links between his nominalist metaphysics and his political outlook as provided by the authors just cited; (2) his derivation of active faculty rights from Gratian and the canonists, as in the *iura* of the imperial electors or the *ius* of the Pope to make new laws is important, but misses the point that such rights were socially conferred according to what was considered to be objective justice and did not rest upon *de facto* ownership or self-ownership as later with Ockham; (3) his linking of non-nominalist thinkers like Bonaventure and Godfrey of Fontaines to an advocacy of something more like rights based upon possession ignores the fact that they still stood within a voluntarist and proto-univocalist lineage of which Ockham was heir: thus these thinkers already thought more in terms of 'private conscience' and will detached from reason and so of motivation and intention as things 'owned' – indeed even one's own poverty was paradoxically 'owned' for the Franciscan theorists and so had a 'claim' upon ecclesial support; (4) his attempt to see continuity from Catholic thought through to Locke forces him, against all the well-known evidence, to see Hobbes as an aberration and to oscillate inconsistently between regarding medieval canonists as 'already liberal', or else Ockham and Locke as 'still corporatist'. In reality, a single theologically voluntarist to liberal tradition, as Villey and

based upon the pursuit of virtue in general and hence the decisive role of the virtuous few tends to lapse.

Moreover, if only individuals are real, then political power must derive from the individual will. This presents us with two options: either a single individual must be all-powerful, or else power can be derived from the many individual wills, provided that they contract with each other in order to delegate sovereign power. In the first case, one may either insist on the derivation of all power from a sovereign centre for pragmatic reasons of securing order in the face of endemic anarchy, as with Jean Bodin and Thomas Hobbes, or else (or yet again in combination with the former option) one may promulgate 'the divine right of kings', a theocratic absolutism which is of course a wholly modern doctrine, unknown to the Middle Ages.[109]

Alternatively, in the second case, one can advocate a distilling of order from many originally isolated wills. This can occur either through the mechanism of the market or that of the state, or more usually both in combination. Here it is taken that an original 'natural' self-interest will be tempered by a reflective 'artificial' self-interest that consents to the operation of a series of mannered, market or legal norms in order to pursue the original self-interest in a securer and more predictable fashion. The 'war of all against all' continues, but it is assumed that most people will trade the relative comfort of engaging in a predictable conflict that is apparently a 'war game' more than a war, for the possibly greater opportunities of victorious gain held out by a more naked, anarchic mode of conflict. Nevertheless, a scarcely concealed *aporia* arises here. If the only basis for submission to the rules is a kind of rule utilitarianism that considers that, on the whole and in the long run, a partial respect for the freedom and desires of others is sensible, then exactly the same calculative logic would endorse an exceptional criminal infringement of these rules if the individual

de Muralt recount, developed the inevitable voluntarist paradox according to which the mark of the absolutely inalienable will is precisely its right to alienate any *content* of willing whatsoever. This resulted in a 'hysterical' oscillation between insistence on liberal freedom on the one hand and exaltation of absolute rule on the other: *both* things being clearly evidenced in Hobbes. Whereas Aquinas thought there was a right to resist tyrants, but that the man justly condemned to death had no absolute right to try to escape from his cell, the voluntarist perspective will tend to lead one to say *both* (with Ockham or Kant) that power has been forever alienated to the king without right of recall, *and* (with Godfrey of Fontaines) that the prisoner may resolve his legal dilemma by reverting to his inalienable natural right of self-ownership – and so by trying to escape. For much more on all this, see Milbank, 'Against Human Rights'.
[109]   De Muralt, *L'Unité de la philosophie politique*, 29–87; on the divine right of kings see Brague, *The Law of God*, 137–139.

can get away with it, and if there is a strong likelihood of stable and permanent benefit thereby accruing to him. And all experience shows that liberal societies also engender pockets, or even dominant aspects, of recidivism and rule by organised crime.

It is true that the 'moral sympathy' tradition deriving from the Cambridge Platonists and Shaftesbury and continued by the Scottish Enlightenment has tempered this liberal contractualism by encouraging the view that 'sympathy' for others is as original as self-concern.[110] Yet since in the Scottish recension sympathy had generally become detached from previously agreed-upon virtues, in the end sympathy is with the self-centred, non-ecstatic concerns of the other. Moreover, Adam Smith was clear that the norms of state government and economic civil society were to refer primarily to the innately stronger negative sympathies based upon fear rather than the positive sympathies based upon empathetic pleasure.[111] Thus a sympathy with those who have been cozened, cheated or assaulted, immediately and before reflection tends to persuade the many to acquiesce in the operation of coercive law and the upholding of economic contract. In this way the ethics of sympathy scarcely qualifies a basic liberal individualism, especially because the sympathising individual has instinctively substituted himself for the other. William Hazlitt's Romantic gloss on this tradition allowed more scope to the 'imagination' of another's predicament that was not one's own, but this predicament remained at base that of an individual, within an individual horizon, not one of shared values or concerns only available to a collective consciousness.[112]

So this alternate favouring of either the one or the many is the ultimate source of our modern political distinctions between 'conservative and right' on the one hand, and 'progressive and left' on the other. But the same genealogy also makes it clear that these apparent opposites are but variations on one metaphysical theme, namely nominalism-voluntarism. The role of the few is here eliminated, because *this* numerical set cannot so readily be construed in nominalistic terms. Unlike the many, a grouping of the few is not merely an aggregate of multiple individuals, but only exists as a corporate unity exceeding the sum of their parts, so long as it is made up of 'aristocrats' bound together by consensus as to virtuous purpose,

---

[110]   See John Milbank, 'The Invocation of Clio', *Journal of Religious Ethics*, 33/1 (Mar. 2005), section 5, 31–36, and Isabel Rivers, *Reason, Grace and Sentiment: A Study of the Language of Religion and Ethics in England, 1660–1780*, vol. 2: *Shaftesbury to Hume* (Cambridge: Cambridge University Press, 2005).

[111]   See Milbank, *Theology and Social Theory*, 28–32; Luigini Bruni, *The Genesis and Ethos of the Market* (London: Palgrave Macmillan, 2012), 87–100.

[112]   Milbank, 'The Invocation of Clio', 35–36.

and not merely by 'oligarchs' unified simply in factional terms of the pursuit and maintenance of landed or moneyed power. In the latter case their factionality is mathematically definable by their merely aggregate character, which borders upon the nature of 'criminal conspiracy' from the perspective of modern politics, since it tends to usurp the proper prerogatives of both central sovereignty and the equal rights of dispersed individuals.

However, this same modern politics is unable to make any discrimination between such prejudicial factionality on the one hand, and the role of guiding, educative bodies on the other. And as I suggested earlier, one can properly extend the semantic scope of the term 'the few' to include all those intermediary associations – family, guild, fraternity, commune, corporation – which only exist at all because of their assumption of, or commitment to, certain (often complex and continuously debated) ethical and vocational norms or aims. These also, like the role of virtuous leadership, run the danger of being de-legalised or even criminalised from a modern political and economic perspective. Thus increasingly the state protects the 'rights' of the individual against all intermediary and voluntary associations – the child against parental authority; the parent against the child's need for a parent to fulfil his or her traditional obligations; the member of a Church or an individual church congregation against ecclesial accusations of heresy or indiscipline; the worker against any requirement that she belong to a vocational association or trade union; the user of a pub or club against any customs, restrictions or health risks that this 'public house' may care to tolerate; businesspeople or business enterprises against any corporate limitations; bankers and financiers against any limitations imposed by traditional codes of practice. But at the same time, this 'liberation' also requires a further extension of *state* regulation of all the individuals, to prevent the emergence of a criminal anarchy, while elements of the latter must now perforce be recruited to the central state interest. For these reasons there is no paradox in the joint extension of 'market freedom' and 'state control' during the recent political epoch dominated by neoliberalism. One should also note that where, as often with Edmund Burke himself, modern conservatism allows a certain role for the aristocratic 'few' and for traditional corporate privileges, this tends to be for fundamentally utilitarian reasons; a fake 'tradition' alone gives substantive stabilising content amidst the dominance of negative formal norms.

However, this conjunction also reveals that, at the deepest structural level, 'right' and 'left' politics always collude, if we take (against the usual now-prevailing taxonomy) the individualist 'market impulse' to be at bottom 'left-liberal', and the controlling collectivist 'state impulse' to be 'right-authoritarian'.

Even if the former takes the more social democratic form of trying to ensure, through health, housing and educational provision, greater equality of opportunity, it still cannot qualify the sway of the free market unless it is prepared to decide upon what is objectively best for all people, or on the co-ordinated variety of what is best for many different aptitudes, and then to promote the full flourishing of all by seeking to encourage the good desires of all. Otherwise, if one is simply giving everyone the maximum chance to express whatever desires they may happen to have, with no sense of assumed norms, there is no real way to encourage an equity of outcomes (ensuring the full realisation of all according to their aptitudes), and instead it becomes inevitable that the excessive and selfish desires of some will continuously erode the conditions for ensuring even an equality of opportunity, never mind acceptable conditions of living and working for all. It follows that any social democracy which has abandoned all sense of objective virtue independent of subjective desire must necessarily remain a variant of liberal philosophy, and moreover one which has no real defences against a more virulent mode of liberalism – as recent history tends to confirm. Even the provision of health, housing and education, on the virtue-neutral account, will have to start to provide equality of provision in terms of 'choice' – an enterprise which of course must favour growing social inequality in these domains.

For one can lay it down as an axiom that only where there is a tacit consensus as to virtue and goal, upheld and promoted by an educated elite, is there any ground for a relatively equal distribution of material and cultural goods. This is exactly why the 'conservative' 1950s exhibited far more economic equality and social mobility than the 'liberated' and 'less deferential' Britain of the early twenty-first century. Or to express the axiom more succinctly: one cannot have equal distribution without a consensus upheld by all, including the powerful, as to the nature and desirability of 'the goods' to be distributed. This consensus will tend to emerge from folk tradition, which more reflective deliberations need critically and yet not slavishly to respect if this entire consensus is not to be undermined.

At this point the post-1960s libertarian left will inevitably issue protests against 'elitism' and 'paternalism', yet this is to beg a large number of questions. Most important of all, there is the point that the conjoint extension of market and state power does not really abolish either paternalism or hierarchy. Instead, it characteristically erects a new hierarchy of 'professional experts' who tend to announce from time to time that some sort of 'empirical research' done by academic functionaries (which a 17-year-old who had read his Feyerabend or Foucault would know how to question) has supposedly undermined yet another time-honoured truth.

In this way folk-wisdom is abandoned in the name of science and the supposed deliverances of nature herself. But in reality it is the self-appointed spokespersons of nature who are assuming in her name vast power over their fellow human beings, while they themselves become slavishly chained to the supposed natural imperatives which they have unearthed.[113]

For example, since the 1960s they have often been in thrall to the idea that the family and the intimate group is necessarily and mainly the site of a game of power-dominance: this very idea dooms one to endless exhausting wariness and the fabrication of new schemes for unleashing this agonistic energy, together with ever newer ones for containing its worst side-effects.[114] Meanwhile, all the traditional tacit controls and encouragements embodied in local associations based upon trust can no longer be appealed to, because they have to be regarded with expert, objective and detached suspicion. In this way one can see how hierarchy has not been abolished or even tempered – because it cannot in principle be abolished at all, unless real anarchy were possible (which is identical with 'pure democracy'). Instead, we now have a far worse hierarchy than in the past – however far short of anything ideal that may have been. A hierarchy of sheer money, force and spectacle; a hierarchy without even any pretensions to virtue, inspired by a merely shallow romance, whose inspiration has quickly faded.[115] The alternative to this is clearly *not* the abolition of stratification. What could that possibly mean? Every hysterical refusal of mastership is always in reality the equally hysterical demand for a new and more absolute master, as Jacques Lacan famously saw.[116] The alternative is rather the re-creation of a social situation in which folk-transmission of norms and educated reflection upon these norms regain a fruitful interaction within a common horizon.

Most forms of social democracy and state socialism, therefore, fail to qualify the norms of liberal individualism. The left, for this reason, remains overwhelmingly defined by liberalism, and this is just why liberalism in our

---

[113] See C. S. Lewis, *The Abolition of Man: Reflections on Education with Special Reference to the Teaching of English in the Upper Forms of Schools* (Oxford: Oxford University Press, 1942), 39–55.

[114] I derive this point from Adam Curtis's excellent BBC TV series *The Trap: What Happened to Our Idea Of Freedom?*

[115] In this respect Scott Fitzgerald's reading of America in *The Great Gatsby* has proved profoundly prophetic.

[116] Lacan's riposte to the revolting students of 1968 was 'As hysterics, you want a new master. You will get one.' History has proved him abundantly right. This is cited from Slavoj Žižek, *The Parallax View* (Cambridge, Mass.: MIT, 2006), 91.

own day has returned as the normative point of left-reference. Previous 'socialist' norms on the left were either semi-coherent attempts to qualify liberalism which too much assumed liberalism's own terms of reference, or else they derived (especially in the case of religious socialisms) from religious and metaphysical perspectives much at variance with those of modern politics and economics.

One needs here to identify and distinguish: first there was pre-1848 socialism (which was still contending with non-socialist Jacobin state-terror tactics during the revolution of that year), together with elements of Marx's thought, which tended to reject 'economic' categories of price, profit, wage, share and interest altogether, in the name of a mystical fraternity with its ultimate roots in the medieval guild tradition, which it deliberately revived and pitted against liberalism, though without wishing to return to the equally modern bastard-feudalist, pre-revolutionary *ancien régime*.[117]

Secondly there arose, at the end of the nineteenth century, post-marginalist socialisms, including both Fabianism and Soviet communism, that now adopted utilitarian versions of economic categories, whether in a state *dirigiste* or free market guise, or in one of a mixture of the two. Arguably, the Italian co-operativist tradition, together with Catholic social teaching, and much of the mutualist and 'Christian socialist' tradition (inspired equally by Methodism, Anglicanism and Catholicism) of the early British Labour Party, as later elaborated by Karl Polanyi, proffers a third model of 'socialism', even if it has not usually, except in the third case, defined itself as such – though it is entirely logical to do so, since all these currents are also based on the primacy of 'the social' as against the economic or the political. For this third model, in contrast to the other two, economic categories are admitted, but it is not accepted (as the first model did negatively, and the second positively) that economics is disembedded as ethically indifferent on the 'political economy' model of Adam Smith. Instead, the 'civil economy' model of the eighteenth-century Neapolitan economist (and student of Vico) Antonio Genovesi, is either implicitly or explicitly – as in the Italian case – embraced, according to which even economic

---

[117]   See Michéa, *The Realm of Lesser Evil*; Milbank, 'On Complex Space'; 'Were the Christian Socialists Socialist?', in *The Future of Love*, 63–74; 'The Narrative of Blue Labour', in Ian Geary and Adrian Pabst, eds., *One-Nation Labour* (Oxford: Oxford University Press, 2013). Victor Hugo's novel *Les Misérables* (and indeed the recent musical and the film of the musical!) is infused with much of this spirit, even if he did not define himself as a socialist. Both his legacy and that of French Christian socialism were later developed by Charles Péguy in the late nineteenth and early twentieth centuries.

contract can be grounded on mutual 'sympathy', as well as upon self-interest.[118] Hence this third model is more realist than the first, yet more idealist and humanistic than the second.

This more accurate, yet almost never stated, classification completely undermines the common alignment of socialism with the Enlightenment and the abandonment of socialism with 'postmodernism'. For, to the contrary, the triumph of the neoliberal and then neoconservative right represents the re-emergence of unqualified enlightenment (late modern or postmodern) after the abandonment of more communitarian and associationist philosophies derived from the nineteenth century.

It is for this reason that the recent unleashing of market forces belongs at least as much to the politics of the left as to that of the right; this is why it could so easily pass from the superintendence of Margaret Thatcher to the superintendence of Tony Blair.[119] And one should construe the emergence of a libertarian new left in the 1960s, plus the conjoined first attempt to 'democratise' (and thereby also to simplify, commodify and corrupt what might have its legitimate place in terms of certain artistic and critical social functions) hitherto 'Bohemian' norms, as fundamentally in continuity with the later conversion of 'the right' to an unfettered capitalism.[120] The 'conservative' form which the latter 'neoliberal' phase appeared to take should be viewed as accidental, since while it pandered to fears of encroaching anarchy in people's private and local lives, it did nothing really to ameliorate this and finally gave way to the 'New Labour' or 'neoconservative' phase of the substitution of direct state paternalism in the interests of predictable order for the earlier government encouragement of 'traditional family values'.

The politics and the economics of the many remain therefore fundamentally 'left' even where they are nominally 'right', and they remain fundamentally left-liberal even when they are nominally social democratic.

Inversely, the politics and the economics of the one remain always fundamentally conservative and right-wing, even when they go under the auspices of the reverse tendency. For the increasing police defence in our own day of the supposed liberties of the majority against the supposed terror or contagiousness of the few necessarily involves also an increasing

---

[118]   See Johanna Bockman, *Markets in the Name of Socialism: The Leftwing Origins of Neoliberalism* (London: Verso, 2011); Luigini Bruni, *The Wound and the Blessing: Economics, Relationships and Happiness* (New York: New City Press, 2012).
[119]   See Bockman, *Markets in the Name of Socialism*.
[120]   See Phillip Blond, *Red Tory* (London: Faber & Faber, 2011).

restriction of the liberty of all for the sake of the unity and strength of the state. One sees this in terms of the extended criminalisation of injuries to one's own health or the extended surveillance and restriction of all forms of human transport, and also in terms of either the outlawing or else the state and market monopolisation of various modes of dubious enjoyment that exploit sexuality and escapist or aggressive impulses.

However, this is not at all to argue that there is always, in structural terms, a clear distinction between right and left. To the contrary, at the very deepest level, they always remain in collusion with each other. The most fundamental reason for this collusion is the principle of *alienation* which undergirds the representationalist paradigm in its socio-politico-economic form, as already discussed. Already, with William of Ockham, nominalism encouraged not just the alternative of the one or the many, but also their unmediated combination. For Ockham claimed that while, initially, sovereignty belongs with the dispersed populace, taken in the aggregate, once the emperor or king has been elected, sovereignty is transferred to him since it is derived directly by him from God.[121] This alienation is also possible because of the fundamental paradox that ensues from the voluntarist understanding of will as 'self-possession'. Formally speaking, one's freedom is entirely one's own possession and therefore inalienable, since it is now defined by pure choice in independence of any willing of a true end which 'sets one free', as Jesus had it (John 8:32). But in substantive terms, precisely because freedom is ours alone, the *content* of any choice can be absolutely and irrevocably alienated: if one's relation to one's birthright degenerates into one of mere unconditional possession, then paradoxically what belongs to one is just the thing that one can get rid of if one so chooses. To be formally self-possessed is to have the material right to self-dispossession. Thus Ockham's populace (rather like Shakespeare's Richard II handing over power to Bolingbroke) is most of all sovereign in its abandonment of this sovereignty.[122]

7　Representation and Mixed Government

Here we see more clearly the political equivalent to the ambiguity of knowledge as 'substitution' in the field of epistemology. Truth as substitution for being can imply that it is a kind of subservient deputy. Or it can imply

---

[121]　De Muralt, *L'Unité de la philosophie politique*, 115–156.
[122]　See n. 108 above, and Jean Bethke Elshtain, *Sovereignty: God, State and Self* (New York: Basic Books, 2008), *passim*.

that it displaces being altogether. In either case what is denied is the equal dignity of truth with respect to being: namely its co-extension with, and yet aspectual qualification of, the entire ontological field: the 'convertibility' of being with truth. Likewise, in the present case, the initial equal dignity of the one with that of the many is denied; the Aristotelian reality that there only exists manifold society because of the unity imposed by architectonic government, in whatever form it takes. Instead, government is already seen in 'American' guise as but an unfortunate necessity. Thus to begin with, the many are fully a social reality in their own terms, but to sort out the endemic anarchy consequent upon an assumed individualist nominalism they must contract with each other to set up a unified central political power in order to 'represent' both their several and their aggregated interests. Yet because the issue of a formal and conventional peace (a mere 'agreement to differ') is always so pressing, this representation must be also an alienation, and the 'royal' power once established must be viewed as sacral and unlimited in its own right, if it is to possess sufficient scope to establish order. So while, initially, the one substitutes for the original rule of the many by deputising for it, in the end it substitutes for this rule through usurpation.

Of course, this alienation process has usually been mitigated in modern times by constitutional or conventional norms which endorse regular processes of election and re-election for the establishment of sovereign rule. However, alienation as a principle continues in force and cannot really be contained. A government, once elected, remains essentially unaccountable for a period of years: many things which it does within that period cannot easily be undone (in the UK, for example, the publicly unwanted privatisation of the railways and various utilities, or the semi-privatisation of health and schooling over the last thirty years). And as has already been discussed, the structurally sovereign 'position' of ruling is of itself unelected, save in terms of the myth of an original moment of collective contracting. Instead, it never ceases to operate in independence of the will of the people, as though, indeed, it were something directly ordained by the will of God. Thus, between the closing of the polling booths on election night and the announcement of the national result in the early hours of the next day, you can still get arrested by the police for a violation of the still operative law, just as a mass violation of ballot papers would not result in a permanent suspension of the governing function. From government to government this unelected positional centre fosters the incremental growth of traditions and norms of ruling amongst a civil service, even in countries (the United States for instance) where the personnel substantially changes when a new party comes to power.

To reiterate, the point of these observations is not to denounce representative democracy altogether. Rather, it is to point out how the process of alienation is endemic to the representationalist model in either its 'mimetic' or 'substitutionary' versions, which lack the true mediating 'between' which is participatory identity. The original European constitutionalism of corporate bodies assumed such mediation, and therefore participatory government was *not* born in the west as a later response to religious division.

To the contrary, outside a metaphysically realist and intellectualist acknowledgement of intrinsic natural justice, the alienated sovereign power exerted by the one must be alternately theocratic, factionalist, or nationalistic in character (that is, seeking to augment the power of the whole, merely for the sake of this augmentation). Only the personal recognition of equity beyond the letter of the law legitimates the necessarily excessive role in the last instance of the sovereign unified authority.[123] If, however, one grants the sovereign centre in this way a proper and specific role, then one also allows that normally it should be restrained by representation and must ultimately and periodically submit to the judgement of the multitude. Moreover, a more traditional social ontology (see further below) will qualify this entire representational matrix that lies between the many and the one with the role of intermediary bodies. Here indeed direct forms of democracy should be exerted: for example at the level of streets (as in Cuba) and villages or urban localities, besides worker co-operatives where these are appropriate to the nature of the economic enterprise. At the same time, other intermediary enterprises – regional government, business enterprises on a larger scale, universities, religious bodies – require more of an interplay between democratic consultation and the advice and guidance of the virtuous and educated few – given that all education must be rethought in terms of a training in the virtues. This interplay is necessary because, beyond the most local level, elements of innovation and the need for wise guidance in the face of the unexpected become more exigent.

Again, the crucial point here is that we *already have* this role of the few, but in a debased form. Such a role is in reality unavoidable, and the choice is between its being played out in an authentic fashion, or its being corrupted and deployed in the interests *only* of the few, again understood in debased 'fleshly' (material and power-seeking) terms. Abolition of this

---

[123]   At his best, under the influence of Catholic personalists like Erich Przywara, this was how Carl Schmitt regarded the proper role of the sovereign exception, even if it remained unclear whether he thought that this could any longer be exercised in the circumstances of modern politics.

role is not an option, and the idea that it should be basically tolerated but mitigated once more falls prey to the 'paradox of substitution' which I have just detailed for the case of the one. In the case of the few, if the role of 'education and guidance' is regarded as merely a kind of makeweight for a more desirable pure self-direction on the part of the general populace – individually and in the aggregate – then this role will be reduced to one of 'propaganda and management', which quickly and overridingly will become a power-interest in its own right. By contrast, where the role of the few is seen as intrinsically desirable and irreducible – on analogy with the cognitive role of the sensory *species* as it mediates between material thing and spiritual mind – then paradoxically it is less liable to get out of hand.[124] As with the case of the central power, we need the idea that ultimately the one, the few and the many are immediately *identified* with each other (like the form as knowing with the form as sensory and the form as material) in terms of their transmission through time of eternal justice. This is only possible in terms of a realist metaphysic, for which the 'collective personalities' of groupings of the few and the unified character of the one fulfil and sustain all individual personalities, to whose singularity and horizontal relatedness they in turn should yield. A new political order which embodied such a metaphysics would thereby abolish the absolute sovereignty of the one centre which is peculiar to modernity, because sovereignty would now lie in the interplay between the three numerical factors. This must be regarded as a desirable goal, as the upshot of modern democracy since the French Revolution has been far more to increase the power of the continuous executive state than to augment the sway of the will of the people. Where politics pivots on the direct relation between the many and the one, alienation will always outreach representation.

The same logic of alienating representation was detailed by Marx for the economic sphere.[125] Money and capital are supposed to 'represent' human needs, desires and productive achievements, but in reality they usurp them, such that control of an amount of money or capital in itself grants primary power to fulfil needs and desires and to realise productive purposes. Again, in this realm, the extraction of a 'surplus' from worker, consumer, investor and citizen in the form of profit, interest and tax is not really avoidable (as some socialisms fantasise, as already mentioned) if there is to be any economy beyond the household level at all, any

---

[124] As Raymond Geuss points out, Karl Marx defended the necessary role of functional hierarchy against French radical egalitarianism, which he treats with derision in his *Critique of the Gotha Programme*. See Geuss, *Philosophy and Real Politics* (Princeton NJ, : Princeton University Press, 2008), 76–80.

[125] For the account of Marx on this topic which I would give see Milbank, *Theology and Social Theory*, 177–205.

collective enterprise and any reserving of forces for future innovation and expansion. However, the representational logic of liberalism, which in the economic sphere is known as 'capitalism', fails in a certain sense to give a *sufficient* justification for the role of money, capital, interest and profit, by pretending that these things are just neutral abstract means of rendering objectively commensurate the intrinsically incommensurate character of different products, goods and desires. This substitutes for the role of subjective judgement as 'diagonally' mediating the incommensurable, as advocated by Aristotle in Book V of the *Nicomachean Ethics*.[126] In a similar way, capitalism fails to give a *sufficient* justification for the role of private property by treating it as simply a *de facto* matter, or the accidental result of successful competition under the neutral rules of the market.

In the first case, the abstract economic markers should not be viewed simply as 'substitutes' for the real things, in exactly the same way that nominalism views the role of concepts or of linguistic symbols, but rather as necessary ideal manifestations of the analogical co-ordination of the apparently incommensurable, according to tacit notions of a just social distribution. There is nothing esoteric about this, because such tacit notions remain still in play within different regions of our world to a greater or lesser extent, and it is impossible for merely abstract capitalist norms ever to attain to a 'degree absolute' without rendering human society completely unworkable – for example by *entirely* overriding the tacit human sense that food should be both universally available and relatively cheap as compared with other commodities.

In the second case of property, its distribution should not be seen as something with which the political order has no proper concern, as if the wielding of power over matter had nothing to do with intrinsic human value (this being a bad upshot of the at once spiritualising and naturalising Franciscan legacy, whose separation of an ideal 'usage' of things from their 'ownership' tended to leave the latter a sheerly brutal, *de facto* affair).[127] Under this scheme, the life of the individual is treated simply as a factual

---

[126]   See Milbank, 'Dignity Rather Than Rights'; Robert L. Gallagher, 'Incommensurability in Aristotle's Theory of Reciprocal Justice', *British Journal for the History of Philosophy*, 20/4 (2012), 667–701.

[127]   See Milbank, *Theology and Social Theory*, 17–18, and n. 108 above. The Franciscan tendency was to see religious poverty as absolute 'not owning' and so paradoxically as a static 'possessed' state, rather than as an austere way of owning things according to minimum personal and charitable usage. David Aers plausibly argues that the English late medieval poet William Langland, speaking on behalf of the 'real poor' in his masterpiece *Piers Plowman*, criticised the Franciscans for making poverty a more important virtue than a charitable 'fyndinge' of one's path through the things of this world towards God. See his *Sanctifying Signs: Making Christian Tradition in Late Medieval England* (Notre Dame, Ind.: Notre Dame University Press, 2004), 99–156. I am indebted to discussions with Arabella Milbank here.

'given' outside of ethical valuation of her appropriate character and role, just as the roles of the few and the one are seen as merely 'substitutes' for this natural level, again outside any valuation of their ethical function within the social totality. By contrast, an authentic political economy would consider, in line with Catholic and other Christian social teaching, that private property is crucial for the creative development of the individual personality and for its being able to participate in the political process without being subject to economic blackmail – in contrast to the vast majority of mortgage-holders who are only simulated property-owners in the contemporary world. This view favours the greatest possible equal distribution of private property and a justification of larger private property always in terms of both the specific needs and capacities of different individuals (because all are *not* equally gifted or responsible) and the fulfilment of functions which genuinely serve the common good.[128]

Finally, in the social sphere also, norms of civil behaviour, whether in terms of manners or styles of clothes and deportment, are supposed simply to 'represent' the tacitly agreed-upon norms of human behaviour which permit all to be democratically 'present' within the civil sphere. Yet in reality these things have displaced older 'ritual' norms which did not merely represent 'the fashion', but rather expressed an entire normative way of social being within the cosmos.[129] Here dress was not something that conveyed social or individual choice – 'following the fashion' at peril of being considered 'eccentric' – but rather the clothing one wore represented a social role which one aspired to fulfil adequately. It was not a 'substitute' for our nakedness, nor a mere lure to its renewed uncovering, but rather belonged to our intrinsic humanity – like the decorative flowers that Eve may have garlanded herself with in Eden, not the rough animal skins she was forced to don against climactic vagaries after her expulsion. Again one is speaking of the 'trans-organic', an animal clothed as animal – and likewise an animal artificially housed as animal, just as the beaver is an animal who erects dams in streams and rivers. In late medieval England, new 'sumptuary' legislation sought to impose strict dress codes for different social castes under penalties for infringement – but this was already a sign that more informal social conventions regarding role and dress were starting to break down, along with the solidarity and effectiveness of local

---

[128] See, most of all, Hilaire Belloc, *An Essay on the Restoration of Property* (Norfolk, Va.: IHS Press, 2002).
[129] For an account of the general shift from social ritual to social manners, see Catherine Pickstock, *After Writing: On the Liturgical Consummation of Philosophy* (Oxford: Blackwell, 1998), 146–149.

feudal unities, guilds and fraternities.[130] Later, the market and the parade of manners proved far more effective at imposing dress codes which now simply married fashion to economic success and political prestige.

8   Bureaucracy and the Formal Distinction

So far, we have considered the vanishing of the role of the few in terms of the political aspect of a nominalist metaphysic. However, there is also a second aspect which derives from an earlier, Scotistic metaphysic.

Following Ibn Sina, as mentioned in the first sequence, Duns Scotus argued, against Aristotle, that there can be more than one unifying form within a single material substance. This perspective tends to imply that there are other 'virtual' realities latent within the given realities with which we have to deal. The unity of these realities would then seem to be extrinsically and arbitrarily imposed, rather than being an expression of integral essence. In the case of Scotus himself this is only mitigated by the operation of a hierarchy of forms within an individual material substance, according to what now appears to be a somewhat 'imposed' sort of order, which could equally well have been otherwise.[131] In consequence there arises the idea of a single reality with 'formally distinct' aspects that hover between a real division which remains unactualised on the one hand and a merely mental categorisation on the other.

In political terms this encourages the idea of hierarchy more as a functional, administrative necessity than as the expression of a natural, edu-cative order. Such a hierarchy (already of a very 'modern' kind) will on the one hand be under-determined in terms of its innate justification, but on the other hand over-determined in terms of its fixity, non-revisability and closure against social mobility. It also encourages what one could describe as a 'brittle holism'. For just because unity, within this political metaphysic, is more contrivance than organism, it has all the more to be insisted upon, imposed and enforced through the operation of a conventional hierarchy which operates as a 'sham aristocracy', a 'quasi-few', as exampled by some modes of eighteenth-century Whiggery. Equally, the formally distinguished parts of a political totality (formally distinguished at least in terms of their legal personality, since they are really distinguished in their actuality) tend to foster centralisation, since they substitute for the horizontal 'real-relatedness' of truly distinct different social bodies. If, as for Aquinas, social relations are real since they in part constitute the terms of the relation

---

[130]   See A.J. Pollard, *Imagining Robin Hood* (London: Routledge, 2004), 82–110, 134–155.
[131]   See de Muralt, *L'Unité de la philosophie politique*, 14–16.

themselves, then organic unity is already in part sustained without mediation through the centre. This would then be somewhat like an imagined
railway system in Great Britain in which all the various provincial centres
were directly connected with each other – as opposed to the reality, in
which very often they are only connected with each other via a detour
through the capital city, London (even though it is situated in the far south-
eastern corner of the island and is only 'central' by virtue of its Continental
proximity), while the north is only connected to the south of Wales via a
detour through the English Marches. The latter, existing, system one could
say, shows parabolically a Scotist and nominalist bias, since both these
metaphysical systems (nominalism of course even more so) tended to deny
the reality of real, constitutive relations, regarding 'relatedness' as being
just as 'nominal' as the notion of 'universal essence'.[132]

9 Form, Matter and Contract

However, still more significant from a political point of view is the Scotist
real distinction between form and matter. For the Aristotelian understanding,
as we saw, form and matter compose an integral unity, such that matter
'in itself' can only be negatively characterised. But for Scotus and his
legacy, matter becomes a kind of 'quasi-act' in its own right, validating the
theological view that God *could* have created a purely material world, given
the primacy of aleatory possibility over ideally normative actuality.

As André de Muralt points out, there is an analogy between this metaphysics
and the Lutheran view that a corrupted potentiality for sin after the Fall is so
complete as to render any actual performance of the good by a fallen human
being without the assistance of grace an impossibility.[133] For just as Scotus
treated the sheer potentiality of matter to be informed as though this were
a mode of virtual actuality, so also Luther treated a corrupted *habitus* as
though, like an actual deed, it could be *entirely* corrupted, whereas such an
idea of total depravity contradicts the very notion of a habit as a potency and
inversely of evil as privation. Such barbarically poor metaphysics cannot
possibly make good theology – quite aside from the entirely non-biblical
and historically implausible character of this version of 'original sin'.

In Luther's political thinking it resulted in the idea that politics can only
deal in a kind of pragmatic disciplining of irremediably perverse wills which
together constitute an intrinsically amoral sphere that cannot be breached.

---

[132] I am indebted here to discussions with Adrian Pabst, now of the University of Kent.
[133] De Muralt, *L'Unité de la philosophie politique*, 42–44.

This view often in effect gave a theological overlay to the more philosophical consequences of the Scotist real distinction of form from matter, as analogously echoed in the socio-political sphere. For now human beings in their material, animal aspect could be seen as formally contemplatable in abstraction from their cultural and legal institutions. In the late Renaissance or early Baroque period, this gave rise to a strong return to Stoic conceptions of a 'state of nature' as the genesis of political order, and of an explanation of political order in terms of this genesis. But notably, as de Muralt also points out, the irresolvable hesitation as to whether this state of nature was historically real, or was rather a counter-factual abstraction, is entirely true to the undecided character of the Scotist 'formal distinction' – given that the contracting individuals cannot be entirely assimilated to 'matter', but are also akin to the lowest rungs on the hierarchy of forms.[134]

This conception was also directly encouraged by the new theological admission of a *natura pura* that is truly complete and fully human in entire disregard of the question of our supernatural destiny.[135] Thus the 'state of nature', as first articulated especially by Francisco Suárez, is, in effect, 'formally distinguished' within actual human, historical reality as something almost but not quite real and fundamental and yet not merely abstracted according to legal convention. Its epistemological status is already rather like the Kantian transcendental *a priori* synthesis in the sphere of theoretical understanding.

In consequence we get the idea, within modern political theory, of a quasi-prehistorical material base of animal humanity, which 'later' engenders an abstractly formal superstructure, according to a conception of form which has inversely separated it in principle from its integral 'informing' of the material world. In jurisprudential terms this tends further to separate law from custom and from the notion of general topical guidance, rather than rigid application without regard to circumstances – the latter now being engineered to fit the terms of the law, rather than the other way around. Not only are the many thought of as initially isolated individuals; they are also thought of as initially material and sensory beings, not as yet subject to the processes of spiritual refinement.

This circumstance gives rise to that intellectual and practical ethos first dubbed the 'biopolitical' by Walter Benjamin, and further explored by Michel Foucault and Giorgio Agamben in his wake.[136] By the operation of

---

[134]   De Muralt, *L'Unité de la philosophie politique*, 115–119.
[135]   John Milbank, *The Suspended Middle: Henri de Lubac and the Debate Concerning the Supernatural* (Grand Rapids, Mich., and London: Eerdmans/SCM, 2005, 2006).
[136]   See Milbank, 'Paul versus Biopolitics'.

a kind of formal distinction, the animal aspect of our human history is seen as fundamental and original, whereas the civil, economic and political aspects of this history are seen as sheerly artificial. This accords also with the fundamental *aporia* of the seventeenth-century scientific revolution as noted by Bruno Latour: on the one hand scientific knowledge is now defined, according to the Hobbesian *verum-factum* as 'maker's knowledge', such that all that we can truly know is what we have constructed – rendering (as for Hobbes and Locke) what one might variously dub the 'machinic organism' of society or 'the general social experiment' the most knowable thing of all, with human experimental and technological manipulations of nature as but the second most knowable thing. On the other hand, knowledge is now defined as contrivance precisely because, increasingly, only natural processes are deemed to be fully real. And this means that, just to the measure that human beings can alter and manipulate nature, especially their own, so also we see that in all that we do it is only really nature at work, and that, in order to succeed, the best we can hope for is attend to nature as closely as possible and be governed by her even as we attempt in certain respects to master her.[137] It is clear that the construction of automata, especially of anthropomorphic kinds, most of all fuses this double aim. But the automaton sustains the *aporia* of the modern: does it display our psychic mastery of nature, or rather the natural mechanisation of the psychic?

The consequence of this *aporia* is that modernity is constantly trying to set nature loose, while equally it is trying to tame and direct her powers and even to discipline her (in the latter respect, the Protestant and Jansenist account of original depravity tends to come into play). In accord with the latter requirement, if human beings are 'originally' isolated and sensory and so tend to conflict with each other, then these very same feral and competitive instincts must be directed towards a more comfortable coexistence and the expansion of economic wealth and state power. This was one of the main endeavours of the 'enlightened' eighteenth century. However, here also and ever since, one sees an oscillation between the idea of channelling and controlling a supposed human animal nature on the one hand, and 'releasing' this animal nature on the other. The main line of antique Stoic reflection had in fact viewed the pre-political human state as belonging to a blissful golden age, and this idea was taken up again by Jean-Jacques Rousseau, who viewed sociality as originally the contamination of envy and

---

[137] Bruno Latour, *We Have Never Been Modern*, trans. Catherine Porter (Cambridge, Mass.: Harvard University Press, 2001); Robert Miner, *Truth in the Making: Creative Knowledge in Theology and Philosophy*, Radical Orthodoxy series (London: Routledge, 2004).

insecurity, and only by artificial contrivance as the erecting of a new sort of *polis* as a way to release a still higher mode of natural liberty, which would be a collective expression of civilisation.[138]

Here again we have a prime source of 'conservative' and 'liberal' attitudes. Human animal nature is either to be held down or else it is to be released into its innocent true expression, however sublimated. At their most extreme, these attitudes supply the contrast of religious 'fanaticism' on the right, encouraging public puritanism, and moral 'libertinism' on the left, calling for the release of all natural instincts, which cannot be anything but innocent, even if innocence is thereby redefined. Yet once more, right and left are thinking within the *same* assumed paradigm: namely, that human animal nature 'precedes' (either historically or *a priori*, and this paradigm cannot really decide which) the human social artifice.

Now a common assumption tends to be that this 'artificiality' coincides with 'historicity' and so with its modern critical recognition: history, as for Marx, is what we have collectively manufactured, if never under conditions of our own choosing. Yet we have seen that the socially artificial as distinguished from the natural is predominantly thought of in modern times in terms of an entirely atemporal and ahistorical Scotistic formal distinction. By contrast, as already remarked, the Romantic discovery of a genuinely historicist dimension to politics actually coincided with a greater recognition of an 'organic' dimension: the rooting of political life in unwritten folk-culture, lying close to the soil.[139] And so, to repeat, this was in effect a redis-covery in a more conscious and relative mode of an Aristotelian-Thomist sense of human 'political animality' as being also 'historical animality'.

This can be further illustrated with reference to Edmund Burke, in the later, more Romantic and less utilitarian, phase of his intellectual career.[140] At this stage, his elevated tirades against basing social, political and

[138]   Rousseau, *The Social Contract*; 'First Discourse', in *The First and Second Discourses*, trans. R.D. and J.R. Masters (Boston and New York: St. Martin's Press, 1964), 32–64.

[139]   See Frederick C. Beiser, ed., *The Early Political Writings of the German Romantics* (Cambridge: Cambridge University Press, 1996), and Thomas Carlyle, *Past and Present* (London: Chapman & Hall, 1870).

[140]   But the careful reader may agree with Coleridge that a utilitarian element in the justification of inheritance as procuring balance never quite disappears from Burke's thought, even if it is now qualified by the argument that inherited property tempers the lust to acquire with truly virtuous social responsibility in the pursuit of a flourishing which exceeds the merely useful. An assessment of this issue turns upon what Burke really means by the 'pleasing illusions' (see below in the main text) on which society traditionally depends. Are these simply 'useful' illusions, or are they rather 'true illusions' in continuity with religious symbols and sacraments? I would suggest that for Burke's earlier political aesthetic it was the former, and that this was just why he downgraded the beautiful to mere diversion while augmenting the sublime, linked to fear and manly courage,

religious duties upon voluntarily entered into contract invoked *at once and inseparably* both our historicity and our created animality. Thus he wrote that 'out of physical causes, unknown to us, perhaps unknowable, arise moral duties which, as we are able perfectly to comprehend, we are bound indispensably to perform. If the social ties and ligaments, spun out of those physical relations [childhood, sexual union and parenthood] which are the elements of the commonwealth, in most cases begin, and always continue, independently of our will, so, without any stipulation on our own part, we are bound by that relation called our country, which comprehends (as has been well said) "all the charities of all".'[141]

In this remarkable passage we can see how Burke's both traditional and romantic Anglicanism (in stark contrast to William Warburton's Whig contractualist reworking of Church-state relations) integrally linked animal nature and supernatural grace as charity beyond post-Suarezian norms, such that he elsewhere declares that 'man is by his constitution a religious animal',[142] precisely because he was appealing to the English reality of a 'Christian Commonwealth' where 'Church and State are one and the same thing',[143] and therefore the ultimate political community is only bound together by the assumption of the diverse workings of supernatural charity.

But just on account of this integralism, Burke is not simply crowning with further religious mystification an already ideological naturalisation of social arrangements. To the contrary, the link which he postulates between the undeniable biological reality of 'natality', as Hannah Arendt would

---

as the nobler because more realist aesthetic sentiment. But for the later political aesthetic it was surely more the latter, and this is why he now linked the attempts of Rousseau and others to achieve a sublime 'shock' in modern literature (in default of traditional appeal to the marvellous realm of *faerie*) to the horrible artistry in blood of the French revolutionaries. Correspondingly, he now regarded the 'beautiful' domain of social ornamentation, linked to the chivalrous adulation of women, as crucial to sociopolitical life. (This makes Mary Wollstonecraft's rejection of the Burkean sublime, and tendency to embrace, like Burke, an aesthetic of picturesque charm as well as dignity, and yet her support the French Revolution arguably an unstable combination.) He justifies the realist reference of this domain by appeal to natural law and supernatural destiny. See the passage on Marie Antoinette in *Reflections on the Revolution in France*, 169–171, and the passage on Rousseau's literary technique (283–284).

[141] Edmund Burke, *An Appeal from the Old to the New Whigs*, in *Works* (London: Henry Frowde, 1906–7), vol. 4, 125–126. I have taken this and some of the other following citations from Burke from Clarke, *English Society, 1688–1832*, 247–258. His account of Burke here is highly instructive.

[142] Burke, *Reflections on the Revolution in France*, 187.

[143] Burke, *Speech on a Motion in the House of Commons by the Right Hon. C.J. Fox, May 11, 1792*, in *Works*, vol. 7, 43.

later call it, and the lure of divine grace, is precisely that historicity which is the result of all the real (not mythical or transcendental) 'contracts' or 'partnerships' into which human beings have entered in time and which serve to compose 'the decent drapery of life' and those 'pleasing illusions which made power gentle and obedience liberal'.[144] In the most famous of all the passages from his writings, he declares that 'Each contract of each particular state is but a clause in the great primeval contract of eternal society, linking the lower with the higher natures, connecting the visible and invisible worlds, according to a fixed compact sanctioned by the inviolable oath which holds all physical and moral natures each in their appointed place.'[145] Hence for Burke the middle term between animal nature and supernatural framework is the human, historical making of society whose reality Lockean liberal contractualism is bound to suppress. For it tries to ground reality in an impossible pure present when all would be foregathered in one place and all would only enter into the social and political order through their own choosing. But in reality, since the human 'partnership' is not in this way both spatialised and biopolitical – not one, in Burke's words, which lies 'in things subservient only to the gross animal existence of a temporary and perishable nature', but a 'partnership in all science, a partnership in all art, a partnership in every virtue and in all perfection' (again the supernatural note) – it follows that 'the ends of such a partnership cannot be obtained in many generations' and therefore 'it becomes a partnership not only between those who are living, but between those who are living, those who are dead, and those who are to be born'.[146]

Burke's teleological perspective was therefore able seamlessly to fuse the animal, the artificial-historical and the human orientation to their final end in God. As animals we do not elect our way of life, but as peculiarly cultural animals we are able to reshape it through time,

---

[144]   *Reflections on the Revolution in France*, 170–171.

[145]   *Reflections on the Revolution in France*, 195.

[146]   *Reflections on the Revolution in France*, 194–195. In the same passage Burke speaks of 'the municipal corporations of that universal kingdom', so linking his refusal of the rights of states altogether to change their political natures to his respect for the liberty of corporate bodies, ecclesiastical and otherwise, beneath the level of the state, which the French Revolution had sought to destroy. Conor Cruise O'Brien rightly suggests (Introduction, 9–76) that a latent Irish Catholic critique of the English Protestant settlement informed Burke's not simply 'conservative' identification of tyranny rather than liberation as being at work in French revolutionary state power. He was certainly disparaging about Henry VIII's seizure of monastic lands, yet here again he is not an entirely thoroughgoing conservative radical (unlike the actual Tory William Cobbett), since he does not criticise, and indeed upholds, that agrarian capitalism which was in part raised in England upon the basis of the monasteries' demise.

although this means that we do not choose the ways in which we have already been shaped by past others. Because through all this reshaping we are prompted by the gift of supernatural charity, political society is not an attempt at minimal mutual interference in space, but rather a collective attempt in time to realise human works (of art and science) which truly fulfil and complete our specific and peculiar mode of animal existence.

By comparison with Burke and the Romantic outlook, the antique-medieval conception of the 'social animal' was not truly historicist. Nevertheless it was *not* spatialising, nor was it biopolitical in character – or at least not in the modern sense. For here what was already seen as specific to the human organism was its achievement of its own mode of animal life through complex and varying artifice – even if the real potential scope of such artifice was as yet but dimly glimpsed. Hence the family, local economic arrangements or religious free associations were for the Middle Ages at once entirely 'natural' and yet equally entirely 'artificial'. (For the medieval recognition of social artifice, see sections 10–15 below.) And it is just this integral combination which, we can anachronistically note, renders us 'historical'. For mere animality on its own would ensure our relative stasis, while if, to the contrary, social structures were entirely artificial, then they would tend to be utopian and precisely repeatable, enabling a far greater degree of control of human life than is truly possible. But in reality, social artifice is constantly the work of unpredictable animal passion which is thereby also reshaped and revealed anew. This is just why human acts run ahead of theories and provide a constant stimulus to new theorising.

It follows from this older conception that one should not and indeed that one cannot coherently think of politics in terms of either 'controlling' or 'releasing' a raw human animality. There is simply no way of distilling 'basic' human instincts from the way humans behave within families and social groups of different specific kinds. For example, much of the enterprise of 'psychoanalysis' is the attempt to think of the impact of family relationships as if these were somehow shadowed by a more primary 'virtual' human life which is non-familial – and which either requires the family for its psychic and social disciplining, or would attain its true ideal flourishing were these family constraints removed. And yet of course they cannot be, since any household unit of nurture, however 'unconventional', remains in some degree as much a family as a conventional one. Given this circumstance, the imagination of the primary life of the psyche which responds to its family history as though it intruded from the outside upon a 'pre-ethical' and material reality (as Freud ultimately thought) is an exercise in sheer fantasy, not subject to any verification or falsification whatsoever.[147]

The older conception, of the integral trans-organic 'social animal', therefore permits us to think beyond the modern alternative of politics, civility and economics as either control or liberation. For it is our specific mode of animality which itself demands that politics pursue instead ideals, and seek to define and realise a true human flourishing.

10   The Antiquity of Historicism

So far I have argued that, for the classical and medieval view, human beings were integrally rational and social; that is to say that they were rational and social *as* animals and not in spite of their animality.

I have also recently implied that, for the same view, humans were integrally natural and 'artistic' (or poetic) and also that it is just this which guarantees human historicity.

Yet were not the Middle Ages 'deficient' both in a sense of human creative artistry and in a sense of human historicity, and did not this double sense first come to the fore in the period dubbed 'the Renaissance'? How can one square that circumstance with my theses already in part adumbrated concerning the essentially anti-historicist character of modernity (built on Counter-Renaissance and classicist notions) and the retrieval of a historicist sense, along with an organicist sensibility, during the medievalising Romantic period? (Though more accurately one should identify a 'pre-Romantic' anti-classicist sensibility, in many ways in continuity with aspects of the Renaissance and encouraging both historicism and the primacy of the poetic sublime as commencing, in Italy, with Vico, Doria, and Muratori, in France with Boileau and Fénelon, in Germany with Hamann and Herder, and in Britain with Shaftesbury, Addison, Hogarth, Lowth, Young and Hume, as far back as the late seventeenth century.)[148]

The way to square these seeming contradictions is to propose two related theses. The first is that, as has already been suggested, the main line of modernity is actually Counter-Renaissance in character, which means that it is also counter-poetic and counter-historicist. A real historicism

---

[147]   See Catherine Pickstock, *Repetition and Identity* (Oxford: Oxford University Press, 2013), 109–126.

[148]   See Milbank, 'Sublimity: The Modern Transcendent', and *The Religious Dimension in the Thought of Giambattista Vico, 1668–1744*, 2 vols. (New York: Edwin Mellen, 1991, 1992); Livingston, *Philosophical Melancholy and Delirium*.

(as opposed to an Enlightenment celebration of an 'exit' from history, defined as the reign of the arbitrary and aberrant, towards its 'end', defined as the release of negative freedom) would require that one see certain contingent human deeds or sets of deeds as true *events* in the sense that they redefine our intellectual and emotional horizons, despite the fact that they are rooted in very specific and non-repeatable circumstances. Such human deeds are *poetic* in the sense that they reframe our sensibilities and reorientate our horizons, rather in the way that *Les Demoiselles d'Avignon* or *The Waste Land* altered forever painterly and literary outlooks in the first half of the twentieth century.

Such a historicism is precluded by the notion that human actions are only variations within a *genus* of human nature already adequately and positively defined in such a way that no example of this nature could possibly be in excess of this nature such as to redefine it without destroying it. For this reason, as we have seen in the first sequence (section 9), a rationalist or idealist constructivism is intrinsically at variance with real historicism, because it is concerned with the unfolding of an *a priori* truth, however many dialectical detours this may undergo. Equally and oppositely, if there is no given human nature whatsoever (as with the most common reading of David Hume) then while human beings may *suppose* that there are eternally significant events, this is an illusion, since all human artifice, as ultimately an expression of natural passion, is equally random and indifferent as regards meaning, from an objective scientific perspective.

So on the one hand the merely natural cannot be historical in the sense of engendering irreducibly time-marked significance. But on the other hand, the entirely artificial can only represent the sheerly arbitrary or aleatory. Its only permanent significance, as with Descartes's 'rules for the direction of ingenuity', would have to be one of exhibiting a formal method that could be reapplied in entirely different circumstances. But in that case what is essential in artifice precludes the realisation of any essentially and irreducibly new content. Where the real mark of *poesis* is identical repeatability, it is reduced to *techne*, and the variations of time and circumstance are likewise reduced to the level of trivia. Hence neither logical reason, a *mathesis* for reforming practice (including language, as with Leibniz), nor strict experimental science in any way nurture a historicist outlook: indeed they were developed in opposition to it, even if aspects of Renaissance historicism, newly aware of 'anachronism', had already evolved in the direction of a merely 'objective' interest in the difference of the past, which the Enlightenment sustained as the curious history of non-reason, now progressively surpassed according to the inevitable unrolling of reason itself.[149] This approach is again not compatible with the continued unique significance of any particular past event: such as the continued and indispensable example of the 'ancient' writers (as later reaffirmed by Boileau and the first recovery of Longinus's aesthetics of the sublime) against the idea that moderns might equal this by pursuing a proper, ironically dubbed 'classical' literary method which strictly observed certain rules.[150]

It follows that the truly historical must concern, as we have already seen, the strange hybrid of the natural-artificial or of the natural-cultural. It must arise, so to speak, within this trans-organic unlikely interval where art is 'added' to nature and yet this addition remains natural. Such art is not 'predictable' by nature, nor deducible from it. It is also more than an 'imitation' of nature. And yet it adds to nature an indispensable new significance which arrives only with this particular 'work of art', and is not reducible to the 'method' by which this work was produced. So it must be said, with many of the Romantics, that true art seems to grow organically, to be not so much produced as engendered. Yet for the same reason this Romantic trope must be balanced by a modernist sense that the work of art does not express (or does not merely express, one should add in qualification) the natural personality of the artist, but rather makes a new thing with its own integrity and its own new disclosure of significance to humanity in general.[151] For this to be the case, then, one must say that nature completes herself by becoming deliberative, contriving and intending. And also that she becomes finally more interested in the fragile symbolisation of what lies beyond both life and death, rather than in the perpetuation of living forms that yet remain for human beings frustratingly deficient in significance or personal welcome. That is why we build garden houses and erect garden statues amongst living plants: if there is pathos in the former there is also pathos in the latter, and the two aspects of the garden – dead but significant artifice and living but ultimately cold nature – expose each other's pathos, while each also supplies the deficiencies of the other in a literally sym-bolic gesture of mutual supplementation.[152] This is why, in every garden, every time one steps out into it, one immediately expects the appearance of a resurrection.

---

[149]   Zachary Sayre Schiffman, *The Birth of the Past* (Baltimore, Md.: Johns Hopkins University Press, 2011), 144–151.

[150]   Milbank, 'Sublimity: The Modern Transcendent'.

[151]   See Rowan Williams, *Grace and Necessity: Reflections on Art and Love* (London: Morehouse, 2005).

[152]   See Pickstock, *Repetition and Identity*, 1–70.

This kind of reflection, on the natural role of the artificial and the 'pathetic' semi-fulfilment of the natural in the artificial, was not, however, sufficiently attained by either Aristotle or Aquinas. For this reason one needs to assert something seemingly precarious, and yet I think demonstrably true. This is that the outlook of Aquinas, while clearly not yet historicist, is nonetheless logically hospitable to historicism in a way that Scotism, nominalism and modern philosophy (in its dominant modes) are not. I have already in part indicated why this should be the case in terms of contrast with 'the four pillars' of modern philosophy: univocity, representation, possibilism and concurrence.

First of all, the excess in Aquinas of an analogically and negatively known *esse ipsum* over the hierarchy of the ways of ontic being allows the possibility that a single event could disclose 'more' of being than any *genus*. This circumstance was for Aquinas hyper-abundantly realised in the Incarnation, in which the being of the Christ-event is identified with the divine *esse* and has no existentiality apart from this.[153] The implication of this radical Christology is that all the aspects of Christ's human life somehow frame those normal ontological categories which appear to include within their scope all historical occurrences.[154] The *états* (to use Pierre de Bérulle's later term) of Christ's life as narrated by the gospels outplay and resituate the situating ontological categories themselves.[155] This has a particularly drastic implication for human ontology: not only is it the case that a significant human event like the trial of Socrates or the life of the Buddha or St Francis can greatly expand our sense of human nature and its capacities, but, in the Christic instance uniquely, we see that human nature

---

[153]   One can also note here that if, as for orthodox Christology, Christ was personified by the second person of the Trinity, then it follows that, while he was an individual human being, he was (uniquely) not an individual person. For God, according to the tradition expressed by Aquinas, was no more an individual than he was a universal, and so it follows that the persons of the Trinity are not individual either, since they fully share the divine characteristics in general. This might appear to remove Christ's exemplarity for us as finite individual persons. Yet even in the human case, 'personality' is contagious, identifiable precisely because it exceeds any locatable point and instance and recognisable as 'the same' on entirely different occasions and under entirely different guises. Even though such a 'characteristic' belongs inseparably to one individual, the stronger it is, the more it proves communicable to others, possible for them to participate in without surrendering their own identity, but rather strengthening it. Thus our participation in Christ which allows us fully to become ourselves naturally implies that 'way of exchange', spoken of by the Anglican lay theologian Charles Williams, or the assuming differently of each others' characteristics, as a crucial aspect of our redemption.

[154]   John Milbank and Catherine Pickstock, *Truth in Aquinas* (London: Routledge, 2001); Riches, Ecce Homo: *On the Divine Unity of Christ*.

[155]   Pierre de Bérulle, *Discours de l'estat et des grandeurs de Jésus* (Paris: Cerf, 1996).

can be entirely revised and re-made and yet remain human nature, or even begin at last to be human nature. But this transfiguration arises not within the bounds of human nature alone, but through a personal unification with the divine nature which reveals that human nature is only fulfilled when, by the grace of deification, it entirely exceeds itself and all the capacities of the created realm as such. Here the trans-organic is surpassed (and yet completed) by the trans-natural.

Secondly, the notion of knowledge by identity suggests that knowledge is the event of a fuller becoming of form in the course of time; it is far less spatialised than the model of knowledge by representation.[156]

Thirdly, the priority of the actual means that, even for God, significance is inseparable from the *factum*, from the work or the deed.

Fourthly and finally, causality by influence means that a historical series of causes has its own, immanent, uninterrupted integrity, which ensures that historical genesis cannot be subordinated to structural simultaneity (as it can within causality by concurrence) when accounting for any created reality. This is partly why Aquinas constantly appeals to authoritative precedent when arguing for his positions, and does not think that this appeal to precedent can be altogether displaced by atemporal argument – and he does so almost as much in terms of his relatively 'philosophical' positions as in terms of his relatively 'theological' ones.[157] In either case, an illustrious forebear is not just seen as someone who happened to stumble in the past upon the same position that Aquinas himself is stumbling upon now; instead this forebear is acknowledged as a prime *cause* of Aquinas holding the position he does and so as someone who made a move within a process of reasoning that has unfolded within a certain not accidental temporal order and in relation to specific cultural circumstances.

At the same time, any historical mode of explanation is here safeguarded against any ultimate reductive appeal to a non-historical natural immanent or 'evolutionary' principle always at work, because all historical causes are themselves 'genetically' derived from a metaphysical origin of higher causality which places things 'in being' as such. Historicism, one might venture to say, is not here foreclosed, because an immanent account of the way things are is not deemed adequate as an account of their existence. In terms of univocity, by contrast, a series of good or true

---

[156]   For 'spatialisation', see Pickstock, *After Writing, passim.*

[157]   See Philipp Rosemann, *Omne ens est aliquid: Introduction à la lecture du 'système philosophique' de Saint Thomas d'Aquin* (Louvain and Paris: Peeters, 1996), and Olivier-Thomas Venard, *Thomas d'Aquin, poète-théologien*, vols. 1–3 (Geneva and Paris: Ad Solem/Cerf, 2003, 2009).

things within this world engendering other good or true things would be explanatorily trumped by the view that this series only exampled at every stage the good or true in general which can be homologically and so ahistorically known in terms of the transcendental 'how' of its essence, deemed as completely accessible without reference to the 'why' of its created, metaphysical origination.[158] If, however, the good and the true are analogical terms, then beyond the historical series of good and true events (or events disclosing the good and the true), there must lie the metaphysical series of still greater truths and goods in excess of the material realm. This series does not then, like univocal meaning, interrupt or transcendentally ground the historical series, but rather confirms its irreducible ultimacy and significance within its own level, which we can never in time fully exceed.

By contrast with Thomism, Scotism and nominalism are emphatically *not* hospitable to historicism (or only in a negatively dialectical sense, as we shall see in the next section). Univocal being is either there or not there; it enjoys no increase and decrease, it exists independently of any derivation, historical or metaphysical. Thus it twice and smugly refuses – in its waistcoated but straitjacketed comically swelling pride – any supposed 'genetic fallacy'. Likewise, the 'substitution' offered by representation cannot function as a historically necessary 'supplement' to given nature. Meanwhile, the possible usurps the significant event by preceding will or logic, and concurrence confines any immanent cause within a synchronous embrace with the ontically reduced transcendent agent. In addition, if general, like particular, names are but artificial conventions, as they are for nominalism, then no linguistic artistry discloses any new or higher realities, but only yields a convenient artificial path to the already given.

11 The Sovereignty of the Artist

For just these reasons, the greatest exponents of Renaissance humanism – Nicholas of Cusa, Pico della Mirandola, Desiderius Erasmus, Pierre de Bérulle – clearly directed their anti-scholastic ire mainly against the nominalist legacy, and when they invoked the metaphysical favoured the realist legacy, often given a still more Neoplatonic tinge than that favoured by Aquinas, and in a mode that tended to return (beyond Aquinas)

---

[158] See John Milbank, 'Only Theology Saves Metaphysics', in Peter M. Candler and Conor Cunningham, eds., *Belief and Metaphysics* (London: SCM, 2007), 452–500.

to the more unambiguous unity of philosophy with theology found in the Church Fathers.[159] The celebration of human artistry found in their works, and of the indispensability of historical example in all its specificity, remained thoroughly in line with this metaphysical traditionalism, even though it is significant that the poetic and the historical were now given a new and unprecedented prominence.[160] The reasons for this we shall try to consider in the next section.

If, however, one wishes to sustain the difficult thesis that a degree of historicism was not alien to the high Middle Ages, even though not clearly expressed by them, then this strange-seeming claim is best supported by Ernst Kantorowicz's famous article 'The Sovereignty of the Artist: A Note on Legal Maxims and Renaissance Theories of Art'.[161] Moreover, this article reveals that the discovery of the humanly creative and historical was not just a medieval achievement, but also, to begin with, an *ecclesiological and political* matter.

For Aristotle and Aquinas, as Kantorowicz confirms, the field of the arts in general was governed by the maxim that 'art imitates nature'. There was little or no suggestion (but see the following section) of human art as something creative, or as adding to the natural, save, significantly, by way of 'adinvention' for Aquinas in the case of legislation, where positive law seeks to adapt general principles to particular circumstances.

The exception to this norm within the high Middle Ages was indeed the field of jurisprudence as dealt with by canonical glossators. Jurisprudence was itself considered to be an art, as Kantorowicz underlines: *ius est ars boni et aequi*. And Aristotle had himself made it clear that, while ethical action in general belongs to doing (*praxis*) and not making (*poesis*), the broader field of 'politics' within which the ethical is situated is indeed governed by art (*techne*) as well as prudence (*phronesis*), since it is an 'architectonic' practice, like shipbuilding, which organises and oversees other, subordinate, arts. Politics, one might gloss, is more transitive and

---

[159]   Here Michael Allen Gillespie fails to recognise that by no means all Renaissance thinkers were nominalists and that, to the contrary, an opposition to nominalist logicism was often a motivating force for humanism. Obviously though, I agree with him that theological nominalism is the most crucial source of the modern outlook and practice. See his *The Theological Origins of Modernity* (Chicago: Chicago University Press, 2008), 19–100.

[160]   See, for example, Johannes Hoff, *Kontingenz, Berührung, Überschreitung: Zur philosophischen Propädeutik chrisitlicher Mystik nach Nikolaus von Kues* (Frankfurt am Main: Albert Karl, 2007).

[161]   In *Selected Studies* (Locust Valley, NY: J.J. Augustin, 1965), 352–365. Also in Millard Meiss, ed., *Essays in Honor of Erwin Panofsky* (New York: NYU Press, 1961), vol. 1, 267–279.

artistic than ethics for Aristotle, because it shapes the behaviour of others, rather than merely one's own behaviour.[162]

As an *ars* therefore, jurisprudence must also 'imitate nature'. The way in which it did so for the medieval glossators, Kantorowicz contended, was in terms of the composition of 'legal fictions'. Thus, for example, the process of adoption involves a fiction of blood relationship, whereby someone can become, through a process of legal gestation, someone else's child.[163] Accordingly, one finds in the gloss of Baldus upon Bartolus the view that not only art but also '*fiction imitates nature*, and for that reason fiction can take place only where *truth* may have its place'.[164] Thus the demand that law, as an art, 'imitate' nature already has the paradoxical consequence that the truth of law must be something artificial, an approximation to nature which is not simply a 'weak form' of the natural, but also an artificial substitute for the natural. This substitute (and here one needs to call to mind the entire series of reflections upon 'substitution' above) can only avoid being a second best (the adopted son being denied the full rights of a son by natural birth) or alternatively a usurpation (the 'elected' child displacing the mere child by birth), if indeed the fiction both performs and discloses a certain 'truth' – certain 'legal consequences' or a new legal-social state of affairs – which nevertheless cannot be made apparent without the aid of fiction. This applies especially to the recognition of a corporate body, beginning with the Church itself, as a *persona ficta*. It is within this line of reflection that notions of *verum-factum* ('the true is the made', or 'the true and the made are convertible transcendentals') first emerge in writers like Coluccio Salutati, and are applied already to medicine (and so encourage the idea that natural philosophical truth is performed, made, or 'experimental') as well as to legal practice.[165]

So because (and I am here glossing Kantorowicz) legal fictions, unlike merely artistic fictions, are *inhabited* fictions – because they are lived out 'for real', as if one performed the stage role of son or father for the entire remainder of one's life, without the curtain ever falling – one can say that

---

[162] Aristotle, *Nicomachean Ethics* 1094a1–1094b22; Aquinas, *De Regno* I. And see Maritain, *Art and Scholasticism*, trans. J.F. Scanlon (London: Sheed & Ward, 1947). Thomas Gilby OP fails to understand this point in his *The Political Thought of Thomas Aquinas* (Chicago: Chicago University Press, 2000).

[163] It is significant that Islamic law does not fully incorporate the notion of adoption. Perhaps the Christian ease with the category has something to do with the adoption of Christ into the Davidic line via Joseph and our 'adoption' through Christ as sons of God in the process of deification.

[164] Cited by Kantorowicz in 'The Sovereignty of the Artist'.

[165] See Milbank, *The Religious Dimension in the Thought of Giambattista Vico*, vol. I, 20–21.

within the jurisprudential realm the maxim 'art imitates nature' starts to edge slightly more towards a constructivist implication, even within the medieval period.

As Kantorowicz suggests, the increasing stress upon the use of fiction within the field of law was echoed by the Petrarchan defence of poetry as fiction rather than lie (a common inherited accusation): 'the office of the poet' is to 'disclose and glorify the truth of things woven, as it were, into a decorous cloud of fiction'.[166] This truth, one can add, could also, for late medieval/early Renaissance poetic theorists like Salutati, extend to the disclosure of divine matters – and here it was very early observed that Moses and other writers of the Scriptures themselves attained to prophecy through poetic means. This observation was then used to vindicate the faint but still genuine theological insights of pagan poets, while already (before the rediscovery of Longinus) this lesser degree of 'revelation' was correlated with a lesser degree of poetic inspiration. Such 'poetic theology' was nurtured within both Franciscan and Dominican-influenced cultural orbits.[167]

Nevertheless, Kantorowicz also pointed out that Thomas Aquinas himself paid some parallel attention to the irreducibly 'literary' character of the Bible and more specifically to its deployment of fictions. The words of Christ cannot possibly be considered lies, and yet he often had recourse to parable and image. Therefore fiction can be a *figura veritatis* and deeds can be 'feigned without falsehood' if, like words, they signify something else which is true: here Aquinas cites Augustine's reflections on the same topic: *Non omne quod fingimus mendacium est … cum autem fictio nostra referetur in aliquam significationem, non est mendacium sed aliqua figura veritatis.*[168] Moreover, Aquinas also cited an instance of apparent 'performed fiction', namely Christ's appearing 'in another shape' to the disciples on the road to Emmaus and his 'pretence of going on further' as though he were a stranger to them. Aquinas, however, denies that Christ was here performing a 'magical illusion' and suggests that the Resurrection body was such as only to be discernible by those who were 'well disposed to belief' and not by those 'who seemed to be already growing tepid in

---

[166]   Cited in Kantorowicz, 'The Sovereignty of the Artist'.

[167]   Patricia A. Emison, *Creating the 'Divine' Artist: From Dante to Michelangelo* (Leiden: Brill, 2004); Sarah Nair James, *Signorelli and Fra Angelico at Orvieto: Liturgy, Poetry and a Vision of the End* (London: Ashgate, 2003) 78–91, 130–146. Emison and James correct E.R. Curtius's claim that only Franciscans favoured poetic theology while the Dominicans opposed it. This was very far from being the case; Aquinas himself had unusually elevated poetry from the status of 'art' to the status of 'science': *ST* I q. 1 a. 9 obj. 1.

[168]   *ST* III q. 15 a. 4 ad. 1.

their faith'. Hence the 'hindrance in their [the disciples] eyes' was really Satan's doing. It follows that the real 'fictioning' element on Christ's part was the pretence of being a stranger and that this had something of the nature of a spiritual test. By contrast, Christ's earlier transfiguration on the mountain was neither magical illusion nor fictional pretence but rather real creative transformation.[169]

We can conclude that, already in the medieval period, there was a certain cautious recognition within the fields of jurisprudence, poetics and theology of the indispensable role of fiction in disclosing truth, and that this thematic subtly modified the meaning of the *topos* 'art imitates nature'.

However, there is more than this. Kantorowicz also showed that there were medieval adumbrations of a notion of art as original and creative. He rightly criticised Ernst Robert Curtius for tracing the notion of the *poeta creator* only back to the eighteenth century, for example in the writings of the English poet Edward Young from 1729 onwards. To the contrary, as Kantorowicz noted, Cristoforo Landino already in the fifteenth century described Dante as a *procreator* with a certain kinship to God, not to mention the exposition of this theme by Philip Sidney in the sixteenth.[170] One might still see the relatively late date of these citations as fitting with the notion that such an idea is a sign of a certain 'neo-pagan' Renaissance hubris. But Kantorowicz also notes that Curtius rightly pointed out that the new *topos* applies not a classical, but a Jewish-Christian metaphor. One can add here that it was more precisely Augustine who elaborated specifically the idea that God as creator is also God as artist.[171] While he did not really reverse this metaphor, the reversal is implicit in its very use, and one can find hints of such a reversal in some of his remarks on the art of music.[172]

In the case of Aquinas there is one isolated instance where he definitely compares the internal emanation of the human conceptual *verbum* with the divine creation of light out of nothingness: 'In things which are made without movement, to become and to be already made are simultaneous, whether such making is the term of movement, as illumination (for a thing is being illuminated and is illuminated at the same time) or whether it is not

---

[169] *ST* III q. 55 a. 4.

[170] See Michael Mack, *Sidney's Poetics: Imitating Creation* (Washington: CUA Press, 2013).

[171] Chrétien, 'From God the Artist to Man the Creator', 94–129.

[172] See Catherine Pickstock, 'Music: Soul, City and Cosmos After Augustine', in John Milbank, Catherine Pickstock and Graham Ward, eds., *Radical Orthodoxy: A New Theology* (London: Routledge, 1999), 243–277.

the term of movement, as the word is being made in the mind and is made at the same time. In these things what is being made, is: but when we speak of its being made, we mean that it is from another and was not previously. Hence since creation is without movement, a thing is being created and is already created at the same time.'[173]

Here it is notable that the context for the notion of a human creative act is not simply imitation of God as creator, but also God as Trinitarian – the implication being that human verbal art as an internally generated or 'made' product is as indispensable to human cognition as is the generation of the Son/Word to divine cognition (a view, which as we have seen, Duns Scotus denied). And in general, Aquinas's sense of the priority of the act of being over form encourages a sense that radically new things emerge within time, even if he reserves this novelty to the divine power of absolute origination of being and does not clearly allow that human modification of existing being can 'share in' this power of origination (though without truly commanding such a power, and indeed only possessing the power relatively to innovate within the created order *because* of this sharing in the also 'imparticipable' capacity to create out of nothing).

Aside from these fragmentary theological hints, the Middle Ages in general saw poetry in classical terms as a blending of rhetorical and musical elements through fictional devices, and painting equally as a visual rhetoric. Neither was regarded as a 'creative' activity, but more as a matter of refined craft. However, Kantorowicz's scholarly tour de force was to note that already in the year 1220 the canonist Tancred glossed the phrase 'Vicar of God' as applied to the Pope in an Innocentian decretal of 1198 to include the idea that, as standing in the place of Christ, the Pope 'makes something out of nothing like God'.[174] This he regarded as an aspect of the papal *plenitudo potestatis* in relation to the affairs of the Church. And what he has in mind is a radical version of the power and reach of legal fiction, as already described. The Pope supremely can invent new law and override existing law in the name of equity, in either case through a kind of fictioning. Examples of this mentioned by Kantorowicz are the Pope retrospectively accepting bishops invalidly elected as though a valid election had taken place; or the granting of a lawsuit of stipulation even though stipulation had never occurred, for the purpose of reclaiming a dowry. After Tancred, Bernard Botone of Parma declared in 1234 that the Pope *de nullo aliquid facere*, and therefore can *naturam rerum immutat*. Citing Tancred, Hostiensis in his *Summa Aurea* (1250–3) announced that

---

[173]   *ST* I q. 45 a. 2 ad. 3.
[174]   Cited in Kantorowicz, 'The Sovereignty of the Artist'.

the Pope 'makes something that is, not be; and makes something that is, come into being'. Finally, in a Roman modification of the *Glossa Ordinaria* to the *Decretals*, it was said that 'to make something out of nothing is to found new law'.[175] So now it was established that law-making as such is a process of creative fictioning.

12   Eucharistic Creativity and Political Power

These claims may seem highly surprising, insofar as they were not as yet, as we have seen, clearly supported by either theology or poetic theory. However, what turns out to be crucial is their *Christological* point of reference. Kantorowicz showed that the source of the decretalists in this instance was Gratian's *Decretals* themselves, wherein he cites a passage from Ambrose of Milan's *De Mysteriis* concerning Christ's institution of the Eucharist. Ambrose here argued that 'the power of blessing is greater than the power of nature, because by blessing nature itself is changed'. He then proceeded to cite a series of Old Testament examples of this phenomenon: Moses turning his rod into a serpent; his restoration of the divinely brought-about blood of Egypt's streams back into water; the dividing of the Red Sea; and the turning back of the Jordan's flow through a miraculous tidal bore, besides Elisha causing iron to swim and Elijah drawing fire down from heaven. Ambrose then asked: 'if the word of Elijah had such power as to bring fire down from heaven, shall not the word of Christ have power to change the nature of the elements?'[176] He then specifically suggests that, since Christ was the *Logos* incarnate, the creative power of the divine word must be communicated to the capacity of Christ's human utterance, which was fully exercised on the evening of Maundy Thursday: 'You read concerning the making of the whole world: "He commanded and they were created". Shall not the word of Christ, which was able to make out of nothing that which was not, be able to change things which already are into what they are not? For it is not less to give a new nature to things than to change them.'[177]

Ambrose here clearly enunciates the idea that radical change is *equivalent* to creation *ex nihilo*, so opening up the possibility of understanding drastic

---

[175]   Cited in Kantorowicz, 'The Sovereignty of the Artist'. On legal fictioning and the creation of corporations in the Middle Ages, see also Michael Wilks, *The Problem of Sovereignty in the Later Middle Ages* (Cambridge: Cambridge University Press, 2008), 23–25.

[176]   Ambrose, *De Mysteriis*, 9.50–52.

[177]   *De Mysteriis*, 9.52.

human action as creative. Of course, in human beings other than Christ there is no absolute co-incidence of the human will with the divine creative will; but nevertheless one can logically speak of a 'participating' in this creative will, where human action brings about something that is generically new, as in the case of a new sort of legal convention or a new sort of artistic idiom. But because the creative human being is 'inspired', and because she does not fully grasp or command the new thing which she has brought about, there is no absolute creation here: the new thing invented is also 'discovered', given to the creator herself as a mysterious new potency. It must be in this sense that the glossators spoke of the power of the Vicar of Christ, who remained entirely a human being. Nevertheless, it is crucial that the papal power radically to innovate, to 'create from nothing', was not understood simply as a sharing in the divine creative act, but rather as a participation in the transmission of this power to humanity in the person of Jesus Christ. Through the entire connection of the Church as the body of Christ to Christ himself, ecclesial deeds are joined to the fully creative act of God.

Ambrose appeared to hint that this is indeed the ultimate 'mystery' which the Church safeguards, and which she should not reveal to unbelievers. (The entire treatise was written for the already catechised and newly baptised.)[178] The crucial mark of grace is that it is creative; though this inversely implies that human creativity only proceeds from grace – an implication with which the decretalists kept faith. Thus Ambrose notes that Jesus's life on earth commenced with a creative alteration of the course of nature in the case of the Virgin Birth. This circumstance then functions as a persuasive argument for the absolute transformation of the eucharistic elements: 'Why do you seek the order of nature in the Body of Christ, seeing that the Lord Jesus Himself was born of a Virgin, not according to nature? If it was the true Flesh of Christ which was crucified and buried, then this is then truly the Sacrament of his Body.'[179] (The missing but implied third term here would seem to be the resurrection as being truly and literally Christ's body, but in entirely altered form.)

On this basis Ambrose articulates what we can anachronistically and yet with exegetical accuracy describe as a theology of transubstantiation: 'The Lord Jesus himself proclaims: "This Is My Body". Before the blessing of the heavenly words another nature is spoken of, after the consecration the Body is signified. He Himself speaks of His Blood. Before the consecration it has another name, after it is called Blood. And you say, Amen, that is,

---

[178]   *De Mysteriis*, Introduction.
[179]   *De Mysteriis*, 9.53.

that is true. Let the heart within confess what the mouth utters, let the soul feel what the voice speaks.'[180]

After this characterisation of the eucharistic event as a more than miraculous creative transformation, Ambrose goes on to speak of an erotic mutual feeding between Christ and the Church, based upon allegorical exegesis of the Song of Songs. Christ feeds the Church with the sacraments; the Church guards the (creative) mystery of the sacraments like 'a garden enclosed, a fountain sealed'. Into this garden of secrets, the Bridegroom alone is invited, citing Solomon's love-poem: 'Arise, O north wind and come thou south: blow down upon my garden, and let my ointments flow down. Let my brother come down to His garden and eat the fruit of his trees.' Like Jesus himself at the Last Supper, or a priest officiating at a Mass, the eternal manhood of Christ continues to feed off his own ecstatically given flesh, just as God himself has come to be incarnate in the creation, whose being is entirely his own being, albeit a given, ecstatic being that has somehow been made (as creation) integrally other to the godhead. The 'mystery' for Ambrose (which of course he does not fully divulge) would then appear to be further explicable as the joint human-divine feasting upon a restored and re-created order of created nature. He further cites Canticles: 'I have entered into My garden, My sister, My spouse; I have gathered my myrrh with My spices, I have eaten My meat with My honey, I have drunk My drink with My milk.' Then he concludes: 'And there is no doubt that He Himself eats and drink in us, as you have read that He says that in our persons He is in prison' (Matthew 25:36).[181]

Ambrose's entire argument is brought full circle when he declares that, through feeding from the sacraments, beginning with baptism, we are brought to 'new birth'. We cannot understand how because, again, this is more than a metaphor: it is, rather, a literal re-creation. Just as humanity was wrought anew through the descent of the Holy Spirit upon the Virgin, so likewise the Holy Spirit comes down upon the font to bring about the generation of drastically reshaped human beings at baptism.

It follows that, for Ambrose, Christ is a new creation in excess of creation (since he is both uncreated and created) and that he himself is able to re-create. The members of the Church participate in both realities: they are recreated in Christ and are themselves able to re-create through the administration of the sacraments; something equivalent to Neoplatonic 'theurgy' would seem to be invoked here.[182] But one should add that if,

---

[180]   *De Mysteriis*, 9.54.
[181]   *De Mysteriis*, 9.56–57.
[182]   See Shaw, *Theurgy and the Soul.*

in a sense, by being joined to Christ we are fully a new 'trans-creation' and are fully and literally creators, nonetheless, insofar as we remain and will always remain separate created persons, we only 'share' in this absolute re-creation, just as the merely 'fictional', signifying characters of the water, the wine and the bread remain for us essential mediations, even during and after the processes of more than miraculous renewal.

From all the above it becomes clear that the very first 'creative artist' in western Europe was taken to be Christ himself and in his wake the figure of the Pope, who then not inappropriately became in the Renaissance period such an enormous patron of the visual arts. It was the Pope, initially, who had the power of drastic creative innovation, because he mediated first of all liturgically, but then legislatively, the trans-creation of Christ himself, Christ's deployment of fictions, Christ's institution of new birth at baptism, and finally Christ's act of transubstantiation on Maundy Thursday. And this means that the notion of *homo creator* did not first arise in the west as an appropriation, displacement or semi-denial of divine power, or in other words as an aspect of secularisation. To the contrary, it first arose as a consequence of reflection upon the nature of miracle, grace and the Incarnation. Curtius was right to say that the very idea of 'creativity' is only supplied by the biblically derived idea of creation *ex nihilo*, but to this one needs to add that this attribute was initially transferred also to human beings under the *aegis* of participation, Christologically guaranteed. Only *because* an absolute non-human origination lies at the bottom of all human reality are humans able to a degree to share in this and to themselves originate. But the power to do this is restored to us in the Incarnation and even newly augmented by it.

And as we have now seen, following Kantorowicz, this transfer occurred initially in the legal-ecclesial sphere of canon law. Quickly, it was extended to the powers of emperors and kings, who sought to rival the Pope in this respect.

13   The Conundrum of Kingship

Here one should advert to what one can describe as 'the conundrum of kingship' in Christian history. The terms of this conundrum originate in the Bible itself: on the one hand kings have relatively to do with the things of this world, while priests are concerned with the things of the next world and therefore, supremely, carry out sacrifices and render purifications and absolutions. In this respect the more material power of kings is clearly subordinate to the more spiritual power of priests. On the other hand, the mediating power of priesthood is destined to fade away, and for this reason God himself is the supreme king (indeed originally the only king in Israel) and is not himself a priest. And so one can conclude that really and penultimately kingship is subordinated to priesthood, but *symbolically and ultimately* priesthood is subordinate to kingship. One can legitimately see this tension as underlying the more explicit uncertainty as to whether the expected messiah would emerge from the royal or from the Levitical, priestly, line.[183]

This conundrum is sustained and intensified in Christological terms. Jesus is a human king by fictional adoption(!), since he is quasi-descended from King David through his foster-father, Joseph, by way of King Solomon (Matthew 1:1–17). On the other hand, Luke traces this lineage from David via the priest Nathan (Luke 3:23), suggesting that Jesus as messiah possesses priestly as much as kingly attributes: a blending much expounded both in legend and in doctrine in the first few Christian centuries.

And in the third place, as divinised man Christ is the 'eternal' priest who performs the 'final' sacrifice to end all sacrifice, and as such he is said to be a 'priest forever after the order of Melchizedek' (Hebrews 5:1–9). This mysterious figure mentioned in Genesis was said to be both priest and king (Genesis 14:18–20), and thus Hebrews links the eternity of Christ's priesthood with his unique eternal fusion of priestly and royal functions. His eternal offering is to the Father in heaven, and so Christ's human priesthood and earthly sacrifice (sustained, according to later Christian doctrine, by the communication of divine attributes through his divine personhood) persist forever, along with (it will later be understood) the conjoined priesthood of all priests and their equally conjoined eucharistic operations. Thus for the first time in the biblical tradition (though there are remote parallels with Hinduism) the quality of sacrificial priesthood was added to deity itself.[184] However, in terms of his divinity and of his final resurrected and ascended triumphal glorification, Christ is once again, in a far more than Davidic sense, a king. Even if he remains eternally a priest in his role as mediator before the Father, this is a mediation that is eternal as entirely accomplished: a humble sacrifice forever overtaken by princely gift.

---

[183] See Gilbert Dragon, *Emperor and Priest: The Imperial Office in Byzantium*, trans. Jean Birrell (Cambridge: Cambridge University Press, 2007), 313–318.

[184] One should stress this in opposition to post-Tridentine ecclesiology, which at times somewhat reduced priesthood to a worldly function, so politicising and bureaucratising it. See P.D. de la Soujeole OP, 'Le Débat sur le surnaturel et l'ecclésiologie contemporaire', *Revue Thomiste*, special issue on the *Surnaturel* (Jan.–Feb. 2001), 329–344.

Now it is often said, and it is no doubt true, that the peculiar shape and problematic of European politics derives from the 'theologico-political problem',[185] or the unique notion of two parallel authoritative societies: a temporal one and a spiritual one (which could not as yet in the Middle Ages be seen as 'state' and 'church', though that is what they later evolved into). However, this problematic was made vastly more difficult and even aporetic by virtue of the inherited 'conundrum of kingship'. In Byzantium the emperor was king in a Davidic sense, and deferred to priestly authority, yet he also claimed to exercise to the optimum the 'royal priesthood' of the laity in general, and to reflect the glory of Christ in majesty where the roles of kingship and priesthood were combined, following the foretype of Melchizedek. For this reason, as Gilbert Dragon has stressed, imperial theology in Byzantium, far from amounting to a kind of theocratic and Caesaro-papist closure, both sustained some acknowledgement of the episcopacy's different and higher authority on earth, yet maintained also the primordial Christian sense of eschatological and messianic expectation.[186] Quite contrary to the story so often told by recent theologians, this mood did not end with the imperial adoption of Christianity (which if anything intensified it by pointing up the inherently messianic fusion of the sacerdotal with the worldly and political,[187]) but rather tended to diminish in the west precisely because of the *end* of the Roman empire in its original guise.

In medieval England, which was most of all the home of 'west Byzantine' notions (fomented at once by the Arthurian legacy and by Anglo-Saxon traditions stemming in part from Bede), the so-called 'Anonymous of York' or 'Norman Anonymous' remarkably argued that, just because the king deals with more material matters than the Pope, it is the king's authority which is highest, since it anticipates our entire deification and the resurrection of the whole human person.[188]

Even where things were not understood in these extreme terms, there remained a kind of reserved eschatological aspect to the king's apparent subordination. For the initial Gelasian outlook in the west there is mutual subordination: of Pope to emperor as regards the things pertaining to

---

[185]   On this problem, see Manent, *An Intellectual History of Liberalism*.

[186]   Dragon, *Emperor and Priest*, 282–312.

[187]   Later in the Latin west also, apocalyptic speculation could often centre round the figure of a coming messianic emperor. This stress could be both in tension and in fusion with a more 'spritualising' mode of messianic hope.

[188]   Sections of this document only are generally available in David C. Douglas, ed., *English Historical Documents, 1042–1189*, vol. 2 (London: Routledge, 1996), 725–728.

time, of emperor to Pope as regarding the things pertaining to eternity.[189] However, this was seen by Pope Gelasius I not simply in Augustinian terms of the secular power being situated in *hoc mundum* relatively outside the Church, on account of its compromised and coercive character, but also in terms of an anti-hubristic division of the conjoined kingly-priestly powers of Christ and his foretype, Melchizedek. Since Christ's Davidic kingship was really swallowed up into his divine kingship, the Christian king only ruled legitimately as anointed (and so even in the west in some sense as a 'quasi-priest', usually held to possess curative powers through his touch) and was supposed to direct his management of the things of this world to the more ultimate concerns of the next. Yet this very direction also anticipates an eschatological time when the things of this world will be renewed and restored.

Although this aspect was more stressed within the eastern legacy, it is still signalled in the early west by a Paternal and Christological iconography which exhibit the Father and the Son always in monarchic, and not as yet in papal, guise.[190] In the end there will be no coercive rule even on this earth, and no imperfect peace of mere 'agreement to differ'. However, just because the ways of peace and forgiveness will then be fully effective, it is also true that at this end-point the worldly hierarchy will be reversed and priesthood will give way to a perfected monarchic rule that will now itself subsume the priestly function.

Arguably, Orthodox and Anglican Christianity (especially the latter, by force of historical circumstance) better retain this 'triple tension' than does Roman Catholic Christianity, since the crucial function of the Holy Roman Emperor was gradually and now, it would appear, finally, lost.[191] Yet the spiritual sway of the Pope over the whole of the Church is an equally essential mark of Christendom. The tragedy of Christian division, which the separate Catholic churches (for my theoretical purpose – at least – meaning those recognising the threefold order of ministry and the ontological efficacy of the sacraments) still all too rarely admit, is that no single one of the three main Catholic churches (Roman Catholic, Orthodox and Anglican) presents an ecclesial aspect which is structurally unblemished

---

[189]   Pope Gelasius I, 'Letter to the Emperor Anastasius' (494) in James Harvey Robinson, ed., *Readings in European History* (Boston: Ginn, 1905), 72–73.

[190]   Kantorowicz, *The King's Two Bodies*, 42–86.

[191]   See Carl Schmitt, *The Nomos of the Earth in the International Law of the Jus Publicum Europaeum*, trans. G.L. Ulmen (New York: Telos, 2003), 59–60. Yet even up to the First World War the assent of the Habsburg emperor was required to the nomination of a pope.

in terms of the co-balancing of the sacerdotal and the 'monarchic-lay'[192] powers in terms which exceed any national boundaries.

In the case of the medieval west, the triple tension of the monarchic conundrum was undone by the gradual collapse of the priestly and monarchic functions into each other, and the accompanying now irresolvable rival claims of Pope and emperor, or Pope and king, to be the sole site and authoritative source of their ultimate combination. There were several stages in this process, which apparently pulled in contradictory directions, yet ended up mutually reinforcing each other.

First of all, there was the fatal transmutation of Gelasius's 'this world' into Jonas of Orleans's 'this church' within which the two powers exercised their sway.[193] This loss of the ambivalent interior/exterior status of secular rule inevitably implied that one aspect of ecclesial rule was brutally coercive and involved in necessary political compromise: Augustine's sense of a necessary but still 'alien' work (to adapt Luther's phrase) of preserving a second-best peace within the 'city of this world' was lost sight of.

But if this tendency seemed 'theocratic', then one might say that the second significant moment, the Gregorian reforms, were intended rather to purge spiritual functions of worldly contamination – of simony, nepotism and debasement of the clerical role, and in the given historical circumstances these reforms seemed entirely necessary and were indeed beneficial in many of their consequences. But their more negative effect was deliberately one of confining the laity to more distinctly worldly functions by removing them from many functions of church government: the appointment of clergy, administration and defence of monastic *familia* in the Celtic lands and so forth. Thereby, one might say, there began a process by which, in the west, the Church began somewhat (and somewhat disastrously) to be identified with a clerical caste, in such a way that opened in principle the space for a lay culture that would come to be regarded as purely 'secular' in the sense of being only concerned with 'natural' matters, without any intrinsic onlook towards the supernatural – such a culture only today exists in the Christian east (from Pushkin to *Pussy Riot*) as the result of importation from the west.

In the wake of the reforms, it started to seem in the west that to be lay was not to be fully Christian, even though the laity then vigorously responded (and indeed one can see a dialectical benefit here, as compared with the Christian east, where the eschatological value given to the body nonetheless allowed its present proper powers to remain too undeveloped)

---

[192]   Obviously this could take many valid forms.
[193]   *A Ninth-Century Political Tract: The* De Institutione Regia *of Joan of Orleans*, trans. R.W. Dyson (Pompano Beach, Fla.: Exposition Press, 1984).

with many creative movements for discovering how one could be a Christian warrior, lover, worker, trader and so forth. Mystical practice also later penetrated far outside conventual walls, and helped in the late Middle Ages and early Renaissance to foment the spirit of Christian humanism. However, the clerical/lay divide, construed as a supernatural/worldly one, was eventually triumphant in the late medieval circumstances of the breakdown of complex order and the rise of merely formalistic solutions to the problem of power.[194] Here a clear division of powers and discrimination of tasks between those of this world and those of the next became paramount, the more that faith and salvation themselves came to be construed in 'extrinsic' terms of 'manageable' items of information and procedure.

In a third and accompanying moment, the claim of Gregory VII (Hildebrand) to a papal 'plenitude of power' was initially, as still with Tancred, cited above, a claim to ultimate overriding power (a power in the last instance, not, as yet, a 'sovereign' power) within the Church alone. However, since the Church had already become, as we have seen, co-extensive with the entire western political world, this already implied a power to override secular authorities if they were imperilling the concerns of salvation. There is still nothing in this idea that is truly at variance with Augustine's political vision, but the impact of the Gregorian reforms encouraged its exercise in terms of what too often appeared to be the protection of the worldly interests of the clerical orders. And later on, with the work of Giles of Rome (and, in a more modified way, that of his pupil James of Viterbo) heavily influenced by Averroist 'possibilism', this plenitude started to mean something more like a possession of sovereign capacity by divine right, such that papal power was now of the same *kind* as secular power, possessed simply to a higher and more absolute, if more refined, degree. The way was then open for claiming that the Pope had an *enforceable* and so in the end 'material' right to override any decree of any secular ruler or any secular ruler him or herself, since secular authority was now held to derive wholly from spiritual.[195]

---

[194] See Brad S. Gregory, *The Unintended Reformation: How a Religious Revolution Secularised Society* (Cambridge, Mass.: Harvard University Press, 2012).

[195] Henri de Lubac, 'The Authority of the Church in Temporal Matters' and 'Political Augustinism', in *Theological Fragments*, trans. Rebecca Howell Balinski (San Francisco: Ignatius, 1989), 199–233, 235–286. In these two crucial articles, de Lubac sought to refuse both Giles of Rome's extreme papalist theory of the 'direct power' of the Church in secular matters and Robert Bellarmine's early modern and more concessionary (to the emerging nation states) theory – as favoured by John Courtenay Murray in the twentieth century – of 'indirect power'. The former he rightly saw as reducing spiritual authority to a matter of legal right and quasi-material force. The latter he saw as denying the ultimate power of the Church

In this way an apparent 'spiritualisation' of political thought disguises a 'secularisation' of the notion of the spiritual itself, whose higher dignity is now reduced to the notion of higher power, based on a notion of prior right as rooted ultimately in the *potentia absoluta* of God and its always reserved and latent primal possibility. Secular rulers soon unmasked this disguise and turned an anti-corporatist papal absolutism against itself, to the benefit of an emerging absolute sovereignty of independent states. The bad implications of Jonas of Orleans's shift now become fully clear: even spiritual rule within the Church may freely stoop to any and every coercive measure. In just consequence an excessive papal claim quickly led to a permanent diminishing of papal authority.

It was at this point that the theological 'division of powers' really started to come unstuck. The Pope, as heir to the emperor of Rome according to the forged 'Donation of Constantine', increasingly assumed the powers of Davidic kingship. At the same time, he also started to assume the powers of divine Christological kingship.

over all human affairs, since all of these affairs ultimately have a spiritual dimension. Bellarmine had argued that the Pope has the right to depose a ruler who violates the religious prerogatives of Catholics. De Lubac correctly denies any such right, which he sees as but a qualified version of Giles's position, since it is still seen in terms of 'secularised' legal coercion. On the other hand, he also thinks that Bellarmine is dangerously confining ecclesial authority properly understood, and in all too modern a way. It must, however, be added that de Lubac's own sense of what constitutes 'the spiritual' in these articles and sometimes elsewhere is not entirely sufficient. For while indeed he had a strong new sense of the Church itself as the true human community, this thematic often exists in tension with a sense that spiritual concerns are fundamentally 'inward'; that God acts mainly on the individual, and that ecclesial 'spiritual' influence should be exercised in a mainly one-to-one, interpersonal way. For this reason his reading of Augustine's *Civitas Dei* in the second of these articles is clearly inadequate. The gap between the City of God and the Church on earth is exaggerated, while both are seen too much as purely 'spiritual' communities and not as embodied, 'political' entities, as the term *civitas* implies. Thus de Lubac arguably underestimates the suasive and exemplary role of the Church in a more collective guise, which tends to direct secular political ends beyond themselves to the 'social' sphere, or the realm of what eventually became 'civil society' beyond the scope of coercive law. Further evidence of this would be the way in which, in the same article, he appears to accord rather too much autonomous sufficiency to the natural law for Augustine, where clearly for him, as for Aquinas later, the ultimate test for whether the natural law is being followed is its orientation to the law of the gospel, which restores to us the sway of 'the eternal law' after the Fall. One can totally agree with de Lubac that there is no unbridgeable difference between the political theologies of Augustine and Aquinas. However, if the former had almost as strong a doctrine of natural law as the latter, then the latter has almost as strong a sense as the former that the grounds of all legitimacy, including the political, lie in the human orientation to the beatific vision. Within this near-concord, one must indeed set both thinkers against the proponents of a misnamed 'political Augustinianism' (here de Lubac is right, against H.-X. Arquillière), that

Gelasius's reciprocal hierarchy was thus entirely undone. It was no longer at all easy to distinguish the supreme functions of Pope and emperor: the former was a mitred emperor, the latter an archpriest on horseback. Through the legal process of *aequiparatio*, as Kantorowicz notes, jurists increasingly transferred the attributes and claims of the one figure to the other.[196] Frederick II, in his *Liber Augustalis*, had claimed divine inspiration in his own right as emperor, citing a similar claim of Justinian, but this was later arrogated to himself by the Pope as the *verus imperator*, by privilege of place and mythical grant. On the other hand, the emperor now gave his divine inspiration a more Christological gloss by borrowing from the papacy the right to creative legislation, in equitable response to changing times and circumstances. And we have seen why to appropriate this right is also to appropriate Christological power in its more priestly aspect (because of the link to the Eucharist). Once more one sees the bad consequences of Jonas's innovation. If the emperor's power lies fully inside the Church, and if the latter is not averse to entirely coercive rule, then why should he not exert priestly functions to the most eminent degree?

This then enables us to see how, because of the history of complications with respect to political Christology, the canonical-theological notion of papal creativity was able to pass over into a general notion of legislative-political

---

was in reality a break with Augustine, partially under Arabic influence, and which proceeded in a far more voluntarist and possibilist direction. It can finally be noted that, in the case of de Lubac, there remains some tension between his theological embrace of an 'integration' of grace with nature, and a political position which too much divorces the two, in an understandable reaction against Charles Maurras et al. It would seem wholly plausible to contend that. were de Lubac still alive today, the yet further sway of secular politics away from the norms of both natural law and the gospel would cause him to stress more strongly the social and corporate nature of the Church as having of itself a 'political' reality. Indeed those contemporary lay Catholic movements such as *Focolare* and *Communione e Liberazione* which are partially inspired by de Lubac would seem to draw just this conclusion in practice. It must also be said here that de Lubac may have under-considered the politically integrative considerations of a radically Cyrilline Christology, stressing the communication of idioms, that is historically and logically of one piece with his integrative understanding of grace and nature (see Riches, Ecce Homo: *On the Divine Unity of Christ*). Aberrant as his understanding of these implications undoubtedly was in certain crucial respects, one must acknowledge here that Carl Schmitt had a particularly strong understanding of their importance. See Carl Schmitt, *Political Theology II: The Myth of the Closure of Any Political Theology*, trans. Michael Hoezl and Graham Ward (Cambridge: Polity, 2008). On the relation of the debate concerning the supernatural to politics, and on the City of God in Augustine see further Milbank, *Theology and Social Theory*, 206–256, 382–442.

[196]   Kantorowicz, 'On the Sovereignty of the Artist'; *The King's Two Bodies*, 193–272.

creativity, intimately linked with the idea of equity and equitable fiction, but increasingly taken in a purely positivist sense.

The sceptical reader might, however, ask whether it is clearly demonstrable that all this has anything to do with the notion of 'creativity' in the artistic and the existential sphere and so, by implication, with a wider cultural sense of the possibility of historical innovation. But Kantorowicz already provided the answer: the same process of *aequiparatio* was applied also between rulers and poets, with increasing frequency in the later Middle Ages/early Renaissance, beginning within the poetry of Dante himself and reaching a culmination with the Capitoline crowning of Petrarch in 1341.[197] The comparison was encouraged by the notion that the poet or artist must be versed in all branches of learning, including jurisprudence, and inversely the idea that jurisprudence draws on and can be applied to all the sciences and arts, including music and literature. But above all, by writing the *Commedia*, Dante had taken it upon himself to assume the political function of judging all men, and, in excess of any known politics, of doing so in a fictional simulacrum of the final, divine, judgement. Only Christologically, in terms of the injunction to 'judge for ourselves' after we have been re-created in Christ, could such an ultimate poetic enterprise itself possibly be justified. Moreover, the apologist for imperial authority (Dante) implies by this enterprise that the royal and priestly authority of Christ primarily devolves (as Kantorowicz suggests) on the *officium* of being human as such.

14   The Truth of Political Fiction

The theological-canonical origin of notions of *homo creator* is therefore, at least to a degree, clearly indicated. But was this origin accidental? I have already given reasons why it should not be so regarded: it is theology and the biblical legacy which by implication gives prominence to creative innovation. And what are the implications of this specific origin? I have already mentioned how it gives the lie to the idea that the rise of *homo faber* is also automatically the rise of secularisation. Now several points can be added.

The 'papal' origin of human creativity shows that the idea is entirely in keeping with the high medieval outlook, even if it also implies a considerable fresh development of this outlook. Since the created fiction is necessary for the adumbration of a certain truth, it cannot be reduced either to a rationalist unfolding of the *a priori*, nor to a pragmatic manipulation of a myriad

197   Kantorowicz, 'The Sovereignty of the Artist'.

given facts. These options tended, however, to be the way in which the *verum-factum* and 'maker's knowledge' were treated in the seventeenth century, until Giambattista Vico's simultaneous restoration of an older perspective upon human creativity and anticipation of a later, Romantic, one.[198] Like the cognitive *species*, or still more the intentional *verbum*, the *fictio* is no mere regrettably necessary 'substitute', but is rather a paradoxically essential 'supplement' in a somewhat Derridean sense. Thus it was perhaps in the ecclesio-legal-political realm that a first inkling of the irreducible requirement of actual language and indeed actual narrative for thought started to emerge, even if Augustine and Aquinas had already started to think of thought itself on a more linguistic model (based upon a Trinitarian pattern).[199] The necessary fiction discloses a new universality, like the possibility of 'adoption', yet only through the re-narration of a concrete instance. And this constitutes a kind of implicit riposte to nominalism, not as yet dominant, although it already existed: certainly the universal norms of equity are constructed by us through language, yet the 'artificiality' of the universal need not mean that it does not disclose a true universality.

The irreducible requirement for the created fiction can also be regarded as a mode of 'singular experiment' which is not identically repeatable, and which to a degree affords its own proof, even if it is subject to the existential test of whether it can be tolerably 'inhabited' by human beings. As such, it also conforms to the four pre-modern antitheses to the four norms of modern philosophy already dealt with. A fictional imitation of nature must be an *analogue* to nature, and if it is indispensable then this analogy is irreducible to either pure sameness or pure difference. Fictions always hover in 'the between'.[200] Again, if it is indispensable, then it must be 'identical with' the truth that it discloses, even if it does not exhaust this truth and so is identical with it under a certain mode or guise. Indispensability also ensures that the actuality of the fiction is not reducible to a logical recipe for the *possible* production of fictions, nor to the mere willed moves that brought the fiction into being. Finally, if a fiction is inspired or discloses a truth to us, then it is as much received as produced, as much granted as engendered, as I have already mentioned. It is fully our own work and yet fully also the work of divine influence; it is not partly our construction and partly something shown to us, according to *concursus*, else we would be able to enumerate just which was which, and we cannot do this.

[198]   Miner, *Vico: Genealogist of Modernity*.
[199]   See John Milbank, 'On Thomistic "Kabbalah"', *Modern Theology*, 27/1 (Jan. 2011), 147–185. And see sections 6 and 7 of the first sequence above.
[200]   See Desmond, *Being and the Between*.

15   The Two Rival Constructions

What should be clear to the reader by now is that I regard *homo faber* as the joker in the pack of my genealogies, and the factor which above all prevents me from simply telling a melancholy story of decline and fall. The exaltation of human creativity is not medieval but modern and Romantic, and yet at the same time it covertly takes its origin in the Middle Ages and is in reality either tamed and suppressed by modernity or else unleashed in a demonically negative form that reduces this creativity either to impersonal force or arbitrary predilection. In political terms this translates as liberalism's combination of elite technological control of the people in terms of a rationalist blueprint (whose arbitrariness of aim is concealed behind a regularity of procedure) with a cultural libertarianism into which all the people are increasingly initiated, according to the precise degree in which it is realised that indulgence can be deployed as an instrument of further manipulation.

This process occurs, both theoretically and politically, because the theologically derived sense of human creativity is actually incompatible with the structures of modern thought. As we saw, these overwhelmingly favour the *passivity* of the human intellect, whereas one can only adequately understand the place of human creativity in terms of an extension of the role of the Aristotelian *intellectus agens* and of Augustinian intentionality.

Modern thought ultimately builds upon a slide towards an *a priorism* that derives in part from Avicennian influence, and ultimately from Plotinus's denial that the human soul is 'fully descended' into the human body.[201] The consequence of this denial was that Platonic 'recollection' of a transcendent sphere through the anamnesic operation of material 'triggers', and Augustinian participatory 'illumination' of the mind by God equally through the mediation of the body, the natural cosmos, human teaching and tradition, were displaced in favour of 'a turn inward in order to go upwards'. The new abandoning of material mediation does indeed eventually, for western intellectual tradition, imply that all genuine understanding is 'constructed' by an unravelling intellect, but this unfolding is essentially fated and inexorable, passive in relation to the transcendent power which it witnesses. It is this pseudo-construction which, as we saw in the first sequence (sections 9–12) is celebrated by modern rationalism and idealism.

---

[201]   See Jacob Schmutz, 'La Doctrine médiévale des causes et la théologie de la nature pure (XIIIe–XVIIe siècles)', *Revue Thomiste*, special issue on the *Surnaturel* (2001), 217–264; Shaw, *Theurgy and the Soul*; Milbank, 'From Sovereignty to Gift'.

By contrast, the 'theurgic' Neoplatonism of Iamblichus, Proclus and Damascius, by insisting that the human soul was 'fully descended' into the human body, remained more loyal to Platonic recollection, and it has been plausibly argued that the equivalent of this turn is present in Origen and Augustine, even prior to the influence of Proclus on Christian theology via Pseudo-Dionysius and Boethius.[202] In this line of thought, the countermanding requirement that the divine reaches graciously down to our embodiment, if we are to be able to reach upwards to the divine, becomes synergically fused with human liturgical performance designed to 'attract' such divine influence. Accordingly, the 'constructive' aspect here is not, as for the ultimately Plotinian-derived model, a reduction of *methexis* to *mathesis*, according to an *a priori* determination, but rather a process of free artistic invention of sacred word, image and hymnody. Equivalently, it is not a construction performed in an interior mental space upon empirically received sensory material, but rather an outward artefacting, performed by the mind and the body in conjunction and guided, not by any established if hidden rational norms, but rather by the lure of a transcendent *telos* which to a degree only makes itself apparent through our own poetic shaping of the limited end which we seek to bring about.[203]

It is this 'realist' model of constructivism which is eventually more explicitly expounded by Nicholas of Cusa and Giambattista Vico and later given a more directly aesthetic application by the early Romantic thinkers (like Novalis and Coleridge) in their critique of their idealist contemporaries.

From this brief analysis one can see how the Plotinus/Proclus contrast, internal to Neoplatonism, helped to generate, and roughly maps onto, the Franciscan/Dominican contrast which throughout this book I am suggesting both shapes and is secretly more fundamental than the modern/pre-modern alternative. Both sets of contrast are in fact more fundamental because to a degree they undercut the very notion of an inevitably 'later' modernity. Instead, because of modernity's deep roots in Plotinianism, Avicennianism and Franciscanism, we can start to see how the modernity we have is just the side of the Middle Ages that happened to triumph. Equally, we can see how the constructivism we have is a sham creativity,

---

[202] Jason B. Parnell, *The Theurgic Turn in Christian Thought: Iamblichus, Origen, Augustine and the Eucharist* (London: Lightning Source, 2011). This equivalence is obfuscated by the fact that Augustine opposed pagan theurgy because it was pagan, and, as he thought, demonically magical.

[203] See John Milbank, 'Sophiology and Theurgy: The New Theological Horizon', in Adrian Pabst, ed., *Radical Orthodoxy and Eastern Orthodoxy* (Basingstoke: Ashgate, 2009), 45–85; 'Platonism and Christianity: East and West', in Daniel Haynes, ed., *New Perspectives on Maximus* (London: SCM, 2013).

that has always prevented the full flowering of an alternative and more genuine constructivism which, while it remains rooted in a metaphysical realism, also offers us in the future an 'alternative modernity'.

Within this perspective one can say that much of the Renaissance was in reality the consummation of the Middle Ages, whereas modernity is the abandonment of the Renaissance and a return to the perversities of the later medieval epoch. Equally one can say that there is something in the spirit of gothic itself that unconsciously realises a sense of human creativity better than the later return to the classical: a sense of breaking with formal rules, of democratic creative expression by all, and of the 'grotesque' combination of aspiration and fantasy with realism which does not ignore the strange, the hybrid, the weak or what is distorted by sin and death.[204] As so many of the early Romantics later argued, creation *ex nihilo* by a personal God suggests at once the release of an inventive freedom into the finite, and the symbolic significance of the strange, different and uniquely detailed.[205] At the same time, given belief in the Fall of Man, human endeavour becomes a constant effort to discern and to repair, rather than an elitist pagan retreat to already given norms. And to say that one should not fall prey to a later 'romance' of the Middle Ages is supremely superficial: for it misses the point that the Middle Ages were themselves to a degree culturally constituted by the spirit of romance – that is to say by a Christian-derived reflexive awareness of distance from their own storied ideals, and even at times from their own distorted and imprisoning attempts to embody those ideals. The medieval era was accordingly already in itself 'Romantic' and the 'gothic' was already 'gothick'.[206]

Grotesqueness also embodies the fourth mode of integration, which I shall come to in section 19, that of the beast-angel. Therefore an art of the grotesque suggests an art whose aspiration is inseparable from the inspiration of its invisible roots. An art which, like that of the gothic, is at once seemingly natural and organic in its endlessly varied adaptation of form to function, and yet also highly artificial in its subordination of structure to ornament and instruction, through modes of technological

---

[204]   See Hugo, *Préface de Cromwell*.

[205]   Erich Auerbach sustained this early Romantic argument in the twentieth century in his *Mimesis: The Representation of Reality in Western Literature*, trans. Willard R. Trask (Princeton, NJ: Princeton University Press, 2003).

[206]   I owe these points to Alison Milbank. She has pointed out to me that there was already a 'gothick' hermitage, with an ornamental hermit, at Warkworth Castle in Northumberland in the later Middle Ages, while John Wyclif already saw monasteries and Church institutions as places of sinister entrapment. It follows that even eighteenth-century *topoi* of narrative reflection upon the medieval past perpetuate medieval narrative tropes.

innovation which yet never obliterate 'natural' form with a decorative covering (as often with the Baroque) but rather permit detail to elaborate form as though for its celebration and even reinforcement. Hence, as has been so often observed, the most extreme gothic ornamentations appear to spring up, to grow, or to flower, or sometimes to catch fire of many colours.[207] By aspiring, they also root geometric structure, as the first, most functional and abstract mode of artifice, back in the natural soil, bringing this mode of art always full-circle, like a rose-window.

In kinship with the art of the gothic, the necessary creative fiction suggests that human life is 'naturally artificial' or 'artificially natural'. It will not allow that we are basically animals without art and that art is something exceptional or reserved to the isolated genius, as aspects of the Renaissance later came to think – though this is not in the main characteristic of the later proto-Romantic and Romantic notions of genius, which tended on the whole to be democratic in character.[208] Once again then, one is dealing here with the 'trans-organic'. But the difference in this instance is that the idea of 'originating animal' was no sooner born than it was half-stifled and perverted.

However, it is above all important that the initial notion of human creativity was a public, legal and political one. For this means that it began with the most radical possible notion of human creative power. Not the power to create illusions, nor even beautiful new colours, patterns and sounds, but rather the power to create new historical realities as such, new modes of living which human beings must perforce inhabit and so in the end a power to reshape humanity itself. Therefore, because human creativity was first of all a political power, or rather an ecclesio-political power, it was also first of all fully a power to make human history and to make structures by which human beings are in turn reshaped, to echo Marx's famous dictum. The canonical invention or discovery of human creativity was therefore also the discovery of human historicity which modernity and liberalism have warped and suppressed according to the canons of 'Plotinian' *a priori* construction.

16   Creativity and Mixed Government

It is at this point that we can link the theme of the political *homo faber* with that of 'the diminishing of the few'. The dominance of the one is equivalent to the dominance of *a priori* reason and of the sway of a *mathesis*.

[207]   John Ruskin, *The Nature of Gothic* (London: Pallas Athene Arts, 2011).
[208]   See Edward Young, *Conjectures on Original Composition* (London: Forgotten Books, 2012).

The dominance of the many is equivalent of the dominance of known 'objects' or empirical 'facts' (in the long-term wake of Scotus and others). Thus modern politics rules in terms of either abstract reason or the gathering of factual information, including the gathering of information about public opinion: through *surveillance*, as Foucault realised.[209] But the role (not the dominance) of the few is more equivalent to 'the pragmatic governance of charity', following the evangelical principle as cited by both Francis Bacon and C.S Peirce: 'by their fruits shall ye know them' (Matthew 7:16). This is not, however, to be understood in a utilitarian or consequentialist way as it was by Bacon and, in the end, by Peirce. For 'success' is not the measure of a good result, but rather the fulfilment of justice in charity which is always surprising and original. To be judged as such, both the one who engenders and the one who enjoys the 'new fruits' must contemplate through them the teleological fullness of the charity to which they tend. If the 'fruits' are the test, then certainly Christ did not believe (with Abelard and Kant) that purity of motive or intention was the benchmark for moral goodness. Nor, on the other hand, does the phrase necessarily suggest that the fruits disclose externally a moral state of being always anticipated by the moral actor taken as essentially a utilitarian calculator. This superficial reading should be rejected in favour of the more disturbing notion that it is indeed only with the outcome that the direction of an intention – or even the formation of an intention – in all its implicit thrust as well as its ambiguity and liability to be derailed by circumstances is disclosed, even to the intending subject herself.[210]

Rationalism therefore, where one 'knows in advance' in the ethical-practical as well as the theoretical domain, is a one-sided distortion of 'maker's knowledge', since here the 'fruit' is but the display of a previous blueprint. Empiricism, on the other hand, is equally a distortion, because here one treats the 'fruits' simply as so many given facts, suppressing their teleology or directedness, which is to say the meaningfulness which they embody. Pragmatism (as with William James in particular) is only a variant of empiricism where it still focuses on facts, but logically insists that the mark of a fact (etymologically *factum*) is its producibility and reproducibility, its achieved holding in reality.[211]

---

[209]   Michel Foucault, *Discipline and Punish: The Birth of the Prison*, trans. Alan Sheridan (London: Penguin, 1991).

[210]   I recall the legendary Cambridge theologian Donald Mackinnon expounding on this theme, with both passion and derision, in undergraduate lectures.

[211]   On this see Arthur Fine, *The Shaky Game: Einstein, Realism and the Quantum Theory* (Chicago: Chicago University Press, 1996).

Yet a more genuine pragmatism, which must in the end be deemed a kind of 'supernatural pragmatism', truly favours neither fact before reason nor reason before fact, but rather the predominant role of the *factum* as *fictio*, or in Peircean terms as always a sign to be interpreted. Beyond Peirce, however, one must not see the 'factual' consensus of interpreters as the test of a true interpretation: the latter, within a metaphysical horizon of participation in final truth, is rather its own criterion, its own self-authentication, its own self-confirming arrival and, as Maurice Blondel understood it, the 'extra' within our action beyond our abstract reasonings which suggests already the human drive towards its supernatural end.[212] Elaborating Blondel, I would suggest that the priority which he gave to the surplus of the achieved act over this innate drive (in contrast to Karl Rahner) implies that the 'inspiration' involved in every cultural product is already the actual work of grace, which alone sustains our very being since the fall of Adam, and which is always a typological anticipation or repetition of the saving work of Christ. The 'cultural supplement' to which our purely animal natural reason is already, through our 'trans-naturality', obscurely drawn by the lure of the supernatural implanted within us, simply *is*, as revealed in the light of the Incarnation, the supplement of grace, the beginning of the work of deification which is always (as Sergei Bulgakov saw, through his eastern appropriation of western experience) the work of a further participation in divine creativity.

If the horizon of the *fictio* remains the ultimate one, then there can be no Kantian distinction between the contribution of reason on the one hand and the contribution of sensory evidence on the other. The two have been always already fused by the integrating work of the imagination, and we arrive cognitively too late to disentangle them. As we saw earlier in the first sequence (section 11) Hume recovered this inescapability of the fictional, if he drew from it ambivalent conclusions. From the perspective of medieval canon law, however, the imaginative analogical synthesis achieved in the fictional formulation has a genuine manifestatory power. Above all it is able to 'create', and to confirm as genuine, certain 'corporate personalities' which are characteristically possessed by bodies of the few. Hence papal authority was sustained at its height, beyond the power of kings, by the direct or indirect acknowledgement of a multitude of free associations – parishes, monastic orders, mendicant orders, universities, manorial and urban communes, orders of chivalry both secular and religious, trade guilds and lay fraternities formed for the purposes of works of charity and intercession. This permitted to some degree a 'gothic' rule of complex and overlapping jurisdictions – a rule by a series of mediations, rather than just

---

[212]   See Milbank, *Theology and Social Theory*, 210–220.

a rule of mediation between the centre and the manifold periphery. Here one had a 'pragmatic' rule of constant 'fictional negotiations' to find new conceptual space between bodies that were themselves fictive and defined in terms of irreducible symbolic purposes rather than the mere achievement of formal order from the 'one' centre, or else the mere representative expression of the 'many' factual circumstances and opinions.

17   Christological Constitutionalism

The collective personalities of the bodies of the few were created fictions – yet they were deemed to be real personalities and could be 'represented' by symbolic personages – beginning with the Pope himself. This does not, however, mean representation in the modern sense of 'necessary substitution', but rather a representation, like that of the cognitive *species*, which is based upon a participatory identity: the king's mystical body *is* the sovereign realm; the abbot *is* the monastery, the Pope *is* the Church in person, and so forth.

All this conceptuality and procedure ultimately had a Christological logic. Christ was considered to be the representative of all humanity, not as a 'substitute' in the sense of a replacement, but rather as identical with all of human nature, such that all human beings, because they potentially participate in him through the sacraments, potentially compose his actual body, his *corpus verum*. This new concept of 'representation based upon participation' was then able totally to transfigure European social and political practice.[213] A woman's husband ceased to be merely her master, but became also the personal, public representative of her female body. The lord of the manor ceased to be the controller of slaves and became the protective 'representative' of the manorial terrain – whose partially free, landowning serfs then embarked upon a series of creative, technological innovations which formed the initial and perhaps most decisive springboard for later European scientific, technological and economic superiority.[214] The king or emperor of a realm ceased to be merely a quasi-divine presence, like Augustus Caesar, and became instead, on a Christological model, only 'divine' and anointed to the measure that he was also a representative of his human subjects and had been constitutionally acclaimed by them, as in John

---

[213]   Burke understood this in terms of 'the politics of chivalry': see *Reflections on the Revolution in France*, 107–108, 112, 170–171.

[214]   Belloc, *Essay on the Restoration of Property*, Susan Reynolds, *Fiefs and Vassals: The Medieval Experience Reinterpreted* (Oxford: Oxford University Press, 1996).

Fortescue's application of the body of Christ or *corpus mysticum* model to the king's relationship to the realm of England.[215]

Certainly one should see in this a medieval origin for the principle of 'representative democracy'. However, the modern notion and practice of the same, while it has desirably developed its sway beyond anything known to the Middle Ages, has also in certain respects perverted this principle. We have already seen how: by metaphysically construing 'representation' as unfortunately necessary 'substitution'. If, however, one views the roles of the one and the few not as 'second bests' in the absence of an impossible yet shadowily desirable direct democracy, but rather as embodying necessary functions of guidance and sub-formation and preservation of equity, then in reality the principle of representation allows not only for democracy to be balanced (and enabled) by 'education in virtue', but also for representative democracy to be blended with elements of much more radical direct democracy.

This is because modern 'pure' representative democracy tends to assume, as we have seen, on grounds of formal fairness and neutrality (but in contrast to medieval, politically Christocentric thinkers like Fortescue) that prior to the state their exists only a mass of isolated individuals. By contrast, a 'corporatist' recognition (in line with Catholic social teaching) of the multiple bodies of the few that are as old as the state and are constantly being newly formed, actually allows far more operation of direct democracy, since this is more possible within small-scale bodies – within a monastery or a workshop for example. In our own day we are beginning to see, on the 'Porto Alegre' model, an extension of direct democracy by meeting and ballot at the micro-level of the

---

[215] Voegelin, *The New Science of Politics*, 41–45. Although, as Henri de Lubac argued, the high medieval change of place between *corpus mysticum* as originally denoting the Eucharist, and *corpus verum* as originally denoting the body of the people of the Church, eventually helped to sever the intimate link between the two bodies, and to reduce the import of 'mystical' to mere metaphor, requiring that collective embodiment be extrinsically produced by the outside and superior authority of Pope or Bible, de Lubac himself recognised that the initial switch, for example in Aquinas, did not necessarily have these connotations. Nor should we read them into Fortescue, who, to the contrary, as Voegelin stressed, saw monarchic authority as organically 'erupting' and then 'prorupting' from the social body of the people as part (there is an Aristotelian element here) of that very sociality itself. Nor does the application of *corpus mysticum* to the realm here denote either metaphorical reduction or secularisation. Instead it means that the realm is considered as lying within the universal, international Church and that it is precisely through this location that a 'constitutional' account of kingship is to be derived. Just as the Pope represents God to the People and the People to God, as *servus servorum Dei*, so likewise the double 'representative' monarch is answerable at once to his subjects and to his divine overlord.

street and neighbourhood. This is much to be welcomed, but at the same time we must note that in former (Russia) and present (Cuba) communist countries such things at times operated successfully and even admirably, and yet did not often go along with powerful representative bodies intermediary between this level and that of the state. The danger is that the latter can all too easily fob people off with power over micro-decision and management to which the objectives of the state and the market may be relatively indifferent, while a resort to plebiscite can also be an opportunity for the increased dominance of propaganda.[216] Instead, at every level, people should be able to shape their own collective lives as much as possible, but the question remains of what *options* are put to them in the first place. To say that these 'should' come from the people themselves is not true to reality: for necessarily it tends to be the dynamic few, from whatever social stratum, who shape and present new options. For this reason, the formation of genuinely educative processes – 'republican' processes in quest of virtue and true human ends – must keep pace with the extension of direct democracy. At the more intermediary levels, where direct and representative democracy are necessarily blended, the role of the true 'representative' should keep the educative and the democratic elements within a fine Christological balance. This representative needs to 'guide' and sometimes to 'decide for' the people with whom she is in a sense 'identical'. A concern for their objective interests has to temper, and yet in turn be tempered by, an attention to what they are freely ready to accept.

Counterwise, a rejection of this explorative and guiding role of the few as 'paternalist' is all too likely to strengthen the role of the one supposedly purely substitutionary centre, and to expose the crucial exercise of direct democracy to propagandistic manipulation.

With respect to the role of the few, especially, one should argue for the decisiveness, even today, of the medieval sense of a corporation. The extension in the Middle Ages of the principle of fictive corporate personality, along with the role of participatory representation, are central aspects of the striking development of 'constitutionalism' within this period, a development which on the whole can also be accounted 'Christological'. For it was not primarily the case, as one might too hastily assume, that the relative removal of sacrality from political legitimacy by the unique existence of 'another', sacral polity, namely the Church, encouraged the growth of constitution-making as an

---

[216] Equally one needs to be wary of the deployment of intermediary associations merely as instrumental *reinforcements* of central state authority. For this is why they were advocated by Jean Bodin, the very inventor of modern sovereignty, and then also to some degree by Althusius.

expression of the insight that human arrangements are but fragile and artificial, still less that humans have been 'abandoned' by God to govern their own worldly affairs through the use of unaided reason. To the contrary, this constitution-making was most of all encouraged within, or under the aegis of, the spiritual power itself, just as the instrumental role of human artifice was theorised (from the twelfth century onwards) as an aspect of the account of the divine government of his creation.[217]

Indeed the model being applied here was ultimately a Pauline one: the ecclesial body of Christ constitutes itself not just by the imbibing of the eucharistic body, but also by the formation of reciprocally beneficial constitutive structures: the exchange of talents and benefits.[218] So although the 'fiction' of the Church's corporate body was charged with a real ontological freight, it was also seen as a canonical convention, an artifice which had to be supported by a host of lesser corporate artifices in order to render the 'true body' ever in time a real one. In theological terms, this expresses the fact that Christ's divine personhood or character was manifest not *despite* his humanity and his fully human capacity to will and to decide, but actually *through* his humanity and his human agency. Because, nevertheless, other human beings are *not* divine, their artificial shaping of human social arrangements is highly fragile and subject to judgement for the medieval outlook – a circumstance that, as Rowan Williams has pointed out, lends a new suspicion of political power to the western legacy.[219] However, this very same precarious process nevertheless carries, in Christological terms, a certain sacral charge through the 'communication of idioms'.[220] The *most* human continues to be the possibility of the *most* divine on earth.

A 'liberal constitutionalism' is therefore, as Williams amongst many others contends, a medieval legacy. The 'patriot Whigs' were by no means wrong about this, even if they sometimes failed to see the discontinuity with 'modern' liberalism, predicated not upon the upholding of the role of the 'few' corporations, but upon a pure suspension between the many and the one. To what degree the modern polity remains covertly 'medieval' and to what degree a 'modern' liberal politics must sap its own real roots remains a very complex and open question.

---

[217] See Marie-Dominique Chenu, *Man and Society in the Twelfth Century* (Chicago: Chicago University Press, 1968), 40–41.
[218] See Milbank, 'Paul versus Biopolitics'.
[219] Rowan Williams, 'Europe, Faith and Culture', in *Faith in the Public Square* (London: Bloomsbury Continuum, 2012), 62–74.
[220] Something that was most of all articulated by Richard Hooker.

It is because this constitutionalism is linked, as we have seen, to the entire issue of 'Christological creativity' and 'Christological fictional artifice' that it exhibits a latent 'medieval historicism' that is usually overlooked. It is not the case, as J.G.A. Pocock avers, that the otherworldliness of the heavenly city removed all interest from the historical during this period.[221] He is certainly right to say that often ideas of the wheel of fortune or of an inexorable linear decline of the aged creation (which the Incarnation scarcely interrupted), together with that of an acyclical political decline, tended to dominate. Nevertheless, the Augustinian idea of the City of God as 'on pilgrimage' in this world allowed also a certain idea of progress, such that Aquinas affirmed that the coming of Christ had improved the character of human existence in every respect.[222] The idea of 'reform' in the sense of 're-formation' had indeed been crucial for patristic Christianity, and it continued to resonate in the medieval era.[223] If the Incarnation permitted a reshaping of the world, then it was to be expected that time would bring forth beneficial innovations, including technological ones, in which the Holy Spirit was at work through human hands.[224] The expectation of the good as new and re-newing therefore went naturally together with the idea of *making* new constitutions and of *creating* new legal entities and new corporate realities. Not secularisation or laicisation was involved here, but to the contrary a extension of the sense of God's working through secondary causes and of human participation in the order of the *Logos* through the inspiration of the *Pneuma*.

18   The Fate of the Fabricating Animal

But what of the ultimate fate of the fabricating animal in modern times?

Much of that has already been hinted at. The suppression of the role of the few is also the suppression of the role of *homo faber* in modernity,

---

[221]   J.G.A. Pocock, *The Machiavellian Moment: Florentine Political Thought and the Atlantic Republican Tradition* (Princeton, NJ: Princeton University Press, 1975); *Barbarism and Religion*, vol. 1: *The Enlightenments of Edward Gibbon* (Cambridge: Cambridge University Press, 2001).
[222]   *ST* III q. 1 a. 2.
[223]   See Gerhart Ladner, *The Idea of Reform: Its Impact on Christian Thought and Action in the Age of the Fathers* (New York: Harper & Row, 1967).
[224]   For example, Gilbert of Porreta, *Notae Super Johannem* (MS London Lambeth Palace), 360, fol. 32r, cited in Chenu, *Man and Society*, 40, where 'God is said to make through the intermediary service of men' 'artificial things' like 'footgear, cheese and like products' and Hugh of St Victor, *Didascalion*, 2:1 'the arts are concerned ... to restore within us the divine likeness'. This newly includes for Hugh the 'mechanical arts' which form a sort of sub trivium-quadrivium of sevenfold fabric-making, armament, commerce, agriculture, hunting, medicine and theatrics (2: 20–27).

especially once its defining Counter-Renaissance, quasi-Augustinian moment had set in in the seventeenth century. Here hubristic claims, as already with Marsilio Ficino and then later with Galileo, that humans could univocally equal divine creativity had they but sufficient materials to command actually betray the thematic (as so often) through hyperbole.[225] For this absolute open power ceases to be a power of exploration through the genuinely 'experimental' contingencies of fabrication, echoing not simply the absolutely powerful divine creator but also the eternal Paternal kenotic generation of the *Verbum*. Ficino's new conception must in truth tend towards an exaltation of the absolute mathematicising power of pre-given reason, as fulfilled with Galileo. Inversely, in Francis Bacon, 'the truth of the made' begins to degenerate into the merely experimental confirmation of the utile working of a well-constructed machine.[226] In consequence, a double passivity of the human mind dominates in the face of both given nature and the given measuring power of reason. Just as the role of the *species* and *verbum* identical with known or intended form vanishes, so too does the role of the indispensable disclosing *fictio*. Or rather it is banished to the realm of a depoliticised rhetoric and poetics where it now discloses merely a decorous 'beauty' whose role tends to be reduced to subservience to either reason or utility or else to an integrating imaginative function that has a merely subjective import – this being Kant's solution.[227] Only with the pre-Romantics – Vico, Shaftesbury, Lowth, Young, Hogarth, Hamann, Herder and others – does its irreducible and metaphysical role for all human knowledge and culture start to be recovered, with an unprecedented self-consciousness that goes well beyond medieval perspectives on creativity and much extends those of the Renaissance.

All this had a political correlate, as I have also already intimated. But here the corruption began within the Middle Ages themselves. The 'fictioning' power of the Pope was, as we have seen, a crucial aspect of his claimed *plenitudo potestatis*. Indeed it was perhaps its very core, since it was the creativity of this power which rendered it plenitudinous. To begin with, however, as in the passage from Tancred cited, the plenitude was defined as extending over the Church and only justified an admonitory overruling of the secular arm insofar as it impinged upon concerns of human salvation (although all human affairs can, of course, assume this aspect). Later, however, and especially with Giles of Rome, as we have seen,

---

[225] See Chrétien, 'From God the Artist to Man the Creator'.
[226] See Miner, *Truth in the Making*. Yet an intense mystique of making and of artefacts survives in the Bohemian philosopher Comenius's later gloss upon Bacon.
[227] See Milbank, 'Sublimity: The Modern Transcendent'.

the Pope's power comes to be defined in more 'physical' terms as a handing over to him by God of both *de iure* and *de facto* authority, through which the same kind of power, though in diminished extent, reaches to the hands of kings.

Within this more voluntaristic conception, the power of the Pope to create new bodies degenerates into a notion of his willed pretence, rather than his confirmation of a kind of social miracle. Above all, after the Church itself came to be seen as a 'mystical body' the connection with the eucharistic origin of this phrase was eventually lost, such that the term came to mean little more than 'a body so to speak'. In these terms, the phrase was now transferred to other corporations, including the state itself, especially in connection with its link to terrain – the 'body of France' and so forth – in a manner that gradually shed the original Christological connotations.[228] Such a mystical body is no longer a 'real inhabited fiction', but rather something sustained by the imposition of the 'one' will upon the bodies of the many who are in reality absolutely diverse.[229] So with the realist role of the *fictio*, the role of the few lapses also. Modern politics ceases at least in principle to be poetic, although the Italian city-states sustained a 'civil poetry' for much longer than elsewhere. But as we have seen, a collective poetry is crucial for the exercise of a more participatory democracy, and one that seeks out, within its various collective expressions, the continued expression of transcendent truth.

19   The Fate of the Beast-Angel

I have argued so far that the Middle Ages sustained an antique sense of the 'trans-organic' which we can also affirm to have been on the whole the perennial wisdom of humanity, which defined it as such – the wisdom of tribes, and of the traditions of India and China, even if the greater humanism of Greece and Rome expressed this in a particularly acute form. Human beings are *as* animals both rational and social. Likewise, they are *as* animals fictioning creatures, or in other terms cultural and historical creatures, whose very nature is artificially to question and reshape (though not thereby to destroy) this nature. But as the Middle Ages merging into the Renaissance became more aware of this last aspect, it was simultaneously undermined. This undermining occurred at the hands of nominalist and voluntarist-inspired thought which created a new cognitive space in which

---

[228]   But see n. 215 above.
[229]   See De Lubac, *Corpus Mysticum*.

our animality could be divided from our rationality and sociality and creative capacity. The latter was then parcelled out between our rational and sensory, empirical nature – thereby ensuring that the 'constructive' or the 'fabricating' is henceforth either predetermined, or contingent and arbitrary, but in either case no longer partially disclosive of eternal truth.

Already, however, in antiquity, this triple integration had been highly unstable. Philosophies tended to divide between a favouring of the naturalistic and a favouring of the spiritual. In the case of the historian Thucydides, as in those of the Sophists and some of the more naturalist philosophers, a sundering between *physis* and *nomos* occurred, which already adumbrated a Hobbesian division between nature and culture.[230] And even for Aristotle (though unlike Plato) the government of self, city and cosmos concerned primarily an individual or collective rational regulation of the more animal passions. By comparison, the Middle Ages secured a far greater degree and stability of integration, allowing them fluidly to link public and material life with processes of spiritual transformation, expressed most vividly in their unprecedented 'infilling' of wild nature, to produce a new 'plotted and pieced' landscape that was far less ecologically wasteful than the more sporadic and distanced exploitations of land by the ancient urban-based empires. The mysteries of initiation had become exotericised and open to all, while the most everyday practices were bound back within a liturgical cycle. A contemplative spirituality rarely seemed to yield to the temptations of a purely private *gnosis*, but rather inspired an unprecedentedly practical religious activity which extended the reach of medicine, knowledge, welfare and protection of the weak beyond anything known in antiquity.[231] The reason for this was the new exaltation of the 'supernatural virtues' of faith, hope and charity which refuse, beyond the ancient cardinal virtues (prudence, courage, temperance and justice) to be content with attainable balance and rather forever yearn for perfection, combined with a spirit of patience that does not seek to institute perfection all at once, or imagine that it is securable according to the recipe of a utopian blueprint. The steady fire of a confident and yet absurdly hopeful charity was the element that fused together the biological with the rational and the communal.[232] Like the Platonic *eros*, but with a greater insistence on the abiding value of specific affinities and yet at the same time a greater

---

[230] Marshall Sahlins, *The Western Illusion of Human Nature* (Chicago: Chicago University Press, 2008).
[231] See David Bentley Hart, *Atheist Delusions: The Christian Revolution and its Fashionable Enemies* (New Haven, Conn.: Yale University Press, 2010).
[232] See Anthony Baker, *Diagonal Advance: Perfection in Christian Theology* (London: SCM, 2010).

insistence on the creative, sacrificially giving capacity of love, charity welled up from a mysterious, passionate animal depth, and yet at the same time it reached even beyond the serene contemplative capacity of reason. For the patristic traditions which the Middle Ages inherited, rational contemplation is surpassed at the point where, through the power of love, we are incomprehensibly united with God himself.

Although these traditions – and, later, Aquinas – recognised a 'natural' love for God, this was seen as little more than the natural unconscious inclination of all creatures towards God as to the 'whole' to which they belong, which in the case of human beings becomes a conscious vague sense of gratitude towards, and curiosity concerning the nature of, the giver of finite benefits and the 'total' reality of one's partial being. By contrast, the deeper intellectual yearning in human beings to be personally united with the source and full reality of their own being cannot be naturally satisfied, and so can only be fulfilled by the grant of grace. Genuine interpersonal love – both erotic and generous – begins as the supernatural love of God for us, which we can share in by loving him in return and by echoing this bond in terms of our mutual relations with other human beings and other creatures.[233]

This true love was 'charity', a 'supernaturally infused *habitus*'. As such, it represents in a sense a third level beyond human nature which, as we have already seen is integrally twofold: animal, but also rational, social and cultural. But this third level upsets any straightforward hierarchy within this duality, and through this upsetting also ensures a newly stable integration. For faith, hope and charity are in a certain fashion the testimonies of our body and of our passions more than of our reason.[234] It is our bodies that have to trust, that will not give up, that spontaneously love and can only love. Our passions protest at the rational defeats of reason, and since these are only defeats inflicted by perceived limits, who can rationally deny that that the witness of our bodily passions may not more truly disclose being than reason itself? This, at any rate, has always been the Catholic wager. By directing reason itself beyond reason or to a higher reason, love also elevates the vital powers of mere animal nature and confirms the truth of their dumb intuitions. In this way the dualism of much antique philosophy is averted, besides the autonomy of reason which always threatens to issue in the nihilism which results from the idea that all that reason can securely know is the rational itself. The higher lure of charity ensures that reason will

---

[233]   *ST* I q. 2 a. 1 ad. 1; q. 60 a. 5; II-II q. 26 a. 3 ad. 2. And see Milbank, *The Suspended Middle*.

[234]   Milbank and Pickstock, *Truth in Aquinas*, 60–87.

not see itself as the alien commander of the body and the passions but can only rule over them by also attending to their promptings, which it cannot of its own resources elicit. Its rule must therefore be 'constitutional', like that of the medieval king within the political realm.

But all this depends upon the idea that human beings of their very nature are paradoxically lured towards the final end of the beatific vision which can nonetheless only descend to them as a gift. During the later Middle Ages and the early modern period this came increasingly to be seen as a contradiction in Aristotelian terms: a genuine natural end must be within the reach of purely natural capacities. In consequence, human 'natural ends' – of goodness, true reasoning, technical practices and political formation – started to be seen as fully achievable without any reference to the anticipation of grace or the always already begun (since the expulsion from Eden) work of actual redeeming grace. For Aquinas, by contrast, the 'right ordering' of these natural ends had not been thought possible outside a more fundamental right ordering of human nature towards the supernatural.[235]

For without the 'clasp of charity', or the third level of integration which not only lies 'above' the first two levels of nature and reason but also mediates between them, these first two levels tended to get prised apart. As we have already seen, human animality became in the early modern period something to be either restrained or liberated by force of reason, and thereby ceased to be something of itself teleologically ordered towards reason. Similarly, human sociality became something either artificially imposed upon 'natural' individuals, or else a mere animal gregariousness and herding instinct. Finally, the fictioning impulse became either a matter of rational control or of random fabrication – a matter of 'taste' to be exploited by the economic market.

Supernatural charity and the culturally constitutive fictioning impulse lie, however, especially close together. The human soul includes a rational capacity, but deeper than the soul, as St Paul and Origen taught, lies our 'spiritual' identity, that unites in one 'character' both soul and body and yet whose depths we cannot plummet – for at the depths we are identical with God, from whom our entire being proceeds. It is for this reason that Augustine significantly used the term *spiritus* for the faculty of the imagination, thereby suggesting that it has a special link with the integrity of the whole person.[236] Our spirit, as the fount of our 'personality' is also, as Edward Young in the eighteenth century declared (in very theological

---

[235]   Milbank, *The Suspended Middle*. And see sections 1 and 2 of the first sequence, above.
[236]   Augustine, *De Genesi ad Litteram* XII.7.16–37.70.

terms), our unique 'genius', whose partially hidden character also means that it functions like our 'double', a benign doppelgänger.[237] As Henri de Lubac declared, it is this Pauline 'spirit' which is naturally called to a supernatural end.[238] Since this is a matter of a passionate 'drive' beyond reason (in the Fathers and still in Aquinas), this clearly exceeds that merely elicited 'curiosity' about final causes to which Baroque Thomism tried to confine this paradoxical orientation. However as Maurice Blondel realised, we especially see this 'spirit of character', this 'personalism', at work in our human actions, which always reach beyond anything rationally planned or rationally fathomable. Our actions are in a sense 'given' to us, just as even our reasons can only 'come' to us through force of inspiration. For this reason Blondel was right to see in the 'excess' of culture itself, as composed by human action, a constant probing towards our final end which is also the gift of the tendency towards supernatural grace.[239] But as he also stressed, every action is a work of love and of sacrificial love, since we cannot act without self-limitation as well as self-extension (as Chesterton also realised). To act, then, is not just ecstatically to anticipate grace, but also actively to receive grace in advance by 'typological anticipation' of the content of the act, besides that subjective anticipation of grace which is somehow neither grace nor nature, and yet both at once. (Just as the created order is at once other than God and yet not in any way outside the divine omnipresence.) For no deed is a good deed unless it tends towards or in some measure embodies charity, even though the latter is the gift of God's being itself to humanity. But if charity is uniquely the work of the spirit extending beyond reason in *action* towards the supernatural end, then it is also a humanly creative work, since it is the work of the spirit as 'genius'. Charity as personal must express our uniquely personal self-giving response towards equally unique others who give themselves to us in turn.

These suggestions, however, are liable to meet with a great perplexity. If charity is integral to human life as such and is also, as I have argued, the key to all the integrations of our dual nature, then how can it *really* be the divine gift of grace? How can the fluidity of the patristic era and the early to high Middle Ages be right as against the strict distinctions of modern theology which seek to preserve at once the autonomy of the secular

[237]   Young, *Conjectures on Original Composition*.

[238]   Henri de Lubac, 'Tripartite Anthropology', in *Theology in History*, trans. Anne Englund Nash (San Francisco: Ignatius, 1996), 117–233.

[239]   Maurice Blondel, *Action (1893): Essay on a Critique of Life and a Science of Practice*, trans. Oliva Blanchette (Notre Dame, Ind.: Notre Dame University Press, 2003).

realm and the gratuity of grace and thereby the purity of the spiritual – a distinction which appears to safeguard the separate integrities of the spiritual and the political? Why argue instead for a seeming muddle which threatens a theocratic contamination of both reason and religion?[240]

So why should we still contend, with the Middle Ages, that genuine love as such is something 'supernatural', descended from above? Is not love, to the contrary, something universal and natural, quite obviously independent of the Church and the mediation of grace? Again, does not the modern perspective on love make far more sense?

20 The Death of Charity

Our contemporary outlook on love has been shaped both by the Reformation and by the Enlightenment. For the former, salvation came primarily by the pathetic gesture of 'faith' and no longer through the infused habit of charity. In this way grace became more a matter of arbitrary election than of loving gift. Charity was now a sanctifying consequence of justification, but since conjoint love towards God and neighbour had ceased to be its prerequisite, the mark of charity became (for the first time, though we now take this for granted) its absolute pure disinterestedness. Supposedly the Protestant 'elect' *will* be charitable, and yet if they happen not to be, this does not really seem to matter all that much. Thereby human charity also takes on some of the quality of divine election and concomitantly loses something of the character of divine gift. Human and divine charity alike are only guaranteed in their character of disinterested gratuity by the contrast of supposedly 'merely just' (and often viciously punitive) actions where the gesture of love is withheld. In accordance with this logic, charity comes to be something that need not inform the public sphere, since the community of Charity, the Church, is now more thought of as merely a collection of individual believers, and the political arm is seen as concerned with either the prudential policing of sins (Luther) or the enforcing of the moral law of the Old Testament (Calvin), now less seen as subject to the equitable revisions of charitable insight. Meanwhile, in the economic sphere, exchanges cease (as a matter of conscious Reformed policy) to be exchanges of gifts in any sense or even intrinsically just exchanges, and become ones of the mere observation of contract.[241]

---

[240] See, again, Milbank, *The Suspended Middle*.
[241] See Marcel Hénaff, *The Price of Truth: Gift, Money and Philosophy*, trans. Jean-Louis Morhange (Stanford, Calif.: Stanford University Press, 2010).

The situation was much less extreme in southern Catholic countries – where, for example, people commonly tried to view interest on loans and profits on commodities in 'gift-exchange' terms, so giving rise to a politico-economic culture which, from a stern northern perspective, is bound to seem lazy and corrupt, confusing 'public' with 'private' interest – as though this very distinction were not the result of the heterodoxy of marginalising *caritas*.[242] But even within Counter-Reformation culture an evacuation of charity from public life had begun, encouraged by a neo-scholastic dualism of justice and mercy, besides an increasingly extrinsicist and judicial concept of grace which, in effect, as with Protestantism, had the result of downgrading works in favour of divine decree, ecclesiastically mediated. Here the impact of the 'concurrence' model of causality meant that all divine action was reduced to an immanent ontic model of efficient causation (as opposed to the ineffable para-causal 'gift' or 'emanation' of being) such that the donation of grace no longer 'informs' and 'reshapes' our freedom from within, rendering it more free without any external pressure of 'determination' whatsoever, but instead coerces it from without. This extrinsic action was often deemed, as with Suárez, to make no essential experiential difference to the human subject.[243]

During the seventeenth-century *de auxiliis* controversy between the Jesuits and the Dominicans (which is officially still extant but suspended) this modern conceptual apparatus was apparent on either side.[244] Thus the Dominican Domingo Báñez understood the Thomist *praemotio physica* to mean that God efficiently predetermines the soul towards grace by special causal intervention, or away from grace by withholding this intervention. The soul here only remains free in the pedantic logical sense that within the order of human activity it might have done otherwise. But in reality this is as predestinarian as Calvin. And not essentially different is the 'opposed' position of the Jesuit Luis de Molina, whose 'middle knowledge' involved God being able to see what would be the response to grace of any particular individual within the *possible world* that God has happened to create. Here no special intervention is necessary, because the 'general'

---

[242] Hénaff, *The Price of Truth*. In our own day liberal newspaper columnists are typically shocked by the idea of employers hiring members of their family or their friends. Yet even in pragmatic terms it makes far more sense to employ a person one knows as able, reliable and apt for the job (if such they be) by force of nurture or training, as opposed to someone only 'up to the job' by testimony of written report. Justice is emphatically *not* fairness.

[243] See Jean Mouroux, *The Christian Experience: Introduction to a Theology*, trans. George Lamb (London: Sheed & Ward, 1955).

[244] Laurence Renault, 'Banezianism-Molinisme-Baianisme', in J.-Y. Lacost, ed., *Dictionnaire critique de théologie* (Paris: PUF, 1998).

dimension of divine causality itself ensures predestination and in effect a double predestination. Here the paradoxical result of 'concurrence' is an absolute divine overriding. For while the free response of our will is in this case entirely our own (too much so, from the point of view of the *influentia* model), it is also entirely predetermined from outside. Its meritorious acts of charity that are the immediate consequences of grace alongside faith are also its own, but are likewise entirely the result of a *habitus* induced in a wholly alien fashion. In ethical and social terms this again has the result, as with Protestantism, of rendering charity gratuitously external to the normal, natural demands of morality and justice.

The above paragraph substantiates a counter-intuition. When love ceases to be given primacy by theology and therefore ceases to be so obviously a theological prerogative, it does not newly flourish in merely natural terms (whose reality theology had always allowed) but rather withers away, becoming at once moralised, sentimentalised and marginalised. Luther already confined erotic, preferential and friendly love to the natural and the trivial, and this view had a long later echo. The Enlightenment, however, as we have already seen, in a more humanist mode, generally sought to naturalise supernatural charity as 'benevolence'. This tended to mean a one-way sympathy towards the other person and as such it lacked the range of resonance of *caritas* in the Middle Ages.[245] The latter was more the establishment of a mutual state of being and as such something subject to positive increase, not in principle dependent upon a state of need or impoverishment. Nor did the French and British Enlightenment, whose central defining project was 'political economy', in any way regard the realisation of benevolence as a primary direct consideration in the operation of the marketplace.[246]

We have started to see, then, that 'love' as an all-encompassing human horizon is not at all something natural (where it tends merely 'to have its place') or readily envisaged in secular terms. Perhaps, after all, it is an intrinsically theological construct, and is enabled by the vision of something 'supernatural'. But just why does love of the neighbour depend upon the love of God in a double sense of the genitive? And why is this passionate love of God (as opposed to a merely natural yearning) deemed a gift of supernatural grace and not simply something consequent upon the natural created order?

---

[245]   Yet a more mutualist sense of sympathy as itself the goal lingers in Shaftesbury, still influenced by the Christian Cambridge Platonists and still retaining his own pagan version of a Platonic-Stoic philosophy. Arguably this sense is actually revived in the case of David Hume.

[246]   See Luigini Bruni and Stefano Zamagni, *Civil Economy* (Oxford: Peter Lang, 2007).

21   Augustine's Three Cities

To answer these questions, a digression linking this issue back to politics may be helpful. In his *Civitas Dei*, Augustine famously distinguished between the 'City of this World', by which he meant, in part, all our inherited political arrangements, and the 'City of God', which is the real realised Church of the saved in heaven, but also the visible Church 'on pilgrimage' through temporal reality.[247] The former he considered to be based on 'love of self' and the latter on 'love of God in despite of self' – in other words, upon charity. A careful reading of passages in Books IV, V and XVIII of this treatise however, suggests that in a way there were for Augustine not two, but *three* cities. Or rather two cities with a subdivision of the City of this World into two further polities.

'The City of this World' is primarily represented by ancient Babylon, which also represents human rule in general. The 'City of God' is of course Israel as a foretype of the Church and then the Church itself as a fulfilment and continuation of Israel. But what of Rome? Primarily it is in a literal sense like Babylon and belongs to it also figuratively. Yet Rome is also given a more privileged and specific providential role, indicating that in this respect Augustine, for all his North African ecclesial singularity in the wake of Tertullian, and Carthaginian political externality, does not in this respect entirely depart from his more centrally located patristic predecessors.

Indeed he explicitly declares that God now exercises his governance partially through the mediation of the Roman imperial office, since he has rewarded the just emperor Constantine with the honour of founding a new city in the east, bearing his name, while he has quickly removed the unjust emperor Jovian from his throne.[248] Yet the measure of the felicity of Christian emperors, in contrast to pagan ones, is not their success but their exercise of justice, which involves primarily a direction of political power towards the promotion of the *ecclesia*, the City of God on pilgrimage through this world. Just rulers 'love that realm where they do not fear to share the kingship', and this involves being 'slow to punish and ready to pardon ... in the hope of the amendment of the wrong-doer'. If they have to use violence and take severe decisions to protect the state, as will often be the case, then unlike pagans they must 'compensate this with the gentleness of their mercy and the generosity of their benefits'. They must prefer to govern their own appetites than to dominate subject peoples, and above all must look towards their eternal share in the divine glory rather than any earthly renown which

247   See Milbank, *Theology and Social Theory*, 382–442.
248   Augustine, *CD* V.25.

involves them in ceaselessly offering to the true God, 'as a sacrifice for their sins, the oblation of humility, sacrifice and prayer'.[249]

In this passage, which was to become the template for myriad 'Mirror for Princes' texts in the Latin west, Augustine shows how, for all that he thinks of secular office as significantly 'outside the Church' because it remains the governance of the fallen and Babylonian City of this World, marked by violence, coercion, self-interested commerce and semi-sordid compromise, he nonetheless (in a fashion not completely dissimilar to that of later Byzantium) thinks of it as now, within a Christian era and after the conversion of Constantine (which he fully regards as providential), as also partially located *within* the Church. The mark of this interiority is the 'ordering' of worldly compromise towards celestial uncompromised charity, and this means that, just to the degree that the emperor or king does *not* operate in one respect within the Church, he is unjust, since the definition of justice is now paradoxically the exceeding of justice in the direction of a charitable order. The phrase 'sharing the kingship' is crucially twofold. Henceforth, in order to reign with validity, a king must do that which most goes against the grain of kingship – namely share his rule; in this case with the heavenly king, which means, of course, to participate in that rule. Yet on the other hand, the earthly king *is* truly granted a share in divine ruling, in the rule of Christ as Melchizedek the king-priest. And the mark of this sharing is that the emperor is spoken of in terms of sacerdotal language: he is ceaselessly to offer sacrifice and oblation. Again, this is two-sided: the emperor only accedes to his 'priesthood' and so to a legitimate kingship, through an unprecedented proneness to penitence; on the other hand, to be granted the power to share in the offering of atonement not only for oneself but for one's realm is actually a heightening of kingly privilege under the Christian dispensation.

From this passage one can conclude two things: horizontally and vertically. Horizontally, it would seem, from Augustine's invocation of the newly founded city Constantinople's 'association' with the Roman empire, that he envisaged ideally a kind of reformed and pluralised empire of shared and overlapping sovereignties, but not a *dissolution* of empire, which would not have favoured the international spread of the charitable *politeia* which was the *ecclesia*.

Although in Book IV of the *Civitas Dei* he affirmed, against the love of imperial expansion for its own sake, the greater desirability of small kingdoms coexisting in peace, to read this passage as simply anti-imperial, or even proto-Westphalian, is to ignore three things.

---

[249] *CD* V.24.

First, the somewhat whimsical counterfactual invocation in a polemical context of such a, rather unlikely, 'golden age' state of affairs, which has never in fact existed in a human history dominated by the rise and fall of empires. Second, Augustine's admission here that 'stern necessity' in the face of injustice will sometimes require 'the good' imperially 'to make war and to extend the realm by crushing other peoples', even though they will by no means, like 'the wicked', regard this as straightforward 'good fortune', causing them perversely 'to worship the injustice of others as a kind of goddess'. Given Augustine's views about the prevailing state of human sin, one cannot seriously imagine that he thought this stern necessity would arise only occasionally, or that the upshot of its successful exercise is not to a degree genuinely good fortune, 'since it would be worse that the unjust should lord it over the just'. Augustine hence unambiguously locates (in contrast to modern theorising after Vitoria and Grotius) just war in a context of international 'policing' and a substantive *ius gentium*. Third, and most decisively, he compares a 'multitude of kingdoms in the world' to 'a multitude of homes in our cities'. Not, that is, to a multitude of nomadic tents in a desert belonging to no one.[250] Instead, the implication is that there should indeed be a concrete *cosmopolis*, an imperial world-city, even under invoked golden-age circumstances. Perhaps, in this whimsical invocation, what is alluded to is simply a disembodied Stoic order of immanent reason, but the strong analogy would seem to suggest more than that. In any case, Augustine now proclaimed the incarnation of *cosmopolis* in *ecclesia*, which, since Constantine, included a new embrace and tempering of an international political order.

The very idea of comparing the world to a city is of specifically Roman lineage and Augustine's perspective would therefore seem to be cognisant of the fact that western as opposed to oriental empire – first in the case of Alexander, second in the case of Rome – was specifically the result of the expansion of the, itself peculiarly western, no longer familiarly based order of the *polis*, after the survival of that institution had been threatened by incessant wars between cities and between cities and oriental empires.[251] Allied to this singularity of western empire was Rome's peculiar (if clearly flawed, as Augustine exposes) claim to provide international peace under the rule of law.

---

[250]   For all three points, see *CD* IV.25.

[251]   See Pierre Manent, *Les Métamorphoses de la cité: Essai sur le dynamisme de l'occident* (Paris: Flammarion, 2012). Manent also points up the unique way in which 'monarchy' in the form of Caesarism returned in Rome after the republic, as it was to do later in post-revolutionary France (and then again in the mode of twentieth-century fascism, Nazism and arguably communism). However, one could read this as an example of the operation of Polybian cycles.

Meshing together his scattered remarks therefore, it seems justified to conclude that Augustine advocated a new 'pluralisation' and 'subsidiarisation' of empire in the direction of a kind of 'international commonwealth',[252] made possible by the cultural and organisational subscription of the various constitutive polities and nations to the new trans-legal supernatural order of the City of God. As Pierre Manent suggests, the *ecclesia* was in effect a kind of new synthesis of the city and the empire and therefore in one respect a new revision of the Roman project itself. For it combined the face-to-face and amity-based character of the city with the quest for an external and universal imperial peace. It can even be seen, as Manent argues, as effectively a response to the crisis of empire, as empire was to the crisis of the city. For the international co-operation provided by the ecclesial structure was able to survive and override internecine warfare within the empire and to reach beyond its insufficient and always threatened boundaries without necessary recourse to arms.[253]

Vertically, one can conclude that the role of secular rule within the *ecclesia* (even though it is in an important sense alien to it) is in fact crucial

---

[252] In his visionary (but sadly belated) advocacy of an international co-operative order based upon a British empire evolved into an international co-operative *respublica* or 'commonwealth' – as opposed to an American-dominated combination of anarchy and both intrusive and impotent formal liberal 'right' – Lionel Curtis more rightly echoed Augustine in his title than he knew, since he wrongly ascribed to him a merely negative view of the role of the state: Lionel Curtis, *Civitas Dei* (London: George Allen & Unwin, 1950).

[253] Manent, *Les Métamorphoses de la cité*. Manent goes on to argue that eventually the nation in turn replaced the Church as the vehicle for the mediation of the civic, imperial and Christian legacies. He thinks the new solution arose because of the intractable gap between verbal aspiration of the Church to power on the one hand and the actions of the secular arm on the other: another way of putting his earlier expressed 'theologico-political problem'. He thinks that the nation 'solved' this problem through the idea of the neutral liberal state and the uniting of word and action through popular representation which gradually shaped a common idiom of word and deed in the form of national languages. He then hesitates between a (correct) indictment of the empty and static humanism of international rights and a continued claim for the necessity of nation-states, on the one hand, and an admission that the 'hyperbolic wars' of the twentieth century require a search for a fifth political solution on the other. I will further pursue these issues in *On Divine Government*, but in partial contrast to Manent I would emphasise (as already in this volume): the contingency and non-necessity of the break-up of Christendom, even if indeed it failed to solve its political problems; the inauthenticity of modern representation (of which Manent gives a somewhat Rousseauian version?) as a solution to a Christian dilemma; the way in which the nation-state itself more or less inevitably engendered hyperbolic warfare and finally the continued need for the imperial dimension in a Christianised form, as anticipated by Augustine, of an 'international commonwealth' linked to shared and overlapping cultures, as opposed to an impotent framework of rules and rights that independent nations are supposed to observe.

for human salvation. For given the requirement of fallen man for the sway of political coercion and somewhat impersonal economic transaction, *unless* these things are self-denyingly ordered towards peaceful agreement and reciprocal exchange, then human beings will remain unredeemed and 'unjustified' as unjust, since we cannot be saved merely in part.

Augustine and the west sustained this grasp of the crucial redemptive role of 'kingship', yet it was later reinforced by Aquinas when he absorbed both the Aristotelian and the Byzantine understanding that even in the golden age or in paradise there would have been some political rule of men over men and not just of men over families and animals, as Augustine, in more typically Latin fashion, tended to think.[254] For this concurs with an allowance that the positive architectonic of human self-organisation (such as the provision of roads and aqueducts for example) requires political rule, however much a huge proportion (and perhaps desirably as much as possible) of this architectonic can be subsumed within Church organisation itself, as occurred so much more extensively in the west, where the Church encountered only primitive existing political structures. This positive aspect of political governance, which is fully in continuity with an unfallen world, remains a lay function, and yet one that can be fully exercised as lay rule within the *ecclesia*, since no alienation from charity is involved here.

It follows that political rule is crucial to the mediation of divine governance, both with respect to sustaining and extending the positive order of creation and in terms of bending a necessarily negative and legal reaction to evil and sin towards the supernatural order of their full positive overcoming. This second aspect of lay ruling therefore has to be exercised both outside and yet within the Church. And this renders it more theologically and ecclesially central than has often been realised: for in an important sense this place of political 'hinge' most acutely reflects the human existential condition in a lapsed reality. Just for this reason a central concern with 'political theology' is not a swerving away from mystical and salvific preoccupations.[255] Equally, the category and operation of human law remain central for a Christian understanding of salvation, and this is why both Byzantine emperors and Anglo-Saxons

---

[254]   *CD* XIX.15.23, and see section 23 below.

[255]   One must beware the contemporary and doubly escapist Christian temptation (much encouraged by certain readings of Bonhoeffer and Simone Weil) to split Christian existence between a marginal 'spirituality' on the one hand (often involving a rather worked-up bourgeois claim to *accidie* and excessive critiques of – unavoidable and necessary – self-imagining) and a political engagement regarded as an entirely secular one in a world 'abandoned by God to its own freedom' on the other. This typical double stance is a surely a very dubious and inauthentic rationalisation of the current Christian predicament.

rulers' preoccupation with the Old Testament can be regarded as a valid consequence of the Christian rejection of Marcionism.

One is dealing here with a paradox that has a double implication. For Christianity the criterion of just law is that it must exceed the law's mere reactivity in the face of an always presumed evil, towards the recovered paradisal horizon of action as gratuitous and unnecessary positive offering, assuming no prior state of affairs to be remedied; this horizon can only be recovered through the ministries of mercy, forgiveness, reconciliation and reciprocal friendship. Thus now, for law to be law as just law, it must point beyond itself. Yet conversely, given the general state of human corruption, we are never, or at least rarely, in a relational condition where we can either act with pure paradisal spontaneity or proceed directly to reconciliation without an initial resort to corrective justice which will most frequently involve the coercive imposition of justice in some degree or other – given that, as the ancient Hebrews correctly thought, the defence of the weak and the abused cannot afford to wait upon the repentance of the wicked. Therefore it follows that the human existential situation, as understood by the gospel, is typically that of needing to bend a necessarily pre-reconciliatory and pre- (fully) restorationary justice towards the *telos* of genuine justice which is full reconciliation and an entire peaceful harmony of right apportioning. This situation and this bending are most acutely, crucially and publicly (but not exclusively) exemplified and manifest in the instance of public law. Without this bending, according to both Augustine and Aquinas, and later the Anglican Richard Hooker – but not according to Scotus, Ockham, Luther and Calvin, who thereby lapsed back into a dualism of the Testaments – justice cannot itself remain just and law cannot itself remain legitimate. And yet exactly this bending of the necessary but imperfect towards the unnecessary but perfect, exactly this Christian politics, actually belongs to the *primary* task of Christian conversion.[256] This is one reason why the idea of Christianity without Christendom is a self-deluding and superficial illusion.

So for Augustine, in a way that merely qualifies the over-enthusiasm of earlier Church Fathers, first political rule in general, then empire or international rule in general, and finally Rome as a providential particular of city-empire, are to do with this vital existential 'hinge'. Primarily in its post-Christian guise, but also, proleptically, before the time of Constantine.

Thus Rome's history is said by Augustine to present many symbolic simultaneities to that of Israel. Providence decreed, he argues, that after the fall of the Assyrian empire, the kingship of Rome, 'the western Babylon', arose to eminence. At the same time, during the reign of Hezekiah in

---

[256] I owe this insight to my undergraduate pupil Francesca Peverelli of the Milan Cattolica University.

Judah, Christ's birth was most strongly foretold, while during the coin-ciding reign of Numa Pompilius in Rome sprang forth the prophecies of the Erithrean or Cumean Sibyl concerning the same event. Augustine thinks that it belongs to the divine plan that the first Hebrew prophecies most explicitly concerned with Christ, whose message was also for the gen-tiles, should have temporally coincided with prophecies concerning his coming made also amongst the gentiles themselves. Moreover, he thinks that these were appropriately made in the Roman dominion because it was later in the course of this dominion that Christ was destined to come.[257] In addition the ending of the Hebrews' Babylonian captivity is said by Augustine to coincide with Roman liberation from monarchic rule, antici-pating empire. All this shows that he had not abandoned the earlier patristic conviction that the unprecedentedly widespread character of Rome's dominion was linked with the universal relevance of the gospel.

Although he will eventually provide a devastating critique of Roman virtue, in Book V he suggests that pagan Roman virtue has a great deal to teach Christians by example, and indeed often puts Christians to shame. This is especially true of the ancient, original Roman virtue, because Augustine thinks that it has undergone a degeneration.[258] In this account, the notion of 'glory' is central. Now, the modern reader might expect that Augustine would contrast an original 'virtue pursued for its own sake' with a virtue pur-sued merely for the sake of honour and glory. But in fact, he contrasts the early Rome, where honour was paramount, with a later Rome, where virtue had been lost in favour of a pure *libido dominandi* that was either (one could say with anachronistic validity) sadistic or masochistic. And the entire logic of the argument of the *Civitas Dei* is that the source of this degeneration is *not* the corrupted pursuit of glory, but rather the following through of a logic implicit in the very idea of Roman *virtue* as such: namely that virtue, whether in the soul or in the city, is a *reactive* response to disordered passion or external enemies and is therefore the *dominance* of reason over passions through the mediation of inner force (the Greek *thumos*) or analogously of Roman law and Roman might over 'foreign injustice'.[259]

By contrast, the pursuit of glory initially *tamed* sheer domination, since the early Romans would have been ashamed in their manliness to use underhand means or to bully the weak.[260] Likewise, they would have been collectively ashamed if the freedom of their city had been constrained from

---

[257]   *CD* XVIII.19–27.
[258]   *CD* V.12–13.
[259]   *CD* IV.15; XIX, *passim*. In the denunciation of virtue as mere reaction to evil (*not* of course to goodness!) Augustine has something in common with both St Paul and Nietzsche.
[260]   *CD* V.13, 18.

without – they were concerned more for their own freedom than with inhibiting the freedom of others.[261] And in the interests of this worldly glory they were often prepared, says Augustine, to make more sacrifices than Christians are in the pursuit of ultimate, heavenly glory.[262] For this reason Augustine gives Rome the status of a kind of rebuking foretype of the Christian order. Compared with the Romans, the Jews more clearly anticipated a distributive justice and above all the worship due in justice to the true good in inhibition of worldly political pretensions. Yet the Romans more clearly anticipated (and of course made possible) both the universal sway of the Church and (by a negative foreshadowing) the new rule of the true heavenly glory which is grace-given sacrificial charity. Under the rule of charity, we are no longer striving to hold back our passions; rather, we are receiving from God an unmerited honour (despite our lack of virtue) and in response to this gift we render praise to God with our whole being, in such a way that our passions are now rightly directed and no longer need to be suppressed, which had been a Sisyphean task. Under this new divine rule we must also love and honour others, willing not simply their fair shares or disciplinary control, but rather their ultimate, infinite human fulfilment which is equal for all. We must then form our entire community upon this basis. If we are not prepared to sacrifice ourselves for this community, then we should indeed be ashamed.[263]

From all this we can conclude that historians of ethics have overlooked something. 'Primitive' ethics is generally taken to be about reputation, how we appear to others, and so to have possessed a concept of shame but no true one of guilt. More 'developed' or philosophical ethics is rather about conscience and our self-judgement before an inner tribunal. Conformity to the abiding form of the Good in Plato allows us a Socratic indifference to public opinion. Some modern philosophers, such as Bernard Williams, seek to vindicate the notion of shame, but by nearly all it is assumed that Christianity in general and Augustine in particular perpetuate the Platonic and Stoic 'interiorisation' of morality.[264]

---

[261] Augustine echoes Cicero in his tale of the decline of Roman virtue, though seems to admire more the early monarchy than did his pagan republican predecessor.

[262] *CD* V.18.

[263] *CD* V.19; XIX, *passim.* My conclusions here are in line with Giorgio Agamben's assertion, in the wake of Eric Peterson and Carl Schmitt, that western politics is archaeologically based upon Christian glory, glorification, praise and acclamation. See his *The Kingdom and the Glory: For a Theological Genealogy of Economy and Government*, trans. Lorenza Chiesa and Matteo Mandarini (Stanford, Calif.: Stanford University Press, 2011), 167–259. I hope to include a discussion of Agamben's theses in *On Divine Government*.

[264] Williams, *Shame and Necessity.*

But now we can see how this might be qualified. For Augustine actually criticises the interiorisation of ethics as a source of violence: at least on the Roman model it dooms one to endless self-division and self-repression, while the fatally expansive imperial violence is to do with trying to subsume the alien within oneself. By contrast, Augustine actually sees the primitive, ur-Roman monarchic register of honour, glory and repute as more interrelational (more interior-exterior) and so as a strange figure of the sway of divine glory. Does this evangelical reality mean for him a glorious reward for virtue rather than virtue pursued for the sake of honour? Not at all: it means rather a *radicalisation of honour*, such that the bestowing of glory is not a response to virtue, but rather the very *condition of possibility* for virtue. To be virtuous is now to receive participation in the divine glory. To be virtuous is now to love and honour each other in a series of appropriate degrees according to closeness of connection and worthiness to be loved. And it is also to love even the worthless in order that they might grow back into their created worth: it is to honour even the dishonoured, and in this way to shape an interval of merciful restraint that will permit them to grow back into virtue. Finally and most crucially, if virtue means love, then it is *not* first of all a matter of internal congratulation and rebuke (only this by secondary reflex), but rather one of recognising the other and being recognised by the other. Our 'reputation' with the other and the other's reputation with us are here more fundamental than an esoteric incommunicable worth, while an absence of love between oneself and others makes one first of all feel ashamed and dishonoured[265] – and again only by secondary reflex gnawed by a sense of *self*-estrangement which is 'guilt'. But above all, to be virtuous now means to live to the measure of that honour given to us by God by which he glorifies us into being and finally deification. This is, as it were, the supernatural chivalry of the order of humanity as such.[266]

22   Church as *Cosmopolis*

So through this significantly political detour we now have an answer as to why love is a 'supernatural virtue'. It is so because it is not primarily virtue as attainment at all, but rather virtue transvalued as the grateful receiving of a gift, from an unknown transcendent source, and then the social

---

[265]   This defines the new tincture given to evil by the word 'sin'. See Ivan Illich and David Cayley, *The Rivers North of the Future: The Testament of Ivan Illich* (Toronto: Anansi, 2005).

[266]   See John Milbank, 'The Ethics of Honour and the Possibility of Promise', in William Desmond, ed., *Forgiveness: Critical Considerations* (New York: SUNY, 2014).

passing on and reciprocal receiving back of this gift. We aspire and make necessary efforts towards mutual love, but when it arises it comes as a gift or as a state of miraculous coexistence and affinity between people. Doubtless the absence of love is due to a human refusal of its multiple offering, but all too often the obstructions to this offering can be hard to locate or to know how to remove: 'Never the time and the place / and the loved one altogether!'[267] This is precisely why, as Origen understood, our own salvific destiny is bound up with the response to us of others and cannot be separated from the assistance that we give to them.[268]

Here, however, we are returned to the first perplexity. If love in this way is the real fulfilment of human ethics and human justice as infinite concern for the other, then how can it be a 'superadded' gift, rather than something which nature demands and so ensures for herself, as part of her created right from God? Should we not distinguish this from that supernatural 'electing' grace which grants salvation and beatitude?

One should approach this issue by asking whether one is so sure that what is 'borrowed' cannot also be innate. In terms of analogues to the completion of nature by grace, Aquinas spoke of the way in which tides are proper to the sea even though they are only drawn by the alien influence of the moon.[269] More decisively, Blaise Pascal's teaching concerning three orders of power, knowledge and love is germane to my thematic of 'triple integration'. Pascal, whose Augustinian humanism mostly transcended the decadent scholastic theology and Jansenism of his time, famously wrote: 'From all material objects taken together no one can ever extract the tiniest thought. That is impossible. Out of all material objects and all spirit no one can ever draw a movement of true charity; that too is impossible; it belongs to a different order, the supernatural order.'[270]

The dictum does not imply that really and truly in the concrete order of things there exists 'spirit' (or one should better say here 'thinking soul', as 'spirit' more traditionally concerns the transition to the supernatural) without charity, since, by analogy to the first transition, there does not really and truly exist a purely robotic, material human being. The point is rather that reason, as an intrinsic aspect of human nature, is nonetheless 'superadded' to matter, like the lunar lure to the maritime waters.

---

[267] Robert Browning, the opening of 'Never the Time and the Place'. It continues: 'This path – how soft to trace! / This May – what magic weather! / Where is the loved one's face?'
[268] Origen, *De Principiis* III.5.6; III.6.1–9; *Homilies on Leviticus*, 7.2. And see Pickstock, *Repetition and Identity*, ch. 9.
[269] *SCG* III, 147 [3], [6]; In *Rom.* Cap. II lect. 3; *De Motu Cordis*. (Though the authenticity of this last work is disputed.)
[270] Pascal, *Pensées* (Paris: Livre de Poche, 1974), §308.

Matter can in no way produce reason or consciousness out of its own resources; rather, the pull of reason shapes matter into a sensory body adapted to reason's requirements. This fits with my notion that the 'rational animal' is a trans-organism, a more-than-organism and yet an organism. Hence the structure of 'superaddition of something nonetheless essential' applies before we reach the instance of the supernatural, just as it applies already at the ontological level to the Thomistic 'real distinction' of essence from being: by divine creation actuality is, as it were, superadded to natural form, but thereby assumes a primacy over it, actualising form itself in the instance of a particular existence. (Although one should be careful here not to think of form-essence as exactly a receiving 'base'; it too is superadded to what is 'nothing' in itself, and finite existence from another perspective limits the fullness of formal ideality as it exists in God.)[271]

But if mind is gratuitously given to matter and then intrinsically belongs to the human material body, then by a parallel we can see how supernatural charity, the ecstatic ordering of the individual self to reciprocal relation with the other – to the mutual honouring of para-ontological chivalry – and finally to erotic union with God, is at once an unanticipated gift and yet the gift most intimately longed for, and so a gift that completes precisely by adding the most apparently superfluous extra.

Supernatural charity, therefore, is the priority of the divine or human other in us, defining us. First of all of the God who is 'other' to us also as 'not-other' and the ground of our identity. Then also of the neighbour with whom we are always already reciprocally related.

Clearly this formulation somewhat echoes Emmanuel Levinas, and one must respect his contribution.[272] Nevertheless it departs from him, first of all in sharply distinguishing these two 'others'; secondly in insisting that the God who purely gives is also a God ontologically beyond any ontic contrast between giving and receiving as he is also beyond any contrast between determining and determined.[273] The Trinitarian God lies at both of these poles at once, because he apophatically exceeds them: as Hilary of Poitiers taught, there is a sense is which, because of 'substantive relationality' (as Aquinas later named it), the generating Father is himself 'consummated' by the Son, or is, reversely, 'constituted' by him.[274]

[271]　See Milbank and Pickstock, *Truth in Aquinas*, 19–59.

[272]　Emmanuel Levinas, *Otherwise Than Being, or Beyond Essence*, trans. Alphonso Lingis (Pittsburg, Pa.: Duquesne University Press, 1999).

[273]　See John Milbank, 'Plato versus Levinas: Gift, Relation and Participation', in Adam Lipszyc, ed., *Emmanuel Levinas: Philosophy, Theology, Politics* (Warsaw: Adam Mickiewicz Institute, 2006), 130–144.

[274]　Hilary of Poitiers, *De Trinitate* VII.31.

Equally, the Son's reception is spontaneously active to such a maximum degree that we can say that he is 'independent' of the Father, precisely *because* of his substantive relation to him, as Pierre de Bérulle suggested.[275] Hence in absolutely giving us to be, but only (as Aquinas declares) from his own point of view within the Paternal action of generating the Son, he also from always receives us back again in the 'return' of the Son to the Father through the Spirit, since what is ontologically constituted as gift (the creation) can only exist at all as the rebound of gratitude.[276] This conception also departs from Levinas in a third way by fully affirming that we cannot give to the human other without having received from her, just as we cannot receive the human other constitutively without having actively made a movement of return love towards her – but a movement which becomes 'ethical' only when we freely judge it to be worthy of our love in some measure.[277] Hence the presence of the other is not pre-ontological 'persecution' by the unknowable and so unlovable, nor is it a unilateral response to this invisible and unknowable other, but rather it is situated within just that ontological relationality which Levinas so adamantly refuses. Precisely as relational this cannot be a closed totality, whereas a one-way response to that which never appears can only be a solipsistic self-enclosure, totalising in its very hypostasised negativity, after all.

From the most ultimate perspective, supernatural charity is the merging of creative art with ethical exchange through gift. For if it concerns spirit or 'genius', the enigma of personality that is forever distinctive in its very elusiveness, and therefore is forever newly original and surprising, yet with the surest consistency, it also concerns the original inter-communication of persons that is co-original with their very originality. The work is from the outset an offering, a token, and can only commence with the reception of a token already contrived and already offered and received.

For this reason, just as love occurs entirely as the gift of God, so also there cannot be any love outside the human community of love, which is to say the Church, understood as covertly embracing all of human history and all of redeemed nature insofar as it is actual at all – that is to say not contaminated by the privations of being which are evil, sin, death and suffering. The visible Church on earth, as the explicit recognition of this true community and thereby its fuller realisation, seeks to shape a trans-community on the basis of metaphysical honour alone.

---

[275] Pierre de Bérulle, *Discours de l'état et des Grandeurs de Jésus* (Paris: Cerf, 1996), VI.7 [1].
[276] See López, *Gift and the Unity of Being*; Rosemann, *Omne ens est aliquid*.
[277] López, *Gift and the Unity of Being*.

But this means that the thesis that human trans-organicism is only completed and sealed by the further supplement of charity is also the thesis that the society of the Church alone completes and seals the integration of natural familial and economic 'society' with political law and government. The Church is emphatically not, on a theological conception, a kind of 'extra' religious organisation which some people happen to belong to; it is, rather, the *sine qua non* for the existence of human society as such, and so for the existence of humanity as such: *nulla humanitas extra ecclesiam*. Were the Church 'to disappear', its trace would still remain, and would still be all-sustaining, since it is the ultimate finite ontological reality beneath all appearances. But even on the historical evidential level, it is clear that the practical project of *ecclesia* in both its cosmopolitan aspect and its aspect as a 'supernatural society' have totally altered the course of human history, such that the questions of international order and of a 'civil society' and a 'culture' beyond the scope of the political or economic as our 'highest human achievement' are now more paramount than ever before.

23   Aquinas and Kingship

For perhaps the most complete understanding of how the politically transorganic is fulfilled and guaranteed by the society of supernatural charity, one should turn to the political thought of Thomas Aquinas, whose import has rarely been well understood.[278] Famously, Aquinas took from Aristotle the view that political government is natural to the human animal and that in consequence there was a political order even in the terrestrial paradise. This view went somewhat beyond the Stoic-inspired conclusions of Augustine and other Latin Fathers, which limited authority in Eden more to the natural tribal predominance of the male, the older and the wiser, without any political structuration.

Generally this innovation has been interpreted as a new 'naturalisation' of politics, combined with a more optimistic sense of political purpose as being to do with a necessary architectonic directed towards positive ends and not just the disciplining of sin. This interpretation is not incorrect, but the discernment of a modern, sunnier outlook on the political is not entirely accurate. What is overlooked here is the way in which Aquinas is

---

[278]   For an English edition of Aquinas's fragmentary and incomplete *De Regno*, see *On Kingship to the King of Cyprus*, trans. Gerard B. Phelan (Toronto: Pontifical Institute of Medieval Studies, 1949).

returning to a *Greek outlook in general* (excepting the Stoics) not just an Aristotelian outlook, on this issue. For the Greek outlook – Plato as well as Aristotle, philosophers of the Hellenistic period, Philo and then the Christian Greek Fathers – political rule, and especially monarchic rule, reflect the general order of the cosmos and there was no 'original anarchy' in the golden age. So in effect and indirectly, by invoking Aristotle, Aquinas is also recognising, like Byzantium, the original created role of human kingship, which he insists is necessary for the production of architectonic order, just as the one God rules the entire created cosmos.[279] In Eden, for Aquinas, Adam was a king, and if this was indeed a 'natural' role, then he could only exercise it with full justice because he was also ordered by grace to supernatural charity.[280] There was no pope in paradise, but there was a king – who typologically and by fictionalised natural lineage foreshadowed Christ's kingship – and he ruled by grace as well as by natural institution.

With respect to this dimension of kingship, we can therefore see that Aquinas was not straightforwardly 'naturalising' the domain of politics. We are, rather, dealing once again with the 'trans-organic' and the 'trans-natural'. First of all, one can note that the new recognition of the Aristotelian *zoon politikon*, rather than simply removing politics unambiguously from the sphere of supernatural influence, instead suggests that within the natural sphere itself there is already an analogue to the paradoxical 'necessary supplementation' of the supernatural in terms of the 'original' supplementation of natural sociality by political artifice. By comparison, Stoic 'natural anarchy' would indeed tend to imply a pure natural self-sufficiency – and it came to be understood in this way after the Renaissance.[281] As has already been noted, Aquinas himself directly suggested that there are natural analogues to the idea that a genuinely final end of something can be outside the reach of that thing's natural capacities. The moon and the tides have been cited, but with respect to humanity Aquinas mentions the way that

---

[279] See Francis Oakley, *The Mortgage of the Past: Reshaping the Ancient Political Inheritance (1050–1300)* (New Haven, Conn.: Yale University Press, 2012), 113: 'Here [in the *De Regno*] one can detect once more echoes and harmonics of that Hellenistic philosophy of kingship which … having been mediated by Philo Judaeus and Eusebius, had come to be domesticated in the political thinking of Christian antiquity and medieval Byzantium. Man, Aquinas points out, is a microcosm paralleling the macrocosm not only of the political community but of the very universe itself. What the soul is to the body, the king ("shepherd of his people") is to the kingdom, and God is to the world.'

[280] *ST* I q. 95 a. 1; 96 a. 4.

[281] See Charles Taylor, *A Secular Age* (Cambridge, Mass.: Harvard University Press, 2007), 114–119.

human beings, uniquely amongst animals, cannot defend themselves with their bodies, but can still achieve the end of self-defence which is required by their animal nature through the 'Protean' production of weapons by the human hand – the latter process thereby being seen as analogous to the innate drive towards the supernatural.[282] In this way Aquinas clearly sees a parallel between art as supplement and the supernatural as supplement, and between the aid provided by grace and the aid that is provided by the products of art. These products which made up for our natural deficiency and defencelessness are supplied by reason and its accompanying gift of language.[283] But the supreme art, in the Middle Ages, as we have already seen, is that of political jurisprudence, such that here Aquinas can compare the role of the king in inaugurating and sustaining his domain as a manifold unity to the role of the astral bodies sustaining the cosmos under the ultimate governance of the creator God.[284] He declares that 'the greatness of kingly virtue also appears in this, that he bears a special likeness to God, since he does in his kingdom what God does in the world'.[285] This participation of the king in the divine creative and providential power is one reason why, compared with Aristotle, Aquinas stressed rather more strongly the way in which political constitutions are artificially contrived by human beings:

> there are two works of God to be considered: the first is creation; the second, God's government of the things created ... Of these works, the second more properly pertains to the office of kingship. Therefore government belongs to all kings ... while the first work does not fall to all kings, for not all kings establish the kingdom or city in which they rule ... We must remember, however, that if there were no one to establish the city or kingdom, there would be no question of governing the kingdom. The very notion of kingly office, then, comprises the establishment of a city and kingdom ... It pertains also to the governing office to preserve the things governed, and to use them for the purpose for which they were established.[286]

Perhaps in accordance with this perspective on ruling as creating and 'economically' providing for, Aquinas, under the influence of Augustine, expanded the *zoon politikon* to *animal politicum et sociale*.[287] This suggests

---

[282] *ST* I-II q. 5 a. 5 ad. 1.
[283] *De Regno* I.1 [5–7].
[284] *De Regno* I.1 [9].
[285] *De Regno* I.10 [72].
[286] *De Regno* I.14 [97–101].
[287] *ST* I-II q. 72 a. 4; *De Regno* I.1 [4].

that the gap between the political and the social is bridged (and always already bridged) by architectonic art, or that humanity is only for Aquinas a 'political animal' insofar as it is also a 'contriving animal', like a kind of 'super bee'.

Accordingly, Aquinas writes to the King of Cyprus:

> every natural governance is governance by one ... Among bees there is one 'king bee' and in the whole universe there is One God ... Every multitude is derived from unity. Wherefore, if artificial things are an imitation of natural things, and a work of art is better according as it attains a closer likeness to what is in nature, it follows that it is best for a human multitude to be ruled by one person ... Of course the founder of a city and kingdom cannot produce anew men, places in which to dwell, and the other necessities of life. He has to make use of those which already exist in nature, just as the other arts derive the material for their work from nature: as, for example, the smith takes iron, the builder wood and stone, to use in their respective arts.[288]

The shaping of tools and weapons, like the shaping of a political constitution, is a productive as well as conserving work of freedom and therefore the work of spirit or of 'genius' (as it later came to be seen). But if, for Aquinas, we are free, then this is ultimately for the sake of our freedom to be lured by the supernatural end, which is all that we can love with absolute, uncoerced freedom. The meaning of our freedom in both its ethical and poetic dimensions is finally the free acceptance of divine grace and the life of charity. It follows that the affirmation of politics in Eden, far from being a handing over of the political to the natural and secular, is, to the contrary, a recognition of the way in which both human lack and human compensating freedom (the Proteus *topos*, found in the Fathers and later pervasive during the Renaissance)[289] already anticipate the drive to the supernatural and the supplementation of grace and is indeed already the obscure double presence of these realities.

This link between 'political supplementation by art' and the divine government of the creation through a necessary 'supplementation' by grace is expounded in Book I, chapter 15, of the *De Regno*. Aquinas develops this analogy first with respect to the teleological governance of the human soul:

> It is the carpenter's business to repair anything which might be broken, while the pilot bears the responsibility of bringing the ship to port. It is the same with man. The doctor sees to it that a man's life is preserved; the tradesman supplies the necessities of life; the teacher takes care that man may learn

---

[288] *De Regno* I.3 [19].
[289] See Milbank, *The Suspended Middle*, 48–55.

the truth; and the tutor sees that he lives according to reason. Now if man were not ordained to another end outside himself, the above-mentioned cares would be sufficient for him. But as long as man's mortal life endures there is an extrinsic good for him, namely, final beatitude which is looked for after death in the enjoyment of God ... Consequently the Christian man ... needs another and spiritual care to direct him to the harbour of eternal salvation, and this care is provided for the faithful by the ministers of the church of Christ.

He then extends the analogy of rule by art with human grace from the governance of the soul to the governance of the human city:

If ... the ultimate end of man were some good that existed in himself, then the ultimate end of the multitude to be governed would likewise be for the multitude to acquire such good, and persevere in its possession ... It is, however, clear that the end of a multitude gathered together is to live virtuously ... Yet through virtuous living man is further ordained to a higher end, which consists in the enjoyment of God ... Now ... we always find that the one to whom it pertains to achieve the final end commands those who execute the things that are ordained to that end. For example ... the ruler of a city, who makes use of arms, tells the blacksmith what kind of arms to make. But because a man does not attain his end, which is the possession of God, by human power but by divine ... the task of leading him to that last end does not pertain to human but to divine government. Consequently, government of this kind pertains to that king who is not only a man, but also God, namely, our Lord Jesus Christ ... Hence a royal priesthood is derived from Him, and ... all those who believe in Christ, in so far as they are His members, are called kings and priests. Thus ... the ministry of this kingdom has been entrusted not to earthly kings but to priests, and most of all to the chief priest, the successor of St. Peter ... To him all the kings of the Christian People are subject as to our Lord Jesus Christ Himself ...[290]

Thomas's political theory is therefore directly *opposed* to the ahistorical 'naturalising' theses that have generally been ascribed to it, which are seen as helping to usher in a modern secular, 'Whiggish' political autonomy. Instead, it incorporates the *interruptus* of revelation, seen as typologically anticipated in specific historical ways, as with the ancient Druidry of Gaul.[291] Holistically his theory is based upon a 'triple integration' of the natural with the social/artificial (the political), and of both with supernatural

---

[290] *De Regno* I.15.
[291] *De Regno* I.15. For the 'Whiggish' reading, see Gilby, *The Political Thought of Thomas Aquinas.*

charity as partially realised in the visible Church. He embraces the Hildebrandine vision of a papal plenitude of power, but confines this to a suasive authority over kings, whose overseeing of natural justice must ultimately be directed towards supernatural charity, and who, significantly are said themselves to enjoy a 'plenitude of power' within their own realms and within the domain of the *saeculum*.[292]

Here one has an example of the translation of the 'eucharistically creative' power of the Pope into the secular, political domain. But this is a translation without corruption, since the monarchic plenitude only exists for Aquinas by participation in the papal plenitude. The point of Aquinas's extension of the canon lawyers' concept of 'plenitude of power' is not (as so often imagined) to so neutralise this idea as to confine it to univocally distinguished 'areas', only co-operating in a 'concurrent' way (though others were soon to extend it in just this fashion), but rather to acknowledge, in a somewhat 'Byzantine' fashion, a certain degree of royal participation in the spiritual power. This acknowledgement involves a subtle double move – while the king is thereby made ultimately answerable to Pope and Church, the power of the latter is itself constitutionally delimited, *in the very measure* that this power, as higher, is a suasive and spiritual one.

If Thomas no longer sees natural political authority as lying entirely within the realm of the Church (yet not entirely outside, since the king is anointed) then again this is not mainly a sign of his 'modernity', but rather of a *return* to Augustine and Gelasius, yet via the prompting of Aristotle: once more political authority is somewhat prior to ecclesiastical authority as 'natural', and yet alien to it in a postlapsarian world as necessarily coercive and drastically punitive in certain circumstances. Aquinas's refusal to the Church (unlike Giles of Rome, shortly after) of coercive or even legal power over the secular arm, here has its counterpart and corollary. A certain exteriority of the political to the ecclesial helps to ensure that the latter will remain true to its vocation to be a society of charity without exception.

For we are talking here not about a simple and potentially oppressive 'organicism', but rather about a 'trans-organicism' in which the ultimate orientation of the political to the supernatural as the guarantee of even natural justice is upheld, *just to the very degree* that one must recognise the natural and fallen ambivalence of the 'purely' political as such.

---

[292] Aquinas, *In Sent.* II, dist. 44 q. 2; IV dist. 20 q. I a. 4 sol. 33. Also the disputed *Sermo in primo dominica adventus 2* (Paris, 1270?), attributed to Thomas by Jean Leclerq in his article 'Un sermon inédit de Saint Thomas sur la royauté de Christ', *Revue Thomiste*, 46 (1946), 152–166. See in addition *ST* II-II. q. 60 a. 6 ad. 3.

Hence the political must be somewhat sequestered paradoxically within the same gesture that it is co-opted by the *ecclesia*. The political, to be more fully its original paradisal self, must exceed itself through gradual entire inclusion within the ecclesial.

Insofar as the political lies in this manner, for Aquinas as for Augustine, both within and outside the City of God, it is clear that the pivotal figure of this ambiguity is the ruler him or herself. On the 'secular' side of rulership, the people have the right to overthrow a tyrannical king or to appeal to a higher authority in the case of a sub-king, because such a monarch is deemed to have broken the tacit 'contract' between king and people.[293] For even though the king derives his authority from 'representing' God to the people, should he fail to do so, then he is taken as also having ceased to 'represent' the people, as his true function is one of service. Aquinas fully recognises that monarchy can readily degenerate into tyranny and that often a republic can more effectively release the energy of a people who now assume a collective responsibility for their polity. (Unlike us moderns, Aquinas does not feel the need ahistorically to 'side' with either monarchism or republicanism.)[294] Indeed he declares that monarchy can be the very worst form of human government.[295] On the other hand he considers that it is also the best form of government, because the pure rule of the few, or 'aristocracy', is more *habitually* subject to the rule of faction, and to what one might call the rule of the 'pseudo-one' or oligarchic tyrant who seizes power from his elite rivals and is peculiarly likely to bend public interest towards private.[296]

By contrast, the very condition for the exercise and holding of monarchic power is a certain eminent exaltation of the king above the aristocratic class, by which he identifies with the common good and the interests of the common people – as was indeed, the case, one may add, of the Roman emperors compared to the earlier republican senators.[297]

It is then the very *isolation* of the king (as Shakespeare so well dramatised) that leans him towards an identification with the cosmic and the universal. Even though he is uniquely subject to the temptations of power, which can shockingly subordinate his subjects' temporal and eternal well-being

---

[293] *De Regno* I.7 [49].

[294] Though one doubts if he would have regarded an *international* non-monarchic republic as viable, precisely because of the necessarily more symbolic and so preferably personal character of international rule and normativity.

[295] *De Regno* I.6 [30–35].

[296] *De Regno* I.6 [38].

[297] I am grateful to my son, Sebastian Milbank, for this point.

to his own natural and corrupted megalomania, it is also true, as Aquinas emphasises, that, because his *own* personal salvation is peculiarly bound up with his exercise of public office,[298] in his very personal isolation he is best able architectonically to direct many particular interests towards the ultimate common goal, which for Christianity has become the personal salvation of each and every one:

> anyone on whom it devolves to do something which is ordained to another thing as to its end is bound to see that his work is suitable to that end; thus, for example, the armourer so fashions the sword that it is suitable for fighting ... Therefore, since the beatitude of heaven is the end of that virtuous life which we live at present, it pertains to the king's office to promote the good life of the multitude in such a way as to make it suitable for the attainment of heavenly happiness, that is to say, he should command those things which lead to the happiness of Heaven and, as far as possible, forbid the contrary ...[299]

So for Aquinas, as for Augustine, the king rules under the priest, but precisely because he does so, his own rule has its legitimacy in partaking of the priestly function which is the final guardian of the law, since now under the new covenant (which Deuteronomy only prefigured) it is the priest of the new law of the gospel who can fully decipher the eternal law of God. By no means does the legitimacy of the king's rule, nor of any secular rule, derive from any merely 'natural' and not grace-given political autonomy.

24   The Theology of Ruling

Since all contemporary government still involves 'one person at the top', there is nothing outdated about these considerations. Nor can any idea that the concerns of the state should be sheerly secular be theologically acceptable, unless we were to embrace a false, early modern theology according to which 'nature' is self-governing without reference to beatitude, or else that the Fall does not chronically impair our natural aptitudes, or else again (the Protestant and 'classical Augustinian' options) that it so drastically ruins them that the political and economic theatres are to be considered pure spectacles of technocratic efficiency.

---

[298] *De Regno* I.10.
[299] *De Regno* I.16 [114–116].

Clearly from the outset with Paul, Christianity has envisaged the possibility of the Church existing alongside pagan political authorities that can still be regarded as legitimate in natural terms. Nevertheless, since the time of Constantine's conversion, it has been assumed that the ruler now *also* exerted his rule within the Church. Even Augustine, who rejected Eusebius's much greater degree of sacralisation of the empire (we have seen that, much more than is usually noticed, there remains a qualified version of this in Augustine), assumes that the ruler in one respect exerts a 'pastoral' function, and this view was sustained in the west during the Carolingian era – indeed without this perspective we would not have had the Christian modification of the Roman law code, nor the imperial and monarchic endowments, east and west, of a manifold number of welfare, monastic and educative institutions.[300] To those 'anti-Constantinian' Christians who would have preferred that the Church remain a quasi-Montanist nomadic puritanical sect, whether in the deserts of North Africa or those of New Mexico, one can only reply that this is to have a somewhat deficient sense of both mission and common humanity.

But in what sense is the secular ruler within the Church a 'king'? A merely Davidic sense or an iconically Christological sense? The complexities of the 'conundrum of kingship' will not readily allow the Anglo-Saxon or Gaulish modesty of a return simply to the former (constitutional acclamation confirmed by anointing) without a dubious reverting to the norms of the Old Testament and a non-ambiguous sacralisation of coercive rule within its own proper domain. For within a Christian perspective, Davidic kingship is fulfilled and surpassed in the divine kingship of Christ – who, as we have seen, is first and foremost a king and only a 'priest forever' after the example of King Melchizedek in Genesis and Psalms, who combined both roles (Genesis 14:18–20; Psalm 110:4). Any claim after Christ by a Christian to be a monarch – that is, to be a secular ruler of any sort – must require (on pain of Nestorianism) that he sees himself as mediating Christological kingship. Certainly, such a person can only be schizophrenic, since he is the 'king of this world' as Christ was not, yet how can he be a Christian king or ruler unless he is trying to conform this world as far as possible to the government of the eternal realm and the eternal government of time? The New Testament is quite clear about all this: while Christic priesthood is primarily a temporal mediating function (which all Christians exercise, but 'presbyters' in particular), Christic kingship belongs more to all Christians as such and so to the laity as much as or more than to the priesthood.

---

[300]   Peter J. Leithart, *Defending Constantine: The Twilight of an Empire and the Dawn of Christendom* (London: Intervarsity Press, 2010).

Christians are already kings, even in independence from apostolic power, and are destined eventually to rule along with the apostles according to St Paul (1 Corinthians 4:8). This means that all Christians inherit Christ's kingly power to judge, in equity, above and beyond the law. If, however, all Christians are literally kings in Christ's name, then, should one of them happen to assume the kingship of this world or a portion of this world, he must all the more exercise his Christic kingship responsibly and representatively – in a somewhat priestly style – on behalf of others. To be a king in Christ's image must mean that every Christian individual takes upon himself to 'represent' his neighbours by standing in active and atoning solidarity with them, and therefore the Christian ruler is simply exercising this role to a supreme degree. For this reason it is *kings* who are eventually to cast their crowns at Christ's feet – as they finally yield up their representative responsibility to his ultimate representation (Revelation 4:10).

Moreover, one should not take this representation (which is not a matter of replacement) to apply solely to 'natural' matters, subordinate to a priestly concern with supernatural ones. Against his own precise intentions, Aquinas's new invocation of Aristotle on politics actually helped open the way in the west to revisiting the logic of the Byzantine position as articulated in Britain or in France (no doubt too extremely) by the 'Anonymous of York'. For if the ruler has responsibility for positive natural functions (co-ordinating the organisation of agriculture, building, manufacture, trade, transport and education) that would exist irrespective of sin, and if he must have an eye to the further co-ordination of these things with the supernatural life of charity, then in a real sense it is the ruler who is most concerned with the whole human person, body, soul and spirit, and the ruler who most anticipates our resurrection in glory, when Jesus will reign forever and ever. The emperor or king as it were 'diagonalises out' of his proper subordination to the Curia and the Pope.

Perhaps for this reason, after Aquinas and more in keeping with him than has often been supposed, Dante advocated a 'Byzantine' view of the Holy Roman Emperor in the west; in his *De Monarchia* this is indeed far too much in naturalistic terms that seem to exhibit some kinship with Marsiglio of Padua; but in the *Paradiso* it is in terms of a sense of the fulfilment of Roman justice as the rule of supernatural charity, *incarnate* here on earth as far as this is possible.[301] Dante's prescient humanism is really suggesting

301   Dante Alighieri, *De Monarchia*; *Paradiso*, cantos 18–20. Whether or not the *Paradiso* is earlier than the *De Monarchia*, it should be taken as embodying Dante's more considered theological view of politics, in contrast to the more occasioned polemic of his prose treatise.

that if Christianity cannot make a difference outside the monastery, then the vision of resurrection is belied. His great poem then holds up a highly corporeal mirror to our failure to incarnate this truth.

The tension therefore between priest and king is still more complex than theology has always allowed, and more germane to the entire nature of Christianity than is usually recognised. The Christological conundrum of kingship means that the king is, for here and now, insofar as he is concerned with natural matters, 'above' the priestly function. But as regards matters pertaining to the ultimate welfare of our soul, the king is subordinate to the priest. Yet in a third sense the latter's role is penultimate, not ultimate. As regards the human 'spirit', the whole person and the ultimate resurrection of the whole person, soul and body, the king and the concerns of kingship are symbolically more ultimate, since they are a remote foreshadowing of the *eschaton*. If Christ is to return, then so too is Arthur, so also Charlemagne, Frederick II and King Sebastian of Portugal (lost in battle against the Moors and one day to return to shore from the sea, where he is rumoured to wander over the waves).[302]

Of course there has always been a danger here of an over-realised eschatology, with the king claiming a plenitude of iconic presence: in Byzantium this was one factor in the iconoclastic attempt to ban sacred images, thereby focusing all mediation in the person of the emperor. The iconophile theologians rightly argued for a deferral of the imperial to the priestly authority in religious matters and for a subordination of imperial kingship to the symbolic authority of the painted icon of Christ and the saints. This ensures that the Christological iconicity of the emperor himself does not proceed from his will, taken as echoing the will of God the Father, but is construed in more orthodox Trinitarian terms as residing in his constitutional symbolic role, to which his actions ought to measure up, by sustaining the filial image of the father in works of justice and mercy.[303]

In the Christian west also, kingship was viewed in Christological terms. Just as Christ had two natures, so also the king was said to posses both a mortal body and a 'fictional', undying body.[304] In this way sovereign power was analogically assimilated to the resurrected body of Christ and sometimes, as in the realist metaphysical theology of John Wyclif, the king was seen as ruling 'by grace' and therefore on condition that he fulfilled the

---

[302]   See Fernando Pessoa, *Message [Mensagem]*, trans. Jonathan Griffin (Exeter: Shearsman, 2007).
[303]   Dragon, *Emperor and Priest*.
[304]   Kantorowicz, *The King's Two Bodies*.

terms of that divine grant.[305] In the seventeenth century Pierre de Bérulle linked the power above the law of the king which sustains the law with the divinity of Christ which paradoxically fulfils and completes our humanity – in this way linking equity to grace and the supernatural infusion of charity.[306]

The monarch therefore stood really and symbolically at the very centre of the four aspects of the trans-organic and the trans-natural. He was supposed to rule nature through reason; by his own body fused with the body of the realm he constituted the *societas*; by the various fictions of his eternal body and his representative power he composed the legal constitution. Finally, by seeking to blend justice with mercy, he stood at the cusp of the relationship between the natural and the supernatural orders. But at the same time, the king was not simply the one furthest removed from animality; to the contrary, as standing 'above' regular reason, social norms and codified law, his creative, fictioning power was also an animal power once more. This is expressed especially in Celtic tales like that of 'Suibhne and the Birds' where a king 'goes feral' – and the same symbolic equation has been attested from West African cultures.[307]

But all this is most supremely expressed by Shakespeare. A large number of his plays turn upon the relationship of kings to justice and to charity or mercy, while they also exhibit the intrinsic proximity of the lawgiver who is half-outside the law to fury, madness and ferality. Today we tend to suppose that kingship is an extraordinary frivolity usurping what should be most serious, or a manifestly deranged subordination of the public interest to the private, biological, hierarchical and dynastic. Yet we thereby overlook the way in which Shakespeare makes it clear that the monarch, by virtue of the unchosen destiny of his birth, and his relatively absolute existential freedom, is in fact more everyman than everyman, and that by dramatically examining the most public of 'thrown' personal destinies, one is also regarding the most acutely private anguish and exuberance.

This is most of all the case in *King Lear*. Here, the ancient British king commits an act of the most monstrous injustice precisely because, within the circle of his immediate family, he has violated charity, in the shape of the Augustinian *ordo amoris*. He has demanded from his youngest daughter Cordelia a degree of absolute love for his own person which

[305]   See Milbank, 'The Gift of Ruling'.
[306]   Stéphane-Marie Morgain, *La Théologie politique de Pierre de Bérulle 1598–1629* (Paris: Publisud, 2001).
[307]   See *Buile Suibhne* [The Madness of Suibhne] in *The Corpus of Electronic Texts* on the internet. For West African kingship, see Luc de Heusch, *Sacrifice in Africa: A Structuralist Approach*, trans. L. O'Brien and O. Morgan (Bloomington, Ind.: Indiana University Press, 1985).

should be reserved for her future husband or for God.[308] On the other hand, Cordelia's refusal to exaggerate for the sake of concord is also subtly questioned in the course of the play. In the elder daughter Regan's puritanical court, the exaggeration that is revelry is banned, and the numbers in the royal retinue are reduced, calling forth Lear's 'Burkean' expostulation in defence of that excess that is endemic to culture as such, the 'clothing' that is natural to cultural man.[309] The result of Lear's abuse of charity and Cordelia's refusal of all rhetorical hyperbole is that Lear deliberately and ironically reduces himself to a naked, feral condition which for a human being cannot be one of being at peace with nature, but of raving insanity and lost wandering.

In his outcast phase (reduced to 'bare life' in Giorgio Agamben's terminology) Lear meets others whom Shakespeare clearly sees as the victims of the Elizabethan Protestant Poor Laws – reduced to sub-humanity by a replacement of integral charity with the rational disciplining of human 'bestial' vagaries.[310] Nevertheless, amongst and between the lost, who are now strangers alike to reason, society and symbolic clothing, Lear rediscovers the fire of the supernatural which is charity as the highest and yet most basic supplement that is inextinguishable in humanity and always able to refuel our rational, social and symbolic processes. Egoism at its most deranged seeks to suppress or command the future and so tends to murder its own children.[311] Charity, by contrast, gives with proportionate measure, and yet invites a gratitude which is without measure in response to gifts which, taken as a whole, are always 'excessive' because gratuitous. Eventually, but too late, Lear and Cordelia rediscover this exchange, which can 'never' return for them in time, but is intimated as something that abides in eternal excess of the creation itself.[312]

These 'integrating' and yet 'alienated' aspects of kingship are, as already emphasised, germane to the role of any ruler, since kingship in the sense of the rule of the one has never been abolished anywhere, and remains in every existing country today in the practice of having 'one person' at the top not merely for symbolic reasons, but also for reasons of final co-ordination, necessary legal innovation and final decision-making. The role of the one is still truly not just substitutionary, but also crucial even within the most conceivably democratic order. Moreover, recent more

---

[308]   *King Lear* I.i.90–95.
[309]   *King Lear* II.ii.330–460.
[310]   *King Lear* III.i–iv.
[311]   See also Anton Chekhov's play *The Seagull*.
[312]   *King Lear* IV.v, V.iii.280–286.

objectively critical discussion of monarchy has started to point out how the monarch, who inherits and hands on his throne and his terrain, tends to be far more identified with both than the temporary ruler who is, by virtue of his mere 'renting' of his realm, somewhat more likely to exploit it in his own interests – remembering that no degree of constitutional control can ever altogether counter the 'alienation effect' of representative democracy which leaves every ruler always to some degree anarchically free.[313] The same thing applies to the hereditary landlord as opposed to the temporary property owner – at every social level. So where supposedly 'radical' politics imagines that it is deposing hierarchy in space, it is in fact ignoring the political dimension of time and the democratic interests of all in sustaining certain representative dynastic and para-dynastic continuities through the ages, if intrinsic values are not to be exchanged for those of abstract wealth and ephemeral prestige.[314] It follows that if we have lost the old dynastic mechanisms we need either to preserve or restore them in a new way or find equivalents for them, as Tocqueville thought – actually in the interests of democracy.

And is it an accident that some of the most egalitarian countries in the world, with the best welfare states and the most respect for civil liberties and due process of law (certainly far more than obtains in the republic of the USA, where the jury system has now more or less collapsed in favour of plea-bargaining)[315] – the Scandinavian and Flemish countries, Canada and New Zealand – are also constitutional monarchies, while France, which also scores relatively well on these registers, preserves much of monarchical substance in its constitutional organisation? It can be added here that the restoration of constitutional monarchy in Spain helped to overthrow Falangist rule, while the monarchies of Morocco and Jordan best contrive with the Islamic world to sustain some sort of separation of secular and sacred, while retaining a pervasive Islamic influence and avoiding the desecration of the Islamic physical and intellectual legacy that has been perpetrated by many political Islamists.

The point may be that constitutional monarchy or its near equivalent (because any dogmatic literal 'monarchism' is an absurdity) sustains a symbolic space of political and legal acting not just as representative of the majority will, nor as the expression of a temporary power interest, but as a 'permanent' power interest of the general will across time by the

---

[313] Hoppe, *Democracy: The God That Failed.*
[314] Hoppe, *Democracy: The God That Failed;* Ankersmit, *Aesthetic Politics.*
[315] William J.Stuntz, *The Collapse of American Criminal Justice* (Cambridge, Mass.: Harvard University Press, 2011).

'democratic' accident of birth,[316] whose only alibi is the promise to the eternal God to attempt to secure justice on earth.[317] This safeguards a sense of the common good and a fulfilment of people's true potential beyond the mere issue of 'what they want', while allowing through the operation of constitutional assemblies that desirable ends need to be freely assented to, and that if the people choose bad ends then they need to realise for themselves the consequences of so doing. At the same time, the sense of a source of law grounded in the timeless search for equity and subject to the directly personal qualification of judgement (by the ruler or his judges) better secures the need sometimes to protect the interests, responsibilities and valid rights of individuals and corporate bodies against the tyranny of mass opinion.

My remarks so far on the 'angelic' aspect of the human animal – its orientation to supernatural charity – have sought to suggest that charity has an irreducibly interpersonal aspect: as a 'state of being' it only exists socially; while, since we are political as well as social animals, it requires a 'representative' exercise by one or a few on behalf of all, within the polity of charity which is the Church.

25 The Ecumenico-Political Problem

However, I have also sought to intimate that 'the conundrum of kingship' has historically unsettled and divided this polity. There remains, then, an 'ecumenico-political problem' which today only becomes all the more evident. In the face of the power of global secular capitalism and technologism, plus the invasion of the west by terror and stealth of a newly modernised and politicised wing of Islam, what was once 'Christendom' remains divided between the Latino-Germanic (largely) Catholic world, the Anglo-Saxon Anglican and sectarian world and, thirdly, the Orthodox world of eastern Europe and northern Asia.

Not one of these three divisions offers an ideal Christian model. Western Christendom gradually lost its Gelasian balance. Popes started to claim to exercise the inherited powers of Roman emperors (as it were 'Davidic kingship') and then eminently to represent the 'royal' and divine aspect of Christ, who concomitantly started to be portrayed in papal garb. Inversely, emperors and then kings began to try to exercise, both before and after the

---

[316]   Ironically this Burkean stress saves what is valid in Rousseau.

[317]   It does not have to be underlined that a purely secular monarchy would be the worst of all possible political monisms, if not a contradiction in terms.

Reformation, a full jurisdiction over the supposedly merely 'external' and temporal aspects of ecclesial organisation – though the Anglican settlement was so ambiguous that, from the early seventeenth century onwards, a sacramental and Christological sense of a spiritual corporate body started to reassert itself, ensuring that the English arrangement started to take on a more 'neo-Byzantine' as well as neo-corporatist shape.[318] Eventually, in the nineteenth century, this encouraged a High Church theology which insisted upon the 'incarnation' of charity in the social and the political aspect of the Church-Nation that is England, while reserving the prophetic judgemental excess of the Church in its spiritual aspect.[319]

This came about partly because of the loss, since the Carolingian period, of the desirable and specifically Latin sense of the semi-externality of the *Saeculum* to the *Sacrum*. Yet one could also argue that excessive papal appropriations were rendered conceivable by an absence of a full sense of the 'conundrum of kingship' that was better preserved in the Byzantine east. In the case of the Latin Gelasian tradition, kingship cannot be usurped by the Pope because of its extra-ecclesial natural aspect. However, in the case of the Byzantine conception of iconic kingship (sometimes echoed in the west, particularly in England), Christological kingship in its supernatural aspect cannot be so usurped either. The effect of the gradual displacement of the latter in the west (despite the respective positions of Aquinas and Dante) was surely to downgrade a sense of the specific 'royal' dignity of the laity in general, whereby it is the baptised human being as such, not the priestly human being, who most anticipates the reign of Christ in glory. (It is also not an accident that it is always priests who favour overly kenotic Christologies, 'disapprove' of the once more militantly Judaic Book of Revelation and so forth – in all this it is easy to see a ruse of power posing as the celebration of weakness.) Thus the effect of early over-clericalisation of the Church in the west was negatively to engender excessively naturalistic accounts of secular rule, and so of a rule of justice without charity. And since, once the supernatural virtues have been revealed, it is not really possible to value the natural ones on their own, this pursuit of natural justice tended in reality to devolve into a pursuit of pragmatic order and voluntary control for the sake of control. This was the institutional space

[318]   One can argue that if England betrayed the gothic by losing the enchanted cosmos of participation (especially led by Oxford), she then saved the Baroque by restoring it in a new guise (especially led by Cambridge, though Oxford played its part).
[319]   See Jeremy Morris, *F.D. Maurice and the Crisis of Christian Authority* (Oxford: Oxford University Press, 2008); S.A. Skinner, *Tractarians and the 'Condition of England': The Social and Political Thought of the Oxford Movement* (Oxford: Oxford University Press, 2004).

in which theories of 'pure nature' were liable to take root, while they in turn helped to define this space as truly conceivable and so inhabitable.

On the other hand, the Byzantine solution on the whole lacked the sense that the natural functions of law and politics were somewhat 'demonic' in terms of a Christian transvaluation of virtue, as Augustine realised in the *Civitas Dei*. It also lacked a sufficiently effective episcopal curia and operation of canon law. Above all, it became (more gradually and stutteringly than is usually supposed) sundered from the representative primacy of the descendant of Peter in Rome.[320] Without these things, the entire Orthodox tradition has tended to lack any critical distance from political rule and has not adequately explored a supernatural social life that exceeds a familial, local and politically administered context (the less collective and organised character of its monasticism is bound up with this). It is to a considerable extent for this reason that the European east remains today deficient in the presence of 'civil society'.

So while, on the one hand, lay life in itself remained in the east more religious than in the west, the preconditions for sectarian breakaways of lay life from the Church, first in religious forms and finally in avowedly atheist and nihilistic forms, were always nurtured. If the west encouraged a gradual secularisation which the east later had to import, the east also of itself helped to make possible a later more abrupt and drastic secularisation whose consequences have persisted beyond the fall of the Iron Curtain.

Anglicanism has tended to partake of both western and eastern faults as much as, or more than, it has also, at its best, combined a Latin sense of the critical function of the Church with a Greek sense of the need to incarnate the mystical.

One can conclude, therefore, that a true ecumenico-political project would aim to join the Byzantine-Anglican sense (which is also an early Latin sense) of the double aspect of kingship (or of worldly rule), and of the need to incarnate charity also in political structures, with the Augustinian-Gelasian sense of the ambivalence of political rule and the need to regard the Church itself as the site of encouragement for trans-political human associations. This conjoined emphasis implies a gradual subsumption of the secular polity, as materially architectonic and so 'royal', into the *ecclesia*, but requires an increased purging of an acquired and excessive priestly dominance.

---

[320]   Often the contemporary Orthodox churches sustain the myth that the 'Uniate' Greek Rite Catholic churches are a post-Reformation phenomenon. In reality their claim to an archaic double fealty is arguably more authentic than the Orthodox abandonment of any subscription to the authority of the Roman Primate. For long into the high Middle Ages many in the east acknowledged both Pope and Byzantine emperor, unperturbed by the rift over the *filioque*.

26 Supernatural Charity and Global Order

From a theological point of view, any true global order must be based upon justice infused by charity, and therefore must require the reunification of the Church in terms of the more adequate logic of the society of the supernatural, as sketched in the previous paragraph. Any new, viable and adequate 'nomos of the earth' (in Carl Schmitt's phrase)[321] would have to involve the emergence of a symbolic and representative centre of world government (the equivalent of the lapsed imperial role) which was at least not opposed to Christian aims, and ideally made explicit acknowledgement of them, and more ideally still recognised the spiritual primacy of the Pope. Given the now rapidly proceeding Christianisation of the globe and the already notable spiritual and intellectual revival of Christianity amongst the more reflective youth of Europe (which despite a general decline in Church attendance, at least until recently, is significant given a background of secular ideological bankruptcy and inactivism) this is not entirely far-fetched, if Christians can recover their inspiration and reignite their will. Even if the prevalence of excessively rigid evangelical forms of Christianity remains at present a problem, this may diminish as the problems of individualist capitalism to which it is linked appear more and more evident.[322]

In this way a genuine ecumenical project is inseparable from the project of establishing a global Christendom – the distinction of Christianity from Christendom being rejected as semantically and theologically confused.[323] And the majority of thinking Christians who now suppose that this distinction *can* be made should reflect upon the evidence that, once Christendom declined and eventually collapsed, so too did the social reality of charity, or the life of the supernatural which is Christianity itself.

For already, with the clericalisation of the Church in the west, one gets also the insidious rise of the implicit idea that charity is primarily something to administrate, as traced by Ivan Illich and Charles Taylor in his wake.[324] Where charity and grace were seen as clerical specialities, then *already,*

---

[321] Schmitt, *The* Nomos *of the Earth.*

[322] See Marcia Pally, *The New Evangelicals: Expanding the Vision of the Common Good* (Grand Rapids, Mich.: Eerdmans, 2011).

[323] The word in fact historically meant the same thing: the body of Christians. Thus to make the distinction is to reduce Christianity to a 'belief system', a notion that only came in during the early modern period. In English, unlike French, the word that denoted this, 'Christianism', never caught on. It can also be noted that Kierkegaard attacked not 'Christendom', as the translations of his work misleadingly suggest, but Danish Lutheran 'official Christianity'. He was less critical, if by no means uncritical, of medieval Christendom.

[324] Taylor, *A Secular Age*; Illich and Cayley, *The Rivers North of the Future.*

in the heart of the high Middle Ages, the clergy started to think of themselves as dishing out disciplinary medicine to recalcitrant, basically 'natural' beings sunk in mere bestiality. So, despite what was said above, one has to acknowledge, even at this early stage, a certain root of the modern 'bio-political' duality, when one looks at confessional and pastoral practices, and even at the organisation of charitable and educative institutions that are admirable in principle, but in practice over-classificatory and tending to engender an excessively passive and predictable response.[325]

Yet these tendencies to the 'bureaucratisation of love', which forget that love is a natural-supernatural passion, were intensified after 1300 and in the early modern period. The gradual loss of any sense of the symbolic participation of the natural in the supernatural led more and more to the extrinsic imposition of ecclesiastical order, which was then mimicked by the secular arm – and tended to extend and intensify by far the instance of those 'gothic horrors' of inquisition, torture and burning which are so routinely invoked today. This loss reached also to the conception of the Church itself, where the informing of the collective physical body of the Church through the supernatural food of the Eucharist started to be displaced by an 'administration of grace' from above, or else, in the Protestant instance, by the external and remotely archaic authority of 'the Scriptures' reinvented as independent of tradition and the gloss of inspired interpretation.[326] In consequence, within Catholicism as well as Protestantism, the organisation of the external practices of the Church was viewed more and more as a matter of administrative efficiency run according to merely rational principles.

This led in consequence to a further 'cold' organisation of charitable works, which were increasingly dominated by a top-down sense of simply 'doing something for others', as if we were not all of us, in the end, 'the poor', rather than aiming eventually for mutuality and reciprocity. The new approach also ensured that such works lost their festive aspect and their link to a series of exchanges which extended all the way from earth to heaven – as for example in the instance of medieval alms-houses which were endowed with the understanding that the beneficiaries would constantly pray for the souls of the benefactors.[327] In the long run the administration of welfare and education have been taken over by the secular state, which has systematically subordinated 'charity' to the interests of its own strength and of economic efficiency in the accumulation of abstract wealth.

---

[325]   Much more will be said about this in *On Divine Government*.
[326]   De Certeau, *The Mystic Fable*; James Simpson, Burning to Read (Cambridge, Mass.: Harvard University Press, 2010).
[327]   Eamon Duffy, *The Stripping of the Altars* (New Haven, Conn.: Yale University Press, 2005).

If, indeed, Ivan Illich exaggerated in almost seeing schools, hospitals and mad-houses as bad *per se*, surely he did not exaggerate in seeing the absolutely unprecedented intrusion of the state and the capitalist market into absolutely every aspect of modern human life as a kind of demonic perversion of the 'extra' of supernatural charity.[328] According to his thesis, it is not so much that the sense of the supernatural has ever gone away as, rather, that it has been grossly perverted, starting with processes at the heart of Christendom itself, as just detailed. The Christian charitable sense of unlimited inter-involvement and creative capacity to give to the other and so transform it has been mis-deployed as an excuse for the state to pry into and regulate absolutely every aspect of human life – apparently in the interests of our now of course merely animal well-being (as, for example, with smoking bans) but really in the concealed interests of the state as an efficiently run machine, and of the extraction from it of the capital of control by those who – for the moment – run it. But equally, the Christian sense that divine love 'economically' adapts itself to our every circumstance[329] has been perverted first of all into a disciplinary mode of the pastoral, and then into the warped anarchic rule of the entirely 'flexible market', in theory reflecting perfectly our every need and wish – but in reality constraining and shaping our desires and opportunities by its innate mechanism of the re-production of arbitrary inequities of wealth.

In terms of international relations also, the tempering of justice with charity has gradually eroded after the self-destruction of Christendom. During the medieval era, as Carl Schmitt described, an enemy might be respected as a 'just enemy' out of a charitable respect for him as a fellow Christian, open to divine grace, even if one considered that he was at ethical fault in this or that respect. But in the era after the peace of Westphalia (1648) and the end of 'religious' conflict, war became more of an out-and-out power struggle, first between dynasties and eventually (rather later than is often thought)[330] between nation-states, competing within a now capitalist international market, under the imposed promptings of the Anglo-Saxon world.[331] Here there was no longer any sense of intrinsic justice or injustice on either side, although wars were still declared and fought within certain clear rules which embodied a mutual respect for the state

---

[328] See Illich and Cailey, *The Rivers North of the Future*.

[329] See Agamben, *The Kingdom and the Glory*, 17–52, 261–287.

[330] Benno Teschke, *The Myth of 1648: Class, Geopolitics and the Making of Modern International Relations* (London: Verso, 2009).

[331] Schmitt, *The Nomos of the Earth; Theory of the Partisan*, trans. G.L. Ulmen (New York: Telos, 2007).

institution as such.[332] Alternatively, with Kant, one gets the idea of an international law which would be able to determine 'violations of rights' between nations, and thereby turn certain enemies into absolute villains, the equivalent of international criminals. Already the 'terrorist' is in sight, and with the rise of globalisation one sees more and more the phenomenon of what Schmitt called 'partisan warfare', in which the advocates of a religious or secular ideology pursue a war without rules against an 'absolute' enemy (of class, race or creed), while equally these partisans can be hunted down by 'international' authorities like vermin. Here either side reduces the other to 'purely animal' humanity, liable to any sort of treatment whatsoever.[333] In this way it turns out that, without the sense of the community of charity, no 'natural' rights are inviolable after all. And increasingly, the 'international authority' itself takes on a 'partisan' guise as we see in our own day, as its increasingly sole obeisance to market and bureaucratic norms permits it to wage absolute war for these causes, as though this were a justified war on behalf of reason itself. Globalisation erodes the in part constitutive relationship of the particular political community to the other, both as enemy and as stimulating influence.[334] Instead, an incipient international polity (and in effect the United States *is*, for the moment the world government) unchastened by the *ecclesia*, has to discover a permanent enemy within, namely 'the Islamic terrorist', while being also secretly captivated, and to a degree captured, by the glamour of absolute political monotheism.

It follows that the only way to end 'partisanship', is to aim for a world order based upon the collective pursuit of innately desirable human goals, whose defence can be justified and whose enemies could now indeed be treated not as 'terrorists', as if we secretly acknowledged the sanity of their own goals to deny our universal order altogether, but rather simply as criminals, who still have souls worthy of saving. But such innately desirable goals are only conceivable if we resume our construction of ourselves as a trans-organism, drawn naturally beyond ourselves. As to the meaning of the presence in us of reason, art and the social instinct, this can be variously interpreted and we *have* to choose, else we fall back upon the merely formal adjudication of differences which is bound to be the 'partisan' reign of capitalist and bureaucratic liberalism which swallows all in its maw, and cannot possibly treat its enemies as human, since it is committed only

---

[332]   See James Turner Johnson, *Just War Tradition and the Restraint of War: A Moral and Historical Inquiry* (Princeton, NJ: Princeton University Press, 1981), 172–189.

[333]   Agamben, *State of Exception*.

[334]   Again I am indebted to Sebastian Milbank here.

to an operative notion of humanity and not to a metaphysical one – such that outside its own practices there are no supra-animal human beings. Even up to the present, the choice of the west has remained faintly the view that reason, society and art are superadded to material animal nature, because they are themselves orientated to the eternal kingdom of love. And indeed once this idea had been spoken in time, from AD 1 onwards, it is in reality obvious at some level to all that no still higher ideal will ever be spoken by anyone. The choice then is really between trying to follow this trajectory (in whatever diverse and unpredictable a fashion) or else to abandon the path to the eternal altogether and so to give up on human reason, fraternity and our disclosive power to imagine.

27   Socialism Beyond the Left

What kind of contemporary political stance though, does this genealogy of the collapse of 'integral humanism' imply? Is it a radical one or a conservative one? Is it 'left' or 'right'?

To answer this I need to recapitulate and elaborate. Fundamentally, we now need to begin with the critical insight that 'left' and 'right' are modern categories, which means that 'the left' is not more 'modern' than 'the right'. Like the old intellectual and aesthetic battle between 'the moderns' and the 'ancients', the battle between 'progressives' and 'traditionalists' is itself a modern one. It follows logically that a certain initial appeal to the 'pre-modern' (of the kind made by Cobbett, Carlyle, Ruskin and Hugo, or many early socialists for example) is not of a 'traditionalist' or 'reactionary' nature, because it is precisely to appeal outside the framework in which such terms make any sense.

To moderns the political issue is always one of a relative favouring of the one or the many, and so of the right or the left. Hence monarchy and dictatorship become matters of absolute advocacy, and likewise with the cause of democracy. Yet in the classical and medieval eras, as already discussed, while there were differing opinions as to the ideal constitution, every sound polity was considered to be in some measure a mixed constitution, and the relative predominance of the one, the few or the many was considered to be a matter of adaptation to circumstance, and especially the circumstance of the distribution and preponderance of virtue.

One could see the sophistic advocacy of democracy in ancient Athens as an exception to this. But here we have an essentially 'cynical' proto-liberal endorsement of a system for the regulation of power politics, linked to an already materialist philosophy and a pessimistic denial of the reality of the human spirit. Nothing of the modern link between socialism and materialism is apparent here, and to the contrary, Platonic 'communism' amongst the Guardian class was linked to collective spiritual participation in an ideal world. Here a shared agreement concerning the good was the precondition for an equal sharing of material resources.

We have seen that the emergence of the left-right, many-one oscillation in modernity is directly the result of the nominalist-voluntarist theological revolution in the late Middle Ages, and that theological notions continue to give a specific colouring to apparently secular understandings. If universals and real relations are sheer fictions (that do not 'disclose truth'), then only the many individuals or the *de facto* one central power upheld by one man are real. If the will defines most truth, then it is only correct procedures of authorisation from God, from the monarch or from the will of the many that can define justice.

The latter option is the 'liberal' one, and for this reason the modern left is always fundamentally liberal; this is its fall-back position to which it will endlessly revert. Socialism, by contrast – the theorisation of society as the work of human personhood manifest as free labour – is the joker in the pack of left-wing options, just as 'creativity' is the joker in the pack of genealogies and of human ontology. This is because its account of society as the upshot of visionary work requires a certain appeal to the 'sacrality of the many' or the 'mystique of the collective' – thereby, as it were, 'theurgically' subverting the natural link of the many with the material. It also requires an appeal to the full realisation of the capacities of each human individual in harmony with the realisation of the capacities of every other individual: the principle of 'solidarity' – originally a socialist term, later adopted by Catholic social teaching. In either case a latent metaphysic seems to be invoked which is scarcely that of nominalism-voluntarism at all, and therefore scarcely that of modernity.

It is arguable, then, and historically evidenced, that socialism is only 'left-wing' in an aberrant sense.[335] Both the reality of the collective (and the inter-relational) and the reality of objectively good and true human ends appear to require a teleology and reality of universals that are rooted in a derivation of all reality from a transcendent source of value as well as being. Not even an immanentist theology can provide this: for in the case of Spinoza, as has been argued, 'the many' that compose the community in reality simply 'are' the self-sustaining impersonal one of 'substance', in their shared and fated 'modal' identity, and democracy is only advocated because it balances out the vagaries of the equally predetermined reactive

---

[335]   Michéa, *The Realm of Lesser Evil*.

imagination of the general populace, who are incapable of ascending to the active philosophical vision of the one, and therefore require for their guidance an adaptation of the imaginary 'religious' outlook to the nearest possible approximation to this vision.

By contrast, the sense of a 'mystical body' and of the compossible mutual realisation of individual flourishings, requires some sense of the *locus* of the mediation in time of transcendent goodness, in order to prevent the merging of real people into an impersonal totality. This has been provided in western history by the idea of the church as the 'Body of Christ' and by the Pauline notion of the social process of the Church as working through the exchange of gifts and the co-operation of diverse *charismata* or talents.[336] After the failure of the French Revolution really to improve the lot of the ordinary person (since it was basically about replacing a set of aristocratic functionaries with a set of bourgeois ones, fully committed to the principles of secular liberalism), the early non-state socialists in France before 1848, along with many more 'organicist' liberals (including Victor Hugo) as well as certain strangely 'kenotic' and visionary Catholic traditionalists (supremely Honoré de Balzac)[337] tended to appeal back to the gothic legacy of guilds and corporations as phenomena which had been nourished within this sense of mystical collectivity and labour.

As we have seen, to invoke this legacy is to re-invoke the role of the few both in the expanded Christian sense of mediating free associations and in the antique Greek and Roman sense of the guidance of the wise. For free associations – from trade unions to universities – tend to be bodies committed to an objective sense of the human good and its promotion. They respect democracy as the importance of free consent and a majority testing of 'aristocratic' proposals, but they resist any idea that what people want *en masse* defines the nature of the good itself. And indeed, sometimes the advice of the few or the will of the one must override the popular will in the interests of equity as applied to the fate of this or that individual or grouping.

But more generally, without the educative role of the virtuous few and the mediate groupings of corporations, the mass of the people – especially in the towns and countryside, where slightly more people still live than in large cities, even in contemporary Britain – is constantly subjected to centrist propaganda from government and the media organisations of capital cities. Their will may be sovereign, but what exactly is presented to them to decide

---

[336]   See Milbank, 'Paul versus Biopolitics'.
[337]   See Balzac's final volume of his *Comédie humaine: The Wrong Side of Paris* [*L'Envers de l'histoire contemporaine*], trans. Jordan Stump (New York: The Modern Library, 2004).

about? The 'educative' dimension cannot be itself democratised without an impossible infinite regression. It is here that, if one regards the role of the few (of educators, of intermediate associations, of political representatives) as but an unfortunate substitutionary necessity, one will undermine and corrupt democracy itself. Instead, for democracy to work, it must be complemented by a non-democratic 'Socratic' sense of the importance of the role of the few as pursuing truth and virtue for their own sake.

Socialism, one could say, involves a relatively 'democratic' version of such a sense. This is because it believes that the most important human goods are in principle achievable by all, even though it *does not* equate these goods with what people – individually or collectively – 'happen to want'.

Such 'democratisation of virtue' is itself also a Christian legacy. For the New Testament makes it clear that the highest wisdom lies in love and so not in esoteric visions or scholarly expertise or mental capacity to abstract from matter (as too often in certain modes of Platonism). Love is always personal and singular, so that the highest thing which *all* can offer is now nothing general to which they should aspire; it is instead simply their given real selves, their own uniqueness, which is inseparable from their unique set of relations to others. In clear continuity with this personalism, later western humanism and Romanticism considered that the really democratic element is 'genius', the 'originality' of each and every one which tends to be suppressed by over-scrupulosity concerning rules, or over-veneration of the specificity of the past productions of acknowledged ability. It is just this creative capacity of all, this 'personality', which socialism aims fully to release. But to release always in and under *judgement*, since the 'truth' of the personal, both 'truth to oneself' and 'truth to the witness of others' remains a matter of constant discernment, both individual and collective. This is not a vision of libertarian anarchy, but of the collective realisation of a collective work of art that is continuously to be built and which all can personally inhabit. Its criterion of aesthetic acceptability is not the negative one of the release of freedom (even if liberal 'emancipation' from unacceptable past positivities, indefensible on the grounds of justice, is an important fruit of its one-sided post-Franciscan account of Christian personal liberty), but rather its unique power to disclose something of eternal verity.

28 Critique of All Materialisms

If socialism is only 'left' in a further rather 'left-handed' way that breaks with liberalism as defining 'leftness' as such (ever since the French Revolution), then it also should not be 'materialist' in any straightforward sense. I have already given reasons why the opposition of 'idealism' and 'materialism' as mapped onto 'right' and 'left' is also specifically modern. Ancient materialism was usually the philosophy of an ascetic elite, who were not atheists, but either (as we saw in section 1 of the first sequence) sought escape from the vagaries of the gods (Epicureanism) or subordinated them to the sacred whole of the cosmos (Stoicism). Moreover, the very idea of 'materialism' has always proved elusive. If it means that the basic components are 'atoms', then how is it that matter comes 'one by one', and does not this suggest, with Plato, that the basic realities are numbers after all (as Ralph Cudworth argued against Thomas Hobbes)?[338] Or if it means rather that basic reality is a kind of vital energy, then is not this force tinged with a certain 'spirituality'? Because we can only apprehend reality in terms of thought, meaningful image and intending will, consequent upon the manifestness or at least manifestability without which the very notion of 'being' would make no sense, it is scarcely possible for us to abstract an idea of 'pure matter' at all. As George Berkeley saw, this endeavour involves something like the privileging of our sense of touch over our sense of vision, and then a forgetting that the registering of 'hardness', for example, is just as subjective as the registering of 'blueness'. Then we further forget that the 'solidity' of matter is only a metaphor and yet a metaphor that is necessary to its very conception. So we land up with the banality of hypostasising 'that which we bump into'.[339]

The problem then, with all 'materialisms', is that the matter which they attempt to see as fundamental is always reversely deconstructible into something ideal or spiritual after all. We tend to assume that Aristotle's or Aquinas's 'hylomorphism' is a kind of compromise between materialism and idealism. But instead, as I have already argued, it is rather the *most materialist philosophy that is possible*, even though it is, indeed, a hybrid ideal-material realism. For if one declares that there is 'only matter', then matter always turns out to be a kind of quasi-form or set of forms (as we have just seen), whereas if one declares, with Aristotle, that there is always, 'beneath the moon' matter-form hybridity, then one can let matter be matter; in Aristotelian phraseology, one 'saves the appearance' of material reality. But one can only do this by *leaving* matter as an inexpressible mystery, outside the full reach of the human mind which is bound to thoughts, images and volitions. Hence Aristotle uniquely avoided the trap of thinking of matter as a vague, unappetising soup, or as infinitesimal

---

[338] See Milbank, 'The Thomistic Telescope: Truth and Identity', in Peter Candler and Conor Cunningham, eds., *Transcendence and Phenomenology* (London: SCM, 2007), 288–333.
[339] See Milbank, *The Word Made Strange*, 97–105.

numbers, or again as a kind of de-volitioned volatility that is a mysterious 'blind will'. Instead, he approached matter through a *via negativa* which respected its mystery and so delivered just that 'mystical materialism' which socialism so often seems to require, yet lacks the ontological resources to articulate. Matter is the degree zero of act, which retains its primacy: hence it is 'pure possibility' which limits the actuality of form as species and gives rise to the individual – though Aquinas's more 'pan-personalist' (so to speak) perspective improved on this to say that it is the very 'existence' of an entity which blends form and potency through the excess of actuality to produce the unique particular thing.[340]

Therefore matter everywhere makes its presence felt as the concreteness of the particular – yet it cannot appear 'in itself', because the particular always has a 'shape', and this shape is *never* entirely unique to it but always exhibits something 'already' known in general and somewhat repeatable otherwise elsewhere, as well as clearly modifiable *in ways which would not destroy but merely confirm the enigma of its uniqueness*. It is like the way in which someone can have a new hairstyle and not only remain recognisable but *still more* disclose their specificity precisely by changing and yet remaining enigmatically 'still the same'. These are the strongest reasons to be urged both against the Scotist *haeccitas* and against nominalism.

Matter 'in itself', therefore, can be but negatively characterised, because it is only ever 'there' when it has been always already 'informed' – by shape, colour, sound, touchability and so forth. The characteristic 'left-wing' attempt to 'liberate' pure matter as force (as found in Gilles Deleuze for example) can only end by losing both matter in its mysterious generality and form in its treasured specificity, subordinating both to a virtual force of indifferent differentiation.

In the case of Aristotle, as with Plato, matter remains nevertheless a strange 'base' that does not itself derive from the transcendent realm. This dualism resonates with the echoes of ancient pagan myth in which originally a divine shaping force overcomes and orders a resistant, dragon-like chaos. But the strange thing about much 'left materialism' is that it is almost as if it accepted the basic terms of this dualism and simply sought to reverse it. Surely a kind of *ressentiment* and aggrieved yet self-vaunting self-abasement is at work here, as Nietzsche correctly realised? It is as if the identity of the worker or the ordinary person with the base, the material, the bestial and the valueless and unaspiring were *accepted*, but it was perversely argued that 'the base' itself (in every sense) should henceforward command.

---

340   See Milbank and Pickstock, *Truth in Aquinas*, 19–59.

Platonic and Aristotelian metaphysics invites this sort of reversal, in which a kind of back-handed tribute is paid to the superiority of the formal and the ideal, even though they are to be overthrown. However, metaphysical tradition knows of later, paradoxical elevations of the material, which upset the ancient Greek dualistic *schemata*. First of all, within late pagan antique theurgic Neoplatonism (Iamblichus, Proclus, Damascius), the mysterious 'simplicity' and non-reflexivity of matter, which can only be negatively characterised, are seen as providing a remote echo of the simplicity and non-reflexivity of the transcendent One itself, and as thereby betokening a 'rebound' to the One from the base of the descending hierarchical series of reality. Matter has in itself a mysterious value *not* given to mind, and this is why the material world can sacramentally remind us of our faults and reinstigate our worship of the divine, as envisaged by the Irish Christian theologian and philosopher John Scotus Eriugena in the ninth century.[341]

In the second place, biblically inspired monotheistic theologies, from Philo onwards, taught that matter is fully created and intended by a personal God. When one combines these two outlooks (and this has so far never sufficiently occurred within the three monotheistic traditions), one can see how matter is a crucial divine gift, complementary to the mystery of mind and spirit. Again, to adopt this outlook (as Stanislas Breton, Catholic philosopher and socialist friend of Louis Althusser, realised)[342] is *the most materialist that one can be*. For instead of trying impossibly to value valueless matter by merely inverting Plato's and Aristotle's dualism, one instead discovers in matter an irreplaceable sacramental significance.

Yet modern materialism traces from just such an inversion, rather than simply from a revival of antique materialism, because it evolves from the Scotist real distinction of matter from form, as described above. Matter that is 'freed' from form, as a quasi-act beyond pure potential, loses its mystery and quickly becomes Descartes's geometric extension which, once again, loses matter to mathematical abstraction. In the political realm the many then come to be identified with this supposedly freed-up materiality and therefore lose their links to reason, sociality and fictioning power. The 'biopolitical' is entered upon, and the typical 'left' perspective is just as complicit with this as is the typical 'right' one.

---

[341] See Milbank, 'Platonism and Christianity: East and West'.

[342] Stanislas Breton, *Du Principe: L'Organisation contemporaine du pensable* (Paris: Cerf, 2011). See also Wayne John Hankey's helpful and informative article. 'French Neoplatonism in the Twentieth Century', *Animus*, 4 (1999), 135–167.

Therefore one should refuse the *pathos* of left materialism. How can an abstract emptiness, a thinned-out formality which has lost both the mystery of identity and the mystery of the ideal, be a source of value or a stimulus to revisionary action? All that this perspective can support is a negative mockery, and a destructive, anti-populist iconoclasm which ironically confirms the view of the powerful that people in general are incapable of nobility. Instead of saying – with a Romantically revisited Christendom, as in Chateaubriand, Hugo, Novalis, Carlyle and Ruskin – that all human beings, men and women, are capable of virtue, of chivalry, of romantic love, of artistry and the contemplation of God and the cosmos, it says, rather, that *there are no such things*, but that we can all be compensated for their lack by the equal distribution of an impoverished remainder. Instead of seeing the vision of the Good, as with Plato, as the basis for an equitable distribution of the echoes of the Good, it seeks, rather, to deny the Good altogether, just as social democracy in Sweden decided that fairness involved the demolition of much of that country's historic architectural legacy along with the fundamental social role of interpersonal reciprocity. It was all just too beautiful and interrupted the endless vista of lakes and pine trees as an appropriately infinite backdrop for the pursuit of private self-realisation. Unsurprisingly, fictional obsessions with mass murder were soon to follow.

Once the goal of 'fairness' has displaced the quest for justice in the light of the Good, then either one must be resigned to the market regulation of competing desires, or else the only 'common good' which remains to be equitably distributed will be the lowest common denominator on which we supposedly all agree, which can therefore be doled out in (ideally) exactly equal shares. John Ruskin advocated the opposite: the extension of chivalry and noble aims to all through the formation of 'knightly' guilds of work and trade which would impose high ideals and standards upon their members as a condition of participation in these various enterprises. But today, instead, we are proceeding in the opposite direction: even the professions have ceased to be guilds built upon high standards, mutual trust and creative innovation to sustain traditions of virtuous practice, and have instead become themselves proletarianised, regulated and routinised in ever more extreme degrees by the increasingly conjoint oligarchy of state and market.

What we require therefore today is a new 'politics of integral trans-organicity' which fuses Christian socialism with a new sense of what is valid in the 'conservative' critique of modernity. One could also take this as a 'left' reading of Catholic social teaching. Fundamentally, we require a (genuinely) 'third way' beyond modern left and right, which recognises the roles of the one and the few if the democratic role of the many is to be properly fulfilled.

The recovery of the role of the few and of the one (as, ideally, a Christian political ruler at local, national and global levels) can permit us to recover in the social order that integration of natural justice and supernatural charity which, as we have seen, is the precondition for the recovery also of our properly human integral but 'trans-organic' existence as rational, social, artistic and grace-imbued animals, on the way to a 'deified' unity with the Triune God.

Yet the leftwards slant to this third way is justified first of all by the Christian democratisation of virtue as love, and secondly by the Renaissance-Romantic demand for the expressive release and fulfilment of the entirety of human creative powers in the most material as well as the most ideal realms.

It is a democratisation of exaltation which we should now seek.

Index

Beyond Secular Order: The Representation of Being and the Representation of the People, First Edition. John Milbank.
© 2013 John Wiley & Sons, Ltd. Published 2013 by John Wiley & Sons, Ltd.